Destiny of the Republic

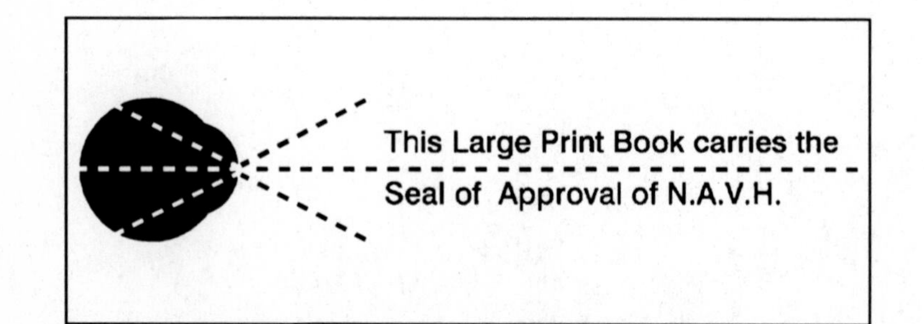
This Large Print Book carries the
Seal of Approval of N.A.V.H.

DESTINY OF THE REPUBLIC

A TALE OF MADNESS, MEDICINE, AND THE MURDER OF THE PRESIDENT

CANDICE MILLARD

LARGE PRINT PRESS
A part of Gale, Cengage Learning

Detroit • New York • San Francisco • New Haven, Conn • Waterville, Maine • London

Large Print Press, a part of Gale, Cengage Learning.

The text of this Large Print edition is unabridged.
Other aspects of the book may vary from the original edition.
Set in 16 pt. Plantin.

LIBRARY OF CONGRESS CATALOGING-IN-PUBLICATION DATA

Millard, Candice.
Destiny of the republic : a tale of madness, medicine, and the murder of a president / by Candice Millard.
p. cm. — (Thorndike Press large print biography)
Originally published: New York : Doubleday, c2011.
Includes bibliographical references.
ISBN-13: 978-1-4104-4625-1 (hardcover)
ISBN-10: 1-4104-4625-5 (hardcover)
1. Garfield, James A. (James Abram), 1831–1881—Assassination. 2. Presidents—United States—Biography. 3. Guiteau, Charles Julius, 1841–1882. 4. Presidents—Medical care—United States—History—19th century. 5. Medicine—United States—History—19th century. 6. Bell, Alexander Graham, 1847–1922. 7. Medical instruments and apparatus—United States—History—19th century. 8. United States—Politics and government—1881–1885. 9. Political culture—United States—History—19th century. 10. Power (Social sciences)—United States—History—19th century. I. Title.
E687.9.M55 2012
973.8'4092—dc23 2011045169

ISBN 13: 978-1-59413-614-6 (pbk. : alk. paper)
ISBN 10: 1-59413-614-9 (pbk. : alk. paper)

Published in 2012 by arrangement with Doubleday, an imprint of Knopf/Doubleday Publishing Group, a division of Random House Inc.

Printed in the United States of America
1 2 3 4 5 16 15 14 13 12

FD268

For my parents,
Lawrence and Constance Millard,
on their fiftieth wedding anniversary

CONTENTS

PART THREE: FEAR

PART FOUR: TORTURED FOR THE REPUBLIC

Prologue: Chosen

Crossing the Long Island Sound in dense fog just before midnight on the night of June 11, 1880, the passengers and crew of the steamship *Stonington* found themselves wrapped in impenetrable blackness. They could feel the swell of the sea below them, and they could hear the low-slung ship plowing through the water, its enormous wooden paddle wheels churning, its engine drumming. At steady intervals, the blast of the foghorn reverberated through the darkness, but no ship returned its call. They seemed to be utterly alone.

Although most of the passengers had long since retired to private cabins or the bright warmth of the saloon, one man stood quietly on the deck, peering into the fog that obscured everything beyond his own pale hands. At five feet seven inches tall, with narrow shoulders, a small, sharp face, and a threadbare jacket, Charles Guiteau was an unremarkable figure. He had failed at everything he had tried, and he had tried nearly everything, from law to ministry to even a free-love commune. He had been thrown in jail. His wife had left him. His father believed him insane, and his family had tried to have him institutionalized. In his own mind, however, Guiteau was a man of great distinction and promise, and he predicted a glorious future for himself.

Just three days earlier, immediately following the Republican Party's tumultuous presidential convention in faraway Chicago, Guiteau had decided to pack his few belongings and leave Boston, his sights set on the party's campaign headquarters in New York. In a surprise nomination, James Garfield, an eloquent congressman from Ohio, had been chosen over a field of powerful contenders, including even former president Ulysses S. Grant. Like Guiteau, Garfield had started out with very little in life, but where Guiteau had found failure and frustration, Garfield had found unparalleled success. The excitement surrounding the unexpected, charismatic candidate was palpable, and Guiteau was determined to be a part of it.

Absorbed in his own thoughts, and blinded by the thick fog that blanketed the sound, Guiteau did not even see the other ship until it was too late. One moment there was the soft, rhythmic splashing of the paddle wheels. In the next instant, before Guiteau's eyes, a 253-foot steamship abruptly materialized from the darkness and collided with Guiteau's ship head-on in a tremendous, soul-wrenching crash of iron and steel. As the *Stonington* recoiled from the blow and tried to pull astern, it compounded the disaster by tearing away the starboard wheelhouse and wheel of the oncoming ship — its sister steamer, the *Narragansett,* which had been headed at full speed in the opposite direction.

On board the *Narragansett,* passengers were suddenly plunged into darkness, confusion, and terror. As the ship listed steeply, the lights went out and rushing water and scalding steam poured over the decks. Several staterooms were swept away entirely, and one man, who had been asleep in an upper bunk, was thrown out of a gaping hole and into the sound. Just as the shocked passengers, who had rushed from their rooms in nightgowns and bare feet, began to comprehend what had happened, another thunderous blast shook the *Narragansett* as its boiler, which had been struck by the *Stonington,* exploded. Flames licked the well-oiled decks, sending a deadly firestorm billowing through the ship.

As the passengers of the *Stonington* watched in horror, the men and women of the *Narragansett,* frantic to escape the fire, began to throw themselves and their children over the sides of the blazing ship into the depths of the sound. One terrified young man raised his gun and shot himself as the boat began to sink. In just minutes, the fire grew in intensity until it covered the length of the ship, from stem to stern, and illuminated the sound for miles.

As the tragedy unfolded before him, Guiteau could hear the screams and desperate cries for help, which continued, disembodied, even after the ship burned to the waterline and then sank, plunging the shell-shocked witnesses, once again, into complete darkness. The frightened and ill-prepared crew of the *Stonington* lowered lifeboats into the water and circled blindly for hours, searching for survivors by their cries and pulling them to safety by arms, legs, clothing, even the hair of their heads. Many, however, had already drowned, or had drifted beyond help, their cries fading as they were carried away by the tide.

When the *Stonington* finally staggered into its home port in Connecticut early on the morning of June 12, the town's stunned inhabitants were met with a scene of destruction that, in the words of one reporter, "beggar[ed] description." The ship's bow had been smashed in, the timber and planking ripped away nearly to the waterline. Three passengers of the *Narragansett* who had been rescued from the sound had already died on board. Twenty-seven more had burned to death or drowned. Those who had survived collapsed on the pier, hysterical, nearly naked, their skin left in shreds by the fire. Parents searched frantically for children as crew members solemnly wrapped two bodies, that of a man and a child, in sailcloth and laid them upon rocks near the shore. Two weeks later another body would wash up on Fishers Island.

As dawn revealed the scale of the carnage, the survivors, even in the midst of their shock and despair, considered themselves extraordinarily fortunate to be alive. Guiteau, however, believed that luck had nothing to do with his survival. As he stepped off a steamship that had come to the *Stonington*'s rescue, Guiteau felt certain that he had not been spared, but rather selected — chosen by God for a task of tremendous importance. Disappearing into the crowd, he dedicated himself to what he now saw clearly as the divine mission before him.

Part One: Promise

Chapter 1
The Scientific Spirit

The life and light of a nation are inseparable.

JAMES A. GARFIELD

Even severed as it was from the rest of the body, the hand was majestic. Sixteen feet tall, with long, tapered fingers holding aloft a twenty-nine-foot torch, it sat on the banks of a small lake in Philadelphia in the summer of 1876. It was all that existed of the Statue of Liberty, and it had been shipped in pieces from France for the United States' Centennial Exhibition, a world's fair celebrating the country's first one hundred years. Ten years later, the complete figure, rising more than a hundred and fifty feet from its pedestal and with a bright skin of copper, would be installed in New York Harbor to the awe and admiration of the world. But in 1876, the Statue of Liberty, like the young country to which it would be given, was still a work in progress. A symbol of promise, perhaps, but not yet of triumph.

Across the lake from the statue, James Abram Garfield walked with his wife and six children under a flawless sky, the scent of a recent rain still hanging in the air. A tall man with broad shoulders and a warm smile, Garfield was, in many ways, the embodiment of the Centennial Exhibition's highest ideals. At just forty-four years of age, he had already defied all odds. Born into extreme poverty in a log cabin in rural Ohio, and fatherless before his second birthday, he had risen quickly through the layers of society, not with aggression or even overt ambition, but with a passionate love of learning that would define his life. That love had brought him to Philadelphia, for the opening day of the centennial fair.

Although he was a congressman, Garfield traveled through the exhibition unaided by guards or guides of any kind. Except for his statuesque height and soldier's posture, he was indistinguishable from the hundreds of thousands of other fairgoers who swarmed the rain-soaked grounds and the eighty miles of asphalt walkways. In just a few weeks, these walkways would be transformed by the summer sun into hot, sticky, lava-like rivers, trapping shoes and small animals. But on that day they felt smooth and solid as the crowd surged through the fairgrounds, headed toward one destination above all others — Machinery Hall.

With fourteen acres of exhibits, Machinery Hall shivered with life. It pulsed and throbbed so irresistibly that the wooden plank floors vibrated underfoot. Conversations were either muffled by a heavy humming or forced to an early and violent end by a sharp, sudden clack. Exhibits included everything from a machine that could weave a customer's name into a pair of suspenders while he waited, to an internal combustion engine that William Ford, Henry Ford's father, had traveled all the way from his farm in Dearborn, Michigan, to see.

These exhibits were finely calibrated to appeal to no man more than James Garfield. A former professor of ancient languages, literature, and mathematics who had paid for his first year of college by working as a carpenter, Garfield's interests and abilities were as deep as they were broad. In fact, so detailed was his interest in mathematics, and so acute his understanding, that he had recently written an original proof of the Pythagorean theorem during a free moment at the Capitol. *The New England Journal of Education* had published the proof just the month before, transparently astonished that a member of Congress had written it.

Despite Garfield's deep admiration for mathematics and the arts, however, he believed that it was science, above all other disciplines, that had achieved the greatest good. "The scientific spirit has cast out the Demons and presented us with Nature, clothed in her right mind and living under the reign of law," he wrote. "It has given us for the sorceries of the Alchemist, the beautiful laws of chemistry; for the dreams of the Astrologer, the sublime truths of astronomy; for the wild visions of Cosmogony, the monumental records of geology; for the anarchy of Diabolism, the laws of God."

After his first day at the exposition, back in the Philadelphia home he and his family had rented, Garfield sat down to write in his diary, just as he had done nearly every night of his life for the past twenty-eight years. With characteristic seriousness of purpose, he wrote that the fair would be a "great success in the way of education." In Garfield's experience, education was salvation. It had freed him from grinding poverty. It had shaped his mind, forged paths, created opportunities where once there had been none. Education, he knew, led to progress, and progress was his country's only hope of escaping its own painful past.

In 1876, the United States, still reeling from a devastating civil war and its first presidential assassination, was far from the country it hoped to become, and faced daily reminders of the hard challenges that still lay ahead. While men like Garfield strolled the aisles of Machinery Hall in Philadelphia, marveling at the greatest inventions of the industrial age, George Armstrong Custer and his entire regiment were being slaughtered in Montana by the Northern Plains Indians they had tried to force back onto reservations. As fairgoers stared in amazement at Remington's typewriter and Thomas Edison's automatic telegraph system, Wild Bill Hickok was shot to death in a saloon in Deadwood, leaving outlaws like Jesse James and Billy the Kid to terrorize the West. As middle-class families waited patiently in line for their chance to marvel at the Statue of Liberty's hand, freed slaves throughout the country still faced each day in fear and abject poverty.

So incomplete and uncertain was the United States that, although it was a hundred years old, it did not yet have a national anthem. At the opening ceremony, the exposition's hundred-piece orchestra, with a chorus of a thousand voices, dutifully performed the anthems of the forty-nine other countries participating in the fair. Only the host country had no official song with which to honor its people, and would not for another fifty-five years. With eight untamed territories and eleven states that still seethed with hatred and resentment and dreamed of secession, a national anthem seemed premature, even presumptuous.

Garfield understood as well as any man what the Civil War had accomplished, and what it had left undone. When he was still a very young man, he had hidden a runaway slave. As commander of a small regiment from Ohio, he had driven a larger Confederate force out of eastern Kentucky, helping to save for the Union a critically strategic state. In Congress, he fought for equal rights for freed slaves. He argued for a resolution that ended the practice of requiring blacks to carry a pass in the nation's capital, and he delivered a passionate speech for black suffrage. Is freedom "the bare privilege of not being chained?" he asked. "If this is all, then freedom is a bitter mockery, a cruel delusion, and it may well be questioned whether slavery were not better. Let us not commit ourselves to the absurd and senseless dogma that the color of the skin shall be the basis of suffrage, the talisman of liberty."

Garfield knew, however, that there was some suffering that no one could prevent, and whose reach no one was beyond. Throughout the centennial fair — in hall after hall, exhibit after exhibit — this suffering was unflinchingly apparent. There were rows of coffins of every variety. There were, in the words of one reporter, "instruments for the curing of diseased and deformed bodies and limbs." An entire exhibit was devoted to a scene of a mother huddled over a crib, crying over the child she had just lost.

Nearly every family Garfield knew had suffered the death of a child, and his own family was no exception. His first child, a bright-eyed little girl named Eliza, had died of diphtheria when she was just three years old. Garfield had adored her, marveling at her precociousness and nicknaming her Trot, after Elizabeth Trotwell in *David Copperfield,* one of his favorite books. Thirteen years had passed since Trot's death, but for Garfield, the pain of losing her was still fresh.

Although he worried for the health of his surviving children, Garfield himself seemed uniquely out of place among the fair's somber scenes of death and disease. He had always been poor — and, even as a congressman, continued to live a simple and frugal life — but he had never been frail. On the contrary, he was the picture of health and vitality. With his quick, crisp stride, he was a striking contrast to the men and women at the fair who, rather than walk, chose to pay the exorbitant price of sixty cents an hour to be pushed through the halls in a cushioned "rolling chair" by a uniformed attendant. In many ways, Garfield had less in common with these people — a group that included the poet Henry Wadsworth Longfellow — than he did the man from Joplin, Missouri, who had loaded a wheelbarrow with minerals from his home state and, over a period of three months, pushed it all the way to Philadelphia for the fair.

It was this kind of gritty determination that impressed Garfield most. He admired men who seemed not to notice even the most insurmountable of obstacles. He saw that caliber of man all around him at the centennial fair, tinkering with an engine or worrying over the strength of a blade. Among this group, eclipsed by the vast shadow of hundreds of other inventors, were two men whose ideas would not only change the world, but had the unique potential to save Garfield's life.

Next door to Machinery Hall, where Garfield spent his first day at the fair, was the Main Exhibition Building, a twenty-one-acre, glass-enclosed behemoth. Inside, at the far east end of the building, past row after row of dazzling exhibits from far-flung nations, was a small staircase that led upstairs to a quiet, easily overlooked gallery. In one corner of that gallery, bent over a rough, wooden table that held a collection of mysterious-looking brass-and-wood instruments, was a serious young Scotsman named Alexander Graham Bell.

The invention Bell had brought with him from Boston was "a new apparatus operated by the human voice" — the telephone. He had won a patent for it just three months earlier, and he knew that the fair was his best opportunity to prove that it really worked. He had come to Philadelphia, however, with great reluctance, and with each passing day he had only grown more convinced that he should have stayed home.

Bell's principal work was not inventing, but teaching the deaf. He had inherited this work from his father, but he loved it with a passion that was all his own, and he was astonishingly good at it. Even the emperor of Brazil, on a recent break from the Centennial Exhibition, had visited Bell's classroom in Boston. Bell's school would administer its annual exams the next day. It was the most important day of the year for his students, and not being there to help them prepare made him miserable.

From the moment Bell had stepped off the train, he had encountered one disaster after another. He suffered from debilitating headaches brought on by extreme heat, and Philadelphia was in the grip of a brutal heat wave. To his horror, when he examined his luggage, he discovered that some of his equipment had been lost in transit. Worse, what had arrived was damaged.

When Bell had finally reached the fairgrounds and entered the Main Exhibition Building, he realized that not only was his telephone broken and incomplete, but his exhibit would be nearly impossible to find. Because of his reluctance to attend the fair, he had missed the official deadline for registering. His fiancée's father, Gardiner Greene Hubbard, who was a member of the Massachusetts Centennial Committee and who had been urging Bell for months to enter his invention, had secured an exhibit space for him at the eleventh hour, but it was arguably the least desirable location in the entire hall. Instead of being taken to the electrical exhibits, Bell had been led upstairs to the Massachusetts educational section, his small table wedged between an exhibit of pipe organs and a collection of educational pamphlets. His invention would not even be listed in the fair's program.

Bell's only hope lay in the cluster of exhausted, sweat-soaked judges that wearily made its way through the Main Exhibition Building one morning, examining a seemingly endless array of inventions. For days, Bell had worked feverishly on his equipment, desperately trying to repair the damage that had been done on the journey from Boston. There was little he could do, however, to make it seem exciting. In comparison to the colossal engines and locomotives in Machinery Hall and the rows of whirring contraptions in the electrical aisles, his small, battered machines seemed hopelessly unimpressive and inconsequential.

Fearing that he would be forgotten altogether if he stayed upstairs, Bell made the long journey down to where the judges were gathered in the central hall. As the sun beat down mercilessly through the glass roof, the judges, sweltering in their stiff, formal suits, suddenly decided that they'd had enough. Unanimously, they agreed to end the day early. They would see only one more exhibit.

Standing near enough to overhear their conversation, Bell realized that he had lost his only chance. All the time, expense, and effort he had poured into the fair, all the frustration and misery, were for nothing. Even if the judges returned the following day, they would never see his invention. By then, he would be back in Boston.

As Bell stood in silence, watching the judges turn their backs to him and begin to walk away, he suddenly heard a familiar voice. "How do you do, Mr. Bell?" Surprised, he turned to find Emperor Dom Pedro II of Brazil, his full, white beard neatly trimmed, his deep-set eyes bright with curiosity, looking directly at him. A passionate promoter of the sciences, Dom Pedro had asked to accompany the judges on their rounds that morning, perfectly happy to be in the tropical-like heat that reminded him of home. When he saw Bell standing in the crowd of some fifty judges and a handful of hovering inventors, he immediately recognized him as the talented teacher of the deaf whom he had met in Boston.

Eager as they were to leave, the judges could not go anywhere without Dom Pedro, who was not only the leader of a large country but, with his irrepressible energy and enthusiasm, had become the darling of the centennial fair. With the judges waiting anxiously nearby, the emperor struck up a leisurely conversation with the young teacher. When Bell told him that he had come to the fair hoping to show an invention, but would have to leave early in the morning, Dom Pedro reacted with characteristic vigor. "Ah!" he exclaimed. "Then we must have a look at it now." Taking Bell's arm in his own, he strode toward the stairs, a long line of judges shuffling resignedly behind.

After the group had crossed the vast hall and climbed to the remote gallery, Bell led them to his table, around which he had optimistically arranged a few chairs. Among the various instruments assembled was something that Bell called an "iron box receiver," a vertical metal cylinder that had a thin diaphragm in the center and had been secured to a square block of wood. Wires leading from the receiver had been strung along the gallery railing, disappearing into a small room about a hundred yards away. As the judges gathered around him, Bell explained his invention, the telephone. It was, he cautioned, but an "embryo of an idea." However, with it, he had achieved something extraordinary — the electrical transmission of the human voice.

With his audience's full attention now, Bell crossed the gallery to the room where the wires led. Leaning into a transmitter he had set up earlier in the day, he slowly began to recite Hamlet's famous soliloquy. For Bell, it was a natural choice. He had known the speech by heart since he was fourteen, when his grandfather had taught it to him in Scotland. As he spoke, Shakespeare's words now traveled by wire, traversing the gallery to where the judges waited in suspense.

Sitting at the table, with the iron box receiver pressed tightly to his ear, Dom Pedro heard an extraordinary sound — Bell's voice, heart-wrenchingly clear. "To be, or not to be," he said. Leaping from his chair, the emperor shouted, "I hear! I hear!" As the knot of judges watched in amazement, he turned toward the room at the far end of the gallery and raced off, "at a very unemperor-like-gait." Moments later, Bell, who was still reciting the soliloquy, with no understanding of the effect it had had, suddenly heard the unmistakable sound of pounding feet. Looking up, he saw the emperor of Brazil charging toward him, flush with excitement.

In that moment, Bell's life was transformed. To the rest of the world, he would no longer be a teacher, or even simply an inventor, but the creator of the telephone. Even as he watched the emperor's eyes flash with joy and amazement, however, Bell knew that he would reach far beyond this one invention. His mind was too crowded, and his heart too hopeful, to stop here.

While Bell's technological innovation caught fire in an instant of understanding, on the same fairgrounds, in a building just yards away, Joseph Lister's discovery, one of the most important advances in medical history, was lightly dismissed. Standing before a crowded hall at the centennial fair's Medical Congress, the British surgeon struggled to convince his audience, a collection of the most experienced and admired physicians and surgeons in the United States, of the critical importance of antisepsis — preventing infection by destroying germs. Although the men listened politely, very few of them believed what Lister was telling them, and almost none of them seriously considered putting his theory into practice.

At a time when many well-respected scientists still scoffed at the idea of germs, Lister's time-consuming and complicated system for destroying them seemed ridiculous. Lister, however, knew that the difference between his method and the old method was nothing less than the difference between life and death. He had developed antiseptic medicine eleven years earlier, after realizing that the same microorganisms that caused wine to ferment in Louis Pasteur's experiments must also cause infection in wounds. Lister applied this theory to his own patients, creating an elaborate system of sterilization using carbolic acid, and transforming his surgical ward from the typical foul-smelling horror chamber that defined nineteenth-century hospitals to a place of daily miracles.

Although the results were dramatic — the death rate among Lister's surgical patients immediately plummeted — antisepsis had provoked reactions of deep skepticism, even fury. In England, Lister had been forced repeatedly to defend his theory against attacks from enraged doctors. "The whole theory of antisepsis is not only absurd," one surgeon seethed, "it is a positive injury." Another charged that Lister's "methods would be a return to the darkest days of ancient surgery."

By 1876, Lister's steady and astonishing success had silenced nearly all of his detractors at home and in Europe. The United

States, however, remained inexplicably resistant. Most American doctors simply shrugged off Lister's findings, uninterested and unimpressed. Even Dr. Samuel Gross, the president of the Medical Congress and arguably the most famous surgeon in the country, regarded antisepsis as useless, even dangerous. "Little, if any faith, is placed by any enlightened or experienced surgeon on this side of the Atlantic in the so-called carbolic acid treatment of Professor Lister," Gross wrote imperiously.

The medical breakthroughs that won the attention and admiration of men like Gross were those they could readily understand. All around the Medical Congress, throughout the centennial fair, were examples of this type of practical progress. There was a much-admired exhibit of artificial limbs, "The Palmer Leg and Arm," which were of particular interest in the wake of the Civil War. Dr. B. Frank Palmer himself wore an articulated leg of his own design, with impressive results. "We did not in the least suspect that he had himself been provided with one of his own artificial limbs," marveled one of the judges. Down another aisle stood a pyramid of eight hundred ounces of pure morphine, and there were table after table of new and improved medical tools.

Admiring a sturdy saw meant for amputations, one surgeon asked rhetorically, "Who has not experienced the annoyance, in the middle of an operation, of the saw breaking or becoming wedged in the bone so tightly as to be disengaged with difficulty?"

The dangers Lister described were very different from, and far more lethal than, broken saws and inadequate prosthetics. They could not be seen by the naked eye, and many of the doctors in the audience still did not believe they existed. Despite the prevailing skepticism about his discovery, however, Lister refused to give up. If the scientific evidence he presented was not enough, he would appeal to something more powerful than logic: vanity. He would remind these doctors who they were, and what they, as a nation, had achieved. "American surgeons are renowned throughout the world for their inventive genius, and boldness and skill in execution," he said. "It is to America that we owe anesthesia, the greatest boon ever conferred upon suffering humanity by human means." After listing several other discoveries that were the result of American intelligence and industry, Lister beseeched his audience to cast aside their egos and listen to him. He was there, he said, in the hope that they would finally accept "the truth, the value, and the practical application of the principles of Antiseptic Surgery."

For three hours, Lister did all he could to persuade his audience. He explained his process, gave examples from his own surgical studies, and met each of the doctors' criticisms, one by one. To the common complaint that antisepsis was "too much trouble," he replied simply, "It is worth some trouble to be able to seal up an amputation, an exsection, or a large wound, with the absolute certainty that no evil effects will follow."

Seated in the audience, listening to Lister, was Dr. Frank Hamilton, a highly regarded surgeon from New York who would one day, quite literally, hold James Garfield's fate in his hands. When given an opportunity to speak, Hamilton assured Lister that he would be "glad to have you convince us that your method is the best." In his own practice, however, Hamilton preferred to use methods that were quite different from antisepsis. Among them was the " 'open-air treatment,' in which no dressings whatever are employed, but the wound is left open to the air, the discharges being permitted to drop into proper receptacles, or to dry upon the surface." Hamilton also highly recommended soaking dressings in warm water, and then applying them directly to open wounds.

A few weeks after Lister tried in vain to persuade men like Hamilton that, without antisepsis, they risked the very real danger of killing their patients, James Garfield was descending, once again, into what he knew as the "darkness of death." At his home in Washington, he watched helplessly as his youngest child, Neddie, a beautiful little boy who had contracted whooping cough soon after attending the centennial fair, died in his small bed.

After he had lost Trot, so many years earlier, Garfield had thought he could never again feel such an all-consuming sorrow. He realized now how wrong he had been. "I am trying to see through it the deep meaning and lesson of this death," he wrote. "God help me to use the heavy lesson for the good of those of us who remain." Despite his belief in the goodness of God, however, Garfield knew that death was cruel, unpredictable, and, too often, unpreventable. Perhaps even harder to accept was that the science he so deeply admired, for all its awe-inspiring potential, seemed powerless in the face of it.

Searching for a way to teach his children this hard truth, to prepare them for what inevitably lay ahead, Garfield had often turned to what he knew best — books. After dinner one evening, he pulled a copy of Shakespeare's *Othello* off the shelf and began to read the tragedy aloud. "The children were not pleased with the way the story came out," he admitted in his diary, but he hoped that they would come to "appreciate stories that [do not] come out well, for they are very much like a good deal of life."

CHAPTER 2
PROVIDENCE

> I never meet a ragged boy in the street without feeling that I may owe him a salute, for I know not what possibilities may be buttoned up under his coat.
>
> JAMES A. GARFIELD

James Garfield's father, Abram, had died on a spring day in 1833, just a few months after his thirty-third birthday. As he had peered out a window that day, surveying the farmland he had just saved from a raging wildfire, he had known that he would not survive the "violent cold" that had so suddenly seized him. The house he would die in was a log cabin he had built four years earlier. It consisted of one room, three small windows, and a rough, wooden plank floor. The windowpanes were made of oiled paper, and the gaps between the logs were filled with clay in a futile attempt to shut out the brutal Ohio winters. The house and the land were all his family had, and he had done everything he could to protect them from the fire.

Like his ancestors, who had sailed from Chester, England, to Massachusetts in 1630, just ten years after the *Mayflower,* Abram had left all he knew in search of a better life. His father had stayed in the East, on a small farm in New York, but as a very young man Abram had set his sights on the West. In 1819, he and his half brother Amos packed their bags and moved to Ohio. After several years of struggling to make a living, Abram took a job helping to build the Ohio and Erie Canal, as he had helped to build the Erie Canal when he was a teenager.

In the early 1800s, Ohio was the American frontier. Wild and largely unmapped, it had not joined the Union until 1803, becoming the country's seventeenth state. Ohio was the first state to be created out of the Northwest Territory. Iroquois and Shawnee tribes were still scattered throughout the Ohio Valley, fiercely fighting for the little land they had left, but time was running out. They had lost their British allies after the War of 1812, and Andrew Jackson would pass the Indian Removal Act less than twenty years later, forcing them all onto reservations.

Although land was available for two dollars an acre, ten years would pass before Abram and Amos had saved enough money for a farm. Soon after their arrival, they met and married a pair of sisters from New Hampshire named Eliza and Alpha Ballou. In 1829 the two couples, now with children of their own, bought a hundred acres of heavily wooded land in Cuyahoga County. They were just sixteen miles from Cleveland but two miles from the nearest road, surrounded by a vast, thick forest. It was the life they had hoped for, but it was far from easy.

When Abram had seen the wildfire racing toward his cabin, he had met it with equal ferocity. He worked all day, digging ditches, hacking away brush, and fighting back the roaring, choking flames. Somehow, miraculously, he had saved his farm, but his victory came at a high cost. Although he was young and strong, he was also poor and isolated. With no medical care beyond an unlicensed, itinerate doctor, he quickly succumbed to exhaustion and fever. Within days, he would die, keenly aware that he was leaving Eliza with four children to feed. Their youngest, James, not yet two years old.

There would come a time when the story of

James Garfield's early life would be widely admired. Throughout the nation and around the world, his extraordinary rise from fatherlessness and abject poverty would make him the embodiment of the American dream. Garfield himself, however, refused ever to romanticize his childhood. "Let us never praise poverty," he would write to a friend, "for a child at least."

Even by the standards of the hardscrabble rural region in which he lived, Garfield was raised in desperate circumstances. His mother, left with debts she could not hope to pay after her husband's death, was forced to sell much of their land. What was left, she farmed herself with the help of her oldest son, James's eleven-year-old brother, Thomas. Between them, working as hard as they could, they managed to avoid giving the younger children to more prosperous families to raise, as their relatives had advised them to do. So little did they have to spare, however, that James did not have a pair of shoes until he was four years old.

Although Garfield understood clearly, and at times painfully, that he was poor, he had inherited from his mother an innate dignity that never failed to inspire respect. His mother was fiercely proud that she and her children had "received no aid, worked and won their living and could look any man in the face." Even as a child, Garfield walked with his shoulders squared and his head thrown back. "If I ever get through a course of study I don't expect any one will ask me what kind of a coat I wore when studying," he wrote to his mother while attending a nearby school, "and if they do I shall not be ashamed to tell them it was a ragged one."

Eliza Garfield's greatest ambition for her second son was a good education. She came from a long line of New England intellectuals, including a president of Tufts College and the founder and editor of a Boston newspaper. She donated some of her land for a small schoolhouse so that her children, as well as her neighbors' children, could have a place to learn. Even when James turned eleven years old, the age at which his brother had begun helping the family by working on neighboring farms, she insisted that he stay home and concentrate on his education — and Thomas wholeheartedly agreed. "Whatever else happens," they said, "James must go to school."

James, unfortunately, had different dreams. Although he could not swim, and admitted that he "knew almost nothing about the water except what I had read," he longed for a life at sea. As he was hundreds of miles from any ocean, the best he could do was the Erie and Ohio Canal, the canal his father had helped to build. At sixteen years of age, he left home to become a canal man, breaking his mother's heart and, she feared, putting an end to her hopes for him.

Garfield's first job on the canal was as a driver, the lowliest position among a group of rough, and occasionally violent, men. As the months passed, he became increasingly comfortable with the life he had fashioned for himself. He knew that the work he was doing, and the men he met along the way, likely made him "ripe for ruin," but he was willing to take that chance.

Before he could "drink in every species of vice," however, the course of his young life took a sudden turn. As he stood alone at the bow one night, struggling with a coiled rope, he lost his balance and, before he could right himself, fell into the canal. He had fallen in before, more than a dozen times, but each time it had been daylight, and there had been men on the deck to pull him out.

Now it was midnight, and Garfield was certain that he would drown. He cried out for help although he knew it was useless. Everyone on the boat was fast asleep. As he searched frantically and blindly for something to save his life, his hands suddenly struck the rope that had been the cause of his fall. Gripping it tightly, he found that, with a "great struggle," he could use it to slowly pull himself up until, finally, he fell heavily onto the boat.

As he sat, dripping and scared, on the deck of the canal boat, Garfield wondered why he was still alive. The rope was not secured to anything on the boat. When he had pulled on it, it should have fallen off the deck, slipping to the bottom of the canal and leaving him to drown. "Carefully examining it, I found that just where it came over the edge of the boat it had been drawn into a crack and there knotted itself," he would later write. "I sat down in the cold of the night and in my wet clothes and contemplated the matter. . . . I did not believe that God had paid any attention to me on my own account but I thought He had saved me for my mother and for something greater and better than canaling."

Although his life would change dramatically in the years to come, Garfield would never be able to tell the story of that night without wonder. Looking back on it, moreover, he would have a much clearer and broader understanding of its importance than he could have hoped to have at sixteen.

"Providence only could have saved my life," he wrote years later, struggling to understand all that had happened to him in the intervening years. "Providence, therefore, thinks it worth saving."

Garfield returned home soon after his near drowning a changed man, but also a very sick one. He had contracted malaria on the canal, and by the time he reached his family's log cabin, he could barely walk. "As I approached the door at about nine o'clock in the evening," he later recalled, "I heard my mother engaged in prayer. During the prayer she referred to me, her son away, God only knew where, and asked that he might be preserved in health to return to her." When Eliza ended her prayer, her son quietly stepped into the cabin.

James had returned, but so ill was he that his family now feared they would lose him for good. Although his fever broke after ten days, three weeks later it was back, stronger than before. For two months, no one knew if he would survive. When he finally began to recover, his mother dared to hope that his canal days were behind him. After asking him to consider returning to his studies rather than to the canal, she told him that she had more than advice to offer. Since he had been gone, she and Thomas had managed to save seventeen dollars, and they hoped that he would use it to go back to school. "I took the money," Garfield wrote, "as well as the advice."

By the fall of 1851, Garfield had transformed from a rough canal man into a passionate and determined student. After studying at local schools, he was accepted to a small preparatory school in northern Ohio called the Western Reserve Eclectic Institute. The school's entire campus consisted of a wide cornfield and, on the crest of a hill, a modest three-story redbrick building with a white bell tower. "It was without a dollar of endowment, without a powerful friend anywhere," Garfield would later write, but to him, it was a chance to become an educated man.

Unable to afford tuition, he convinced the school to allow him to work as a janitor in exchange for his education. He swept floors, hauled wood, and made fires, and he never tried to hide his poverty from his fellow students. As he walked to the tower every morning, having left the first lecture of the day early so he could ring the school's enormous bell, his "tread was firm and free," a friend would recall years later. "The same unconscious dignity followed him then that attended him when he ascended the eastern portico of the Capitol to deliver his Inaugural address."

Garfield quickly realized that he was an extraordinarily talented student, and the more he learned, the more ambitious he became. "The ice is broken," he wrote as he began his academic life. "I am resolved to make a mark in the world. . . . There is some of the slumbering thunder in my soul and it shall come out." His day began at 5:00 a.m., as he immersed himself in Virgil before breakfast, and it continued, unabated, with studying, classes, work, and more studying until just before midnight. No one worked harder, and if they came close, Garfield took it as a personal challenge. "If at any time I began to flag in my effort to master a subject," he wrote, "I was stimulated to further effort by the thought, 'Some other fellow in the class will probably master it.' " As determined as Garfield was to outpace his fellow students, his fiercest competition was with himself. "He had a great desire and settled purpose to conquer," a classmate and student of his wrote. "To master all lessons, to prove superior to every difficulty, to excel all competitors, to conquer and surpass himself."

So vigorously did Garfield apply himself during his first year at the Eclectic that, by his second year, the school had promoted him from janitor to assistant professor. Along with the subjects he was taking as a student, he was given a full roster of classes to teach, including literature, mathematics, and ancient languages. He taught six classes, which were so popular that he was asked to add two more — one on penmanship and the other on Virgil.

In 1854, Garfield was accepted to Williams College in Williamstown, Massachusetts, where the competition was greater than he had ever experienced, stirring in him an even fiercer ambition. "There is a high standard of scholarship here and very many excellent scholars, those that have had far better advantages and more thorough training than I have," he wrote to a friend soon after arriving in Williamstown. "I have been endeavoring to calculate their dimensions and power and, between you and me, I have determined that out of the forty-two members of my class thirty-seven shall stand behind me within two months."

After graduating with honors from Williams two years later, Garfield returned to the Eclectic Institute to teach. By the time he was twenty-six, he was the school's president.

■ ■ ■ ■

Two things ended Garfield's academic career: politics and war. When an Ohio state senator died unexpectedly in the summer of 1859, Garfield was asked to take his place in an upcoming election. He accepted the nomination, but not without concern. "I am aware that I launch out upon a fickle current and am about a work as precarious as men follow," he wrote in his diary the night of the nomination. Two months later he won the election by a wide margin, quietly beginning a career that, in the end, would lead him to the White House.

Little more than a year after Garfield entered politics, the country was plunged into civil war. Garfield, anxious to leave the legislature for the battlefield, wrote to a friend that he had "no heart to think of anything but the country." Four months after Confederate forces fired on Fort Sumter, he was made a lieutenant colonel in the Union Army. Soon after, at thirty years of age, he was promoted to colonel and enthusiastically began recruiting men from Ohio to join the ranks of his regiment — the 42nd.

As he looked into the eager faces of his

recruits, many of them students of the Eclectic Institute, Garfield shared their excitement, too young himself to understand that, before the war had ended, he would be filled with "pride and grief commingled." The 42nd's first commission was to fight back the growing rebel incursion into Kentucky. Every soldier, Union or Confederate, understood the critical role Kentucky would play in the outcome of the Civil War. As a border state, and Abraham Lincoln's birthplace, it was the constant target of military and ideological attacks from the North and the South. "I hope to have God on my side," Lincoln reportedly said, "but I must have Kentucky."

Garfield's regiment did not have a hope of succeeding. The Confederate force it faced was two thousand men strong, fortified with a battery of four cannons and several wagonloads of ammunition, and led by Humphrey Marshall, a well-known, well-seasoned brigadier general who had graduated from West Point the year after Garfield was born. In sharp contrast, the 42nd had five hundred fewer soldiers and no artillery. Worse, its commander was a young academic who had spent the past decade thinking about Latin and higher math and had absolutely no military experience, in war or peace.

Although he was hopelessly inexperienced, outmanned, and outgunned, Garfield accepted the assignment. After he received his orders, he worked through the night, hunched over a map of eastern Kentucky. By the light of a lantern, he traced the ragged mountains and deep valleys that marked the six thousand square miles of territory he and his men had been asked to defend. By morning, he was ready to set out.

In the end, the struggle for Kentucky's allegiance came down to a single, seminal battle — the Battle of Middle Creek — and a military strategy that some would call brilliant, others audacious. In January of 1862, after weeks of marching through fog and mud, shivering under thin blankets in snow and sleet, and surviving largely on whatever could be found in the countryside, the 42nd finally reached Marshall's men. Despite the Confederate force's size and artillery, Garfield refused to wait for additional troops. Instead, he divided his already small regiment into three even smaller groups. The plan was to attack the rebels from three different sides, thus giving the impression, Garfield hoped, of a regiment that was much larger and better equipped than his.

Incredibly, Marshall believed everything Garfield wanted him to, and more. When Garfield's first detachment attacked, the Confederates, as expected, confidently rushed to meet them. Then a second force fell upon the rebels from a different direction, throwing them into disarray and confusion. Just as they were beginning to figure out how to fight on two fronts, Garfield attacked on a third. "The [Confederate] regiment and battery were hurried frantically from one road to another," recalled a young private, "as the point of attack seemed to be changed." Finally, convinced that a "mighty army" — a force of four thousand men with "five full regiments of infantry, 200 cavalry, and two batteries of artillery" — had surrounded him, Marshall ordered his men to retreat, leaving Kentucky solidly in Union hands.

Although the Battle of Middle Creek made Garfield famous, and resulted in his swift promotion to brigadier general, he would always remember the battle less for its triumph than for its tremendous loss. When the fighting had ended, when his gamble had paid off and the 42nd stood victorious, Garfield learned the truth about war. Stepping into a clearing, he saw what at first he took to be soldiers sleeping, "resting there after the fatigue of a long day's march." He would never forget how they looked, scattered over the "dewy meadow in different shapes of sleep." However, just as quickly as the impression of peace and tranquillity had formed in his mind, it was replaced by the sickening realization that the young men before him were not resting but dead. His own clever plan, moreover, was responsible for this carnage. It was in that moment, Garfield would later tell a friend, that "something went out of him . . . that never came back; the sense of the sacredness of life and the impossibility of destroying it."

As painful as it was for Garfield to witness the death of his young soldiers, he remained firmly committed to the war, determined that it would end in Confederate defeat. "By thundering volley, must this rebellion be met," he wrote, "and by such means alone." For Garfield, however, the Civil War was about more than putting down a rebellion or even preventing the country from being torn in two. It was about emancipation.

Throughout his life, Garfield had been an ardent abolitionist. As a young man, he had written feverishly in his diary that he felt "like throwing the whole current of my life into the work of opposing this giant evil." In an attempt to help a runaway slave, he had given him what little money he could spare and urged him to "trust to God and his muscle." In the darkest days of the Civil War, he had wondered if the war itself was God's punishment for the horrors of slavery. "For what else are we so fearfully scourged and defeated?" he had asked.

Although Garfield had chosen a life of calm, rational thought, when it came to abolition he freely admitted that he had "never been anything else than radical." He found it difficult to condemn even the most violent abolitionists, men like John Brown whose hatred of slavery allowed for any means of destroying it. In 1856, Brown had planned and participated in the brutal slaying of five proslavery activists near the Pottawatomie Creek in Kansas. Three years later, he raided the federal armory at Harper's Ferry, Virginia, in a desperate attempt to form an "army of emancipation."

Garfield had felt a profound sense of loss when, in 1859, he learned that Brown was to be hanged. "A dark day for our country," he wrote in his diary. "John Brown is to be hung at Charleston, Va. . . . I do not justify his acts. By no means. But I do accord to him, and I think every man must, honesty of purpose and sincerity of heart." On the day of the execution, Garfield wrote in his pocket diary, *"Servitium esto damnatum."* Slavery be damned.

Despite the fact that, since winning his state senate seat two years earlier, Garfield had spent far more time on the battlefield or in a military encampment than in his office, his political career continued to take on a life of its own. In the fall of 1862, just ten months after the Battle of Middle Creek, he was elected to the U.S. Congress, receiving nearly twice as many votes as his opponent, although he had done nothing to promote his candidacy. Before the results were even announced, he had set out for Washington — not to prepare himself for Congress, but to seek his next military appointment.

Garfield would not take his congressional seat until more than a year later, when Abraham Lincoln asked him to. "I have resigned my place in the army and have taken my seat in Congress," Garfield wrote home, clearly conscious of his unique role. "I did this with regret, for I had hoped not to leave the field till every insurgent state had returned to its allegiance. But the President told me he dared not risk a single vote in the House and he needed men in Congress who were practically acquainted with the wants of the army. I did not feel it right to consult my own preference in such a case."

Although he worried that it would seem as if he were abandoning the war, and his men, Garfield soon learned that he could fight more effectively, and win more often, on the floor of Congress. He introduced a resolution that would allow blacks to walk freely through the streets of Washington, D.C., without carrying a pass. Appealing to reason and the most basic sense of fairness, he asked, "What legislation is necessary to secure equal justice to all loyal persons, without regard to color, at the national capitol?" After the war ended, he gave a passionate speech in support of black suffrage. By denying freedmen the right to vote, he argued, the United States was allowing southerners extraordinary and unconscionable power over the lives of their former slaves. They were placing every black man at the mercy of the same people "who have been so reluctantly compelled to take their feet from his neck and their hands from his throat."

Having known intimately the cruelties and injustices of poverty, Garfield found ways to help not just the despairing, but even the despised. As head of the Appropriations Committee, he directed funds toward exploration and westward expansion, the only hope for thousands of men much like his father. It was to Garfield that the geologist and explorer John Wesley Powell turned when he needed support for a surveying expedition. Powell, who navigated rapids and climbed cliffs with one arm, having lost the other to a lead bullet in the Civil War, published a full report of his historic exploration of the Colorado River, and the first non-native passage through the Grand Canyon, only after Garfield insisted that he do so.

Garfield even defended enemies of the Union. In his only case as a lawyer, which he argued before the U.S. Supreme Court in 1866, just a year after the Civil War had ended, he represented five Indiana men who had been sentenced to death for stealing weapons and freeing rebel prisoners. The men, who were fiercely hated throughout the North, claimed not that they were innocent but that, as civilians, their court-martial had been unconstitutional. To the horror and outrage of his Republican friends and colleagues, Garfield agreed, accepted their case, and won.

Inexplicably, it seemed that the only cause for which Garfield would not fight was his own political future. In an early-adopted eccentricity that would become for him a central "law of life," he refused to seek an appointment or promotion of any kind. "I suppose I am morbidly sensitive about any reference to my own achievements," he admitted. "I so much despise a man who blows his own horn, that I go to the other extreme." From his first political campaign, he had sternly instructed his backers that "first, I should make no pledge to any man or any measures; second, I should not work for my own nomination." The closest he had come to even admitting that he was interested in a political office was to tell his friends, when a seat in the U.S. Senate became available in 1879, that "if the Senatorship is thus to be thrown open for honorable competition, I should be sorry to be wholly omitted from consideration in that direction." After a landslide victory, his campaign's expenses amounted to less than $150.

When it came to the presidency, Garfield simply looked the other way. He spent seventeen years in Congress, and every day he saw men whose desperate desire for the White House ruined their careers, their character, and their lives. "I have so long and so often seen the evil effects of the presidential fever upon my associates and friends that I am determined it shall not seize me," he wrote in his journal in February 1879. "In almost ever[y] case it impairs if it does not destroy the usefulness of its victim." Aware that there was talk of making him a candidate in the presidential election of 1880, Garfield hoped to avoid the grasp of other men's ambitions, and to be given a chance to "wait for the future." However, he had already lived a long life for a young man, and he knew that change came without invitation, too often bringing loss and sorrow in its wake. "This world," he had learned long before, "does not seem to be the place to carry out one's wishes."

Chapter 3
"A Beam in Darkness"

Quiet is no certain pledge of permanence and safety. Trees may flourish and flowers may bloom upon the quiet mountain side, while silently the trickling rain-drops are filling the deep cavern behind its rocky barriers, which, by and by, in a single moment, shall hurl to wild ruin its treacherous peace.

JAMES A. GARFIELD

When Garfield made his way through the crowded streets of Chicago to the Republican National Convention on the evening of June 6, 1880, he felt not excitement, but a heavy sense of dread. The convention was about to begin the second session of its fourth day, and he had no illusions about what it would hold. Each day had been more bruising than the last, as the crowd had grown louder, the tensions higher, and the delegates angrier. The viciousness of the convention dismayed Garfield, but it did not surprise him. His first night in Chicago, he had written home asking for help in the days ahead. "Don't fail to write me every day," he wrote to his wife. "Each word from you will be a light in this wilderness."

In 1880, the Republican Party was sharply divided into two warring factions. At the convention, delegates had little choice but to choose a side — either the Stalwarts, who were as fiercely committed to defending the spoils system as they were opposed to reconciliation with the South; or the men whose values Garfield shared, a determined group of reformers who would become known as the Half-Breeds. The Stalwarts had nothing but contempt for their rivals within the party, particularly Rutherford B. Hayes, who was about to complete his first term in the White House. President Hayes's attempts to replace government patronage with a merit system had been met with such fury from the Stalwarts, and had led to such bitter contention and open rebellion, that he had made it clear to anyone who would listen that he did not want to be nominated for a second term. "The first half of my term was so full of trouble and embarrassments as to be a continual struggle," Hayes wrote, "and I do not propose to invite a new season of embarrassment."

Hayes's abdication and the escalating battle for control of the party had aroused such intense interest in the nomination that, for the first time in Republican history, every state had sent a representative to the convention. The Half-Breeds had two top candidates: John Sherman, General William Tecumseh Sherman's younger brother and secretary of the treasury under Hayes, and James G. Blaine, who had been speaker of the house and was now a senator of such charm and influence that he was known as the Magnetic Man from Maine. The Stalwarts, on the other hand, had only one serious candidate — Ulysses S. Grant.

If anyone was considered a safe bet in this turbulent convention, it was Grant. The idea of a third term, for anyone, was controversial, and the two terms Grant had already served as president had been notoriously rife with corruption. He was, however, still a national hero. Not only had he commanded the Union Army in the Civil War, but he had personally accepted Robert E. Lee's surrender at Appomattox. In 1868, and again in 1872, he had been given the Republican nomination for president on the first ballot. No one believed he would win the nomination as easily this time, but few believed he would lose.

Although the Republican Party had controlled the White House for more than ten years, and their leading candidates in 1880 were all widely known and well worn, they had wisely chosen as the setting of their convention a city that, more than any other city in the nation, then symbolized rebirth and renewal. Less than ten years earlier, Chicago had been devastated by the worst natural disaster in the country's 104-year history — the Great Chicago Fire. Since then, the city had not only recovered, but had literally risen from the ashes to become one of America's most modern metropolises.

As Garfield made his way toward the convention hall, he saw all around him evidence of the path the fire had taken. The street he was walking on, Michigan Avenue, had been leveled for ten blocks, from Congress Avenue north to the Chicago River. Every building, every lamppost, even the sidewalks themselves had been destroyed.

At the time of the fire, in the fall of 1871, Chicago had been a tinderbox. A hundred days had passed with little more than an inch of rain. The buildings were made of wood, wooden planks covered the streets and sidewalks, and, in anticipation of the coming winter, cords of wood, gallons of kerosene, and mounds of hay had been stockpiled throughout the city. The fire, which had started in a cow barn on the city's west side, raged for almost two days, destroying thousands of buildings and more than seventy miles of street, killing at least three hundred people, and leaving a hundred thousand homeless.

As wide-ranging and devastating as the damage had been, Chicago had sprung back to life with astonishing speed. Rebuilding efforts started so quickly that the ground was still warm when the first construction began. Within a year of the fire, nearly $50 million worth of buildings had been erected, and by 1879 the city had issued some ten thousand construction permits. By the time Garfield saw Chicago, its skyline was dotted with beautiful modern buildings, and it was just five years away from being home to the world's first skyscraper.

While Chicago brought a sense of progress and innovation to the Republican convention, the convention in turn brought money, excitement, and worldwide attention to the city. Delegates, reporters, and curious citizens streamed in by the thousands. There were no vacant rooms at the hotels, no free tables in the restaurants. The streets were clogged with people, horses, and carriages. "Fresh crowds arriving by every train," Garfield marveled, "and the interest increasing every hour."

When Garfield finally reached the convention hall, he stood before one of Chicago's most extravagant buildings. The Interstate Industrial Exposition Building, the city's first convention center, had been built in 1872, on the heels of the great fire. Instead of wood, it was made of gleaming, fire-resistant glass and metal. It was a thousand feet long and seventy-five feet high, with elaborate ornamental domes inspired by the grand exposition halls of London and New York.

Leaving the warmth of a mild summer evening, Garfield stepped into the hall's vast, richly decorated interior. Hundreds of red-white-and-blue flags papered the walls and swung from the arched, raftered ceiling. From huge, open windows, "the cool air of the lake poured in," one reporter wrote. It "shook the banners, bathed the heated galleries, and then fought for mastery with the sewer-gas, which, in some mysterious way, seemed 'entitled to the floor.' " In the center of the hall was a long, narrow stage bordered on one side by rectangular tables covered in heavy white cloths. On the other side of the tables, facing the stage, were tight rows of chairs arranged in alphabetical order for the more than 750 delegates. Above the delegates' heads swayed enormous portraits of George Washington and Abraham Lincoln, and along the hall's curved back wall stretched a wide banner bearing the final words from the Gettysburg Address: "And that government of the people, by the people, for the people shall not perish from the earth."

Although the hall could accommodate thousands of people, it was full to overflowing. Every seat was taken — both on the floor and in the balcony, which rose to the ceiling in steep, vertiginous layers — and every inch of standing room had been claimed. Mortal enemies sat shoulder to shoulder. Reporters hunched over six long tables, elbowing for room. Men even sat on the edge of the stage, their black, highly polished shoes dangling over the side, threatening to tear the bunting with every swing.

As crowded as the hall was, it sounded as if it held twice as many people as it actually did. Beyond the typical raucous, partisan singing and chanting that took place at every convention, a deafening vitriolic battle was being waged between the party's opposing factions. The day before, a woman from Brooklyn, who, despite her great girth, had somehow managed to hoist herself onto the stage, had to be forcibly removed from the hall as she shrieked, over and over again, "Blaine! Blaine! James G. Blaine!" Whenever a Stalwart spoke, whether to argue a position or simply to note a minor point of order, he was met by angry hisses from the Half-Breeds. The Stalwarts, in turn, greeted declarations from Half-Breeds with a chorus of boos so loud they drowned out every other sound in the hall, from the thunderous scuffing of wooden chairs on the wooden floor to the jarring screeches of trains along a track just a few blocks away.

As Garfield quietly found his seat on the convention floor, he took in the spectacle around him with weary eyes. Not only had he already spent four days in the crowded, roaring hall, but his hotel room offered no refuge at night. So crowded was the city that many people who wanted to attend the convention, and even some who were obliged to attend, found themselves with no place to sleep. At one in the morning following the convention's opening day, just as he was finally about to collapse into bed, Garfield had heard a knock on his door. He opened it to find a friend with a favor to ask. He "asked me to allow his brother (a stranger) [to] sleep with me," Garfield sighed in a letter home the following day. He could not bring himself to say no, but he wished he had. "My bed is only three quarter size and with a stranger stretched along the wall," he wrote. "I could not [get] . . . a minute of rest or sleep."

Perhaps even more to blame for keeping Garfield up at night was the nominating speech he knew he had to give for John Sherman. Before becoming secretary of the treasury, Sherman had been a powerful senator from Ohio, and he was keenly aware that there was more enthusiasm within his state for Garfield's nomination than his own. Nicknamed the "Ohio Icicle," Sherman had been determinedly working behind the scenes for years, waiting for an opportunity to win the White House. He was confident that, this time, it was his turn. "It is evident," said William Henry Smith, a former Ohio state secretary, that Sherman "thinks Heaven is smiling upon him." First, however, Sherman had to dampen interest in Garfield, and the best way to do that, he reasoned, was to have Garfield nominate him at the convention.

Nor, certainly, had it escaped Sherman's

notice that Garfield was one of the best speakers in the Republican Party. From a very young age, Garfield had realized that he had one skill above all others — the ability to capture a crowd. When he was just twenty-one, he had humiliated a well-known traveling philosopher named Treat who made his living by going from town to town attacking Christianity and those who would defend it. After Treat had addressed one of the professors at the Western Reserve Eclectic Institute in Hiram, Ohio, with taunting disrespect, Garfield had stood up and, to the surprise of no one but Treat, quietly and calmly eviscerated him. "It is impossible," a man who attended the debate would later recall, "for me to give any idea of his speech or of its effect upon his audience. . . . The applause was constant and deafening. He spoke with readiness and power and eloquence which were perfectly overwhelming. I do not think that Mr. Treat ever attempted another speech at Hiram."

By the time Garfield entered Congress, he was a highly skilled rhetorician. The only problem was that, as good as he was at speaking, he enjoyed it even more, perhaps too much. It was not unheard of for him to speak on the floor of Congress more than forty times in a single day, and when he gave a speech, it was rarely a short one. Over the years, he had tested his colleagues' patience on more than one occasion, prompting some of them to complain that he was "too fond of talking." Even Garfield himself admitted that, when it came to words, he had a "fatal facility."

However, when the fate of a bill lay in the balance or there was a moment of grave national importance, Garfield's colleagues often turned to him to speak for the Party. On the first anniversary of President Lincoln's assassination, he had been asked to give an impromptu eulogy, even though he was then one of the most junior members of Congress. Garfield had resisted, arguing that someone with substantially more seniority should give the address, but his colleagues would not relent. With only a few minutes to prepare, he delivered a speech that would be remembered not only for its eloquence but also for the powerful emotion it conveyed. At one point, he recited from memory Alfred Lord Tennyson's poem *In Memoriam,* which he had not read in many years. "We have but faith: we cannot know; / For knowledge is of things we see / And yet we trust it comes from thee, / A beam in darkness: let it grow."

■ ■ ■ ■

Yet despite his ability, Garfield dreaded the speech he was about to give. He was obliged to support Sherman, a fellow Ohioan, but he did not believe Sherman was the best candidate for the nomination. So reluctant was Garfield to deliver the speech that he had hardly given any thought to what he would say. "I have arisen at 7 this morning to tell you the peril I am in," he had written home in desperation just a few days earlier. "I have not made the first step in preparation for my speech nominating Sherman and I see no chance to get to prepare. It was a frightful mistake that I did not write [it] before I came. It now seems inevitable that I shall fall far below what I ought to do."

Garfield's agonizing situation was made far worse by the fact that he would be competing for the attention and sympathies of the rabidly partisan crowd with Roscoe Conkling, a senior senator from New York and the undisputed leader of the Stalwarts. Conkling was not only a famously charismatic speaker, but arguably the most powerful person in the country. Ten years earlier, then President Grant had given Conkling, his most fiercely loyal supporter, control of the New York Customs House, which was the largest federal office in the United States and collected 70 percent of the country's customs revenue. Since then, Conkling had personally made each appointment to the customs house. Any man fortunate enough to receive one of the high-paying jobs had been expected to make generous contributions to the Republican Party of New York, and to show unwavering loyalty to Conkling. So powerful had Conkling become that he had cavalierly turned down Grant's offer to nominate him to the U.S. Supreme Court six years earlier.

Like Garfield, Conkling had been an outspoken abolitionist and was a powerful defender of rights for freed slaves. He had helped to draft the Fourteenth Amendment, which gave African Americans citizenship and equal rights under the Constitution, and he argued vehemently for taking a hard line toward the defeated South. To no cause, however, had Conkling committed himself more passionately than the spoils system, the source of his personal power. When Rutherford B. Hayes, as part of his sweeping efforts at reform, had removed Conkling's man, Chester Arthur, from his position as the collector of the New York

Customs House, Conkling had attacked Hayes with a vengeance, ensuring that he was thwarted at every turn for the rest of his presidency. Finally, defeated and exhausted, Hayes had bitterly complained that Conkling was a "thoroughly rotten man."

Hayes was not alone in his assessment of Conkling's character. As is true of most men who wield their power like a weapon, Conkling was widely feared, slavishly obeyed, and secretly despised. He offended fellow senators with impunity, ignoring their red-faced splutters even when they threatened to challenge him to a duel.

Conkling was also exceedingly vain. He had broad shoulders and a waspishly thin waist, a physique that he kept in trim by pummeling a punching bag hanging from the ceiling of his office. He wore canary-yellow waistcoats, twisted his thick, wavy blond hair into a spit curl in the center of his high forehead, used lavender ink, and recoiled at the slightest touch. When he had worked as a litigator, he had often worried that he would lose a case after flying into a rage when "some ill-bred neighbor" put a foot on his chair.

Conkling's most open detractor was James Blaine, with whom he had had a famous fight on the floor of Congress fourteen years earlier, and to whom he had not spoken since. In front of the entire House of Representatives, Blaine had attacked Conkling as no man had ever dared to do, ridiculing "his haughty disdain, his grandiloquent swell, his majestic, supereminent, overpowering, turkey-gobbler strut." Clutching a newspaper article that compared Conkling to a respected, recently deceased congressman, Blaine, brimming with sarcasm, spat, "The resemblance is great. It is striking. Hyperion to a satyr, Thersites to Hercules, mud to marble, dunghill to diamond, a singed cat to a Bengal tiger, a whining puppy to a roaring lion."

Conkling, with cold fury, had vowed that he would "never overlook" Blaine's attack, and he had since done everything in his power to deny Blaine the one thing he wanted most in this world: the presidency. Even Garfield, who admired Blaine and considered him a friend, believed that the senator had become "warped" by his all-consuming quest for the White House, willing to sacrifice any cause, even his own honor, in the pursuit of this one, overriding ambition. Four years earlier, at the last national convention, Conkling and Blaine had both been candidates for the presidential nomination. When it became clear that he could not win, Conkling had made sure his votes went to Hayes, not because he liked Hayes but because he hated Blaine. Conkling was now determined to win the nomination for Grant. He was fighting for his own benefit as much as Grant's, but he would have done it for the pure pleasure of watching Blaine lose.

That night in the convention hall, all eyes were on Conkling, as he expected them to be. Every morning, he had entered to wild cheers. Each time he had risen to speak, he had been "cool, calm, and after his usual fashion, confident and self-possessed," breaking into his "characteristic sneer" only when he could no longer suppress it. Sitting in an aisle seat at the front of the New York delegation, he now looked, in the words of one reporter, "serene as the June sun that shone in at the windows." He slowly ran his fingers through his thick hair, which, but for the ever-present spit curl, was swept dramatically up from his head in carefully styled waves. Occasionally, he glanced around coolly or leaned over, almost imperceptibly, to consult with Edwin Stoughton, the minister to Russia, to his right, or Chester Arthur, who sat directly behind him.

From his seat, Conkling watched the proceedings with growing delight. The session was called to order at 7:15 p.m. with the sharp rap of a gavel, the head of which was fashioned from the doorsill of Abraham Lincoln's Illinois home and the handle made of cane from George Washington's Mount Vernon estate. Soon after, James Joy, a little known delegate from Michigan, walked reluctantly to the podium to give Blaine's nominating speech. Blaine's heart must have sunk, and Conkling's sung, as Joy mournfully began: "I shall never cease to regret the circumstances under which the duty is imposed on me to make the nomination of a candidate in the Convention." Complaining that he had been out of the country for months and, since arriving in Chicago, had been very busy on the convention floor, he vowed to bring Blaine before the convention in "as brief a manner as possible." After an extremely modest, stumbling assessment of his candidate's qualities, Joy quickly concluded by nominating for president "that eminent statesman, James S. Blaine," prompting howls of frustration from Blaine's supporters, who screamed that his middle initial was "G! You fool, G!"

After Joy had scurried back to his seat in profound relief and another man had nominated William Windom of Minnesota, Conkling at last had the floor. Hardly waiting for

New York to be called, he sprang from his seat and strode down the aisle — shoulders back, chest out, face already arch with victory. Leaping onto one of the tables where reporters sat, astonished and delighted, Conkling "folded his arms across his swelling breast, laid his head back with a kingly frown upon his cleanly washed face, and settling his left foot with a slight stamp of his right," said, in a slow, clear, supremely confident voice, "When asked whence comes our candidate we say from Appomattox."

As the crowd roared its approval, Conkling went on, never deigning to qualify or explain, never hesitating to ridicule the competition or to use the most extravagant praise for his candidate. "New York is for Ulysses S. Grant. Never defeated — in peace or in war — his name is the most illustrious borne by living man. . . . Show me a better man. Name one, and I am answered." When his attacks on the other candidates evoked shouts of outrage, he pulled a lemon from his pocket and, striking a regal pose, calmly sucked it until the hall had quieted enough for him to continue his blazing theatrical speech. When he had finished, Grant's supporters abandoned themselves to sheer hysteria.

■ ■ ■ ■

It was in the midst of this mania that Garfield was called upon to give his nominating speech for John Sherman. He rose slowly and walked to the stage, the hall still reverberating with screams of "Grant! Grant! Grant!" Earnest and modest, Garfield was Conkling's opposite in every respect, and he had no intention, or desire, to compete with the flamboyant senator.

Those in the hall who knew Garfield, however, did not underestimate him for a minute, least of all Conkling. Earlier in the week, Conkling had tried to have expelled from the convention three delegates from West Virginia who had defied him. Garfield had spoken in their defense, forcing Conkling to withdraw his motion and winning widespread admiration for his courage and eloquence. After this very public defeat, Conkling had kept his silence, but handed Garfield a biting note: "New York requests that Ohio's real candidate . . . come forward."

Although Garfield had entered the hall that night with essentially nothing to say, Conkling's nominating speech for Grant had inspired even him — if not in the way

Conkling had intended. "Conkling's speech," he would write home that night, "gave me the idea of carrying the mind of the convention in a different direction." Stepping onto the same reporters' table that Conkling had just left, its white cloth still creased by Conkling's expensive shoes, Garfield looked calmly into the sea of flushed faces before him and began to speak in a measured voice.

"I have witnessed the extraordinary scenes of this Convention with deep solicitude," he said. "Nothing touches my heart more quickly than a tribute of honor to a great and noble character; but as I sat in my seat and witnessed the demonstration, this assemblage seemed to me a human ocean in tempest. I have seen the sea lashed into fury and tossed into spray, and its grandeur moves the soul of the dullest man; but I remember that it is not the billows, but the calm level of the sea, from which all heights and depths are measured."

As the crowd, which just moments before had been whipped into an almost helpless frenzy by Conkling, grew quiet, Garfield continued. Counseling the steady hand of reason, asking for reflection rather than fervor, he said, "Gentlemen of the Convention, . . . when your enthusiasm has passed, when the emotions of this hour have subsided, we shall find below the storm and passion that calm level of public opinion from which the thoughts of a mighty people are to be measured, and by which final action will be determined. Not here, in this brilliant circle, where fifteen thousand men and women are gathered, is the destiny of the Republic to be decreed for the next four years . . . but by four millions of Republican firesides, where the thoughtful voters, with wives and children about them, with the calm thoughts inspired by love and home and country, with the history of the past, the hopes of the future, the reverence for the great men who have adorned and blessed our nation in days gone by, burning in their hearts — there God prepares the verdict which will determine the wisdom of our work to-night."

His voice echoing in the now silent hall, Garfield asked a simple question. "And now, gentlemen of the Convention," he said, "what do we want?" From the midst of the crowd came an unexpected and, for Garfield, unwelcome answer. "We want Garfield!"

Although caught off guard by this interruption, and the rush of cheers that followed it, Garfield quickly regained control of his audience. "Bear with me a moment," he said firmly. "Hear me for my cause, and for a moment be silent that you may hear." After a short pause, he picked up the thread of his narrative and went on, detailing the triumphs of the Republican Party and sending out a clear and unwavering message to the South: "This is our only revenge — that you join us in lifting into the serene firmament of the Constitution . . . the immortal principles of truth and justice: that all men, white or black, shall be free, and shall stand equal before the law."

By the time Garfield finally began to talk about Sherman, he was speaking to an utterly tamed and transfixed audience. Every man and woman in the hall listened to him intently until his final words, and then, as he said, "I nominate John Sherman, of Ohio," the crowd burst into the kind of ovation that, until that moment, only Conkling had received. When a reporter leaned over to Conkling to ask him how he felt after Garfield's speech, with its stirring analogy of the storm-tossed sea, Conkling answered snidely, "I presume I feel very much as you feel — *seasick!*"

Not only did the applause that followed Garfield's speech rival Conkling's in intensity, it lasted even longer. The convention chairman, George Hoar, who secretly believed that Garfield should be the nominee, sat motionless and silent on the stage, his gavel within easy reach, as the cheers continued unabated. "The chair," wrote one reporter, "did not seem to feel called upon to make any effort to check [the applause], and so, much additional time was wasted, until finally a storm of hisses reduced the unruly to comparative quiet."

By the time the final nominating speeches were given, it was nearly midnight, and the Stalwarts, nervous now that their victory could be stolen from them, pressured Hoar to allow the balloting to begin, even though the following day was a Sunday. "Never," he responded indignantly. "This is a Sabbath-keeping nation, and I cannot preside over this convention one minute after 12 o'clock."

This particular Sunday, however, was a day of rest for no man in the Republican Party, least of all Garfield. While Conkling and his men battled Blaine and Sherman supporters in fierce, behind-the-scenes negotiations, and frightened delegates were coaxed, flattered, bribed, and threatened, Garfield spent the day desperately trying to tamp down a growing movement to make him the nominee. Over the course of the day, three different delegations from three different parts of the country came to him, asking him to allow his name to be put into contention. Finally, a concerned friend spoke to Garfield in confidence. "General," he said, "they are talking about nominating you." Garfield, feeling his duty to Sherman pressing heavily on him, replied, "My God, Senator, I know it, I know it! and they will ruin me." To his would-be supporters he said simply, "I am going to vote for [Sherman] and I will be loyal to him. My name must not be used."

The balloting began at ten on Monday morning. After the vitriol they had witnessed the preceding week, no one in the convention hall believed that their candidate, or any candidate, would receive on the first ballot the 379 votes necessary to win. Neither did they imagine, however, that they were at the beginning of a grueling process that would stagger on for two days, requiring far and away the most ballots ever taken in a Republican convention.

Grant, as had been expected, came closest to the winning number after the first ballot, receiving 304 votes to Blaine's 284 and Sherman's 93. Three other, lesser known, candidates together received 74 votes. Little changed on the second ballot, but on the third, two new names suddenly appeared — a single vote for Benjamin Harrison, a senator from Indiana who would become president of the United States nine years later, and another for James A. Garfield.

As the balloting continued, the solitary delegate from Pennsylvania who had cast his vote for Garfield refused to withdraw it, even though his candidate did not give him the slightest encouragement, or even acknowledgment. He shifted his vote to another candidate for five ballots — the fourteenth through the eighteenth — while the Grant and Blaine men fought tooth and claw over every delegate, but then rededicated himself to Garfield on the nineteenth ballot, and never wavered again.

While tensions rose to an excruciating level inside the convention hall, outside, crowds watched the proceedings with equal intensity. Hundreds of men and women, largely Grant and Blaine supporters, but also those who had no interest beyond mere curiosity, gathered in Printing House Square, where Chicago's biggest newspapers had promised to post the balloting results as they received them. "By high noon, the time when the first returns were expected," a reporter wrote, "the whole of the square, including the space about the Franklin statue, was filled with an eager throng, who awaited the appearances of the vote with ill-concealed impatience. The sun shown out hotly, and the buzz increased each minute."

A reporter from the *Boston Globe,* who had been forced to "elbow [his] way through the throng" to enter the convention hall, watched the balloting with growing astonishment. As the results of the nineteenth ballot were announced, he listened with the feverish interest of a man at a racetrack, his last dollar on a horse hurtling toward a receding finish line. "Grant holds his own and gains one," he wrote, as fast as he could. "Blaine has dropped down to 279, the lowest figure he has struck yet. Sherman gained a bit, and scores 96. . . . The twentieth ballot follows rapidly. It runs much the same as the others. Blaine loses three votes in Indiana, and the remark seems sound that Blaine is breaking up. Grant gains a notch in Tennessee, which is important, and the vacillating North Carolina delegate happens to swing on to Grant's aid this time, making a gain of two. The call is over, and still there is no result." The voting continued for twelve hours, with twenty-eight ballots, but when the convention hall finally emptied at nearly ten that night, the party was no closer to a nominee than it had been that morning.

The next day, as the delegates made their weary way back to the hall, few of them held out any hope for a quick conclusion. They could not have helped but be dismally reminded of the Democratic convention of 1860, which took not only fifty-nine ballots but two conventions in two different cities before it had a nominee — a nominee who would go on to lose to the Republican candidate, Abraham Lincoln. When the first ballot of the day, the twenty-ninth, showed little change from the day before, their fears were only confirmed. The thirtieth through thirty-third were equally stagnant, and the hall was filled with a thick feeling of desperation.

On the thirty-fourth ballot, however, an extraordinary thing happened. As the votes were being taken, the delegates from Wisconsin made a shocking reversal. Their eighteen votes, which on the preceding ballot had been distributed between Grant, Blaine, Sherman, and Elihu Washburne, who had served briefly as Grant's secretary of state, were now divided between just two men — Grant and Garfield. More extraordinary still, Grant received only two of those votes. Suddenly, the single vote from Pennsylvania that Garfield had chosen simply to ignore had grown to seventeen, which was a serious bid for the nomination and a situation of genuine concern for Garfield.

Stunned, Garfield leaped to his feet to protest the vote. "Mr. President," he began. Hoar, who was privately delighted by this unexpected turn of events, reluctantly acknowledged Garfield. "For what purpose does the gentleman rise?" he sighed. "I rise to a question of order," Garfield replied. "I challenge the correctness of the announcement. The announcement contains votes for me. No man has a right, without the consent of the person voted for, to announce that person's name, and vote for him, in this convention. Such consent I have not given . . ." Cutting Garfield off midsentence, Hoar responded stiffly, "The gentleman from Ohio is not stating a question of order. He will resume his seat."

Hoar quickly ordered another ballot to be taken, leaving Garfield no choice but to do as he was told and sit back down. As each state was called, nothing more changed until Indiana stood to give its thirty votes. Two for Blaine, its chairman announced, one for Grant, and twenty-seven for Garfield. Before Garfield could even absorb this news,

Maryland had given him four more votes, and Minnesota and North Carolina one each. With Pennsylvania and Wisconsin holding steady at seventeen, Garfield suddenly had fifty votes — still far less than Grant or Blaine, but uncomfortably close to Sherman. At this point, several men rushed to Garfield, begging him to speak, but he quickly waved them away. "No, no, gentlemen," he said sternly. "This is no theatrical performance."

When Hoar called for the thirty-sixth ballot and the convention clerk cried out, "No candidate has a majority," a hush fell upon the great hall. "Instinctively, it was known, perhaps felt would be a better word," a journalist wrote, "that something conclusive was about to be done." The Ohio delegation was suddenly surrounded by the chairmen of other delegations, demanding to know if they were going to shift their allegiance to Garfield. Garfield, horrified, insisted that they remain loyal to Sherman. "If this convention nominates me," he said, "it should be done without a vote from Ohio."

The votes for Garfield, however, continued to mount. Eleven from Connecticut, one from Georgia, seven from Illinois. "And then," a reporter wrote with awe, "then the stampede came." Iowa stood and declared all twenty-two of its votes for James A. Garfield. Kansas then gave him six, Kentucky three, and Louisiana eight. The tension in the hall continued to grow until Maine, before a shell-shocked crowd, utterly abandoned Blaine, its native son. "Slowly came the call of the State of Maine," the reporter wrote, "and [Senator] Eugene Hale, white of face but in a clear, sharp, penetrating voice replied, 'Maine casts her fourteen votes for James A. Garfield.' "

Blaine was finished, and Sherman, who had been waiting miserably in his office in the Treasury Department, desperately studying every ballot as it came across his telegraph, finally admitted that he was as well. Sitting down at his desk, he wrote a telegram to be sent to the Ohio delegation on the convention floor. "Whenever the vote of Ohio will be likely to ensure the nomination for Garfield," it read, "I appeal to every delegate to vote for him. Let Ohio be solid. Make the same appeal in my name to North Carolina, and every delegate who has voted for me."

When the telegram was received, Garfield frantically shouted, "Cast my vote for Sherman!" But it was too late. He could not stop what was happening. The last state was called, and Garfield was left with 399 votes, 20 more than were needed to win. Having never agreed to become even a candidate — on the contrary, having vigorously resisted it — he was suddenly the nominee.

All that was left was to make it official. Hoar, standing before the breathless crowd, shouted, "Shall the nomination of James A. Garfield be made unanimous?" and none other than Roscoe Conkling slowly stood. In a hoarse whisper almost unrecognizable as the voice that had so brazenly nominated Grant just three days before, he said, "James A. Garfield of Ohio, having received a majority of all the votes, I arise to move that he be unanimously presented as the nominee of this convention."

As soon as the nomination was seconded, the hall exploded in a cheer so deafening the very air seemed to tremble. "The delegates and others on the floor of the Convention hall seemed to lose all control of themselves," a reporter wrote. "Many of them cheered like madmen. Others stood upon their seats and waved their hats high above them. . . . 'Hurrah for Garfield' was cried by a thousand throats." The band began to play "The Battle-Cry of Freedom," and the delegates joined in singing as they grabbed their state banners and joyfully marched them through the hall. Faintly, through the tall windows, they could hear the battery of guns on the shore of Lake Michigan that announced the news to the crowds waiting in suspense outside.

The Ohio delegation was immediately engulfed by a sea of grinning men, eager to shake the candidate's hand or pound his back. Garfield, shocked and sickened, turned in desperation to a friend and asked if it would be inappropriate for him to leave. Told in no uncertain terms that he must stay, he did, sitting quietly in his seat, looking at the floor and responding with a simple "Thank you" to the hearty congratulations showered upon him from every direction. "Only once," a reporter recalled, "did he express anything like emotion, and that was when Frye of Maine came up and said: 'General, we congratulate you.' Garfield replied: 'I am very sorry that this has become necessary.' " Across the hall, in the New York delegation, another man sat in stony silence. As the celebration whirled around him, Senator Conkling was "an unmoved spectator of the scene."

Finally, as the crowd threatened to crush Garfield, his friends decided that it was time for him to make his escape. Simply getting out the door, however, was much more difficult than they had anticipated. As crowded as the hall was, the sidewalk outside was even worse. They managed to find a carriage and step inside, but the throng was not about to let Garfield go that easily. "As Garfield entered the carriage in company with [Ohio] Gov. Foster," a reporter wrote, "the crowd surged around in a state of intense enthusiasm, and shouted: 'Take off the horses; we will pull the carriage.' The driver, who at the time was not aware whom he was carrying, whipped up to get away from the men, who had already commenced to unfasten the harness. He cleared the space several feet, but was overhauled again, and the dazed driver, now thoroughly frightened, applied his whip with renewed energy, and, clear[ed] the crowd."

Violently bounced along the brick streets by the nervous horses and terrified driver, Garfield sat in silence, a "grave and thoughtful expression" on his face. He would not talk about the nomination, or even respond to the congratulations offered by the men seated next to him. "He has not recovered from his surprise yet," one man said. When the carriage pulled into the Grand Pacific Hotel, where Garfield and most of the Republicans had been staying, everyone in the carriage could see the NEW YORK SOLID FOR GRANT banner still waving from its roof.

Garfield quickly made his way to his room, although he knew that if it had offered no refuge in the past, it certainly would not now. The small room in which, just the night before, he had struggled to sleep as he shared his three-quarter-size bed with a stranger, was already filled with six hundred telegrams and seemingly as many people. As men talked excitedly all around him, Garfield, "pale as death," sat down in a chair and stared at the wall, absentmindedly holding a GARFIELD FOR PRESIDENT badge that someone had thrust into his hands.

Chapter 4
God's Minute Man

Theologians in all ages have looked out admiringly upon the material universe and . . . demonstrated the power, wisdom, and goodness of God; but we know of no one who has demonstrated the same attributes from the history of the human race.

JAMES A. GARFIELD

Four days after the Republican convention, and a day after he had stepped aboard the ill-fated *Stonington,* Charles Guiteau arrived in New York. While the other survivors of the deadly steamship collision in Long Island Sound huddled with family and friends, wondering at the twist of fate that had spared their lives, Guiteau walked through the city alone, unburdened by guilt or doubt. To his mind, which had long ago descended into delusion and madness, the tragedy was simply further proof that he was one of God's chosen few.

From an early age, Guiteau had been confident of his importance in the eyes of God. Motherless by the time he was seven years old, he had been raised by a zealously religious father, a man so certain of his relationship with God that he believed he would never die. "My mother was dead and my father was a father and a mother to me," Guiteau said, "and I drank in this fanaticism from him for years. He used to talk it day after day, and dream over it, and sleep over it." Charles's own fanaticism grew until, when he was eighteen years old, he left the University of Michigan in Ann Arbor to join a commune in upstate New York founded by his father's religious mentor, John Humphrey Noyes.

The central tenet of Noyes's doctrine — and the idea that appealed most to men like Guiteau's father — was perfectionism. Noyes believed that, through prayer and the right kind of education, a person could become intellectually, morally, and spiritually perfect, and so would be free from sin. Noyes believed that he had reached perfection and was anointed by God to help others shed their own sins. With this goal in mind, he had founded his commune, the Oneida Community, named for the town in which it was established in 1848. Oneida would last more than thirty years, becoming the most successful utopian socialist community in the United States.

Like most of Noyes's followers, Guiteau moved into the "Mansion House," a sprawling brick Victorian Gothic building that, over time, would grow to ninety-three thousand square feet. It held thirty-five apartments for the nearly three hundred members of the commune. Although the private rooms were small and unadorned, the property had a wide variety of fairly elaborate communal amenities — from theaters to a photographic studio to a Turkish bath.

Guiteau's father dreamed of living in the Mansion House, but his second wife refused to follow him, perhaps in part because of the community's practice of "complex marriage," or free love — a concept that Noyes had developed himself, and practiced liberally. According to Noyes, monogamous love was not only selfish but "unhealthy and pernicious," and the commune's members were encouraged to have a wide variety of sexual partners in the hope that they would not fall in love with any one person.

In an effort to avoid too many pregnancies, Noyes preached what he called "male continence." Intercourse, "up to the very moment of emission," he insisted, "is *voluntary,* entirely under the control of the moral faculty, and *can be stopped at any point.* In other words, the *presence* and the *motions* can be continued or stopped at will, and it is only the final *crisis* of emission that is automatic or uncontrollable. . . . If you say that this is impossible, I answer that I *know* it is possible — nay, that it is easy." It was like rowing a boat, Noyes said. If you stay near the shore, you'll be fine. It's only when you row too near a waterfall that you find yourself in danger.

Guiteau was enthusiastic about complex marriage, and was willing to try male continence, but he quickly found that life at Oneida required far more humility than he could tolerate. Members of the commune were not only expected to help anywhere they were needed — from the kitchen to the fields — doing work that Guiteau found tiresome and demeaning, but to accept the work gratefully and humbly. Guiteau felt that Noyes and his followers should be grateful to him, rather than the other way around. In a letter to Noyes he wrote, "You prayed God . . . to send you help, and he has sent me. *Had he not sent me, you may depend upon it, I never should have come.*"

Believing that he should be shown special deference, and offended by the disapproval and, at times, disdain with which he was treated in the community, he said, "I ask no one to respect me *personally,* but I do ask them to respect me as an envoy of the true God." He was, he believed, "God's minute man."

Although Guiteau claimed to work directly for God — to be "in the employ of Jesus Christ & Co., the very ablest and strongest firm in the universe" — he expected more than heavenly rewards. He wanted all the pleasures the world had to offer, chief among them fame. On one occasion, a member of the commune picked up a slip of paper he had seen Guiteau drop. On it Guiteau, uneducated, isolated, and friendless, had written a strangely grandiose, utterly delusional announcement: "Chas. J. Guiteau of England, Premier of the British Lion will lecture this evening at seven o'clock."

Guiteau's extravagant dreams and delusions persisted in the face of consistent and complete failure. Although the commune promised the pleasures of complex marriage, to Guiteau's frustration, "the Community women," one of Oneida's members would later admit, "did not extend love and confidence toward him." In fact, so thorough was his rejection among the women that they nicknamed him "Charles Gitout." He bitterly complained that, while at the commune, he was "practically a Shaker."

Guiteau also frequently found himself the object of "criticisms," a method Noyes had designed to help his followers identify and overcome their faults so that they could reach perfection. During a criticism, Guiteau was forced to sit in a room, encircled by the men and women with whom he worked and lived most closely, and listen in silence as they described his faults. Again and again, he was accused of "egotism and conceit."

In Guiteau's case at least, the criticisms apparently had little effect. When, in 1865, he finally left the commune, after having lived there for nearly six years, he announced that his departure was necessary because he was "destined to accomplish some very important mission." "God and my own conscience," he proclaimed, "drive me to the battle and I dare not draw back."

Guiteau's plan was to start a religious newspaper called *The Theocrat,* which he said would be a "*warm friend of the Bible,* though it may develop many new and strange biblical theories, differing widely from the teachings of popular theologians." His brother-in-law, George Scoville, recalling Guiteau's outsized enthusiasm and confidence, said that he "labored there for weeks and months to start that project, supposing that he was going right into the matter with entire success, and that this newspaper was going to take its place every morning at every breakfast table in the land." After just four months, Guiteau gave up and begged Noyes to allow him to return to the commune. A year later, however, he left again, sneaking out at night so as to avoid another criticism.

Although Guiteau would never again return to Oneida, his life outside the commune was far from what he had envisioned. Rather than achieving success on a grand scale, he suffered a series of disappointments, rejections, and disasters. Even his brief marriage, which took place soon after he left Oneida, ended in divorce.

Guiteau spent nearly an entire year doing nothing at all, living on a small inheritance while he struggled to free himself from his fear that, by leaving the commune, he had "lost [his] eternal salvation." "The idea that I was to be eternally damned haunted me and haunted me and haunted me every day, and day and night," he said. "So I was unable to do any business."

Finally, desperate for money, Guiteau decided to take up a profession, choosing one that he thought would be lucrative — the law. In a time when law school was encouraged but not required he read a handful of books, served as a clerk for a few months, and then stood for the bar. His examiner was a prosecuting attorney named Charles Reed, who, according to Guiteau's brother-in-law, himself a lawyer, was a "good-hearted fellow," if not particularly discerning. Reed "asked him three questions and he answered two and missed one," Scoville recalled, "and that was the way he got to be a lawyer."

In the courtroom, Guiteau was as unpredictable and egotistical as he had been at Oneida. "The style and plea of his conduct," reported a psychiatrist who would later study his life, "were such as to convince all the lawyers who were present that he was a monomaniac." Arguing on behalf of a client in a criminal case, Guiteau "talked and acted like a crazy man." After he leapt over the bar that separated him from the jury and put his fist directly in the face of one of the jurists, prompting an explosion of laughter in the courtroom, "his client was convicted, without the jury leaving their seats." In another case, Reed, Guiteau's bar examiner, recalled that, instead of addressing the petty larceny of which his client was accused, Guiteau "talked about theology, about the divinity, and about the rights of man. . . . It was a very wandering speech, full of vagaries and peculiarities."

Much more than the work itself, Guiteau enjoyed the prestige that accompanied his new profession. He would frequently take out his business cards simply to admire them. There were eight lines of text on the front of the cards alone, including a proud note that his office building had an elevator. The back had fourteen lines, which made up a reference list, separated by city, of businessmen Guiteau had met only briefly, if at all.

Over the next fourteen years, Guiteau opened, and then quickly abandoned, a succession of law practices in Chicago and New York. In between, he tried his hand at more exciting lines of work. Among his most ambitious endeavors was a plan to purchase one of Chicago's largest newspapers — the *Inter Ocean.* He hoped to convince some of the city's wealthiest citizens to give him $75,000 to fund the project. In exchange for their investment, he promised to use the paper to win for them any statewide political office they desired. "I asked Mr. John H. Adams to put money into it," Guiteau openly admitted. "He was the president of the Second National Bank . . . worth about half a million dollars. I offered to make him governor of Illinois [but] he didn't have any political aspirations. I wanted to get hold of these men that had money and political aspirations. They were the kind of men to help me in that scheme."

After two months of fruitless searching for a financier, Guiteau decided it was time to return to religion, this time as a traveling evangelist. As he did with each new venture, he threw himself into evangelism with astonishing passion and complete confidence. For nearly a year, he traveled to dozens of cities across several states, from Buffalo, New York, to Milwaukee, Wisconsin. Adopting as his own Noyes's theory that the second coming of Christ had already occurred, in AD 70, he gave lectures to anyone who was willing to listen — and pay a small fee.

People "have been in the habit of looking way off into the indefinite future for the second coming," Guiteau would explain. " 'Hold!' I say, 'it occurred eighteen hundred years ago.' "

Guiteau would later admit that his attempt at evangelism was a "failure all the way through," but, he said, "I stuck to it like a hero." After arriving in a town, he would find the business district and walk through it, scattering handbills announcing his lecture and trying to sell printed copies for twenty-five cents. On most nights, only a handful of people showed up, and after Guiteau began to speak they either heckled him or simply left. After he gave a lecture titled "Is There a Hell?" to an unusually large crowd at the Newark Opera House, the *Newark Daily Journal* ran a jeering review with the headline "Is there a hell? Fifty deceived people are of the opinion that there ought to be."

Whatever his occupation, Guiteau survived largely on sheer audacity. As he traveled between towns by train, he never bought a ticket. "You may say that this is dead beating, and I had no business to go around in this kind of style," he argued. "I say I was working for the Lord and the Lord took care of me, and I was not to find fault with the way he took care of me." When the conductor asked for his ticket, Guiteau would simply explain that he was doing God's work and had no money for train fare. Frequently, the man would take pity on him and let him ride for free, but occasionally he would meet a conductor who "was not a Christian man evidently," and would be roughly put off the train at the next station.

Guiteau took the same approach to board bills that he did to train fares. Each time he entered a town, he would choose the nicest boarding house he could find, never planning to pay for his room. "I had no trouble all this time in getting in first-class places," he proudly recalled. "They always took me for a gentleman." When he was ready to move on, he would sneak out under cover of night, or simply leave town immediately following his lecture.

This strategy, however, was riskier than traveling on a train without a ticket. In Michigan, Guiteau learned to his great discomfort, "you can arrest a man for a board-bill the same as you can for stealing a coat." One night in Detroit, he was arrested after his lecture and sent back on the express train to Ann Arbor, where, as always, he had left without paying his bill. Fortunately for Guiteau, the deputy sheriff assigned to travel with him fell asleep on the train. "I kept watching him and he kept bobbing his head," Guiteau later recalled. "When we got to Ypsilanti I says, 'I guess I will get out of this,' and I jumped up and ran off just as tight as I could for about a mile. I had not been gone more than a minute by the clock before I heard them whistle down-brakes; the fellow had missed me."

Guiteau was not always so lucky. In 1874, after not paying rent on the office space for his law firm in New York, he spent a month in the grim lower Manhattan prison that would become known as the Tombs. "I never was so much tortured in my life," he said of the experience. "I felt as if I would go crazy there. I was put in a little miserable hole, and three or four of the nastiest, dirtiest bummers were put in there with me." As searing as the experience had been, the first thing Guiteau did upon release — after "soak[ing] my body in the hottest kind of suds I could find" — was to open another law office, this time in Chicago, and begin again.

As Guiteau's life careened out of control, he began asking anyone he knew — even the most distant acquaintance — for money. His most reliable source was his sister, Frances, and her husband, George Scoville, whom he badgered incessantly with requests for loans they knew he would never repay. At one point, he wrote to Frances, "If Mr. Scoville would let me have a hundred dollars for a month or two, it would greatly oblige me, and I would give him my note with interest for the same." Never subtle, Guiteau ended the letter with an appeal that was strikingly direct even for him. "But to leave this: *money,* to meet my personal wants, is what I desire now," he wrote. "Write *soon.*"

Much larger sums of money, Guiteau believed, might be acquired through lawsuits. At one point, he attempted to sue the *New York Herald* for $100,000, accusing the newspaper of libel after it ran a story warning its readers of his unethical practices as a lawyer. The *Herald* cited one occasion in which Guiteau, acting as a bill collector — the primary work of his practice — had collected $175 of a $350 bill, and then refused to turn any of it over to his client. He claimed that he had been unable to collect anything beyond his own fee, and so owed his client nothing. After another enraged client stepped forward with a complaint against him, however, Guiteau quickly dropped the suit and fled the city.

Searching for another target, Guiteau even tried to sue Oneida. Ignoring the fact that he had signed a waiver of compensation when he joined the commune, he claimed that he was owed $9,000, plus interest, in back pay for the six years he had worked there. When Noyes learned of the suit, he replied drily that, while at Oneida, Guiteau had been not only "moody [and] self-conceited" but "a great part of the time was not reckoned in the ranks of reliable labor." After speaking with Noyes, Guiteau's lawyer realized that his client had lied to him and resigned from the case.

Undeterred, Guiteau continued to rail against the commune. In a series of letters to Noyes, he threatened to expose Oneida's controversial sexual practices and to send the founder himself to prison. "If you intend to pay my claim say so," he warned. "If you want to spend 10 or 20 years in Sing Sing and have your Communities 'wiped out,' don't pay it." When Noyes did not reply, Guiteau quickly wrote again. "I infer from your silence that you do not intend to pay the claim. All right. If you find yourself arrested within a week, it will be your own fault."

Noyes's reaction to these threats mirrored the thoughts of nearly everyone who came into contact with Guiteau: He was certain he was insane. "I have no ill will toward him," Noyes wrote to Guiteau's father. "I regard him as insane, and I prayed for him last night as sincerely as I ever prayed for my own son, that is now in a Lunatic Asylum." Luther Guiteau, furious with his son and ashamed of his behavior, did not hesitate to agree. Only the lack of money to pay for an asylum, he assured Noyes, prevented him from having his son institutionalized. Luther's oldest son, John, who was a successful insurance salesman in Boston and had been repeatedly humiliated by Charles, wrote with restrained fury that he believed his brother "capable of any folly, stupidity, or rascality. The only possible excuse I can render for him is that he is absolutely insane and is hardly responsible for his acts."

Throughout Guiteau's life, the only person who remained his unwavering ally was his sister, Frances. After their mother's death, Frances, who was six years older than Charles, had done her best to fill the void in her brother's life. She had not wanted him to join Oneida, but after he left the commune, she had tried to help him when no one else would. As well as giving Charles money, she and her husband allowed him to live with their family on several occasions, even after he was released from the Tombs.

Finally, though, even Frances had to admit that her brother was deeply disturbed, and likely dangerous. This painful realization came in the summer of 1875, when Charles was living with her family in Wisconsin. One hot afternoon, as he lay on his back on her sofa, she called out to him from the kitchen, asking if he would "cut up a little wood for us." He "immediately said, 'Yes,' " Frances remembered, "and got up and went out and did it willingly." After he cut the wood, however, instead of taking it to the shed, he dumped it on a walkway leading to the house. Since his arrival, Charles had been sullen and easily angered, so when Frances saw the wood, rather than chastising him, she quietly bent down to pick it up herself. "As quick as I did that he raised the ax, without any provocation or words," she would recall years later, still shaken by the memory. "It was not so much the raising of the ax as it was the look of his face that frightened me. He looked to me like a wild animal." Terrified, she dropped the wood and ran into the house.

Fearing as much for her own safety as for Charles's sanity, Frances reluctantly admitted that her brother needed to be institutionalized. Before taking such a drastic step, however, she asked her family physician to examine him. After one conversation with Guiteau, the doctor, deeply concerned about the young man's "explosions of emotional feeling," strongly advised Frances to place him in an asylum without delay. Frances planned to travel with Charles to Chicago, where he would be tried by a jury and, she was certain, found insane. "I had no doubt then of his insanity," she said. "He was losing his mind." Before the trip could even be arranged, however, Charles made his escape.

For the next five years, Guiteau continued his peripatetic life, moving from city to city and scheme to scheme until, in 1880, he drifted to Boston, where he developed a new, all-consuming obsession: politics. A voracious reader, he followed the political machinations of men like Ulysses S. Grant and Roscoe Conkling with intense interest and growing admiration. It did not take long for him to decide that he was a Republican Stalwart, and that the best way to enter politics was through the spoils system.

The upcoming presidential election was irresistible to Guiteau. By forcibly inserting himself into the Republican campaign, he believed, he would win not only the gratitude of high-ranking men in the party, but, ultimately, an important political appointment. In the weeks leading up to the national conventions, Guiteau spent every day in a Boston library, feverishly working on a campaign speech. Believing, as did most of the country, that the Republicans would nominate Grant, and knowing that Winfield Scott Hancock, a highly decorated Union general, was heavily favored among the Democrats, he titled his speech "Grant against Hancock." After Garfield's surprise nomination — and Hancock's predictable one, on the second ballot — he changed the title, and virtually nothing else, to "Garfield against Hancock."

Three days later, clutching his speech and a small, frayed bag, Guiteau had boarded the *Stonington,* his sights set on the Republican campaign headquarters in New York. "I remember distinctly," he would later say, "that I felt that I was on my way to the White House." Garfield's sudden rise to prominence, he was certain, only foreshadowed his own.

CHAPTER 5
BLEAK MOUNTAIN

This honor comes to me unsought.
I have never had the Presidential fever;
not even for a day.

JAMES A. GARFIELD

That night, as Guiteau's steamship collided with the *Narragansett,* the object of his ambitions, James Garfield, slept in the farmhouse he shared with his wife and five children in Mentor, Ohio, far removed from the tempestuous workings of his presidential campaign. The house, which the reporters who stretched out on its wide lawn that summer christened Lawnfield, sat on 160 acres of land about twenty miles from the log cabin Garfield's father had built half a century before. Mentor, as one reporter described it, was less a "regular town [than] a thickly settled neighborhood." A few houses and small farms, encircled by orchards and gardens in heavy bloom, were scattered along a dirt road that ran for two miles between the train station and Lawnfield. While traveling along this road in 1877, Garfield had been impressed with the area's "quiet country beauty" and decided it would be a good place to teach his sons the lessons he believed they could learn only on a farm.

For the past three years, Garfield had worked on his farm every chance he got. He built a barn, moved a large shed, planted an orchard, and even shopped for curtains for the house. To the house itself, which was one and a half stories high with a white exterior and a dark red roof, he added an entire story, a front porch, and a library. Even with the new library, Garfield's books filled every room. "You can go nowhere in the general's home without coming face to face with books," one reporter marveled. "They confront you in the hall when you enter, in the parlor and the sitting room, in the dining-room and even in the bath-room, where documents and speeches are corded up like firewood."

Although Garfield enjoyed improving the farmhouse, his greatest interest lay in the land, which he approached as if it were an enormous science experiment. His first large project had been to build a dam to irrigate the fields. Then, the summer before his nomination, he experimented with a fertilizer made up of a carefully calibrated combination of pulverized limestone and ground bone. "I long for time," he lamented in his journal, "to study agricultural chemistry and make experiments with soils and forces."

Garfield finally got his wish during his presidential campaign. Although he argued that he should "take the stump and bear a fighting share in the campaign," traveling from town to town and asking for votes was considered undignified for a presidential candidate. Abraham Lincoln had not given a single speech on his own behalf during either of his campaigns, and Rutherford B. Hayes advised Garfield to do the same. "Sit crosslegged," he said, "and look wise."

Happily left to his own devices, Garfield poured his time and energy into his farm. He worked in the fields, planting, hoeing, and harvesting crops, and swung a scythe with the confidence and steady hand he had developed as a boy. In July, he oversaw the threshing of his oats. "Result 475 bushels," he noted. "No[t] so good a yield as last year."

While Garfield worried over his crops, political war was being waged in his name.

The principal target of attack was the Democratic nominee, Winfield Scott Hancock. Widely known as "Hancock the Superb," he was famous for his courage and resounding success during the Civil War, but he had never held an elected office and was perceived to have little more than a clouded understanding of his own platform. The Republicans, naturally, did everything in their power to encourage this perception, including distributing a pamphlet that was titled "Hancock's Political Achievements" and filled with blank pages.

Hancock's greatest liability, however, was his own party. Although he had been a Union hero, he could do nothing to change the fact that, in the minds of the American people, the Democratic Party was still inextricably linked to the South. Garfield himself referred to it as the "rebel party" and growled that "every Rebel guerilla and jayhawker, every man who ran to Canada to avoid the draft, every bounty-jumper, every deserter, every cowardly sneak that ran from danger and disgraced his flag, . . . every villain, of whatever name or crime, who loves power more than justice, slavery more than freedom, is a Democrat." At every opportunity, Republicans reminded voters of the Democratic Party's ties to the South, and accused Hancock of having, at best, divided loyalties.

Democrats, in turn, focused their attentions on Garfield, who, unlike Hancock, had a long public career to plumb. As Garfield had known it would be, the Democrats' first point of attack was the Crédit Mobilier scandal of 1872. At that time, Garfield had been accused, along with several other members of Congress, of accepting from a fellow congressman a good deal on stock in a railroad company called Crédit Mobilier of America. In fact, Garfield had turned down the stock, but soon after had accepted a $300 loan from the same congressman. Although he had repaid the loan before he was aware of the shadow that had fallen over Crédit Mobilier — which, as well as attempting to bribe congressmen, was involved in fraud — and a congressional committee had absolved him of any intentional wrongdoing, Garfield knew that his name would always be linked with the scandal. "There is nothing in my relation to the case for which [the] tenderest conscience or the most scrupulous honor can blame me," he wrote to a friend at the time. But "it is not enough for one to know that his heart and motives are pure, if he is not sure but that good men . . . who do not know him, will set him down among the list of men of doubtful morality."

In the end, the effort to renew public interest in the scandal failed, but it was not for lack of trying. In an impressive, nationwide campaign to remind voters of Crédit Mobilier, and to exploit any lingering questions about Garfield's role in it, Democrats covered every available surface in every major city with the numbers 329 — the amount of money Garfield had been accused of earning in stock dividends. The numbers were on sidewalks, buildings, streets, and barns. Somehow, they even made their way into the homes and offices of members of the incumbent Republican administration. When the secretary of war sat down to breakfast one morning, 329 was scrawled on his napkin. The secretary of the treasury found the numbers on a piece of mail addressed to him, the secretary of agriculture on a beet someone had placed on his desk, and the secretary of state on his hat and, incredibly, the headboard of his bed.

When dredging up an old scandal proved ineffective, zealous Democrats invented a new one. At the height of the campaign, the editor of a New York newspaper found on his desk a letter supposedly written by

Garfield professing his support for Chinese immigration. "Individuals or companys [sic] have the right to buy labor where they can get it cheapest," the letter, which was written on congressional stationery, read. The issue of Chinese immigration was then highly inflammatory, guaranteed to inflame racist sentiment, incite the anger of American labor forces, and threaten the future of any presidential candidate who argued for it. The signature on the letter, however, did not remotely resemble Garfield's, and after some investigation, the plot behind the forgery was revealed. After the election, a man from Maryland would confess his role in the plot in a New York courtroom, and be sentenced to the Tombs.

Throughout the campaign, despite an onslaught of attacks and accusations, and Garfield's silence in the face of them, his supporters steadily grew. In New York, Garfield campaign clubs sprang up among completely disparate groups, from 52 students at the University of the City of New-York, to 150 German immigrants in Manhattan, to 50 young ladies from Jefferson County, who "raised a pole 50 feet high, and swung out a handsome streamer." The *New York Times* reported that a judge who had been a lifelong Democrat announced his intention of switching party allegiance so that he could "support Gen. Garfield for President, as the best and fittest thing for an honest and patriotic citizen to do." In Washington, D.C., a former slave named John Moss lost his job at the Library of Congress when he pummeled a fellow worker who had torn to pieces a lithograph of Garfield that Moss had sitting on his desk.

Freed slaves were arguably Garfield's most ardent supporters. One of the best-known, and most enthusiastically sung, election songs of the contest was "The Battle Cry of Freemen." Americans could hear the final stanza ringing through the convention halls and city streets, sung with joy and determination:

> Now we'll use a Freemen's right, as thinking freemen should.
> Shouting the battle cry of Garfield.
> And we'll place our ballots where they'll do the toiling millions good.
> Shouting the battle cry for Garfield.
> Hurrah! Boys for Garfield.

On October 25, a political meeting of "colored citizens" at the Cooper Institute in New York filled an entire hall to overflowing. "It could not have been larger," a reporter said of the gathering, "for every inch of space in the large hall was crowded. The seats were filled almost as soon as the doors were opened, and in a very few minutes all the standing room was taken." Even more remarkable than the size of the crowd was its complete racial integration, just fifteen years after the end of the Civil War. "Black men and white," a newspaper reported, "were in almost equal proportion throughout the hall and on the platform."

The keynote speaker that night, and the cause of all the excitement, was Frederick Douglass. After climbing to the platform, the august former slave, now a human rights leader and marshal of the District of Columbia, wasted no time in telling his audience which presidential candidate would receive his vote. "James A. Garfield must be our President," he said to riotous cheers. "I know [Garfield], colored man; he is right on our questions, take my word for it. He is a typical American all over. He has shown us how man in the humblest circumstances can grapple with man, rise, and win. He has come from obscurity to fame, and we'll make him more famous." After pausing once more as the cheers reverberated through the hall, Douglass went on. Garfield, he said, "has burst up through the incrustations that surround the poor, and has shown us how it is possible for an American to rise. He has built the road over which he traveled. He has buffeted the billows of adversity, and to-night he swims in safety where Hancock, in despair, is going down."

Although Garfield did not allow himself to campaign, he could not resist addressing the thousands of people who traveled to Mentor to see him. In what came to be known as "front porch talks," he would stand on his wide veranda, talking to enormous groups — from five hundred members of an Indianapolis Lincoln Club, to nine hundred women who had traveled together from Cleveland. On a single day in October, despite the rain, five thousand people converged on Garfield's farm. When a group of Germans stood before him, he spoke to them in their native language, delivering the first speech by an American presidential candidate that was not in English.

The most stirring moment in the campaign came in late October, when the members of a singing group from an all-black university in Nashville, Tennessee, stood before Garfield's modest farmhouse and sang for him. "As the singers poured out their melodious and at the same time vibrant but mournful spirituals, the little audience became increasingly emotional," Garfield's private secretary later recalled. "Tears were trickling down the cheeks of many of the women, and one staid old gentleman blubbered audibly behind a door." When the performance ended, Garfield stood to address the group. Squaring his shoulders and straightening his back, he said, in a voice that rang through the still night, "And I tell you now, in the closing days of this campaign, that I would rather be with you and defeated than against you and victorious."

A few weeks later, on the afternoon of November 2, a bright, cloudless day, Garfield traveled down the dusty road from Lawnfield to the town hall to cast his vote. Aside from this one concession to the election, and an occasional trip to the office behind his house to see what news had come over the telegraph, he went about his normal routine. He wrote some letters, made plans for a new garden near the farm's engine house, and settled his dairy account in town. That evening, he visited with neighbors.

Although Garfield did not show a great deal of interest in the election, the rest of the country did. Voter turnout was 78 percent, and as the results began to come in, it quickly became clear that it was going to be a close race. Interest was particularly high in the wake of the previous presidential election, when Rutherford B. Hayes was widely believed to have stolen the presidency from Samuel J. Tilden. Tilden, the governor of New York, had won the popular vote by a clear and undisputed margin, and, with all but four states accounted for, had 184 electoral votes to Hayes's 165. However, when the remaining four states reported two different sets of returns, Congress formed an electoral commission to distribute their votes. The commission, a highly partisan group made up of eight Republicans and seven Democrats, awarded all twenty of the disputed votes to Hayes, handing him the presidency by one electoral vote.

In 1880, no commission threatened to steal the presidency, but so close was the race that there was uncertainty until the final hours. At 3:00 a.m. on the morning of November 3, with the nation still anxiously waiting to learn who its next president would be, Garfield went to bed. When he woke up a few hours later and was told in no uncertain terms that he had won the election and was to be the twentieth president of the United States, he was, one reporter noted with astonishment, the "coolest man in the room." Later that day, Garfield gave his election to the presidency little more mention in his diary than he had the progress of his oat crop a few weeks earlier. "The news of 3 a.m.," he wrote, "is fully justified by the morning papers."

In the days that followed, surrounded by celebrations and frantic plans for his administration, Garfield could not shake the feeling that the presidency would bring him only loneliness and sorrow. As he watched everything he treasured — his time with his children, his books, and his farm — abruptly disappear, he understood that the life he had known was gone. The presidency seemed to him not a great accomplishment but a "bleak mountain" that he was obliged to ascend. Sitting down at his desk in a rare moment to himself, he tried to explain in a letter to a friend the strange sense of loss he had felt since the election.

"There is a tone of sadness running through this triumph," he wrote, "which I can hardly explain."

Part Two: War

Chapter 6
Hand and Soul

To a young man who has in himself the magnificent possibilities of life, it is not fitting that he should be permanently commanded. He should be a commander.

JAMES A. GARFIELD

As Garfield tried to accept the new life that lay before him, Alexander Graham Bell, working in a small laboratory in Washington, D.C., struggled to free himself from the overwhelming success of his first invention. Only five years had passed since the Centennial Exhibition, but for Bell, everything had changed. While the telephone had lifted him from poverty, made him famous, and won him the respect of the world's most accomplished scientists, it had also robbed him of what he valued most: time.

Bell had always believed in the telephone, not just its inventiveness but its usefulness. But even he had not anticipated how quickly and widely it would be embraced. “I did not realize,” he would admit years later, “the overwhelming importance of the invention.” By the summer of 1877, more than a thousand telephones were already operating in Philadelphia, Chicago, and as far west as San Francisco. That same year, President Hayes had one installed in the White House, and Queen Victoria requested a private demonstration at her summer retreat on the Isle of Wight. “A Professor Bell explained the whole process,” she wrote in her diary that night, “which is most extraordinary.”

With astonishing speed, the telephone won over not just presidents and queens but skeptics and Luddites. Even Mark Twain, who complained that “the voice already carries entirely too far as it is,” talked his boss at the *Hartford Courant* into putting a telephone in the newsroom. Then, still grumbling that “if Bell had invented a muffler or a gag he would have done a real service,” he had two installed in his own home, one downstairs for his family and a second in the third-floor billiard room just for himself.

Requests for public demonstrations poured in, and Bell’s audiences never failed to be amazed and delighted by what they heard. One night, while giving a presentation in Salem, Massachusetts, Bell directed his audience's attention to the strange, wooden box before them. Suddenly, they heard the voice of Bell's assistant Thomas Watson coming from the box — thin and tinny but unmistakable and, incredibly, speaking directly to them. "Ladies and gentlemen," Watson said, "it gives me great pleasure to be able to address you this evening, although I am in Boston, and you in Salem!" The crowd erupted in laughter and applause.

Bell would quickly learn, however, that a successful invention, especially one that held as much financial promise as the telephone, attracts not only admirers but bitter competitors. Had Samuel Morse been alive to witness the birth of the telephone, he could have warned Bell of the legal nightmare that awaited him. After Morse developed his telegraph in 1837, more than sixty other people claimed to have invented it first. Morse, whose long life was marked by a series of painful disappointments, spent nearly a quarter of a century fighting dozens of lawsuits.

As harassed as Morse had been, his troubles paled in comparison to what Bell would endure. The challenges to Bell's patent began almost immediately, although few of his accusers had anything to support their claims beyond their own fantasies. One man filed suit not only against Bell for the telephone, but against Thomas Edison for the transmitter and David Edward Hughes for the microphone. Another man eagerly hauled his invention into court to prove his claim against Bell. When it simply sat there, silent, his frustrated and humiliated lawyer exclaimed, "It can speak, but it won't!"

Although Bell deeply resented these accusations and the time and thought the lawsuits demanded, three years after his patent was issued, he entered a courtroom for the first time as a plaintiff rather than a defendant. In late 1876, he had offered to sell his patents to Western Union for $100,000, but had been soundly rejected. Just a few months later, the powerful company, worth an estimated $41 million, realized it had made a disastrous mistake. Instead of approaching Bell, however, and striking a deal, it decided to become his direct competitor. After establishing the American Speaking Telephone Company, Western Union bought the patents of three leading inventors in telephony, one of whom was Thomas Edison.

Bell had little hope of competing with this behemoth. Not only did it have seemingly limitless financial resources to fund experiments and improvements, but it had an existing network of wires that stretched across the country. To add insult to injury, Edison, who was partially deaf, developed a telephone transmitter for Western Union that was better — both louder and clearer — than Bell's.

In a court of law, however, Bell had two things that Western Union did not: irrefutable evidence that he had developed the first working telephone and, more important, a patent. When the company began to attack Bell personally, suggesting in the press that not only did he not have the skill necessary for such an invention but had stolen the idea, he set aside his hatred of lawsuits and fought back. The legal battle lasted less than a year, beginning in the spring of 1879 and ending in the fall, with Western Union admitting defeat and agreeing to shut down the American Speaking Telephone Company. In the end, it would hand over to Bell everything from its lines and telephones to its patent rights, receiving in return only 20 percent of the telephone rental receipts for just seventeen years.

With Western Union's defeat, stock in the Bell Telephone Company skyrocketed from $50 a share to nearly $1,000. The fighting, however, continued. In the end, Bell would face more than six hundred lawsuits, ten times as many as Morse. Five of them would reach the U.S. Supreme Court. One rival in particular, a brilliant inventor named Elisha Gray, would insist to his dying day that the telephone had been his invention. Years later, Gray's own partner would sigh, "Of all the men who didn't invent the telephone, Gray was the nearest."

While hundreds of men fought to be recognized as the inventor of the telephone, Bell feared he would never again be anything else. This one invention, he was convinced, would consume his life if he let it. "I am sick of the Telephone," he had written to his wife in 1878, just two years after the Centennial Exhibition. He yearned for the freedom he had lost, for time to think about other things. "Don't let me be bound hand and soul to the Telephone," he pleaded. Not only did Bell chafe under the yoke of his invention, complaining bitterly that the business that had sprung up around it was "hateful to me at all times" and would "fetter me as an inventor," but he worried that it would prevent him from helping those who needed him most.

His "first incentive to invention," he would often say, had been a neighbor's "injunction to do something useful." Rising to the challenge, Bell, just fourteen years old, had built a contraption that used stiff-bristled brushes mounted to rotating paddles to scrape the husks off wheat. To his delight, the machine had worked, and, in the thump and thwack of his first invention, he had witnessed the potential of his own ideas.

Bell soon realized that, through invention, he could change things, make them better. It was clear to him, moreover, that the world needed to be changed. In a time of widespread illness and early death, he understood grief and suffering as well as any man. Before his twenty-fourth birthday he had lost both his brothers to tuberculosis, leaving him an only child and the sole object of his parents' dreams and fears. "Our earthly hopes have now their beginning, middle and end in you," his father had written him after his older, and last, brother's death. "O, be careful."

From painful personal experience, Bell also knew how difficult life could be for those fortunate enough to survive disease or injury. His mother, who had homeschooled him and his brothers and had taught him to play the piano, was almost completely deaf. Eliza Bell had spent most of her life separated from the world around her by the ear trumpet she relied on to hear even faint fragments of words. Her second son, however, refused to be distanced from his mother by her handicap. Instead, he would put his mouth very close to her forehead and speak in a voice so low and deep she could feel its vibrations.

While Bell's mother had been left with some whispers of sound, his wife could hear absolutely nothing. Mabel Hubbard, whose father, Gardiner Greene Hubbard, had been Bell's earliest backer, had lost her hearing after contracting scarlet fever when she was five years old. As a teenager, she had been one of Bell's first students, and he had quickly fallen in love with her. Although Mabel was then only seventeen years old, ten years younger than Bell, he knew with an unshakable certainty that she was the only woman he wanted to marry. "I should probably have sought one more mature than she is — one who could share with me those scientific pursuits that have always been my delight," he had written to Mabel's mother. "However, my *heart* has chosen."

Although, in the public mind, Bell was now an inventor, he still thought of himself, and would always think of himself, first and foremost as a teacher of the deaf. Not only did he teach, but he trained new teachers.

This work, which he knew would never bring him wealth or fame, meant more to him than anything else he had ever done. "As far as telegraphy is concerned," he confided to Mabel, "I shall be far happier and more honoured if I can send out a band of competent teachers of the deaf and dumb who will accomplish a good work, than I should be to receive all the telegraphic honours in the world."

What concerned Mabel, however, was not what her husband worked on, but the feverish intensity with which he worked. Soon after their engagement, she had written to her mother that the endless hours Bell devoted to the telephone frightened her. "He has his machine running beautifully," she wrote, "but it will kill him if he is not careful."

Bell's parents, terrified that they would lose their only surviving child, had long pleaded with him to slow down. In the summer of 1870, just a month after the death of their oldest son, they had convinced Bell to emigrate with them from Scotland to Canada, where, they hoped, he would live a quieter life. To their frustration and despair, he had only worked harder, conceiving the telephone and then moving to the United States, where he worked day and night to give substance to his ideas. Ten years after they had left Scotland, Bell's mother wrote to him to ask if, now that he had accomplished so much, he would finally rest. "I wish very much . . . that you would for a time, turn away your thoughts altogether from the subject you have so long been poring over, and give your mind a rest," she wrote. "I am dreadfully afraid you are overstraining it."

Bell, however, wanted nothing more than to strain his mind, and could not bear to be interrupted when in the thrall of his thoughts. Now that he was married, he begged his wife to let him work as long as he needed to, even if he disappeared for days at a time. "I have my periods of restlessness when my brain is crowded with ideas tingling to my fingertips when I am excited and cannot stop for anybody," he wrote her in 1879. "Let me alone, let me work as I like even if I have to sit up all night or even for two nights. . . . Oh, do not do as you often do, stop me in the midst of my work, my excitement with 'Alec, Alec, aren't you coming to bed? It's one o'clock, do come.' Then . . . the ideas are gone, the work is never done."

When struggling with an invention, the only respite Bell would allow himself was to play the piano deep into the night. Although he had been taught by a mother who could not hear the music, he had quickly learned to play by ear, picking up tunes and then changing them, making them his own. As a boy, he had even dreamed of becoming a composer, but his father had discouraged him from pursuing a profession that, he believed, would reduce his son to little more than a "wee bit fiddler." Although he followed his father's advice, Bell never gave up music, clinging to it with a particular ferocity in times of stress and anxiety. It was a habit that may have given him some release but little rest, as he succumbed to what his mother described as a "musical fever."

Even to Bell's father, a highly regarded elocutionist who for years had worked in his study until two in the morning, developing a universal alphabet, his work habits seemed not just extreme, but dangerous. "I have serious fears that you have not the stamina for the work your ambition has led you to undertake," Alexander Melville Bell wrote his son. "Be wise. Stop in time. . . . I feel so strongly that you are endangering your future powers of work, and your life, by your present course, that I can write on no other subject. . . . Break your pens and ink bottles. . . . Wisdom points only in one direction. Stop work."

As much as he loved his wife and his parents, Bell either would not stop or could not. He tried to explain to Mabel why he worked such long hours, refusing to stop to eat or rest. He had, he said, a "sort of telephonic undercurrent" in his brain that was constantly humming. "My mind concentrates itself on the subject that happens to occupy it," he wrote, "and then all things else in the Universe — including father — mother — wife — children — *life itself* — become for the time being of secondary importance."

By 1880, so frustrated had Bell become with the Bell Telephone Company — the time it stole from his laboratory work and the battles that he now realized it would always be fighting — that he simply quit. "I have been almost as much surprised as grieved at the course you have taken," his father-in-law, who had become the company's president, wrote him that summer. "My mortification and grief are only tempered by the hope that you do not realize what you have done." Bell, however, understood exactly what he had done, and he would never regret it.

Renting a small house in Washington,

D.C., where his parents had settled, Bell at first tried to write a history of the telephone, to at least acknowledge the singular role it had played in his life. To no one's surprise, however, the temptation to return to his work quickly became too strong to resist. "However hard and faithfully Alec may work on his book," Mabel wrote, "he cannot prevent ideas from entering and overflowing his brain." Before long, Bell had opened a new laboratory.

In February of 1881, just a month before Garfield's inauguration, Bell eagerly moved his equipment and notebooks into a small, two-story brick building that stood in the middle of a large, open stretch of land on Connecticut Avenue. He christened the building the Volta Laboratory, in honor of the science prize that Napoleon Bonaparte had created at the beginning of the century and that Bell had won that past summer. Along with the prize had come a substantial sum — 50,000 francs, or $10,000. With the money, he was able not only to lease the building but to hire an impressive young inventor named Charles Sumner Tainter. Bell had found Tainter in Charles Williams's electrical shop in Boston, the same shop where he had met Thomas Watson six years earlier. Watson had left the Bell Telephone

Company about the same time Bell did, announcing his intention to travel and enjoy his modest wealth, and leaving Bell in great need of a man like Tainter.

Although by now even Bell admitted that he needed rest, he could not ignore the ideas erupting and colliding in his mind. "These are germs of important discoveries yet to come," he wrote his parents early that year, "and I find it hard to rest here with the laboratory so close at hand." One of these ideas was the photophone, a wireless telephone that relied on light waves to carry sound. So feverishly did he work on the invention that he finally had to seek medical care for an ailment that he described as "functional derangement of the heart brought on by too much Photophone."

At the same time that Bell was fretting over his new invention, he was also settling an old score. He had not forgotten that Thomas Edison had made and patented improvements to the telephone, and he now realized with delight that he could return the favor. A few years earlier, Edison had invented the phonograph, but had set it aside before it was finished. Bell and Tainter were certain it could be made into something practical, and valuable. "Edison was completely absorbed in the work of perfecting the electrical light, and seemed to have lost all interest in the phonograph and had failed to appreciate its importance," Tainter wrote. "But we had faith in its future."

Since he had freed himself from the telephone, Bell had been desperately looking not just for a new project, but for work that would capture his heart and imagination, work that had meaning. When Mabel had complained that a school for the deaf he had founded in Scotland took too much of his time, Bell, frustrated that she could not understand what seemed so obvious to him, had snapped, "I trust you will . . . see that I am *needed.*" Nothing, not fame or wealth or even international recognition of his work, was as important to him as this. "I have been absolutely rusting from inaction," he tried desperately to explain, "hoping and hoping that my services might be wanted somewhere." The work he was now doing in the Volta Laboratory might not ease suffering or save a single life, but in this cramped and cluttered little building he knew that, if he were needed, he would be ready.

CHAPTER 7
REAL BRUTUSES AND BOLINGBROKES

Tonight, I am a private citizen.
To-morrow I shall be called to assume
new responsibilities, and on the day after,
the broadside of the world's wrath will
strike. It will strike hard. I know it, and
you will know it.

JAMES A. GARFIELD

At 2:30 in the morning on March 4, 1881, the day of his inauguration, Garfield sat at a small desk in his boardinghouse in Washington and wrote the final sentence of his inaugural address. Although he had been thinking about the speech since his election and had read the addresses of every president who had preceded him, he had not put pen to paper until late January. Over the past month, a friend recalled, he had written "no less than a half-dozen separate and distinct drafts of the address in whole or in part, each profusely adorned with notes, interlineations, and marginalia." Then, three days before, Garfield had swept aside all these drafts, dismissing them as "the staggerings of my mind," and had begun again. When he finally finished, just hours before his inaugural ceremony, he laid down his pen, pushed back his chair, and prepared to bid "good-by to the freedom of private life, and to a long series of happy years."

Not long after Garfield climbed into bed that morning, tens of thousands of people left their homes and hotels and began walking toward the Capitol, determined to see the inauguration despite falling snow and bitter cold. With very few exceptions, presidential inaugurations had been held on the same day in March for nearly ninety years, since George Washington's second inauguration in Philadelphia. The four-month delay between the election and the inauguration was then thought necessary to allow the president-elect sufficient time to travel to the capital. As transportation improved dramatically, however, and circumstances such as the Civil War made the delay not just difficult but dangerous, the date had not changed, and would not for another fifty-two years.

By the time a crowd had gathered on the National Mall for Garfield's inauguration, the snow lay an inch and a half thick over the broad greensward and on the buildings that stood, in various stages of completion, along its edges. To the east lay the Capitol, which, waylaid by two wars, one fire — set by the British during the War of 1812 — multiple architects, and bad reviews, had taken seventy-five years to complete. Farther west, on the Mall's southern side, was a building of great interest to Garfield — the National Museum, now known as the Smithsonian's Arts and Industries Building. Although the roof had only recently been finished and the museum would not be open to the public until October, its temporary pine floors had been laid and waxed months earlier, in anticipation of the inaugural ball it would host for Garfield that night.

Just beyond the Mall stood the painfully incomplete Washington Monument, which, in the words of Mark Twain, looked like "a factory chimney with the top broken off." Although it had been proposed in 1783, construction had not begun until sixty-five years later. By 1854, when the monument had risen to just 152 feet, the project ran out of money, and before work could begin again, the country was plunged into civil war. Even now, sixteen years after the end of the war, the monument still sat abandoned, cowsheds erected in its shadow and sheep and pigs milling around its marble base.

When the sun emerged from the clouds at 8:00 a.m., however, glinting off the white marble and new snow, even the blunt, unfinished Washington Monument seemed dazzling and inspiring. Two hours later, Pennsylvania Avenue was finally "free from snow," a journalist wryly noted, "if not from mud." It was also overrun with people. "The sidewalks could not contain them," one reporter wrote. "The crowd was so dense from the White House to the foot of Capitol Hill that they not only filled all the reserved seats, but all the windows, the sidewalks, . . . and much of the space of the roadway." Those who could afford to spent anywhere from fifty cents to a dollar for a place in the roughly built tiered seating that, although "without cover and exposed to the full sweep of the keen west wind," gave the best view of the parade route.

Determined to make up for the last inauguration, when there had been only a short procession and no inaugural ball because Hayes hadn't been declared the winner until March 2, the city had begun planning Garfield's procession immediately after his election. The fighting had started soon after. So bitter was the war between the various factions that President Hayes himself finally had to intervene. "The momentous question as to who shall ride the prancing steeds and wear broad silk sashes in the inauguration procession, and who shall distribute tickets of admission to the inauguration ball," a reporter wrote mockingly, "is now in a fair way of peaceful if not happy solution."

The moment General William Tecumseh Sherman appeared on Pennsylvania Avenue, leading the presidential procession, any lingering disappointment or wounded pride was instantly forgotten. Straight-backed, almost regal on his spirited gray horse, Sherman was, a reporter wrote, "the very picture of an old soldier in his slouch hat and great coat," his orderlies "dash[ing] up to him on horseback from all directions." Behind him marched twenty thousand militia, including thirteen companies of artillery, the red-lined capes of their coats carefully pinned over their shoulders and their bayonets glittering in the sun. Soon after, the first strains of music from the Marine Corps Band could be heard. The band, which had accompanied the inaugural procession since Thomas Jefferson became president in 1801, was now led by the twenty-seven-year-old John Philip Sousa.

Suddenly, from within the crowd, a shout of joy rang out as the presidential carriage pulled into view. Garfield, with President Hayes at his side, rode in the back of an open carriage pulled by a team of four horses and driven by a legendary presidential coachman named Albert, who had trained under Ulysses S. Grant. As Garfield appeared, he was greeted with a cheer that rose "in a deafening chorus, and . . . was carried along the line without interruption." A well-known and -loved minstrel named Billy Rice waited patiently in the crowd until the president-elect was within earshot and then, in a salute to his boyhood days on the canal, yelled out, "Low bridge!" Breaking into a broad grin, Garfield grabbed his silk hat and ducked.

At precisely noon, a pair of massive bronze doors opened onto the eastern portico of the Capitol, and the presidential party, which had disappeared inside an hour earlier, could be seen filing out. Although nearly a dozen people stepped onto the portico, all eyes were on only three: Frederick Douglass, who led the procession; the president-elect; and his mother, Eliza. It was an extraordinary scene, a testimony to the triumph of intelligence and industry over prejudice and poverty, and it was not lost on those who witnessed it. "James A. Garfield sprung from the people," a reporter marveled. "James A. Garfield, who had known all the hardship of abject poverty, in the presence of a mother who had worked with her own hands to keep him from want — was about to assume the highest civil office this world knows. As the party so stood for a moment, cheer after cheer, loud huzzas which could not be controlled or checked, echoed and reechoed about the Capitol."

After the crowd had finally quieted and he had been sworn into office, Garfield stepped forward to deliver the inaugural address he had finished just that morning. He felt deeply the importance of this speech, and he approached it with a seriousness of purpose that was almost didactic. He talked about education, which, he believed, was the foundation of freedom. He discussed the national debt, the challenges facing farmers, and the importance of civil service reform — at which point, a journalist noted, Roscoe Conkling, sitting directly behind Garfield, "smile[d] quietly at the hard task which Gen. Garfield had marked out for himself."

It was when he spoke about the legacy of the Civil War, however, that Garfield was most passionate. With victory, he told the crowd standing before him, had come extraordinary opportunity. "The elevation of the negro race from slavery to the full rights of citizenship is the most important political change we have known since the adoption of the Constitution," he said. "It has liberated the master as well as the slave from a relation which wronged and enfeebled both." Listening to Garfield speak, a reporter in the crowd of fifty thousand realized that, all around him, "black men who had been slaves, and who still bore upon their persons the evidence of cruel lashings," were standing peacefully, even cheerfully, next to "Southern white men, who had grown poor during the war but who seemed, nevertheless, to harbor no ill-feelings."

The painful past, however, had not been forgotten, nor did Garfield believe it should be. As he spoke, former slaves in the crowd openly wept. "The emancipated race has already made remarkable progress," he said. "With unquestioning devotion to the Union, with a patience and gentleness not born of fear, they have 'followed the light as God gave them to see the light.' . . . They deserve the generous encouragement of all good men. So far as my authority can lawfully extend they shall enjoy the full and equal protection of the Constitution and the laws."

When he finished his address, Garfield stood for a moment on the portico, his hands raised to the sky. "There was the utmost silence," one reporter wrote, as the new president appealed "to God for aid in the trial before him."

The trial, in fact, had already begun. The rivalry between the two factions within the Republican Party had only deepened since the convention in Chicago nine months earlier. Roscoe Conkling's fury at Grant's defeat had turned to outrage when it became clear that Garfield would not bow to his every demand. In August, in a desperate attempt at reconciliation, party bosses had arranged a meeting at the Fifth Avenue Hotel in New York. Garfield had traveled all the way from Mentor for it, but Conkling, who lived in New York, had not even bothered to appear. "Mr. Garfield will doubtless leave New York thoroughly impressed with the magnanimity of our senior Senator," a journalist sneered.

Conkling, it was later discovered, was in another room in the same hotel while the meeting was being held. He did not miss the opportunity, however, to let Garfield know what was expected of him. Through his minions, Conkling laid out his expectations, which, not surprisingly, revolved around patronage — its continuation and his control over it. Not hesitating to make the most audacious demands, he insisted that Garfield let him choose the next secretary of the treasury. Conkling would later claim that Garfield had agreed to everything, but Garfield said he offered nothing more than the assurance that he would try to include Stalwarts in his cabinet and, when appropriate, consult with Conkling. "No trades, no shackles," Garfield had written in his diary after the meeting, "and as well fitted for defeat or victory as ever."

Since Garfield's election, Conkling had decided to take a more direct approach. If Garfield would not let him personally select the cabinet, he would dismantle it, one appointee at a time. In a letter he had written to Garfield just days before the inauguration, Conkling had warned the president-elect that he would be wise to keep in mind who was really in charge. "I need hardly add that your Administration cannot be more successful than I wish it to be," he wrote. "Nor can it be more satisfactory to you, to the country, and to the party than I will labor to make it."

Garfield saw the truth in this threat before his administration even began. On March 1, Levi Morton, a Stalwart who had accepted his nomination as secretary of the navy, was pulled from his sickbed in the middle of the night, forced to drink a bracing mixture of quinine and brandy, and driven to Conkling's apartment — known widely as "the morgue" — to answer for his betrayal. At four the next morning, exhausted and defeated, Morton wrote a letter to Garfield asking him to withdraw his nomination.

Two days later, on the morning of his inauguration, Garfield lost yet another cabinet member to Conkling. At 8:30 a.m., he learned that Senator William Allison, who, just the day before, had agreed to be his secretary of the treasury, had also changed his mind. "Allison broke down on my hands and absolutely declined the Treasury," Garfield wrote in his diary. Like Morton, Allison was clearly unwilling "to face the opposition of certain forces."

Almost as maddening as Conkling's sabotage of his administration was the fact that Garfield's efforts to reunify the party and, he hoped, to reassemble his cabinet were thwarted at every turn by the men who were supposed to be on his side. The Capitol building, where Garfield had spent seventeen years of his life, suddenly seemed a snake pit, a place where vicious, small-minded men lay in wait, ready to attack at the first sign of weakness. "The Senate," Henry Adams would write a few years later in his memoir, *The Education of Henry Adams,* "took the place of Shakespeare, and offered real Brutuses and Bolingbrokes, Jack Cades, Falstaffs and Malvolios, — endless varieties of human nature nowhere else to be studied, and none the less amusing because they killed."

Although John Sherman had tried to forgive Garfield for winning the nomination, he remained deeply bitter over the loss of his best chance at the White House, and he wanted revenge. "The nomination of Garfield is entirely satisfactory to me," he had written after the convention. "As it has come to him without his self-seeking, it is honorable and right and I have no cause of complaint." Sherman did, however, complain loudly and often about the Stalwarts, doing what he could to punish those who had voted for Grant, and deepening the divide between them and Garfield. So transparent were Sherman's motives that the *New York Times* openly accused him of "using his influence and power to gratify personal revenge upon men who fought him at Chicago."

The only person who had wanted the presidential nomination more than Sherman, and whose hatred of the Stalwarts — and in particular of Roscoe Conkling — ran even deeper, was James G. Blaine. Although fifteen years had passed since their famous fight on the floor of Congress, Conkling and Blaine had never forgiven each other, nor did they intend to. Blaine was well aware that Conkling had stopped at nothing to deny him the power of the presidency, and now that his man, not Conkling's, was in the White House, Blaine looked forward to repaying the favor.

Blaine and Garfield had begun a lasting, if at times strained, friendship nearly two decades before, when they had entered Congress at the same time. Although Garfield liked and admired Blaine, he had learned over the years that his friend could be "a little reckless of his promises, and a little selfish withal." As Blaine had risen to power, becoming speaker of the house in 1868, he had made and broken commitments to Garfield with a nonchalance that Garfield found astonishing. Nevertheless, Blaine was a highly skilled tactician and had a political acumen that Garfield knew he lacked. “As a shrewd observer of events, he has few equals in the country,” he had written of Blaine. “As a judge of men, he is equally sagacious.”

As aware of Blaine’s faults as he was his attributes, Garfield decided to offer his friend the most coveted position in his cabinet: secretary of state. The offer, however, came with an absolute and, for Blaine, painful condition: he could never again run for president. “I ask this,” Garfield told him, “because I do not propose to allow myself nor anyone else to use the next four years as the camping ground for fighting the next Presidential battle.” Blaine accepted the condition, knowing that, at this point in his life, he had very little chance of being nominated anyway. More important, as secretary of state he would be in a powerful position not only to influence the president, but to shut Conkling out.

Knowing that Garfield wanted to have men from both factions of the party in his cabinet, Blaine tried everything in his power to convince him that this was not just a bad idea but a dangerous one. When Garfield asked Blaine what he thought about offering the position of secretary of state to Conkling instead, with the idea of keeping his friends close and his enemies closer, Blaine had been horrified. "His appointment would act like strychnine upon your Administration," he promised, "first bringing contortions, and then be followed by death." While Blaine was determined to keep Stalwarts out of Garfield's administration, he knew that he had to resist the temptation to rush in as Sherman had. Conkling and his men were formidable adversaries. To succeed, an attack would have to be both clever and quiet. "They must not be knocked down with bludgeons," Blaine brooded. "They must have their throats cut with a feather."

Although he had dangerous enemies and problematic friends, Garfield's biggest problem was his own vice president — Chester Arthur. Not only had the Republican nomination been thrust upon Garfield without his consent, but so had his running mate. Flush with victory, Garfield's supporters had begun to plan the campaign while still at the convention hall, and without consulting their candidate. Knowing that without New York it would be difficult to win the presidency, and that without Conkling it would be almost impossible to win New York, they had decided to offer the vice presidential nomination to one of Conkling's men. No one in the Republican Party was more Conkling's man than Chester Arthur.

Politically, Arthur was wholly Conkling's creation. The only public position Arthur had held before becoming vice president of the United States was as collector of the New York Customs House, a job that Conkling had secured for him and which paid more than $50,000 a year — as much as the president's salary, and five times as much as the vice president's. Even then, he had been forced out of office amid widespread allegations of corruption. "The nomination of Arthur is a ridiculous burlesque," John Sherman had spat after the convention. "He never held an office except the one he was removed from."

Conkling had at first been as furious as Sherman about Arthur's nomination. After he was approached by Garfield's supporters, Arthur had searched the convention hall for Conkling, finally finding him in a back room, pacing the floors in an apoplectic rage in the wake of Grant's defeat. "The Ohio men have offered me the Vice Presidency," Arthur told him. Conkling, with barely suppressed fury, replied, "Well, sir, you should drop it as you would a red hot shoe from the forge." For the first time in his life, however, Arthur defied his mentor. "The office of the Vice President is a greater honor than I ever dreamed of attaining," he said. "I shall accept the nomination."

Although Conkling had stormed out of the room that night, it had not taken him long to realize that having Arthur in the office of vice president was nearly as useful as having Grant in the White House. Perhaps even more so. While Grant was very much his own man, Conkling had complete control over Arthur. Arthur was one of the two men Conkling sent to drag Levi Morton out of bed and force him to resign from Garfield's cabinet — just days before Arthur's own inauguration. A bachelor since the death of his wife five months before the Republican convention, Arthur even lived in Conkling's home at Fourteenth and F Streets in Washington. By the time Conkling witnessed his protégé's swearing in, in a private ceremony that took place inside the Capitol just before Garfield's inauguration, he was thrilled at the prospect of advising Arthur in his new role in Washington.

As strong a grip as he had on the vice president, Conkling was confident he would have little difficulty controlling the president. Even Garfield's friends worried that he was an easy mark. He was too interested in winning over his enemies to be able to protect his own interests. "For his enemies, or those who may have chosen thus to regard themselves," a friend had said of him, "he had no enmity — naught but magnanimity." When challenged in Congress by men for whom "no sarcasm was too cutting, no irony too cold," Garfield never rose to the bait. He would reply with such earnestness that, in the words of an early biographer, "a stranger entering the House after Garfield had begun his speech in answer to some most galling attack would never suspect the speech was a reply to a hostile and malignant assault."

Nor was Garfield capable of carrying a grudge, a character trait that neither Conkling nor Blaine could begin to understand. Years before, Garfield had resolved to stop speaking to a journalist who had tried to vilify him in the press. The next time he saw the man, however, he could not resist greeting him with a cheerful wave. "You old rascal," he said with a smile. "How are you?" Garfield realized that, in a political context, the ease with which he forgave was regarded as a weakness, but he did not even try to change. "I am a poor hater," he shrugged.

What Conkling did not understand, however, was that while Garfield was a poor hater, he was a very good fighter. As president, he wrote in his diary, he was "determined not to be classified the friend of one faction only," and he vowed to "go as far as I can to keep the peace." That said, he had never before walked away from a fight, and he was not about to do so now. He had fought everyone from hardened canal men to unruly students to Confederate soldiers, and he knew that, whether he liked it or not, he now had another battle on his hands.

"Of course I deprecate war," he wrote, "but if it is brought to my door the bringer will find me at home."

Chapter 8
Brains, Flesh, and Blood

I love to deal with doctrines and events.
The contests of men about men
I greatly dislike.

JAMES A. GARFIELD

From an open window in his office in the White House, Garfield could smell the honeysuckle in full bloom on the southern portico, and he could see the broad stretch of the south lawn, dotted with diamond-, circle-, and star-patterned flower beds. In the distance was a lake, a glittering glimpse of the Potomac River, and the Washington Monument. Inside his office, which was on the second floor, just steps from his bedroom, a life-size portrait of George Washington hung on the north wall. "The eyes of Washington," wrote a reporter who visited the new president, "look out upon the unfinished monument, and there is marked sadness in their expression." Since Garfield's inauguration, however, a derrick now sat on the flat top of the truncated monument — the promise of progress.

The White House itself was also about to receive some much-needed and long-awaited attention. Soon after she moved in, Garfield's wife, Lucretia, "sat down to a good rattling talk over the dilapidated condition of this old White House" with two journalists, one of whom was Joseph Harper, a founding brother of *Harper's Magazine.* With their help, she convinced Congress to appropriate $30,000 for renovation and restoration, funds it had withheld for four years from President Hayes. As the structure had slowly disintegrated around them, Hayes and his wife had used rugs to cover holes in the Brussels carpeting and steered visitors away from rooms with curtains that were stained and torn.

With a family to raise in a dangerously neglected house, Lucretia was eager to get started, but she refused to paint a wall or replace a curtain before she did her research. Garfield accompanied her on her trip to the Library of Congress so that he could see his old friend Ainsworth Rand Spofford. Spofford, who had been the Librarian of Congress since 1864, knew Garfield well, ranking him among the most diligent researchers he had ever met and marveling at how, in the midst of a hectic work schedule, Garfield managed to keep "abreast of current literature, allowing no good book to escape him." Whenever Spofford received a box of books from New York or Europe, he would send word to Garfield so he could have the first look. Garfield enjoyed this proximity to knowledge so much that, when in Ohio one summer, he confided to a friend, "Every day I miss Spofford and our great Library of Congress."

As much as Garfield loved books, however, he spent the great majority of his time between congressional sessions not reading but playing. He and Lucretia had five living children: Harry, Jim, Mary — who was known as Mollie — Irvin, and Abe, who was named for his grandfather, Abram. While home in Mentor, Garfield had always made the most of his time with them, swimming, playing croquet, working on the farm, correcting their Homer recitations from memory, or simply reading to them by lantern light after dinner. With his daughter and four sons gathered at his feet, he read for hours without rest, eager to introduce them to his favorite works, from Shakespeare's plays to *The Arabian Nights* to Audubon's detailed descriptions of the woodchuck, the brown pelican, and the ferruginous thrush. His summers and holidays at home, however, always seemed too short, and he regretted deeply the time he was away from his family. "It is a pity," he wrote, "that I have so little time to devote to my children."

For Garfield, being able to work from home was one of the few advantages of being president. He could check in on Harry and Jim as their tutor prepared them to attend Williams College, their father's alma mater, in the fall. He could give fourteen-year-old Mollie a quick hug before she scurried out of the house, books tucked under her arm, on her way to Madame Burr's School, which she walked to alone every day. His youngest sons, Irvin and Abe, were more easily heard than seen, their laughter echoing through the house. While nine-year-old Abe liked to race his friends through the East Room on his high-wheeled bicycle, with its enormous front wheel, Irvin preferred to ride his bike down the central staircase and over the slippery marble floor, startling visitors and carving deep scratches into the wainscoting his mother was trying to carefully restore.

Garfield adored his children, but he was

determined not to spoil them, or allow anyone else to. "Whatever fate may await me, I am resolved, if possible, to save my children from being injured by my presidency," he wrote. "'*Hoc opus, hic labor est.*' Every attempt, therefore, to flatter them, or to make more of them than they deserve, I shall do all I can to prevent, and to arm them against." In this endeavor, he had the help not only of his wife but of his practical and disciplined mother, Eliza, who had moved into the White House with the family. "I am the first mother that has occupied the White House and her son President," she wrote to a friend. "I feel very thankful for such a son. I don't like the word proud, but if I must use it I think in this case it is quite appropriate."

Although Eliza found the White House "cozy and home like," settling into it with her usual quiet confidence, she worried for her son's safety. During the campaign, she had noticed two strangers in Mentor who looked suspicious to her and had warned James about them. "Dear old mother," Garfield later told a friend, "she takes such an interest in her son." The new president and first lady, however, were too overwhelmed by political battles and social obligations to worry about anything else.

"Slept too soundly to remember any dream," Lucretia wrote in her diary after her family had spent its first night in the White House. "And so our first night among the shadows of the last 80 years gave no forecast of our future."

While living in the White House allowed Garfield to see his children more often, it made it impossible for him to escape the long lines of office seekers who waited outside his front door. A few hoped to impress the president with their skills or knowledge, but the great majority of them simply intended to wear him down with dogged determination and lists of influential friends. "This is the way in which we transact the public business of the Nation," a New York newspaper had recently complained. "No man has the slightest chance of securing the smallest place because of his fitness for it. . . . If your streets are so unclean to-day as to threaten a pestilence, it is because those in charge were appointed through political influence, with no regard to their capacity to work."

On March 5, Garfield's first day at work, a line began to form before he even sat down to breakfast. By the time he finished, it snaked down the front walk, out the gate, and onto Pennsylvania Avenue. When he learned what awaited him, he was dismayed but not surprised. Office seekers had begun showing up at his home in Mentor the day after the election, parking themselves on his front lawn, his porch, and, if they could get in the door, even his living room sofa. Most painful to Garfield was the fact that, within the throng, he often found his own friends. "Almost everyone who comes to me wants something," he wrote sadly, "and this embitters the pleasures of friendship."

Those who waited outside the White House, moreover, did not want simply to apply for a position. They wanted to make their case directly to Garfield himself. As the leader of a democratic nation, the president of the United States was expected to see everyone who wanted to see him. In 1863, a journalist close to President Lincoln and his wife had given his readers a tour of the White House. "Let us go into the Executive mansion," he wrote. "There is nobody to bar our passage, and the multitude, washed and unwashed, always has free egress and ingress."

Garfield realized with a sinking heart that a large portion of his day, every day, would be devoured by office seekers. His calling hours were 10:30 a.m. to 1:30 p.m., Monday through Friday, and he faced about a hundred callers every day. "My day is frittered away by the personal seeking of people, when it ought to be given to the great problems which concern the whole country," he bitterly complained. "Four years of this kind of intellectual dissipation may cripple me for the remainder of my life. What might not a vigorous thinker do, if he could be allowed to use the opportunities of a Presidential term in vital, useful activity?"

For Garfield, who treasured time not just to work but to read and think, the situation was untenable. "My God!" he wrote after a day spent wrestling with office seekers. "What is there in this place that a man should ever want to get into it?" So voracious were the people who prowled the halls of the White House searching for a job, that they sounded to one member of the administration like nothing more than "beasts at feeding time." "These people would take my very brains, flesh and blood if they could," Garfield wearily told his private secretary.

Nor was the White House the only point of attack. In the opening days of Garfield's administration, so many people came to see Blaine at the State Department, asking for an appointment, that before the week was out their audacity no longer surprised him. "Secretary Blaine is especially sought after," reported the *Washington Post*, "and it requires all the paraphernalia of messengers and ante-rooms for which the State department is noted, to protect him."

Conkling, naturally, was delighted. The annoyance that the spoils system caused Blaine and Garfield only made him more determined to defend it. Not that he needed any encouragement. During Hayes's administration, Conkling had taken every opportunity to belittle the president's efforts at civil service reform, which he jeeringly dubbed "snivel service." "When Dr. Johnson defined patriotism as the last refuge of a scoundrel," Conkling told reporters, "he was unconscious of the then undeveloped capabilities and uses of the word 'Reform.' "

Although Garfield found the relentless flow of office seekers maddening and time-consuming, he did not consider them dangerous, and he brushed off any suggestion that he might need protection. Even had he wanted bodyguards, he would have had a difficult time finding them. The Secret Service had been established sixteen years earlier, just a few months after President Lincoln's assassination, but it had been created to fight counterfeiting, not to protect the president. Over the years, the agency's duties had broadened to include law enforcement, but no particular attention was given to the White House. Then, the year before Garfield took the oath of office, Congress cut the Secret Service's annual budget nearly in half, to just $60,000, and restricted its agents, once again, to investigating counterfeiting cases.

While the president of the United States was allowed to walk the streets of Washington alone, as Garfield often did, news of assassinations continued to come in from across the sea. In 1812, the British prime minister, Spencer Perceval, had been shot and killed while he was standing in the House of Commons. A series of assassins had tried to kill Queen Victoria at least half a dozen times. Emperor William I of Germany survived an assassination attempt in the spring of 1878, only to be seriously wounded in another one just a month later. Soon after taking office, Garfield sent a "strong dispatch of sympathy and condolence" to Russia following the assassination, on March 13, of Czar Alexander II. The czar, despite the fact that he had abolished serfdom in his country twenty years earlier, had been the target of several previous assassination attempts.

Americans, however, felt somehow immune to this streak of political killings. Although in his dispatch to Russia, Garfield made "allusion to our own loss in the death of Lincoln," Lincoln's assassination was widely believed to have been a tragic result of war, not a threat to the presidency. Americans reasoned that, because they had the power to choose their own head of state, there was little cause for angry rebellion. As a result, presidents were expected not only to be personally available to the public, but to live much like them. When President Hayes had traveled to Philadelphia five years earlier for the opening ceremony of the Centennial Exhibition, he had bought a ticket and boarded the train like everyone else.

The general consensus in the United States, moreover, was that if the president did happen to be at a slightly greater risk than the average citizen, there was simply nothing to be done about it. "We cannot protect our Presidents with body guards," an editorial in the *New York Times* read. "There is no protection with which we can surround them that will ward off danger or disarm it more effectively than our present refusal to recognize its existence." Garfield, unwilling to forfeit any more of his liberty than he had already lost to political enemies and office seekers, could not have agreed more. "Assassination can no more be guarded against than death by lightning," he wrote, "and it is best not to worry about either."

Beyond a doorman and the occasional presence of an aging police officer who had worked in the White House for nearly two decades, the only buffer between the president and the public was Garfield's twenty-three-year-old private secretary, Joseph Stanley Brown. Brown had met Garfield two years earlier, when he was doing secretarial work for the legendary explorer John Wesley Powell. Powell was anxious to get funding from Congress for his survey of the American West and was counting on Garfield's help. Garfield was deeply interested in Powell's work, but his secretary had been ill for quite some time, and he was buried under stacks of correspondence. Powell's solution was to lend him his own secretary.

The next morning, on his way to work, Brown stopped by Garfield's house in Washington, D.C. When Garfield was told that a young man was waiting for him, he crossed the hall and, entering the room, said in his characteristically cheerful and booming voice, "Good morning, what can I do for you?" His casual smile quickly turned to a look of surprise as Brown, then just twenty-one, replied boldly, "It is not what you can do for me, General Garfield. It is what I can do for you."

Over the following weeks, as Garfield came to know Brown, one of the things he liked best about the young man was that he relied on his own intelligence and ingenuity. Like Garfield, Brown had come from humble origins but had risen through hard work and disciplined study. "Aspirations for the reflected glory of a long lineage of illustrious progenitors — the solace of ignoble minds," he would later write, "furnishes no part of the 'motif' of my ancestral inquiries." Brown's grandfather Nathaniel Stanley had come to the United States from England in 1819 in order to avoid debtor's prison, changing his name to Brown upon arrival in Baltimore. In America, Nathaniel's son became a carpenter, and his grandson, Joseph, was expected to do the same. Although Joseph dutifully learned carpentry during the day, he studied Latin at night. When he was twelve, he also began to teach himself shorthand, recording the speeches of every public speaker he met, most of whom were ministers. He won his first job with Powell by offering to work for free.

Soon after Brown began working for Garfield, Powell won his funding from Congress, but lost his secretary to Garfield, who had come to rely on him. Brown, who was not much older than Garfield's oldest sons, quickly became part of the family. He traveled to Mentor, joined family dinners and croquet tournaments, listened as Garfield tried out his speeches, and even gave him advice on relating to his teenagers. "The gracious, affectionate home life of the Garfield family was a revelation to one whose own home life was rather severe and austere," Brown would later recall. "It was like having two homes."

Garfield made it clear to Brown from the beginning that he not only liked him, but genuinely needed his help. When Garfield had returned to Washington for a few days after his nomination, Brown decided not to call on him, worried that his boss would think he was just another person asking for a favor. He realized how wrong he had been when he ran into Garfield on the street. "Where have you been," Garfield asked him. "I need all my friends now." Exhausted and worried, Garfield was in earnest, but he roared with laughter when Brown, who knew that he had had hardly a moment to himself since his nomination, replied, "General, I do not think you could have been very lonesome."

As much as Garfield had come to rely on Brown, when it was time to fill the position of private secretary to the president, the young man who had served him so well was not even a candidate. The position, which was one of great influence and proximity to power, traditionally went to men of considerable political skill and experience. Thomas Jefferson's private secretary had been Meriwether Lewis, whom he soon after entrusted with exploring and charting the Pacific Northwest. Garfield wanted for his private secretary John Hay, who had been Lincoln's assistant private secretary twenty years earlier, and would, in another twenty years, be Theodore Roosevelt's secretary of state. He felt strongly that Hay was the right man for the job, but Hay, who had greater ambitions, delicately declined. "He is very bright and able," Garfield wrote in discouragement. "I more and more regret that I cannot have him for my private secretary."

When Garfield finally offered the job to Brown, it came as a surprise to no one but Garfield. One night, as the family sat before a fire in the farmhouse in Mentor, he ruminated aloud on his options for private secretary after the disappointment of Hay's refusal. Suddenly, he turned to Brown and said, "Well, my boy, I may have to give it to you." The young man replied drily, "Well that *is* complimentary, to say the least, when all these other fellows have been first considered." Everyone in the room burst into laughter.

As prestigious as it was to be the president's private secretary, Brown had no illusions about what the job would entail. Immediately following Garfield's nomination, more than five thousand letters had poured into Mentor from all parts of the country, and Brown had been forced to quickly devise a system to deal with them. On the morning of Garfield's inauguration, when the president-elect had collapsed into bed after finally finishing his speech, Brown had stayed up to make a clean copy of it, leaving him too tired to attend any of the day's events until the ball that night. Since then, he had been opening, sorting, and responding to as many as three hundred letters every day, and there was no one to help him. "There was no organized staff . . . with expert stenographers and typists," he later recalled. "Only one pair of hands."

Although Brown insisted that everyone who called on the president at the White

House be treated with courtesy and respect, regardless of influence or station, he became very adept at shielding Garfield from office seekers. His first official act as private secretary was to issue an order that anyone who wished to see the president had to go through him first. This rule applied to even high-ranking politicians and old friends, many of whom exploded in rage when asked to wait in an anteroom filled from wall to wall with office seekers. "How the President and his Private Secretary stand the pressure of the many callers seems a mystery," one reporter marveled. "They must have nerves of steel, muscles of iron, and brains with more extent of cell and surface than fall to the lot of most mortals."

In a small room across town, Garfield's most persistent office seeker grew more determined and delusional with each passing day. The day after Garfield's inauguration, Charles Guiteau had taken a train from New York to Washington, D.C. With only a few dollars in his pocket and no intention of looking for a job outside the White House, he quickly resumed his habit of moving from boardinghouse to boardinghouse when the rent came due. While he was forced to flee some rooms after just a day or two, he was able to keep others for several weeks by assuring his landlady that he was about to be given an important political appointment.

Guiteau had begun laying the groundwork for his appointment as soon as Garfield was elected. In November, he had sent a note of congratulations that sounded as though he and Garfield were the oldest of friends. "We have cleaned them out just as I expected. Thank God!" A few days later he had written to then secretary of state William Evarts, asking if he was correct in assuming that President Hayes's foreign ministers would step aside to make way for Garfield's appointments. "Please answer me at the Fifth Ave. Hotel at your earliest convenience," he instructed one of the highest-ranking men in the country. "I am solid for General Garfield and may get an appointment from him next spring."

Assuming that Garfield would soon be handing out appointments, Guiteau wanted to be first in line. After deciding that the position to which he was best suited was minister to Austria, he again wrote to the president-elect. "Dear General, I, Charles Guiteau, hereby make application for the Austrian Mission. . . . On the principle of first come first served, I have faith that you will give this application favorable consideration." Although Garfield received hundreds of letters every day from people asking for government appointments, this letter in particular impressed him as an "illustration of unparalleled audacity and impudence."

Guiteau, however, believed not only that he was entitled to a position of importance, but that he had the necessary credentials for one. "I have practiced law in New York and Chicago," he wrote, "and presume I am well qualified for [the position]." He also let it be known that he expected to come into some money. "Being about to marry a wealthy and accomplished heiress of this city," he told Garfield, "we think that together we might represent this Nation with dignity and grace." The heiress in question, however, knew Guiteau only as an annoying and potentially dangerous stalker. After spotting her in church and learning that she came from a wealthy family, he had begun sending her letters, following her on the street, and knocking on her front door. Despite his vigorous efforts, or perhaps because of them, she had never spoken a word to him.

While still in New York, Guiteau had done all he could to make himself known to anyone of importance in the Republican

Party. Every day, he had gone to campaign headquarters or the Fifth Avenue Hotel, a regular meeting place for Republicans. He had been in the hotel when Garfield arrived from Mentor for the meeting that Conkling refused to attend, and he had stayed all day, eagerly greeting senators and cabinet members whenever they happened to pass through the lobby. "All those leading politicians . . . knew me," Guiteau would proudly recall, "and were very glad to see me."

Even Chester Arthur had met Guiteau, who had made it a point to seek out the vice president–elect wherever he happened to be — at campaign headquarters, on the street, even in his home. "I have seen him at least ten times," Arthur would later recall, "possibly as often as twenty times altogether." On several occasions, Arthur's butler opened the door to find Guiteau standing before him, clutching his "Garfield against Hancock" speech. Although he never set foot in the door, Guiteau believed that he had developed a close relationship with Arthur and was "on free-and-easy terms" with him.

The most fail-proof way to secure an appointment, Guiteau had decided, was to convince Arthur to let him stump for Garfield. Finally, Arthur agreed, giving Guiteau an opportunity to deliver a single speech at a small gathering in New York. Guiteau had spoken for only a few minutes, explaining later that it was too hot, he didn't like the torch lights, and there were plenty of other speakers waiting to talk. He was convinced, however, that the speech he gave that night had played a pivotal role in putting Garfield in the White House, and that it should certainly guarantee him a position of prominence in the administration.

Within days of his arrival in Washington, Guiteau was at the White House. As he entered the waiting room, he handed the doorman his calling card and quietly took his place among the dozens of other office seekers, perched on wooden tables and chairs before a large, unlit fireplace. The day Guiteau chose to make his first visit to the White House was, even by the standards of the time, an exceptionally busy one. "No day in 12 years has witnessed such a jam of callers at each Executive Dep't," Garfield would write in his diary that night, complaining that "the Spartan band of disciplined office hunters . . . drew paper on me as highway men draw pistols."

After waiting for a few hours without seeing anyone, Guiteau put his hat back on and left, disappointed but not discouraged.

Since November, he had had a change of heart about the Austrian Mission, and he wrote to Garfield that day to deliver the news. "I think I prefer Paris to Vienna, and, if agreeable to you, should be satisfied with the consulship at Paris," he wrote from the lobby of a hotel where he was not staying but which had more impressive stationery than his own. "Senators Blaine, Logan, and Conkling are friendly to me, and I presume my appointment will be promptly confirmed. There is nothing against me. I claim to be a gentleman and Christian."

Guiteau also made the case to Garfield that he had been instrumental in his election. He argued that the speech he had delivered in New York, and had handed to every man of influence in the Republican Party to whom he had access, including Garfield's own vice president, had not only won votes, but had been the source of an idea that was central to the campaign's success. "The inclosed [*sic*] speech was sent to our leading editors and orators in August," he argued. "Soon thereafter they opened on the rebel war-claim *idea,* and it was *this* idea that resulted in your election."

Not long after Guiteau began visiting the White House, he met Garfield face-to-face. One day, after entering the anteroom as usual and handing the doorman his card, he was led upstairs to Brown's office, which connected directly to the president's office. A moment later, he found himself standing before Garfield, watching silently as he spoke with Levi Morton, one of the men Conkling had forced to resign from the cabinet. Guiteau waited for the two men to finish their conversation, and then, introducing himself as an applicant for the Paris consulship, handed Garfield the campaign speech he had been carrying in his pocket for the past year. On the first page of the speech, he had written "Paris Consulship" and drawn a line between those words and his name, "so that the President would remember what I wanted." "Of course, [Garfield] recognized me at once," Guiteau would later say. He watched with satisfaction as the president glanced down at the speech, and then left, confident that his appointment was now only a matter of time.

After that day, Guiteau quickly became a familiar face at the White House. "His visits were repeated . . . quite regularly," Brown would remember. "I saw Mr. Guiteau probably fifteen times altogether at various places, about on the street and about in the Executive Mansion and on the grounds." When he wasn't waiting in the president's anteroom, Guiteau was sending notes into him by the doorman, or simply sitting on a bench in Lafayette Square, staring at the White House.

Before the end of March, Guiteau found another opportunity to insert himself into Garfield's life, this time even more intimately. The White House held an afternoon reception that was open to anyone who wished to attend, and there was, Garfield would write in his diary that night, a "very large attendance." Guiteau quietly joined the immense crowd, watching as, for two hours, the president and first lady smiled and shook hands with what Lucretia later referred to as "the great roaring world."

Suddenly, Lucretia heard someone say, "How do you do, Mrs. Garfield?" Looking up, she saw a small, thin man in a threadbare suit who, although he had spoken to her with a strange urgency, did not meet her eyes. Guiteau had a strikingly quiet walk, so quiet that people who knew him often complained that he seemed to appear out of nowhere. Now, standing close enough to the first lady to touch her, he told her that he had recently moved to Washington from New York, where he had been "one of the men that made Mr. Garfield President." Although Lucretia, a very private woman who dreaded receptions, was "aching in every joint," and "nearly paralyzed" with fatigue, Guiteau would remember her as "chatty and companionable," clearly "quite pleased" to see him. Before giving way to the crush of callers impatiently waiting to meet the first lady, Guiteau leaned in closely to Lucretia, handed her his card, and carefully pronounced his name, determined that she would not forget him.

CHAPTER 9
CASUS BELLI

I would rather be beaten in Right than succeed in Wrong.

JAMES A. GARFIELD

On the morning of May 3, Lucretia woke with a fever. "She is not well . . . almost a chill," Garfield wrote in his diary that night. When she was not better the next day, he fretted over her, blaming the pressures of his presidency. "Crete," as he called her, "has been too hard worked during the past two months." As the week progressed and Lucretia's fever rose, Garfield's concern turned to alarm. He sent for four different doctors, sat at her bedside late into the night every night, and then stumbled through the day, trying with little success to tamp down a growing terror. "My anxiety for her dominates all my thoughts," he wrote on the night of May 8, "and makes me feel that I am fit for nothing."

Lucretia was the center of Garfield's world. They had met thirty years earlier, while attending the same rural school in Ohio when he was nineteen and she was eighteen. Like Garfield's mother, Lucretia's parents were determined that their children would receive a good education. Her father, Zeb Rudolph, was a farmer and carpenter, but he was also one of the founders of the Western Reserve Eclectic Institute. When the school opened in 1850, he enrolled Lucretia in its first class, watching with pride as she edited the school magazine, helped to start a literary society, and studied Latin with a discipline, if not a passion, that would rival Garfield's.

When Garfield arrived on campus the following year, the boy Lucretia had known in high school transformed before her eyes. She would tell her daughter years later that James at first seemed to her just a "big, shy lad with a shock of unruly hair . . . as awkward and untutored as he was dead in earnest and determined to learn any and everything that came his way." As he immersed himself in his studies, however, the last traces of his life in the log cabin and on the canal seemed to vanish, not just from his mind, but from his face. "Mental development and culture," Lucretia marveled, "seemed, literally, to chisel fineness and delicacy into features that were, if not rugged, at least unformed."

Although Lucretia and James shared a common background and desire for education, they were very different people. Bighearted and cheerful, Garfield was nearly impossible to resist. Throughout his life, he was just as likely to give a friend, or even a determined enemy, a bear hug as a handshake, and he had an enormous, booming laugh that was unfailingly contagious. Years later, the son of a friend of Garfield's would remember watching as his father and Garfield laughed their hearts out, literally rolling "over and over upon the ground and stirring the very trees with their Olympian laughter."

Lucretia, in stark contrast, was softspoken and very private. Her parents, although kind and deeply interested in her education, had never been demonstrative. Zeb Rudolph's neighbors would remember him as being almost without emotion, "never elated and never greatly depressed." Although Lucretia would at times complain that James let the "generous and gushing affection of your warm impulsive nature" affect his good judgment, she worried that she leaned too far in the opposite direction.

"The world," she feared, would judge her to be "cold," even "heartless."

Their courtship was long, awkward, and far more analytical than passionate. It began with a painfully polite letter from Garfield to Lucretia when he was on a trip to Niagara Falls in 1853. "Please pardon the liberty I take in pointing my pen towards *your* name this evening," he began stiffly, "for I have taken in so much scenery today I cannot contain it all myself." As the years passed and they slowly moved toward marriage, Garfield waited impatiently for Lucretia to express her love for him, but she remained distant. Finally, in frustration, he wrote to her, "It is my desire to 'know and be known.' I long to hear from you . . . to know your heart and open mine to you. . . . Let your heart take the pen and your hand hold it not back." Lucretia, however, could only ask James to try to understand. "I do not think I was born for constant caresses, and surely no education of my childhood taught me to need them," she would one day tell him. "I am only sorry that my own quiet and reserve should mean to you a lack of love."

In 1855, when Garfield returned to Ohio from Massachusetts, where he was attending Williams College, Lucretia seemed to him as cold and remote as the first time he met her. "For the past year, I had fears before I went away, that she had not that natural warmth of heart which my nature calls so loudly for," he wrote dejectedly in his diary. "It seems as though all my former fears were well founded and that she and I are not like each other in enough respects to make us happy together. . . . My wild passionate heart demands so much." When he visited her again the following day, however, Lucretia bravely handed him her diary. To Garfield's astonishment, it was filled with the love that she had always felt but had never been able to express. "Never before did I see such depths of suffering and such entire devotion of heart as was displayed in her private journal which she allowed me to read," he wrote that night. "For months, when I was away in the midst of my toils, her heart was constantly pouring out its tribute of love."

Although Garfield now believed that Lucretia loved him, when they finally married in 1858, they both knew that he was not yet in love with her. "I am not certain I feel just as I ought toward her," he had admitted in his diary. "I have the most entire confidence in her purity of heart, conscientiousness and trustfulness and truly love her qualities of mind and heart. But there is no delirium of passion nor overwhelming power of feeling that draws me to her irresistibly." Lucretia was painfully aware that Garfield's feelings toward her had not deepened over the years, and she was tormented by the thought that he was marrying her because he felt he had to. The summer before their wedding, she wrote miserably to him, "There are hours when my heart almost breaks with the cruel thought that our marriage is based upon the cold stern word *duty.*"

If their courtship was difficult, the first years of their marriage were nearly unbearable. Between the Civil War and Garfield's congressional duties in Washington, they spent only five months together during the first five years. The constant separation made it almost impossible for Lucretia to overcome her natural reserve, although she tried in earnest. "Before when you were away my heart missed you," she wrote after they had been married for four years. "Now my whole self mourns with it and longs and pines for your presence, my lips for your kisses, my cheek for the warm pressure of yours. In short, I understand what you meant when you used to say, 'I want to be touched!' "

Finally able to express herself in a letter,

Lucretia still struggled to show physical affection, and Garfield's frustration deepened until he confessed that he had grave doubts about their marriage. "It seemed a little hard to have you tell me . . . that you had for several months felt that it was probably a great mistake that we ever tried married life," Lucretia wrote to James while he was in Columbus, working in the state senate, and she was home, expecting their first child. "I am glad you are coming home so soon, but you must come with a light face, or the shadow of those hours of terrible suffering, which are so surely and steadily coming upon me, will steal over me with its chill of death."

Not even Trot, whose birth in 1860 brought James and Lucretia joy, and whose death, just three years later, knit them in a shared grief, could help them overcome their differences. The divide that had always separated them continued to widen until, in 1864, Garfield nearly destroyed any hope they had ever had of happiness together. In the spring of that year, he had an affair with a young widow named Lucia Gilbert Calhoun. He had met her in New York, where she was a reporter for the *New York Tribune,* and they had fallen in love, the kind of love he had for so long yearned to feel for Lucretia.

A month after meeting Lucia, James went home to Ohio and confessed the affair. Although angry and heartbroken, Lucretia forgave him, demanding only that he end the relationship immediately. Garfield agreed. He was certain he was walking away from his one chance at real love, but he was deeply ashamed of his infidelity. "I believe after all I had rather be respected than loved if I can't be both," he wrote sadly. He thanked Lucretia for her "brave words of good sense," adding, "I hope when you . . . balance up the whole of my wayward self, you will still find, after the many proper and heavy deductions are made, a small balance left on which you can base some respect and affection."

Garfield feared that, in the wake of his confession, Lucretia would lose all faith in him. Instead, his own feelings began to change. As he watched her bravely endure the pain and heartbreak that he had caused, Garfield suddenly saw Lucretia in a new light. She was not cold and unreachable but strong, steady, and resilient. Slowly, he began to fall in love with his wife.

As the years passed, Garfield's love for Lucretia grew until it eclipsed any doubts he had ever had. His letters, which once alternated between terse, cold replies and painfully honest confessions, were now filled with passionate declarations of love. Lucretia was finally the object of James's "gushing affection." "We no longer love because we ought to, but because we do," he wrote to her one night from Washington. "The tyranny of our love is sweet. We waited long for his coming, but he has come to stay." A few months later, he again poured out his heart to her. "I here record the most deliberate conviction of my soul," he wrote. "Were every tie that binds me to the men and women of the world severed, and I free to choose out of all the world the sharer of my heart and home and life, I would fly to you and ask you to be mine as you are."

During the Republican convention, Garfield missed Lucretia desperately. "You can never know how much I need you during these days of storm," he wrote to her just days before his nomination. "Every hour I want to go and state some case to your quick intuition. But I feel the presence of your spirit." When he won the nomination, the first thing he did after making his escape from the convention hall was to send Lucretia a telegram. It said simply: "Dear wife, if the result meets your approval, I shall be content."

By the time Garfield became president, Lucretia was completely confident of his love for her. For years, she had waited at home for him, asking when he would return, wondering if he missed her, questioning his devotion. Now she knew that her husband felt her absence as strongly as she did his. "It is almost painful for me to feel that so much of my life and happiness have come to depend upon another than myself," he had written to her. "I want to hear from you so often, and I shall wait and watch with a hungry heart until your dear words reach me."

For Garfield, Lucretia had become the "life of my life," and as he now sat by her bed in the White House, watching as her temperature steadily climbed, he realized with a helpless desperation that he could do nothing to save her. She was "the continent, the solid land on which I build all my happiness," he had once told her. "When you are sick, I am like the inhabitants of countries visited by earthquakes. They lose all faith in the eternal order and fixedness of things."

On the night of May 10, after Lucretia had been moved to a room on the north side of the house, "to get her further from the river air," Garfield sat with her until

4:00 a.m. A few hours later, news of her illness appeared in the newspapers, stirring dark memories of President John Tyler's wife, Letitia, who had died in the White House less than forty years earlier. "I am sorry to say that I have grave fears about Mrs. Garfield," James Blaine's wife, Harriet, wrote to her daughter. "She is very sick, and after hearing exactly how she is, I confess I am very uneasy."

Garfield could think of nothing but Lucretia. "I refused to see people on business," he wrote in his diary on May 11. "All my thoughts center in her, in comparison with whom all else fades into insignificance." Having buried two children, he knew far too well the devastation of losing someone he loved. After Trot's death, he had been so paralyzed with grief that he had nearly left Congress. "I try to be cheerful, and plunge into the whirlpool of work which opens before me," he had confided to a friend, "but it seems to me I shall never cease to grieve."

Every day, Garfield consulted with the group of doctors he had gathered around Lucretia. They had come to the conclusion that she was suffering from a combination of exhaustion and malaria. Sixteen years before malaria was finally traced to mosquitoes, Lucretia's doctors did not know what caused the disease, but they did have ways to fight it. They gave her "fever powders," presumably quinine, which had been used to treat malaria in the West since the early 1600s, and bathed her with alcohol and ice water. As Lucretia's fever worsened, rising ominously to 104 degrees, Garfield hovered over her, helping however he could. "If I thought her return to perfect health could be insured by my resigning the Presidency," he wrote to a friend, "I would not hesitate a moment about doing it."

While the White House did what it could to protect Lucretia from the outside world, banning carriages from the grounds and occasionally even closing the front gates, Charles Guiteau inched closer. When he had first submitted his application for an appointment, he had been told, as was every office seeker, that it would be put on file and considered. "In the majority of cases there was not the slightest possibility of any position being granted," a White House employee who helped shepherd callers through the president's anteroom later explained. "It was just the usual human method of saving trouble and avoiding a scene." Guiteau, however, believed that the president was carefully studying his application and that his appointment was only a matter of time. When, after handing the doorman a note for Garfield one day, he was told, "The President says it will be impossible to see you to-day," he seized on the word "to-day." This was Garfield's way, he thought, of telling him that, "as soon as he got Walker [the current consul-general to France] out of the way gracefully then I would be given the office."

While he waited for his appointment, Guiteau survived as he always had. As well as skipping out on board bills, he had a long history of convincing people to lend him money, and he was proud of his straightforward approach. "I will tell you how I do it," he would later explain. "I come right out square with a friend. I do not lie and sneak and do that kind of business, or anything. I say, 'I want to get $25; I want to use a little money'; and the probability is that if he has got the money about him he will pull the money right out and give it to me. That is the way I get my money. I take it and thank him, and go about my business."

The technique had worked often enough that Guiteau was reluctant to abandon it, but he was quickly running out of lenders.

In mid-March, he finally tracked down a man named George Maynard, whom he barely knew and had not seen for more than twenty years. He had met Maynard in 1859, when he was a student boarding at Maynard's mother's home in Ann Arbor, Michigan. Maynard had been living in Washington for the past seventeen years, working as an electrician, and knew nothing of Guiteau's life since he had seen him last. He was the perfect person to ask for a loan.

When Guiteau suddenly appeared in Maynard's office, he did not waste time with pleasantries but came quickly to the point. "Mr. Guiteau came into my office and said that he wanted to borrow $10 for a few days; that he was very hard up for money to pay his board bills," Maynard would later recall. Guiteau told him that he was expecting a check for $150 and would pay him back as soon as he received it. Taking pity on the small, shabbily dressed man, Maynard gave him the money and in return accepted a card on which was written: "March 12th, $10 until the 15th." He would not see Guiteau again until June.

In the meantime, Guiteau went about his solitary life. He had very little contact with people outside of his boardinghouse and the White House waiting room, and no social interaction at all. He had lived this way for most of his adult life, with the surprising exception of the four years he had been married.

Soon after leaving Oneida, Guiteau had met and married a young librarian named Annie Bunn, launching her into the most desperate and frightening period of her life. "I lived," Annie would later say, "in continual anxiety and suspense of mind." Not only was she forced to flee boardinghouse after boardinghouse, often leaving behind her clothing and belongings when her husband did not pay the rent, but she was constantly dunned by his creditors and a string of furious clients whom he had cheated.

Despite the constant humiliations, Annie likely would have stayed with Guiteau had he not treated her so cruelly. If she disagreed with him in the smallest way, he would literally kick her out the door and into the hallway, even if other boarders were walking by. On more occasions than she could count, he wrenched her out of bed in the middle of the night and locked her in a bitterly cold closet until morning. Although Annie was convinced that her husband was "possessed of an evil spirit," it was not until he openly visited a prostitute that she finally filed for divorce.

Had Annie seen Guiteau now, almost ten years after she left him, she would hardly have recognized him. He had always been "very proud and nice and particular about his dress and general appearance," she said. "He always dressed well, wore the best of everything." While Annie begged the landlords her husband had deceived to let her have one of her dresses so that she might have a single change of clothes, Guiteau shopped as though he were a wealthy man. "He would not think that a suit of clothes was fit to wear that did not cost at least sixty or seventy-five dollars," Annie remembered. He would obtain the clothes by paying part of the price up front and then never return to pay the balance.

After years of living as a traveling evangelist, however, Guiteau no longer had enough money even for a down payment. His clothes were frayed, torn, and too light for the early-spring weather. He pulled his sleeves down over his hands and, in an effort to conceal the fact that he did not have a collar, buttoned his coat to the very top. While everyone else was wearing boots or heavy shoes, he walked around in rubber sandals. Always a small, slight man, he had grown even thinner and was pale and drawn.

To George Maynard, he looked "somewhat haggard and weak . . . as I have seen many a man look when they haven't had a good square meal for two or three days." When Guiteau did have an opportunity for a meal at a boardinghouse, the other guests recalled him eating with a savage determination and a distinct reluctance to pass the plates.

Despite his desperate circumstances, Guiteau did what he could to give the impression that he was a man of influence and means. When writing letters, he used the stationery either of the well-respected Riggs House, the hotel where Garfield had stayed on the night before his inauguration, or the White House. One day, when a White House staff member refused to give him more stationery, Guiteau slapped one of his enormous business cards down on a table and shouted, "Do you know who I am? . . . I am one of the men that made Garfield President."

He also continued to try to associate himself with powerful men. He found out where John Logan, a Republican senator from Illinois, was staying and took a room in the same boardinghouse. One morning, hearing footsteps in the outer room of his suite, Logan stepped out from his bedroom to find Guiteau sitting in a chair near the door. When he saw the senator, Guiteau quickly stood up, greeted him by name, and handed him a copy of his "Garfield against Hancock" speech. Logan, who had no idea who this strange man was, found himself listening helplessly as Guiteau told him that the speech he was holding had "elected the President of the United States, Mr. Garfield," and that he was now waiting to be appointed consul-general to France. Secretary Blaine, Guiteau said, had promised him the appointment if Logan would give him a recommendation. He then pulled from his pocket a piece of paper on which he had written a three-line recommendation in large print and asked Logan to sign it. Logan declined. "He did not strike me as a person that I desired to recommend for an office of that character, or for any other office," he would later say. "I treated him as kindly and as politely as I could; but I was very desirous of getting rid of him."

A few days later, however, Guiteau was back. This time, he was more forceful in his request, insisting that, as he had once lived in Chicago, Logan was his senator and so was obliged to recommend him for the position. Again he thrust the handwritten recommendation at Logan. The senator ignored the piece of paper but assured

Guiteau, "The first time that I see the Secretary of State I will mention your case to him." While he did intend to mention Guiteau's application to Blaine, Logan later explained, "I intended to mention it probably in a different way from what he supposed I would. . . . I must say that I thought there was some derangement of his mental organization."

As was his habit with the president at the White House, Guiteau followed up his frequent visits to the State Department with letters to the secretary of state. Late in March, he wrote to Blaine that it was his understanding that he was "to have a consulship" and that he hoped it was "the consulship at Paris, as that is the only one I care for." After making the argument that he was entitled to the office and that it should be given to him "as a personal tribute," he ended the letter by suggesting to Blaine that he too owed his position to Garfield's generosity. "I am very glad, personally, that the President selected you for his premier," Guiteau wrote. "It might have been someone else."

In the end, Blaine was the only man to give Guiteau an honest answer. He had received his letters and seen him on dozens of occasions at the State Department, brushing off his persistent questions about the consulship with a terse "We have not got to that yet." So frequent were Guiteau's visits to the State Department that the chief clerk had instructed the messengers not to forward his notes and to do what they could to shield the secretary of state.

Finally, after nearly two months of being chased by Guiteau, Blaine had had enough. When Guiteau cornered him one day, the secretary of state abruptly turned and addressed him directly. He told Guiteau that "he had, in my opinion, no prospect whatever of receiving" the appointment. Determined to end the matter once and for all, he snapped, "Never speak to me about the Paris consulship again." Guiteau watched in shock as Blaine walked away, and then he returned to his boardinghouse, determined to warn Garfield that his secretary of state was a "wicked man" and that there would be "no peace till you get rid of him."

Blaine forgot Guiteau as soon as he turned his back on him. The war that Conkling had been waging against Garfield's administration had taken a sudden and unexpected turn, and the secretary of state could smell blood. Before Lucretia had fallen ill, Garfield, still trying to find common ground with the Stalwarts, had appointed five of Conkling's men to New York posts. He believed, however, that Grant had made a fatal mistake in surrendering New York to Conkling, and he was not about to put himself in the same position. The day after his appointments of Conkling's men, he announced another appointment. This one was only a single recommendation, but it was for the post that Conkling prized above all others, the one he had bestowed upon Chester Arthur — the collectorship of the New York Customs House.

Shocked and enraged, Conkling spluttered that the nomination was "perfidy without peril." Not only had Garfield not consulted him, but the man he had chosen, Judge William Robertson, was high on Conkling's long list of enemies. At the Republican convention, Robertson had been the first delegate to abandon Grant, thus, Conkling believed, causing the hemorrhaging of votes that had ultimately resulted in Grant's defeat. Robertson had, Conkling raged, "treacherously betray[ed] a sacred trust," and he demanded that Garfield withdraw the nomination.

By nominating Robertson, Garfield knew, he had given Conkling his *"casus belli,"* his justification for war, but the president was prepared for battle, and confident of victory. "Let who will, fight me," Garfield wrote in his diary after making the nomination. This battle was about more than Robertson or even Conkling. It was about the power of the presidency. "I owe something to the dignity of my office," he wrote. This post was critical to the nation's financial strength, and he was not about to let someone else fill it. "Shall the principal port of entry in which more than 90% of all our customs duties are collected be under the direct control of the Administration or under the local control of a factional Senator," he asked. "I think I win in this contest."

The American people agreed. Garfield's refusal to back down was widely hailed as a courageous and necessary stand against a dangerous man. Even Conkling's own state turned against him. Of the more than one hundred newspapers in the state of New York, fewer than twenty supported their senior senator, the rest lining up behind the president. Garfield, the *New York Herald* argued, "has recognized Republicans as members of a great party and not of mean factions. He has chosen men for office because of their fitness and ability, and not because they have stuck to the political fortunes of loved leaders." Conkling, in stark contrast, "would be Caesar or nothing." He "makes the mistake of supposing that he, and not Gen. Garfield, was elected President," the newspaper chided. "He declares war, and the President accepts the situation."

Conkling, however, was much more experienced at political warfare than Garfield. Every time he had gone into battle, no matter how bruising, he had emerged even stronger than before. He seemed unaffected even by highly public humiliations, shrugging off scandals that would have ruined another man. Just two years earlier, he had been caught in a brazen affair with Kate Chase Sprague, the wife of William Sprague, a U.S. senator and former governor of Rhode Island, and daughter of Salmon P. Chase, secretary of the treasury under Lincoln and the chief justice of the United States. Newspapers had gleefully reported that Senator Sprague had chased Conkling from his home with a pistol. In the end, however, the only reputation that had been damaged by the scandal was Kate's.

It was not until early May, as Lucretia lay near death, that Conkling finally overreached. Fearing that public sympathy for her would derail his campaign against Garfield, Conkling decided that it was time to call in some favors. He had long before solicited the support of James Gordon Bennett, the founder, editor, and publisher of the *New York Herald.* As Bennett was then out of the country, his managing editor, Thomas Connery, would have to do. Conkling sent word to Connery that he wished to meet with him in Washington. Connery realized that he was about to step into a snake pit, but he had little choice but to do as Conkling asked.

When Connery arrived at Conkling's house on the corner of Fourteenth and F Streets, he was received not by the senator but by the vice president of the United States. Although Chester Arthur was now part of Garfield's administration, his allegiance to Conkling was stronger, and more obvious, than it had ever been. He continued to share a home with him, frequently joined him on long fishing trips, and did not hesitate to criticize Garfield at every opportunity. "Garfield has not been square, nor honorable, nor truthful with Conkling," Arthur told a reporter. "It's a hard thing to say of a president of the United States, but it is, unfortunately, only the truth." After Robertson's appointment, Arthur had even signed a petition of protest against the president.

Connery, unsure why he was there and extremely ill at ease, quickly asked Arthur what Conkling wanted. The vice president, he would later recall, "smiled and looked at me as if doubting the innocence of my question." Soon after, Conkling arrived and launched into a "lengthy and impassioned harangue" against Garfield, at the end of which he asked Connery to pledge the support of the *Herald* in his war against the president. Connery agreed, although he knew there was not much he could do to save Conkling from himself.

While Conkling and Arthur carefully plotted their next move, Garfield, well aware that he was under attack, gave his enemies little thought. Lucretia had slowly begun to recover, and he was overwhelmed with gratitude. On May 15, he finally allowed himself to believe that "God will be merciful to us and let her stay." Her fever had fallen to just over 100 degrees, and Garfield's "hope almost reached triumph." Over breakfast that morning, the normally happy, boisterous family laughed for the first time since Lucretia had fallen ill. "The little ones have been very brave but very still," Garfield wrote. "The house has been very still."

The Capitol, on the other hand, had been roiling. The day after Lucretia began to rally, Conkling made a last, desperate attempt to regain the upper hand from a president who had dared to defy him. The idea came to him from Senator Tom Platt, a Stalwart who had, months earlier, promised to confirm any appointment Garfield made in exchange for help in winning a Senate seat. Now, expected to vote for Robertson, Platt feared Conkling's wrath. The only honorable response to Garfield's outrageous nomination, he told Conkling, was to "rebuke the President by immediately turning in our resignations." The New York legislature would quickly reinstate them, and they would return to the Senate triumphant.

It was a bold, dramatic move, and Conkling, who valued showmanship nearly as much as he did power, seized on it. On the morning of May 16, after the chaplain finished the morning prayer, Arthur, who had entered the Senate chamber late and visibly nervous, handed the clerk a note. Few people in the hall even noticed the exchange, and those who did assumed it was an ordinary, uninteresting communication. As the clerk began to read, however, those who were only half listening, idly sifting through their mail, suddenly sat straight up in their seats, a look of pure astonishment on their faces. The letter was addressed to Arthur, and it read, "Sir, Will you please announce to the Senate that my resignation as Senator of the United States from the State of New-York has been forwarded to the Governor of the State. I have the honor to be, with great respect, your obedient servant, Roscoe Conkling."

The brief note, one reporter wrote, "seemed to stupefy" everyone in the chamber, and it quickly caused a "sensation." The reaction that followed, however, was not at all what Conkling had envisioned. After recovering from their initial shock, Stalwarts in the Senate merely mumbled their support, while delighted Half-Breeds, hardly believing their luck, immediately went on the attack. This was nothing more than a stunt, they jeered, and an impotent one at that. Conkling, scoffed one congressman, was just "a great big baby boohooing because he can't have all the cake."

When he was told of Conkling's resignation, Garfield simply shrugged. It was, he wrote in his diary, "a very weak attempt at the heroic. . . . I go on without disturbance." His first concern was for Lucretia. Any time and energy he had left were put toward creating a balanced administration and freeing himself from office seekers so he would have time to do his job. A few days later, he announced that he was limiting his calling hours to one hour a day, from 12:00 noon to 1:00 p.m. Conkling, he knew, was still capable of doing tremendous damage, but Garfield was no longer interested in compromise. "Having done all I fairly could to avoid a fight," he wrote, "I now fight to the end."

As the final, fatal blow had been self-inflicted, Conkling's long political career came to a shockingly swift end. Immediately following their dramatic resignations, Conkling and Platt left for New York. After years of controlling every aspect of New York politics, and every man involved in it, Conkling was confident that the legislature at Albany would reelect them both. However, on the last day of May, the same day that Lucretia's doctors finally pronounced her well — telling Garfield, "with emphasis, it is ended" — both men were soundly defeated. Conkling received just a third of the Republican votes, and Platt six fewer than Conkling. "Stung with mortification at his inability to control the President, and believing that the people of this State shared his disappointment," wrote the *New York Times,* Conkling "has thrown away his power, destroyed his own influence."

For the first time since his nomination

nearly a year earlier, Garfield was hopeful. Lucretia, who, just days earlier, had been so close to death, was every day gaining in health and strength. No longer forced to surrender half his day to the demands of office seekers, he suddenly had time to think and plan. And, in a turn of events that no one could have predicted, the legendary senator who had declared himself Garfield's enemy, and whose iron grip on his administration had threatened to destroy it before it had even begun, was alone and powerless in Albany. Three months after his inauguration, Garfield was finally free to begin his presidency.

"A deep strong current of happy peace," he wrote that night, "flows through every heart in the household."

CHAPTER 10
THE DARK DREAMS OF PRESIDENTS

History is but the unrolled scroll
of Prophecy.

JAMES A. GARFIELD

The idea came to Guiteau suddenly, "like a flash," he would later say. On May 18, two days after Conkling's dramatic resignation, Guiteau, "depressed and perplexed . . . wearied in mind and body," had climbed into bed at 8:00 p.m., much earlier than usual. He had been lying on his cot in his small, rented room for an hour, unable to sleep, his mind churning, when he was struck by a single, pulsing thought: "If the President was out of the way every thing would go better."

Guiteau was certain the idea had not come from his own, feverish mind. It was a divine inspiration, a message from God. He was, he believed, in a unique position to recognize divine inspiration when it occurred because it had happened to him before. Even before the wreck of the steamship *Stonington,* he had been inspired, he said, to join the Oneida Community, to leave so that he might start a religious newspaper, and to become a traveling evangelist. Each time God had called him, he had answered.

This time, for the first time, he hesitated. Despite his certainty that the message had come directly from God, he did not want to listen. The next morning, when the thought returned "with renewed force," he recoiled from it. "I was kept horrified," he said, "kept throwing it off." Wherever he went and whatever he did, however, the idea stayed with him. "It kept growing upon me, pressing me, goading me."

Guiteau had "no ill-will to the President," he insisted. In fact, he believed that he had given Garfield every opportunity to save his own life. He was certain that God wanted Garfield out of the way because he was a danger to the Republican Party and, ultimately, the American people. As Conkling's war with Garfield had escalated, Guiteau wrote to the president repeatedly, advising him that the best way to respond to the senator's demands was to give in to them. "It seems to me that the only way out of this difficulty is to withdraw Mr. R.," he wrote, referring to Garfield's appointment of Judge Robertson to run the New York Customs House. "I am on friendly terms with Senator Conkling and the rest of our Senators, but I write this on my own account and in the spirit of a peacemaker."

Guiteau also felt that he had done all he could to warn Garfield about Blaine. After the secretary of state had snapped at him outside of the State Department, he bitterly recounted the exchange in a letter to Garfield. "Until Saturday I supposed Mr. Blaine was my friend in the matter of the Paris consulship," he wrote, still wounded by the memory. " 'Never speak to me again,' said Mr. Blaine, Saturday, 'on the Paris consulship as long as you live.' Heretofore he has been my friend."

Even after his divine inspiration, Guiteau continued to appeal to Garfield. On May 23, he again wrote to the president, advising him to demand Blaine's "immediate resignation." "I have been trying to be your friend," he wrote darkly. "I do not know whether you appreciate it or not." Garfield would be wise to listen to him, he warned, "otherwise you and the Republican party will come to grief. I will see you in the morning if I can and talk with you."

Guiteau did not see Garfield the next morning, or any day after that. Unknown to him, he had been barred from the president's office. Even among the strange and strikingly persistent office seekers that filled Garfield's anteroom every day, Guiteau had stood out. Brown, Garfield's private secretary, had long before relegated Guiteau's letters to what was known as "the eccentric file," but he continued to welcome him to the White House with the same courtesy he extended to every other caller. That did not change until Guiteau's eccentricity and doggedness turned into belligerence. Finally, after a heated argument with one of the president's ushers that ended with Guiteau sitting in a corner of the waiting room, glowering, Brown issued orders that "he should be quietly kept away."

Soon after, Guiteau stopped going to the White House altogether. He gave up trying to secure an appointment, and he no longer fought the press of divine inspiration. For two weeks, he had prayed to God to show him that he had misunderstood the message he had received that night. "That is the way I test the Deity," he would later explain. "When I feel the pressure upon me to do a certain thing and I have any doubt about it I keep praying that the Deity may stay it in some way if I am wrong." Despite his prayers and constant vigilance, he had received no such sign.

By the end of May, Guiteau had given himself up entirely to his new obsession. Alone in his room, with nowhere to go and no one to talk to, he pored over newspaper accounts of the battle between Conkling and the White House, fixating on any criticism of Garfield, real or implied. "I kept reading the papers and kept being impressed," he remembered, "and the idea kept bearing and bearing and bearing down upon me." Finally, on June 1, thoroughly convinced of "the divinity of the inspiration," he made up his mind. He would kill the president.

The next day, Guiteau began to prepare. Although he believed he was doing God's work, he had been driven for so long by a desire for fame and prestige that his first thought was not how he would assassinate the president, but the attention he would receive after he did. "I thought just what people would talk and thought what a tremendous excitement it would create," he wrote, "and I kept thinking about it all week."

With his forthcoming celebrity in mind,

Guiteau decided that his first task should be to edit a religious book he had written several years ago called *The Truth: A Companion to the Bible.* The publicity it would bring the book, he believed, was one of the principal reasons God wanted him to assassinate the president. "Two points will be accomplished," he wrote. "It will save the Republic, and create a demand for my book, The Truth. . . . This book was not written for money. It was written to save souls. In order to attract public attention the book needs the notice the President's removal will give it." There would be a great demand for the book following Garfield's death, he reasoned, so it should be "in proper shape."

As was true of most things in Guiteau's life, *The Truth* was largely stolen. In a single-sentence preface, he insisted that "a new line of thought runs through this book, and the Author asks for it a careful attention." There was, however, nothing new about *The Truth.* The ideas, most of them copied verbatim, came from a book called *The Berean,* which John Humphrey Noyes, the founder of Oneida, had written in 1847, and which Guiteau's father had treasured, believing that it was "better than the Bible."

Even *The Truth*'s publication had been fraudulent. Guiteau had tried to persuade

D. Lothrop & Co., one of the most respected publishers in Boston, to publish the book, but they had declined. Determined to see *The Truth* in print, and for it to have the illusion, if not the reality, of respectability, he hired a printing company to produce a thousand copies, all with "D. Lothrop and Company" on the binding and cover page. After trying unsuccessfully to sell the book for 50 cents apiece on the streets of Boston, he left town without paying the printer.

The next stage of Guiteau's plan was more difficult than the first. If he was to assassinate the president, he realized, he would need a gun. Guiteau knew nothing about guns. Not only had he never owned a gun, he had never even fired one. On June 6, he left his boardinghouse and walked to a sporting goods store that he had spotted on the corner of Fifteenth and F Streets, on the ground floor of a tavern. Upon opening the door, his eyes immediately fell on a showcase that held a selection of revolvers. He walked directly to the case, pointed to the largest gun, and asked the store's owner, John O'Meara, if he could hold it. He "did not call it by name or ask for any special pistol," O'Meara would later recall. "He examined it carefully, and inquired as to its accuracy, and made a few commonplace remarks." After a few minutes, Guiteau handed the revolver back to O'Meara and told him that he would return in a few days.

Two days later, George Maynard, the man from whom Guiteau had borrowed $10 three months earlier, was at work when he looked up to find the small, thin man standing once more in his office. He had walked in so quietly that Maynard had not even heard him. Looking at Guiteau, he noticed that he held his head at an unusual angle, tilted slightly forward. "He had a peculiar manner," Maynard would later say, "a peculiar attitude, a peculiar walk." What struck Maynard most of all, however, was the desperation he saw in the man standing before him. "The principal thing," he remembered, "was that he looked hungry."

Guiteau explained that he had received the $150 he had been expecting in March, but had used it to pay other bills. He was now, he said, awaiting an even larger check, this one for $500. In the meantime, he needed money to pay his board bill. If Maynard would give him $15, he would pay him back the full $25 as soon as he received his next windfall. Although by this point Maynard could not have had any hope of being repaid, he was, as Guiteau knew, "a good fellow." Three minutes after he had walked in the door, Guiteau left with enough money to buy a gun.

That same day, Guiteau returned to John O'Meara's shop, as he had promised he would. The last time he was there, he had seen two revolvers that interested him — one with a wooden handle that he could have for nine dollars, and another that cost a dollar more but had an ivory handle. He was drawn toward the more expensive gun, picturing it on display in the State Department's library. Cradling the revolver in his hands, he asked O'Meara about its force. It was, the shop owner said, a self-cocking .44 caliber British Bulldog. "One of the strongest pistols made."

After striking a deal with O'Meara — ten dollars for the revolver, a box of cartridges, and a two-bladed, pearl-handled penknife that had caught his eye — Guiteau asked him where he could take the gun to test it. O'Meara warned Guiteau that he would need to leave the city limits, and suggested he try the river's edge. Taking his advice, Guiteau went to the Potomac one evening and shot ten cartridges with his new gun, sometimes aiming for the river, other times trying to hit a sapling growing nearby. Everything about the gun, from the feel of it in his hand to the damage it wrought, was utterly new and unfamiliar to him. "I knew nothing about it," he would later say, "no more than a child."

In his letters and, he would later insist, his thoughts, Guiteau never referred to what he was about to do as murder, or even assassination. He was simply removing the president — in his mind, an act not of violence or cruelty but practicality. Garfield was a danger to his party and his country, and God had asked Guiteau to correct the situation. "The Lord inspired me to attempt to remove the President in preference to some one else, because I had the brains and the nerve to do the work," he would explain. "The Lord always employs the best material to do His work."

Guiteau had no illusions about what would happen to him after he assassinated the president. He had been twenty-three years old when John Wilkes Booth shot Lincoln, and he could not have forgotten the manhunt that had led to Booth's death. Prepared to kill for God but not to die, his only other option, he suspected, was imprisonment. As he had spent a month in the Tombs, he knew how bad jail could be. He felt, therefore, that it would be wise to make a trip to the District Jail. "I wanted to see what kind of a jail it was," he would later say. "I knew nothing about where it was, nor the character of the building, nor anything."

One Saturday morning, Guiteau took a streetcar from the Riggs Hotel as far as he could and then walked another three-quarters of a mile before reaching the prison. Walking "leisurely" to the warden's office, he rang the doorbell and waited calmly. When a guard arrived, he asked for a tour. Although the jail did not allow tours on Saturdays, Guiteau felt that he had gotten a good enough look at the building. "I thought it was a very excellent jail," he said. "It is the best jail in America, I understand."

Satisfied that the prison where he would be taken was far superior to the Tombs, Guiteau had nothing left to do but track down his prey. All the time and energy he had once spent trying to secure an appointment, he now devoted to following Garfield. Guiteau knew that the president, who had no Secret Service agents and was in frequent contact with the public, was an easy target, especially outside the White House. "It would not do to go to the White House and attempt it, because there were too many of his employés about," Guiteau wrote. "I looked around for several days to try and get a good chance at him."

Finally, Guiteau chose the one place in Washington where Garfield had always felt safe and at peace: his church. Killing the president in church was not sacrilegious, Guiteau argued. On the contrary, "there could not possibly be a better place to remove a man than at his devotions."

Garfield, moreover, could be counted on to attend church. A member of the Disciples of Christ since childhood, and himself a minister, he had faithfully attended the Vermont Avenue Christian Church in Washington since he entered Congress nearly twenty years earlier. He had been an active and involved parishioner, teaching Sunday school and, in 1869, helping the congregation raise enough money to build a larger church. The church's pastor, Reverend S. D. Power, said that he felt God had "a wise and holy purpose" for Garfield "and had raised him up as a Christian leader of a great people."

Guiteau knew exactly where Garfield's church was because he had been there before. Several months earlier, drawn to the church out of curiosity, he had watched from one of the pews as Garfield entered with Lucretia and their five children. Garfield had missed many Sundays since then, choosing instead to stay home with Lucretia during her illness. As she had begun to recover, however, he had come back, grateful to the congregation for their many prayers.

Guiteau returned to Garfield's church on June 12. The sermon had already begun, and Garfield had settled into a pew next to Lucretia's doctor and the doctor's wife, when Guiteau stepped inside. Although he was late, he paused at the door, scanning the congregation for the instantly recognizable figure of the president, who was taller and had broader shoulders than nearly any other man in the church. Quickly locating him, Guiteau noted that he was sitting next to an open window that stood about three feet from the ground. "That," he judged, "would be a good chance to get him." By standing just outside the window, Guiteau thought, he could aim the gun so that the bullet would travel through the back of the president's head and into the ceiling without endangering anyone around him.

Although he had his revolver in his pocket and, had he stepped outside the church, a clear shot through the window, Guiteau stayed seated throughout the sermon. It was, Garfield would later write, "a very stupid sermon on a very great subject."

Guiteau apparently agreed with the president. At one point, no longer able to restrain his frustration, he shouted out, "What think ye of Christ?" Garfield heard Guiteau's outburst and mentioned it in his diary that night, referring to him as "a dull young man, with a loud voice, trying to pound noise into the question."

When the sermon was over, Guiteau had missed his opportunity, but he had not given up on his plan. After watching Garfield step into a carriage and ride away, Guiteau walked to the side of the church to examine the window near which the president had been sitting. Standing in the summer sun, Guiteau could picture the moment when he would raise his gun and take aim. "Next Sunday," he thought, "I would certainly shoot him."

Before the next Sunday sermon, however, another opportunity presented itself to Guiteau. On Thursday he read in the newspaper that the president would soon be traveling to New Jersey with his wife. That same night, Garfield mentioned the trip in his diary, writing that, in an attempt to help Lucretia's recovery, "we have concluded to take her to the sea shore for its bracing air." The family, Guiteau knew, would be leaving from the Baltimore and Potomac Railroad

Station the following Saturday.

A train station, Guiteau thought, might even be better than a church. That Saturday morning he woke up around six, put his gun in his pocket, and walked down to the Potomac to practice his aim one last time. After shooting off another ten cartridges, he made his way to the train station. He arrived before Garfield, and so was able to watch as the president stepped out of the carriage with Lucretia.

It was the sight of the first lady, Guiteau would later say, that prevented him from carrying out God's work that day. "I was all ready," he said. "My mind was all made up; I had all my papers with me; I had all the arrangements made to shoot him." When he saw Lucretia, however, he could not go through with it. She looked "so thin," he said, "and she clung so tenderly to the President's arm, that I did not have the heart to fire on him." Garfield walked right past his would-be assassin, his attention focused on Lucretia.

After returning to his boardinghouse that day, Guiteau wrote a letter to the American people. He had, he explained, "intended to remove the President this morning at the depot," but after seeing Garfield with Lucretia, he decided it would be best to "take him alone." Although he wanted to spare the first lady the horror of witnessing her husband's fatal shooting, Guiteau argued that, when he did kill the president, his death would not be any more painful to Lucretia because it was the result of assassination. "It will be no worse for Mrs. Garfield, to part with her husband this way, than by natural death," Guiteau reasoned. "He is liable to go at any time any way."

Garfield arrived back in Washington on June 27, in the midst of a heavy storm. He had been reluctant to leave Lucretia, worrying that the "sea air is too strong for her," but he was thrilled by the progress she had made. He also knew that he would see her again soon. In less than a week, while his two youngest boys headed to Ohio for the summer, he would leave for New England with his older sons. The plan was to meet up with Lucretia and Mollie and then go on to Massachusetts, where they would attend his twenty-fifth class reunion at Williams College and help Harry and Jim settle in for the upcoming academic year.

Before Garfield could leave, however, he needed to meet with his cabinet. With Conkling out of the way, he had finally been able to establish a strong, if at times contentious, cabinet, which, as he had always intended, included Stalwarts as well as Half-Breeds. The most prominent of the Stalwarts was Robert Todd Lincoln, Garfield's secretary of war and Abraham Lincoln's oldest and only surviving son.

On June 30, as the cabinet was about to adjourn for the last time before the president's trip, Garfield suddenly turned to Lincoln with an unusual question. He had heard, he said, that his father had had a prophetic dream shortly before his assassination, and he wondered if Robert would describe it. Although a private and reserved man, Lincoln agreed to tell the story.

After he had fallen asleep late one night, Abraham Lincoln had had a dream in which, he later told his wife and an old friend, there was a "death-like stillness about me." Within the stillness, however, he could hear "subdued sobs." Leaving his room, he searched the White House for the source of the weeping, but every room he entered was empty. Finally, stepping into the East Room, he saw a coffin that was guarded by soldiers. "Who is dead in the White House?" he asked. "Why, don't you know?" one of the soldiers replied. "The President has been assassinated."

Lincoln had believed deeply in dreams,

seeing in them omens that he dared not ignore. After having "an ugly dream" about their son Tad, he had advised his wife to put Tad's pistol away. Another time, while in Richmond, Virginia, he had asked her to return to Washington after he dreamed that the White House was on fire. When questioned about his belief in dreams, Lincoln had often cited the Bible as support. He pointed to Jacob's dream in Genesis 28, as well as several other chapters in the Old and New Testaments. These passages, he said, "reveal God's meaning in dreams."

Although Garfield did not share Lincoln's reverence for dreams, he had had a few that seemed strange or powerful enough to record. In late January, little more than a month before his inauguration, he had written down a dream he had had in which Chester Arthur drowned. He and a close friend, General David Swaim, had escaped a sinking ship, only to watch Arthur, who was lying on a couch, very pale and obviously ill, disappear under the surface of the water. "I started to plunge into the water to save Arthur," Garfield wrote, "but Swaim held me, and said he cannot be saved, and you will perish if you attempt it."

It was his own death, however, that was often on Garfield's mind. Although he was by nature a cheerful and optimistic man, like Lincoln, he had long felt that he would die an early death. When his friends tried to talk him out of this grim conviction, his only answer was that the thought seemed to him "as foolish as it does to you." Nonetheless, he could not shake it. "I do not know why it haunts me," he said. "Indeed, it is a thing that is wholly involuntary on my part, and when I try the hardest not to think of it it haunts me most." The feeling, he said, came to him most often at night, "when all is quiet." It was then that his mind would turn to his father, who died "in the strength of his manhood," when his wife and children needed him most. At those times, Garfield said, "I feel it so strong upon me that the vision is in the form of a warning that I cannot treat lightly."

The night after his cabinet meeting, July 1, Garfield had dinner with Captain Charles E. Henry, the marshal of the District of Columbia, and invited his guest to join him in the library afterward. As the conversation drifted, Henry would later recall, Garfield began to talk about the times in his life, particularly his boyhood, when he had miraculously escaped death. Just days before, he had received word that his uncle Thomas Garfield had been killed when his carriage was struck by a train, and the tragedy had brought back not just memories of his own near-drowning years before on the canal, but the deaths of his father and children, and Lucretia's recent, nearly fatal illness. As Henry sat in the candle-lit library, listening to Garfield, he realized that he "had never heard him speak . . . in the way he did that night." Garfield was, Henry said, "undoubtedly dwelling upon the uncertainty of life."

After Henry left, Garfield, wishing to talk to Blaine, decided to walk to the secretary of state's house, just a few blocks away. As the president stepped out of the White House, Charles Guiteau, sitting on a park bench across the street in Lafayette Park, looked up. When he saw Garfield, he stood and began to follow him, staying on the opposite side of the street. He had been sitting in the same park two nights earlier and had watched as Garfield left the White House by carriage. After half an hour had passed and the president had not returned, Guiteau had decided to "let the matter drop for the night." Now, as he shadowed Garfield, he removed the loaded revolver from his pocket, carrying it stiffly at his side.

When Garfield reached Blaine's house, Guiteau stepped back into the shadows of a hotel alley. Happening to glance out a window, Harriet Blaine caught sight of the president and ran to open the door. As he waited for Blaine, Garfield gave Harriet a present — a bound and signed copy of his inaugural address — and talked to her about the trip he would be making the following day.

When Blaine finally appeared, he and Garfield stepped out together for a walk. From the alley, Guiteau, who had passed the time examining his gun and wiping it down, watched as the two men walked down the street arm in arm, their heads close together as they spoke. Garfield's camaraderie with his secretary of state enraged Guiteau, proving, he said, that "Mr. Garfield had sold himself body and soul to Blaine."

Guiteau followed Blaine and Garfield all the way to the White House, his gun at his side. He could have easily killed either man at any moment, but he never raised the revolver. After watching the president disappear inside the White House, he walked back to his boardinghouse through the dark streets of Washington. The image of Garfield and Blaine "engaged in the most earnest conversation" haunted him, and the hesitancy he had shown for weeks hardened into resolve. He would not let another opportunity to kill the president pass without taking it. “My mind,” he would later say, “was perfectly clear.”

Chapter 11
"A Desperate Deed"

There are times in the history of men and nations, when they stand so near the veil that separates mortals and immortals, time from eternity, and men from their God, that they can almost hear their breathings and feel the pulsations of the heart of the infinite.

JAMES A. GARFIELD

On the morning of July 2, Harry and Jim Garfield were still in bed when their father bounded into their room, a broad smile on his handsome face. Singing "I Mixed Those Babies Up," from his favorite song in the new Gilbert and Sullivan opera *H.M.S. Pinafore,* he plucked his teenage sons out of bed, tucked one under each arm, and swung them around "as if we were in fact two babies," Jim would later recall. Wriggling free, Jim turned a flip over the end of his bed and said triumphantly to his father,

"You are President of the United States but you can't do that." To his sons' astonishment and delight, Garfield, six feet tall and just a few months shy of his fiftieth birthday, not only did the flip but then hopped across the room balanced only on his fingers and toes.

Despite the strain of the past year, Garfield still looked strong, vigorous, and, on this day, thoroughly happy. Each blow — from his unexpected and unwanted nomination to the battle with Conkling to Lucretia's illness — had taken its toll, but he remained the man he had always been. "There are a few additional lines about the eyes, perhaps," a reporter for the *New York Tribune* noted, "but he wears his old robust hearty frank look, stands straight as a soldier, and greets his friends with the same cordial, strong, magnetic grip of the hand."

After rousing his sons, Garfield had breakfast with his private secretary, who had just returned from a trip to London that Garfield had arranged. "The work of the campaign and the pressure of the first three months at the White House had made pretty severe inroads on my vitality," Brown admitted. When Garfield needed someone to shepherd $6 million in U.S. bonds to London, therefore, he had sent his young friend.

The president had been delighted to give the opportunity to Brown, who had come from a family of modest means and had traveled very little, but he was happy to have him back. Brown had become essential not just to Garfield but to everyone who came into contact with him. Despite the fact that he was the youngest man ever to hold the office of private secretary to the president, he had, in the words of one journalist, "the tact and ability of age and experience." As well as organizing Garfield's voluminous correspondence and personal papers, he made arrangements for presidential receptions and dinners, attended to the countless problems that occurred each day in the White House, and oversaw the entire staff. He had even impressed a hard-bitten political reporter for the *Washington Post,* who wrote that Brown was "perfectly master of the situation and handles his office . . . with ease and dexterity."

As the president's right-hand man, Brown was the last person in the White House to see him before he left for the train station that morning. He was working quietly in his office when, just before 9:00 a.m., he heard the door open and looked up to see Garfield walking into the room. Over the years, he had come to know the president well, and he could tell that he was looking forward to this trip "with an almost pathetic longing." Clapping a hand on his secretary's shoulder, Garfield said, "Goodbye, my boy, you have had your holiday, now I am going to have mine. Keep a watchful eye on things."

After warmly shaking Brown's hand, Garfield stepped outside the White House and climbed into a waiting carriage. It was the State Department carriage, a small coupe with just one seat for the president and the secretary of state, whom Garfield had asked to ride with him to the station. There were no guards, not even an assistant. Just two old friends riding in a modest, one-horse carriage. Behind them, Garfield's army buddy Captain Almon Rockwell drove Harry and Jim in the president's carriage, which Garfield had borrowed from Rutherford Hayes because he could not afford his own.

The small caravan was in no hurry to reach its destination. Garfield, although looking forward to seeing Lucretia and visiting his alma mater, wanted to discuss with Blaine his plans for the end of the summer. He had scheduled a tour of the South and planned to give an important, and very likely controversial, speech on reconstruction and race while in Atlanta, Georgia. As they talked, Blaine kept his horse clopping along at a leisurely pace, "in conscious enjoyment of the beautiful morning."

Like Garfield, Guiteau woke early that morning, excited and restless. When he opened his eyes at 5:00 a.m., he saw not the small, shabby interior of Mrs. Grant's boardinghouse, where he had been staying for the past six weeks, but a much more elegant room. After reading about the president's trip in the newspaper two days earlier and deciding that this was the opportunity he had been looking for, Guiteau had moved to the Riggs House, the hotel where Garfield had stayed on the night before his inauguration. For months, Guiteau had spent entire afternoons in the Riggs House lobby, reading the newspapers, using the hotel stationery, and keeping an eye out for the many politicians and prominent men who met there. Now he finally had a room of his own at the prestigious hotel, and need not concern himself about the bill.

As Guiteau dressed for the day in his new, well-appointed room, Mrs. Grant, the owner of his previous boardinghouse, was desperately trying to track him down. For weeks, Guiteau had met her requests for payment with excuses and promises. "I can't do anything for you to-day, but I certainly will in a day or two," he had written to her two days earlier. "Please do not mention this to any one, as it will do me harm, as I will settle in a day or two. You can depend on this." The next day, Mrs. Grant had found his room empty and his bag gone. She refused, however, to admit defeat. In fact, she had placed an advertisement in the *Daily Post* that was to appear that day: "WANTED: Charles Guiteau, of Illinois, who gives the President and Secretary Blaine as reference, to call at 924 14th St., and pay his board bill."

Unaware and unconcerned about Mrs. Grant's advertisement, and filled with a satisfying sense of his own importance that day, Guiteau allowed himself a leisurely morning. It was too early for breakfast, so he walked to Lafayette Park as he had done nearly every day for the past four months. He rested, read the paper, and "enjoyed the beautiful morning air." At eight, he returned to the Riggs House and had a large meal. "I ate well," he would later say, "and felt well in body and mind."

After breakfast, Guiteau returned to his room to retrieve a few items. Over the past few weeks, as he prepared to assassinate the president, he had written a series of letters that he took great satisfaction in knowing would be published to wide readership. One of those letters, however, he had addressed to just one man — General William Tecumseh Sherman. Scrawled on the back of a telegraph sheet, it read:

> To General Sherman:
> I have just shot the President.
> I shot him several times, as I wished him to go as easily as possible.
> His death was a political necessity.
> I am a lawyer, theologian, and politician.
> I am a Stalwart of the Stalwarts.
> I was with Gen Grant, and the rest of our men in New York during the canvas.
> I am going to the jail.
> Please order out your troops, and take possession of the jail at once.
>
> Charles Guiteau

Folding the letters into an envelope, Guiteau put them with his edited copy of *The Truth.* To the cover of his book, he attached a note to the *New York Herald.* "You can print this entire book, if you wish to," it read. "I would suggest that it be printed in sections, *i.e.,* one or two sections a day. . . . I intend to have it handsomely printed by some first-class New York publisher, but the Herald can have the first chance at it."

There was one last letter, which Guiteau had written just that morning and now tucked safely into his shirt pocket. Addressed to the White House, it attempted to explain what he was about to do. "The President's tragic death was a sad necessity, but it will unite the Republican party and save the Republic. Life is a fleeting dream, and it matters little when one goes," he wrote. "I presume the President was a Christian and that he will be happier in Paradise than here."

His affairs in order, Guiteau was finally ready to leave. He was wearing a dark suit with a "nice, clean shirt," and he looked, he was confident, "like a gentleman." Before stepping out the door, he picked up his revolver, carefully wrapped it in paper, and slid it into his hip pocket.

Although he had taken his time that morning, Guiteau arrived at the Baltimore and Potomac station at Sixth and B Streets half an hour before Garfield. He decided to use the time to complete a few last tasks. Aware that he would soon be the focus of great attention, and concerned that his shoes looked a little dusty, he had them brushed and blacked. Then he approached a line of hack drivers outside the station. Thinking it best to arrange for a ride to the jail ahead of time, in case there was any danger to him personally, he asked one driver what he would charge to take him to the Congressional Cemetery, which was near the prison. "Well, I will take you out there for $2," the driver answered. Guiteau, who did not have two dollars but did not plan to pay for the ride anyway, told the driver he would let him know in a few minutes if he "wanted his services."

Once inside the station, Guiteau turned his attention to the items he had carried with him from the Riggs House. Approaching a newsstand, he asked the young man behind the counter, James Denny, if he could leave some packages with him for a few minutes. "Certainly," Denny replied, and, taking the packages from Guiteau, placed them on top of a pile of papers stacked against a wall. Satisfied that his letters and book were in good hands and would be found by the authorities when the time came, Guiteau walked to the bathroom to examine his revolver one last time. He unwrapped it from the paper he had used to protect the powder from his perspiration, tested the trigger, and looked it over carefully "to see that it was alright." Five minutes after he stepped back into the waiting room, Garfield and Blaine arrived.

When the State Department carriage rounded the corner onto B Street, Garfield was seated nearest the sidewalk and so had an unimpeded view of the station. Although eager to begin his trip, the president did not relish the sight of the three-story redbrick building with its imposing Gothic design, nor had he ever.

So strongly did Garfield object to the station that, while in Congress, he had argued that it should be torn down. Nine years earlier, the government had given the Baltimore and Potomac Railroad fourteen acres of the National Mall, and the company had quickly built the station and laid tracks across the broad greensward. To the Mall, which Pierre-Charles L'Enfant had designed as a place for quiet contemplation, the station brought soot, smoke, noise, and even danger. Trains frequently killed and maimed people as they walked or rode in carriages along the Mall. People "will wonder," one senator railed, "why an American Congress should permit so foul a blotch to besmirch the face of so grand a picture."

Garfield, who referred to the Baltimore and Potomac as a "nuisance which ought long since to have been abated," also had personal reasons for disliking the station. In his mind, it would always be inextricably linked with one of the most painful experiences of his life — the death of his youngest son, Neddie. Just five years earlier, Garfield and Crete had watched as their little boy's body was carried through the station so that he might be buried in Mentor, next to his sister Trot, whom they had lost thirteen years earlier. "I did not know, since that great sorrow," Garfield had written in his diary after burying Neddie, "that my heart could be so wrung again by a similar loss."

As the carriage carrying Garfield came to a stop in front of the station entrance, Patrick Kearney, an officer with the Metropolitan Police, quickly walked in front of it to see if he could be of assistance. The president and his secretary of state, however, remained seated while they finished their conversation, Garfield's hand resting on Blaine's shoulder. Finally, Garfield called out the window to Kearney, asking him how much time he had before his train departed. Kearney, who had been leaning against a lamppost while he waited for the president, walked over to Garfield and showed him his watch: ten minutes.

Before stepping out of the carriage, Garfield turned to say goodbye to Blaine, who would not be traveling with him. The secretary of state, however, insisted on escorting him to the train. "I did not think it was proper for a president to go entirely unattended," he would later explain. As the two men ascended the steps into the station, arm in arm, Garfield suddenly stopped and turned back to Kearney, who had lifted his hat and saluted. Responding with a warm smile and tip of his hat, the president disappeared inside the door.

As Garfield entered the station, Sarah White, the matron for the ladies' waiting room, looked up from her position next to the room's heater. She watched as the president and secretary of state strode by, Blaine slightly ahead of Garfield, Harry and Jim trailing behind them. Garfield walked with an easy, natural confidence — "absolutely free from any affectation whatever."

He must have made a striking contrast to Guiteau, whom White had also been watching that morning. Not only was Guiteau nearly half a foot shorter than the president and seventy-five pounds lighter, but he seemed as uncomfortable and nervous as Garfield was at ease. As he shuffled soundlessly between the gentlemen's and ladies' waiting rooms, his shoulders bent, his head tilted at an odd angle, and his dark slouch hat sitting low over his eyes, Guiteau had seemed suspicious to White. "He would look in one door and pass on to the next door and look in again," she remembered. "He walked in the room once, took off his hat, wiped his face, and went out again."

When Garfield walked in, Guiteau was standing right behind him. This, Guiteau realized, was his chance to kill the president, and this time he was not about to let it slip away. Without a moment's hesitation, he raised the revolver he had been carrying with him for nearly a month and pointed it at Garfield's back. So complete was his composure that he might have been standing at the edge of the Potomac aiming at a sapling, instead of in a crowded train station about to shoot the president of the United States.

The Venezuelan chargé d'affaires, Simón Camacho, happened to be standing next to Guiteau at that moment, and he could clearly see the assassin's face as he stood looking at Garfield, arm outstretched and unwavering. "His teeth were clenched and his mouth closed firmly," Camacho would later recall. "His eye was steady, and his face presented the appearance of a brave man, who is determined upon a desperate deed, and meant to do it calmly and well."

Garfield had walked only a few steps into the room, and was just three feet away when Guiteau pulled the trigger. The bullet sliced through the president's right arm, passing through his jacket and piercing the side of a tool box that a terrified worker was carrying through the station. The sudden impact made Garfield throw up his arms in surprise and cry out, "My God! What is this?"

As Garfield turned to see who had shot him, Guiteau fired again. By now, however, his courage had abandoned him, as his thoughts seemed to have suddenly shifted from the president's fate to his own. "The expression on [his] face had now changed," Camacho said. "His calmness had disappeared. . . . He fired wildly this time and with a hurried movement."

Despite the wave of fear that had washed over Guiteau, the lead bullet hit its mark, ripping into the president's back. The force thrust Garfield forward, his long legs buckling underneath him and his hands reaching out to break his fall. As he sank heavily to the carpeted floor, vomiting violently and barely conscious, a bright red stain blossomed on the back of his gray summer suit. There was a moment of stunned silence, and then the station erupted in screams.

■ ■ ■ ■

Part Three: Fear

■ ■ ■ ■

Chapter 12
"Thank God It Is All Over"

If there be one thing upon this earth
that mankind love and admire . . .
it is a brave man.

JAMES A. GARFIELD

As cries of "Catch him!" echoed through the train station, Guiteau's face "blanched like that of a corpse," the Venezuelan chargé d'affaires, Camacho, would remember. Literally trembling with fear, his eyes rolling "from side to side as if he was a hunted man," Guiteau sprang for the door that led to B Street and his waiting carriage. Before he could reach it, however, Camacho, who was closer to the exit and had suddenly realized what was happening, lunged forward, blocking the door and desperately waving his arms in the air for help. Guiteau spun around and darted for the Sixth Street exit just as Blaine, who had instinctively raced after him, shouted for the doors to be barred.

The first man to catch Guiteau was a ticket agent named Robert Parke. As the assassin raced past him, Parke grabbed him by the back of his neck and his left wrist, calling out, "This is the man." Officer Kearney, who had exchanged a smile and a tip of the hat with Garfield just minutes earlier, ran to Parke's side, seizing Guiteau powerfully and shaking him.

At first Guiteau twisted and turned, trying to free himself, but as the crowd surged around him, pulsing with shock and fury, he realized that, on his own, he would not survive. Across the station, a group of enraged black men, joined by a growing chorus, began shouting "Lynch him!" and the lethal momentum of the mob became all but unstoppable. "I truly believe that if they hadn't been so many officers present," a porter would later say, "the man would have been strung up then and there." Guiteau, fear "in his eyes, in his color, in his every movement," turned to Kearney and said, "I want to go to jail."

Guiteau gladly acquiesced as Kearney dragged him outside the station and onto the street, but he had something he wanted to say, and he repeated it over and over, in a desperate refrain. Taking the letter he had written to General Sherman out of his breast pocket and waving it frantically in the air, he said, "I have a letter that I want to see carried to General Sherman. I want Sherman to have this letter." As they hurried along, Kearney assured Guiteau that his letter would be delivered. By the time they reached police headquarters, Guiteau, surrounded by policemen and safely away from the raging mob, had recovered the calm, determined expression he had had before firing the first shot. "He had a rather fierce look out of his eyes," one of the officers would later recall, "but he did not appear to me to be excited at all."

The men who had arrested Guiteau, on the other hand, had lost all professional bearing in the face of a presidential assassination. So excited and flustered were they that not one of them had thought to take the gun. They did not discover their extraordinary oversight until they emptied Guiteau's pockets. Kearney found his papers first, then a couple of coins — which amounted to all the money he was carrying with him, and likely all he had — and then finally, reaching into his hip pocket, he pulled out the weapon Guiteau had used to shoot the president, still loaded with three thick cartridges.

Just ten minutes after he had arrived at

police headquarters, as word of the shooting spread and the streets began to fill with angry men searching for the assassin, Guiteau was moved to the District Jail. To his mind, he was going to jail only for his own protection, not because he was an accused murderer who would face trial. "I did not expect to go through the form of being committed," he would later say. "I went to jail for my own personal protection. I had sense enough for that."

By the time he stepped into a police department carriage, Guiteau had little thought for the crime he had just committed, or the man he assumed he had killed. His mind was too preoccupied with the celebrity that awaited him. Sherman, he was confident, would soon receive his letter and send out the troops to free him, and Vice President Arthur, overwhelmed with gratitude, would be eager to be of any assistance. Until they could reach him, however, he would need the help of someone less exalted to make his prison stay as comfortable as possible. Recalling what he knew about the District Jail from his trip there the week before, he turned to the detective seated next to him and attempted to strike a deal. "You stick to me and have me put in the third story, front, at the jail," he said. "Gen.

Sherman is coming down to take charge. Arthur and all those men are my friends, and I'll have you made Chief of Police."

Although he was in police custody, on his way to prison, Guiteau could not have been more pleased had he been bound for Paris, the consulship to France finally his. He complained that, for weeks, he had been "haunted and haunted and oppressed and oppressed, and could get no relief." Now that he had finally carried out his divine mission, he could relax and enjoy what was to come. He believed he was about to shake off the poverty, misery, and obscurity of his former life, and step into the national spotlight. He felt happy for the first time in a long time. "Thank God it is all over," he thought.

For Harry Garfield, who stood in the train station waiting room, desperately trying to fend off the crush of people pressing in upon his father, the nightmare into which Guiteau had plunged his family was only beginning. "Keep back! That my father may have air!" he cried, as his younger brother knelt beside Garfield, sobbing. "Keep them back!" Garfield's eyes were open, but it was not clear if he was conscious. He "was very pale, and he did not say a word," Jacob

Smith, a janitor who had been the first person to reach the president, would later recall. Smith tried to help Garfield to his feet, but quickly realized that he could not stand and lowered him back to the floor. Garfield looked "very hard" into his eyes, as if trying to make sense of what was happening.

Watching Smith struggle to help Garfield, Sarah White, the ladies' waiting room attendant, rushed over and placed the president's head in her lap. Although he was able to ask her for water, and drink what she gave him, he immediately began vomiting again, turning his head so that he would stain his own suit rather than her dress. As tears streamed down White's face, a station agent leaned over her to remove Garfield's collar and tie.

Although it seemed to everyone in the station that the president was surely dying, the injury he had sustained from Guiteau's gun was not fatal. The second bullet had entered his back four inches to the right of his spinal column. Continuing its trajectory, it had traveled ten inches and now rested behind his pancreas. It had broken two of Garfield's ribs and grazed an artery, but it had missed his spinal cord and, more important, his vital organs.

Just five minutes after the shooting, Dr. Smith Townsend, the District of Columbia's health officer, arrived at the Baltimore and Potomac. Although he was the first doctor to reach the station, within the hour he would be joined by a succession of nine more physicians, each of whom wanted to examine the president.

Townsend's first concern was simply keeping Garfield conscious. After asking White to place his head back on the floor so that it would not be elevated, he gave the president half an ounce of brandy and aromatic spirits of ammonia. When Garfield was alert enough to speak, Townsend asked him where he felt the most pain, and Garfield indicated his legs and feet.

What Townsend did next was something that Joseph Lister, despite years spent traveling the world, proving the source of infection and pleading with physicians to sterilize their hands and instruments, had been unable to prevent. As the president lay on the train station floor, one of the most germ-infested environments imaginable, Townsend inserted an unsterilized finger into the wound in his back, causing a small hemorrhage and almost certainly introducing an infection that was far more lethal than Guiteau's bullet.

After he made his initial examination, Townsend, finally realizing that he needed to get his patient away from the crowd, asked for help moving Garfield. A group of men who worked at the station disappeared into a nearby room and walked out a few minutes later carrying a mattress made of hay and horsehair. As they lifted the president onto the mattress, a groan of pain escaped from his lips, but he did not speak. The conductor of the train Garfield was supposed to be on had run to the scene of the shooting and now cleared the way as the men carried the president out of the waiting room and up a set of winding stairs that led to a large, empty room over the station.

As Garfield lay on the crude mattress, vomiting repeatedly and falling in and out of consciousness, he worried about Lucretia, who expected to see him that day. She was still recovering from an illness that had nearly killed her, and he was terrified that when she learned of the shooting the shock would be too much for her to bear. There was nothing he could do to protect her from the news. The best he could hope for was to somehow tell her himself. Motioning for his old friend Almon Rockwell to come close, he said, “I think you had better telegraph to Crete.” Rockwell listened intently to Garfield, determined to faithfully convey his words, and then left to send the most difficult telegram he had ever had to write.

On his way to the telegraph station, Rockwell passed the members of Garfield’s cabinet who had intended to travel with the president. They had been walking on the train station platform, waiting for Garfield to arrive, when Colonel John Jameson, an agent of the Postal Railway Service, came running up to them, shouting that the president had been shot. So unexpected and shocking was the news that at first they did not believe him. It was not until they heard the chaos and screaming in the station that they realized that Jameson was telling the truth, and quickly followed him to the somber room above the tracks.

As soon as the cabinet members appeared, Blaine pulled them aside and told them that he knew the assassin. “I recognized the man . . . before, I think, the police had even discovered his name,” Blaine would later say. He had not seen Guiteau pull the trigger, but he had caught sight of him as he fled toward the exit, and with a shock of recognition had realized that he was the same man who had sat in the State Department waiting room day after day, insisting that he be given a consulship.

While the cabinet members discussed Guiteau, a second doctor entered the room — Charles Purvis, surgeon in chief of the Freedmen's Hospital. Although he was only thirty-nine years old, Purvis had already made history several times over. He was one of the first black men in the country to receive his medical training at a university, had been one of only eight black surgeons in the Union Army during the Civil War, and was one of the first black men to serve on the faculty of an American medical school. Now, as he leaned over Garfield, recommending that blankets be wrapped around his body and hot water bottles placed on his feet and legs, he became the first black doctor to treat a president of the United States.

As the tension rose, and everyone around him spoke in hushed, panicked voices, Garfield remained "the calmest man in the room," Robert Todd Lincoln marveled. Lying on his left side, his coat and waistcoat removed so that the wound was exposed, Garfield turned to one of the doctors closest to him and asked what chance he had of surviving. "One chance in a hundred," the doctor gravely replied. "We will take that chance, doctor," Garfield said, "and make good use of it."

Secretary Lincoln watched the events unfolding around him with an all-too-familiar horror. His memory of standing at his father's deathbed sixteen years earlier was vivid in his mind, and he was shocked and sickened by the realization that he was now witnessing another presidential assassination. "My God," he murmured, "how many hours of sorrow I have passed in this town."

Suddenly, Lincoln decided that he would not simply stand by and watch Garfield die. Remembering that his own carriage was waiting just outside the station, he rushed out of the room, down the stairs, and to the door. Calling for his driver, he instructed him to find Dr. D. Willard Bliss, one of the doctors who had tried without hope to save his father.

Lincoln chose Bliss in part because he knew he would be a familiar sight to Garfield. Bliss had lived near the president's childhood home in Ohio, and had known him as "an earnest, industrious boy . . . whose ambitions were evidently far above his apparent advantages." Years later, when he was a congressman, Garfield had supported and encouraged Bliss when the doctor was expelled from the powerful District of Columbia Medical Society after disagreeing with its policy to bar black doctors and showing an interest in the relatively new medical field of homeopathy. When the society repeatedly and openly attacked Bliss, accusing him of conferring with "quacks" and seriously damaging his reputation, Garfield had written to him, praising his actions. By their condemnation, the society had "decorated" Bliss, Garfield insisted. "I have no doubt it will do you good."

In the end, Bliss could not hold up under the pressure. After six years he had buckled, apologizing to the society, returning to its fold, and turning his back on the men he had once championed. By doing so, he had regained his reputation and lucrative medical practice. By the time of Garfield's shooting, Bliss had been a practicing surgeon for thirty years. He had had a thriving practice in Michigan, had served as a regimental surgeon during the Civil War, and had run the Armory Square Hospital across the street from the Smithsonian Institution. Over the years, he had won the respect and admiration of a wide segment of the population, including even Walt Whitman, who had been a steward at the Armory Square Hospital and had described him as a "very fine operating surgeon."

Bliss's record, however, was far from spotless. Although it seemed that his occupation had been determined at birth, when his parents named him Doctor Willard, giving him a medical title for his first name, Bliss's desire for recognition and financial compensation was nearly as all-consuming as Guiteau's. While at the Armory Square Hospital, he had been accused of accepting a $500 bribe and was held for several days in the Old Capitol Prison. Just ten years earlier, he had been heavily involved in a controversy surrounding a purported cure for cancer called cundurango, a plant native to the Andes Mountains. Believing that cundurango would be to cancer what quinine was to malaria, he had staked his professional reputation on it, selling it wherever he could and even posting hyperbolic advertisements: "Cundurango!" one ad read. "The wonderful remedy for Cancer, Syphilis, Scrofula, Ulcers, Salt Rebum, and All Other Chronic Blood Diseases."

More ominous for Garfield was the fact that Bliss had very little respect for Joseph Lister's theories on infection, and even less interest in following his complicated methods for antisepsis. Although he had once been open to working with not only black doctors but also homeopaths, physicians who believed in using very small doses of medicine, Bliss's approach to medicine had changed dramatically after his battle with the Medical Society. Now, like most doctors at that time, he was a strict adherent to allopathy, which often involved administering large doses of harsh medicines that, they believed, would produce an effect opposite to the disease.

As soon as Bliss arrived at the station in Lincoln's carriage, he assumed immediate and complete control of the president's medical care. Striding into the room where Garfield lay, he briefly questioned Townsend and Purvis and then quickly began his own, much more invasive examination of the patient. Opening his bag, Bliss selected a long probe that had a white porcelain tip. Fourteen years before the invention of the X-ray, doctors used these probes to determine the location of bullets. If the tip came against bone, it would remain white, but a lead bullet would leave a dark mark.

With nothing to even ease the pain, Garfield lay silent as Bliss searched for the bullet inside him. Pressing the unsterilized probe downward and forward into the wound, Bliss did not stop until he had reached a cavity three inches deep in Garfield's back. At this point, he decided to remove the probe, but found that he could not. "In attempting to withdraw the probe, it became engaged between the fractured fragments and the end of the rib," he later wrote. He finally had to press down on Garfield's fractured rib so that it would lift and release the probe.

Although the probe was finally out, Garfield had no respite. Bliss immediately began to explore the wound again, this time with the little finger of his left hand. He inserted his finger so deeply into the wound that he could feel the broken rib and "what appeared to be lacerated tissue or comparatively firm coagula, probably the latter."

By this time, Purvis had seen enough. With a boldness that was then extraordinary in a black doctor addressing a white one, he asked Bliss to end his examination. Ignoring Purvis, Bliss removed his finger from the wound, turned once again to his bag, and calmly selected another probe, this one made of flexible silver. Bending the probe into a curve, he passed it into Garfield's back "downward and forward, and downward and backward in several directions" while Purvis looked on, unable to stop him.

Chapter 13
"It's True"

It is one of the precious mysteries of sorrow that it finds solace in unselfish thought.

JAMES A. GARFIELD

Lucretia was packing her bags in her hotel room in Elberon, New Jersey, preparing to meet James for their trip to New England, when General David Swaim knocked on her door. At one point during the Civil War, when Garfield had been too sick to walk, Swaim had literally carried him home. Now, he held only a telegram in his hands, but his words made Lucretia's heart miss a beat. There has been an accident, he said. Perhaps she should return to Washington.

Lucretia took the slip of paper and slowly read the message that her husband had dictated to Rockwell in the train station:

THE PRESIDENT WISHES ME TO SAY TO YOU FROM HIM THAT HE HAS BEEN SERIOUSLY HURT — HOW SERIOUSLY HE CANNOT YET SAY. HE IS HIMSELF AND HOPES YOU WILL COME TO HIM SOON. HE SENDS HIS LOVE TO YOU.

Looking up at Swaim, she said, "Tell me the truth."

As Swaim attempted to tell Lucretia the little he knew, Ulysses S. Grant appeared at the door. He had been staying in his son's cabin just across the street for the past two weeks, but, still nursing a grudge, had done nothing before now to acknowledge the president and first lady beyond a stiff bow and tip of his hat. "I do not think he can afford to show feeling in this way," Garfield had written in his diary just the week before. "I am quite certain he injures himself more than he does me."

As soon as Grant learned of the assassination attempt, however, the hard feelings and wounded pride of the past year were forgotten. Taking Lucretia's hand in his, the former president and retired general was at first "so overcome with emotion," one member of Grant's party would recall, "he could scarcely speak." Finally, he was able to tell Lucretia that he had brought with him something that he hoped would give her a measure of comfort. He had just received a telegram from a friend in Washington who was certain that the president's wounds were not mortal. From what he knew of the injury, Grant agreed. He had known many soldiers to survive similar wounds.

Although he did not stay long, Grant's words and, perhaps even more, his kindness were an emotional life raft for Lucretia, something to cling to until she could see James. Hurriedly finishing her packing, she left the hotel with Mollie to catch a special train, made up of just an engine and one Pullman car, that had been arranged to take them to Washington as quickly as possible. By the time they reached the station, a crowd had already gathered, many of the women crying as the men stood in silence, hats in hands.

As Lucretia's train sped south toward Washington, another train, traveling west, carried her youngest sons to Mentor, Ohio, where they were to spend the summer. By telegraph and telephone, news of their father's shooting had raced ahead of them, stirring fear and confusion throughout the country. "All along the route . . . crowds collected at the stations we passed, and begged for news," one conductor would later say. "The country seemed to become more feverish as the day advanced."

Thanks to an extraordinary, spontaneous act of sympathy that united passengers and rail workers all along their journey, however, ten-year-old Irvin and eight-year-old Abe remained completely unaware of what had happened to their father. Even as citizens throughout the country struggled with their own reactions to the news of Guiteau's crime, the president's children became a focus of national concern. No one could bear the thought of them alone on the train, learning that their father had been shot.

While the boys gazed out the railcar window, watching trees and towns flash by, stationmasters and railroad officials passed ahead instructions not to discuss the assassination attempt. Passengers and even newsboys showed astonishing restraint. "Conductors passed quietly through the train that carried the boys westward, requesting silence as they whispered the news," Garfield's granddaughter would write years later. "The children reached Mentor unaware of the dark cloud that was enveloping their family."

When the boys finally arrived it was noon,

more than an hour after news of the assassination attempt had reached the little town. They were quickly bundled into a carriage and brought to their family farm. While neighbors and friends slipped in and out of the farmhouse, hoping to be told that the rumors were untrue, a reporter spoke to Lucretia's father. "We have not said a word to the [boys]," Zeb Rudolph admitted. "We hoped that it may not be true, and now that it is true we almost fear to tell them." Struggling to keep his composure in the presence of a stranger, he watched as his grandsons played "in happy ignorance" on the wide, sun-soaked lawn.

In the second-story room above the Baltimore and Potomac station, Garfield asked only one thing of the more than a dozen men who hovered over him — that they take him home. After enduring Bliss's excruciating examinations and listening to ten different doctors discuss his fate, Garfield finally convinced the shell-shocked members of his cabinet that, although the White House, with its rotting wood and leaking pipes, was no place for a sick man, anything was better than this room. As gently as they could, eight men lifted the president and carried him back down the steep stairs while he lay on the train car mattress, now stained with vomit and blood.

When they reached the waiting room, the men could hardly believe their eyes. In the brief time they had spent upstairs, trying to understand the extent of the president's injuries, the once orderly station below them had transformed into a madhouse. "The crowd about the depot," one man would recall, "had become a swaying multitude, with people running from every direction in frantic haste." Within ten minutes of the shooting, a mob had gathered on Sixth and B Streets. An attempt to storm the building, in the hope of finding the assassin and lynching him, had been prevented only by a desperate telephone call to the police.

As soon as Garfield appeared, however, the character of the crowd immediately changed. Men and women who had been screaming with fear and fury just moments before suddenly recovered their reason, quietly urging each other to make room for the president as he was carried out of the station and carefully put into a makeshift ambulance. "I think I can see now," one of Garfield's doctors would write years later, "the sea of human faces that completely filled the space in and around the depot, as we carried him down the stairs, and through the depot, with the mingled expressions of pity and consternation that sat upon each of them." Once settled on the mattress and a pile of hastily arranged cushions, Garfield, his right arm lifted over his head and his face "ashy white," looked silently out the window.

Hoping to spare the president any additional pain, the ambulance driver guided his horse so slowly over the broken brick streets that hundreds of people were able to keep up with his wagon, somberly walking just behind it. Whenever they came to a pothole, policemen would carefully lift the ambulance, trying their best not to jar it. Garfield's "sufferings must have been intense," one reporter wrote, "but he gave no sign of it, and was as gentle and submissive as a child."

Joseph Stanley Brown was working alone in his office, just as Garfield had left him, when one of the White House doormen suddenly appeared before his desk. There was something about the way the man walked in, "haltingly and timidly," that made Brown uneasy. "Mr. Secretary," he said, "there is a rumor that the President has been shot."

Years later, Brown would struggle to explain how he felt when he heard those words. It was as if he were "suddenly congealed," he said, as if his hectic, bustling world had lurched to a stop. Desperately trying to dismiss the idea, and to sound more confident than he felt, he snapped at the doorman. "Nonsense!" he said. "The story cannot possibly be true."

The man quickly shuffled away, but Brown could not shake the sickening feeling that had settled over him, nor would he have a chance to. Just moments after he had managed to return his attention to his work, his office door suddenly burst open, and a messenger staggered into the room. "Oh, Mr. Secretary," he cried, "it's true, they are bringing the President to the White House now."

Although Brown would later admit that he was more shocked than he had ever been, or would ever again be, he instinctively sprang into action, reacting with the same intelligence and pragmatism that had convinced Garfield to trust him with such a critical job. "Even in moments of greatest misery," he would later write, "homely tasks have to be performed, and perhaps they tide us over the worst." If the president was injured, a bed must be made ready at once. There was a suitable room in the southeast corner of the house, and Brown ordered a steward to prepare it "with all speed."

Then Brown personally took charge of the fortification of the White House and the protection of the president. With complete confidence and authority, he ordered the gates closed and sent a telegram to the chief of police, requesting a "temporary but adequate detail of officers." Next he contacted the War Department and arranged for a military contingent for Garfield, a man who had never had so much as a single bodyguard.

Although Brown's first priority was to secure the White House, he knew that he could not seal it off completely. The American people deserved "full and accurate information" about their president, and he was determined that they would get it. With astonishing speed and efficiency, he had passes issued to journalists and government officials so that they might have access to his office at any time, day or night.

As he raced through the halls of the White House, giving orders, inspecting rooms, and turning an entire wing into a "miniature hospital," Brown paused for a moment to glance out the window. Below him, he saw a modest wagon trundling up Pennsylvania Avenue. It looked suitable for neither a president nor a wounded man, but as it slowed to enter the gates, he suddenly noticed the crowd gathered around it. Garfield, he knew, was inside.

With his staff watching from the windows, Brown raced down the stairs and out the door to where the wagon had rolled to a stop. As he stood there, still trying to understand what was happening, a group of men reached into the wagon and carefully carried the president out. When he saw his young secretary, Garfield waved weakly and tried to smile. Looking at the president, drained of color, his handsome gray suit torn and soaked with blood, Brown could not believe this was the same man who, just an hour before, had left the White House "abounding in health and the joy of living."

A dozen men lifted above their heads the mattress on which the president lay, carrying him into the White House, through the Blue Room, up the broad, central staircase, and to the room that Brown had had prepared for him. As his son Jim, no longer able to contain his fear and grief, began to cry, Garfield grasped his hand tightly. "The upper story is alright," he promised. "It is only the hull that was damaged."

Just eighteen miles outside of Washington, Lucretia, terrified that she was already too late, suddenly heard a deafening, high-pitched squeal and saw sparks flying outside her window. The twelve-foot-long parallel bar connecting the wheels of the special train that had been arranged for her, thundering along at 250 revolutions per minute, had suddenly snapped. Unable to stop, the engine dragged the broken rod for two miles, ripping up railroad ties and gouging the side of the train. The railroad men who would later arrive on the scene pronounced it a miracle that the engine had not jumped the tracks. Had that happened, "the Pullman car would have been splintered into kindling-wood," the *New York Times* reported, "and all on board would have been killed."

More frustrated than frightened, Lucretia was forced to wait until a second engine could arrive to take her the rest of the way into Washington. By the time she finally reached the White House, it was nearly 7:00 p.m. Garfield had waited for her for hours without complaint, but he knew the moment she arrived. Hearing the crunch of her carriage wheels over the gravel driveway, he broke into a broad smile and, turning to his doctors, said, "That's my wife!"

Lucretia's face was streaked with tears when she stepped out of the carriage, but she quickly wiped them away, determined to show only strength and confidence to James. "Mrs. Garfield came, frail, fatigued, desperate," Harriet Blaine wrote to her daughter the next day. "But firm and quiet and full of purpose to save." Until that moment, Secretary Blaine, although very pale and "evidently . . . making a strong effort to keep up his strength," had managed to stave off grief, allowing himself to think only of what could be done to save his friend. When he saw Lucretia and Mollie, however, he "broke completely," a reporter who had been waiting outside the White House gates wrote, and "wept for several minutes."

Lucretia went straight to Garfield's room, escorted up the stairs by her son Jim, his arm wrapped protectively around her as he whispered in her ear, trying to reassure her as his father had reassured him. Although she was surrounded by people desperate to protect her, to soften the blow, few of them believed her husband would live. Colonel Abel Corbin, President Grant's brother-in-law, had seen Garfield lying on the train station floor and told a reporter that he had watched "too many men die on the battlefield not to know death's mark." "In my opinion," Corbin said, Garfield was "virtually a dead man from the moment he was shot." Even the man who had assumed control of the president's medical care admitted that he held out little if any hope. Garfield "will not probably live three hours," Bliss said, "and may die in half an hour."

Lucretia, as she had done throughout her life, insisted on the truth, no matter how painful, but she was not about to abandon hope. Resolutely opening the door to the room where her husband lay, she left her children and friends behind and stepped inside with dry eyes and a warm smile. She would admit fear, but not despair. When Garfield, the memory of his own fatherless childhood weighing heavily on his mind, tried to talk to her about plans for their children if he were to die, she stopped him.

"I am here to nurse you back to life," she said firmly. "Please do not speak again of death."

Chapter 14
All Evil Consequences

Great ideas travel slowly, and for a time noiselessly, as the gods whose feet were shod with wool.

JAMES A. GARFIELD

While most of the country heard newsboys crying "Extra!" in the streets or overheard the frantic whispers of friends, news of the president's shooting reached the Volta Laboratory by telephone call. Alexander Graham Bell's assistant, Charles Sumner Tainter, was in the laboratory in Washington, working on a row of wax impressions for the phonograph, when his telephone suddenly sprang to life, its sharp ring shattering the silence and wrenching him away from his work. Although by now the invention had been installed in thousands of homes, for most Americans, it was not yet part of the everyday world. Even Bell did not often hear it ring.

If Tainter was surprised to receive a telephone call, he was astonished by the news it brought. "President Garfield," the caller said, had "just been shot while in the Baltimore and Potomac." When they learned what had happened, the members of Bell's family were struck by the cruelty and senselessness of the act, and reminded of the losses they had suffered in their own lives. As his mother would write in the following days, there was a sense of shock and grief, as heavy as if the president "belonged to us."

The Volta Laboratory was on Connecticut Avenue, a main thoroughfare in the heart of Washington, and Tainter and Bell's cousin Dr. Chicester Bell watched as the city seemed to descend into madness. People flooded the streets, dodging carriage wheels and horses' hooves as they raced toward the train station in disbelief, or away from it in terror. "Everybody ran hither and thither without method," one contemporary writer would remember of that day. "Men forgot hat and coat, and ran into the streets and wandered about, apparently anxious only to be near somebody else, but shocked and bewildered." Determined to find out for himself what had happened, Tainter began to make his way toward the Baltimore and Potomac. So crowded and chaotic were the streets, however, that by the time he reached the train station, Garfield was already gone.

In Boston, Bell had been in frequent contact with Tainter, as they worked long distance. His wife, pregnant with their third child, and his daughters needed him, but his thoughts had never been far from his work. As soon as he heard the news of the president's shooting, however, Bell's mind immediately shifted away from Edison's phonograph, and even his own invention, the photophone, to the president. Although he was not a doctor, Bell knew that, in the case of a gunshot wound, "no one could venture to predict the end so long as the position of the bullet remained unknown." It sickened him to think of Garfield's doctors blindly "search[ing] with knife and probe" for Guiteau's bullet. "Science," he reasoned, "should be able to discover some less barbarous method."

Science would soon exceed even Bell's expectations. Had Garfield been shot just fifteen years later, the bullet in his back would have been quickly found by X-ray images, and the wound treated with antiseptic surgery. He might have been back on his feet within weeks. Had he been able to receive modern medical care, he likely would have spent no more than a few nights in the hospital.

Even had Garfield simply been left alone, he almost certainly would have survived. Lodged as it was in the fatty tissue below and behind his pancreas, the bullet itself was no continuing danger to the president. "Nature did all she could to restore him to health," a surgeon would write just a few years later. "She caused a capsule of thick, strong, fibrous tissue to be formed around the bullet, completely walling it off from the rest of the body, and rendering it entirely harmless."

Garfield's doctors did not know where the bullet was, but they did know that it was not necessarily fatal. Just sixteen years after the end of the Civil War, hundreds of men, Union veterans and Confederate, were walking around with lead balls inside them. Many of the soldiers, moreover, had sustained wounds that seemed almost impossible to survive. For the better part of his life, the man who delivered Guiteau to the District Jail, Detective McElfresh, had had a bullet in his brain, a wound also sustained during the Civil War. He appeared to be, one reporter mentioned offhandedly, "none the worse for it."

The critical difference between these anonymous men and Garfield was that they had received little if any medical care. If Garfield "had been a 'tough,' and had received his wound in a Bowery dive," a contemporary medical critic wrote, "he would have been brought to Bellevue Hospital . . . without any fuss or feathers, and would have gotten well." Instead, Garfield was the object of intense medical interest from a menagerie of physicians, each with his own theories and ambitions, and each acutely aware that he was treating the president of the United States.

For one doctor in particular, this national crisis was a rare and heady intersection of medicine and political power — an opportunity for recognition he would never see again. Although ten different doctors had examined Garfield at the train station, as soon as the medical entourage reached the White House, Dr. Doctor Willard Bliss made it perfectly clear that he was in charge. Striding into the room where Garfield was to stay, Bliss immediately began issuing orders. In the chaos and confusion that marked the first hours after the president was shot, Bliss's complete confidence in his position convinced even his most determined competitors that he had been given full authority over Garfield's case.

Taking on the role of chief physician, Bliss's first orders were to isolate the president. In this he had the help of armed military sentinels. The policemen whom Joseph Stanley Brown had requested to secure the White House had been forced to fan out into the city, where, according to one journalist, "the crowds were rapidly increasing in angry excitement." In their place stood a company of soldiers, refusing entry to even Garfield's closest friends and advisers and discouraging the most determined visitors. "The glance of their bayonets flashing in the sunlight as they walked with measured tread the several paths to which they were assigned," one reporter wrote, "recalled the last hours of President Lincoln, when the same astonishment and horror were reflected on the faces of the crowds about the Executive Mansion."

Inside the White House, Garfield was confined not to just one wing, or even one room, but to a small space within that room. At Bliss's direction, his bed was pushed to the center of the room and encircled by screens. Even if a visitor were able to make it past the locked gates and armed guards, through the house, up the stairs, and into

Garfield's room, he would still be separated from the president.

To anyone standing beyond the White House gates, it seemed that the president had simply disappeared. So completely removed was he from sight, and so impossible was it to get any information about him, that rumors quickly began to circulate that he had already died. The rumors were so convincing, in fact, that the *Washington Post* published an extra edition, claiming that "President Garfield was shot and killed this morning." New Yorkers sorrowfully lowered their flags, only to raise them again a few hours later when they learned that the president was still living.

Having strictly limited Garfield's visitors to just a handful of family members and friends, Bliss turned his attention to what he considered to be the greatest threat to his newly won position — the other doctors. At the top of his list of potential competitors was Dr. Jedediah Hyde Baxter, the chief medical purveyor of the army and Garfield's personal physician for the past five years. When Garfield was shot, Baxter had been in Pennsylvania visiting a friend, but he had taken the first express train into Washington as soon as he heard the news. Bliss had been expecting him.

When Baxter arrived at the White House at 9:00 the next morning, he raced up the stairs, expecting to be immediately ushered in to see the president. Instead, he was stopped cold by the sight of Bliss, lying on a sofa in a room adjacent to Garfield's. Bliss was in the midst of dictating a letter that he intended to have copied and distributed to the other doctors. When Baxter stepped into the room, Bliss greeted him pleasantly and invited him to take a seat, gesturing to the foot of the sofa on which he was lying.

Exhausted from his frantic trip and astonished by the scene before him, Baxter refused to sit down, demanding to see Garfield. "Why, doctor," Bliss said cordially, "it would not be proper for me to take you to the bedside of the President at this time." Beginning to understand what was happening, Baxter made it clear that he would not be turned away. "He is my patient," he said, "and I want to see him." "Your patient," Bliss replied. "You astonish me." "Yes, my patient," Baxter growled. "I have been his family physician for five years, and I wish to see him." Tossing aside any pretense of professional concern, Bliss said coldly, "You may have been his physician for *ten* years, for aught I know, but you are not his physician this morning."

Still stretched out on the sofa, Bliss looked up at Baxter with contempt. "I know your game," he spat. "You wish to sneak up here and take this case out of my hands. You just try it on. . . . I know how you are, sneaking around to prescribe for those who have influence and will lobby for you." Enraged, Baxter shouted, "That is a lie!" At this, Bliss sprang to his feet, and his son, who had witnessed the entire exchange, leapt to his father's defense, shouting at Baxter to leave. Baxter, painfully aware of "the impropriety of having any disturbance in a room next to that in which the President lay so grievously wounded," snatched up his hat and strode out of the room, leaving Bliss standing, triumphant, outside Garfield's door.

Bliss's coup, he felt, was complete. In comparison to Baxter, the other doctors would be easy to discourage. That day, he sent out copies of his dictated letter to each of them:

Dear Doctor,

At the request of the President, I write to advise you that his symptoms are at present so favorable, as to render unnecessary any further consultations, until some change in his condition shall seem to warrant it.

Thanking you most cordially for your kind attention and skillful advice, and for which the President and family are deeply grateful.

I remain

very respectfully
D. W. Bliss

As expected, the men who had followed Garfield from the train station — even Townsend, the first man to treat the president after he was shot — left quickly and quietly after reading the letter, taking Bliss at his word that the president had chosen to trust his case, and his life, solely to him.

Later, when concern about the quality of the president's medical care began to grow, journalists would ask how Bliss came to be in charge of the case. "He just took charge of it," one doctor would say. "He happened to be the first man called after the shooting, and he stuck to it, shoving everybody else aside. Neither the President nor Mrs. Garfield ever asked him to take charge." Outraged by this accusation, Bliss would insist that, in a private meeting, both Garfield and the first lady had asked him to be the president's principal doctor and to "select such counsel as you may think best." To his mortification, however, Lucretia herself publicly contradicted his statement. No such discussion had ever taken place, she said. Neither she nor her husband had chosen Bliss.

Lucretia, in fact, had taken matters into her own hands, securing for James two doctors of her choosing. The first was Dr. Susan Ann Edson, one of the first female doctors in the country and Lucretia's personal physician. The stout, bespectacled doctor with the ring of tight gray curls had become such a familiar figure at the White House that even the Garfields' youngest son, Abe, knew her well, referring to her as "Dr. Edson, full of Med'cin."

Although James had chosen Baxter for his own physician, Lucretia knew that he trusted Edson as much as she did. Just a month earlier, when Lucretia was near death, Edson had been among the handful of doctors he had asked to come to the White House. Not only did he know that her presence would be a comfort to Lucretia, but he had seen her skill and compassion six years earlier, when she had struggled to save his son Neddie's life.

Edson, who was referred to in the press as "Mrs. Dr. Edson," had only just returned to her home and practice when her brother and sister, who had been shopping at a market near the Baltimore and Potomac, rushed to her with news of the president's shooting. Quickly packing a small bag, she had reached the White House just as Garfield was being carried in on the train car mattress. His first words to her had been of concern not for himself but for his wife. "What will this do for Crete?" he had asked her anxiously. "Will it put her in bed again? I had rather die."

To Edson, however, Lucretia seemed stronger and more determined than she had ever been. The first lady not only welcomed the sight of her own doctor and insisted that she stay, but immediately sent for yet another physician, a man her husband knew well. Dr. Silas Boynton was James's first cousin and had grown up "tramping through the woods" with him. Lucretia's telegram to Boynton was brief but firm: "Please to have you come as soon as possible."

Bliss found to his surprise and frustration that, despite his determined efforts, neither Edson nor Boynton would leave. Annoyed by their persistence, and hampered by their connection to the first lady, Bliss informed them that, if they must stay, they would be permitted to perform only nursing duties, and would not be consulted as physicians in their own right. Ignoring this pointed insult to their education and experience, both doctors agreed to Bliss's conditions, determined to remain close to the president so that they might watch over him when Lucretia could not.

Very much aware that the world was watching, Bliss was determined not to make any missteps. His temporary ouster from the District of Columbia Medical Society years earlier for consulting with "irregulars" — physicians who were outside the mainstream of medical thought — had led him to shun any association with what he considered to be experimental medicine. In this case above all others, dangerous new ideas were to be avoided at all costs.

High on Bliss's list of suspect medical theories was Joseph Lister's antisepsis — a fact that would surprise no one less than Lister himself. "I had a taste of what has been alas! experienced so largely by our profession," he had lamented years earlier, "how ignorant prejudice with good intentions may obstruct legitimate scientific inquiry." This prejudice persisted despite the fact that, in the sixteen years since Lister had introduced it, antisepsis had fundamentally changed the way British and European doctors practiced medicine, and had saved countless lives. In his own hospital in London, Lister had not seen a single case of hospital gangrene or pyaemia, a particularly virulent and common form of septicemia, since he had begun using antisepsis. He was certain that, were antisepsis to be adopted in the United States, "all evil consequences might be averted."

Although five years had passed since Lister presented his case to the Medical Congress at the Centennial Exhibition, many American doctors still dismissed not just his discovery, but even Louis Pasteur's. They found the notion of "invisible germs" to be ridiculous, and they refused to even consider the idea that they could be the cause of so much disease and death. "In order to successfully practice Mr. Lister's Antiseptic Method," one doctor scoffed, "it is necessary that we should believe, or act as if we believed, the atmosphere to be loaded with germs."

Why go to all the trouble that antisepsis required simply to fight something that they could not see and did not believe existed? Even the editor of the highly respected *Medical Record* found more to fear than to admire in Lister's theory. "Judging the future by the past," he wrote, "we are likely to be as much ridiculed in the next century for our blind belief in the power of unseen germs, as our forefathers were for their faith in the influence of spirits, of certain planets and the like, inducing certain maladies."

Not only did many American doctors not believe in germs, they took pride in the particular brand of filth that defined their profession. They spoke fondly of the "good old surgical stink" that pervaded their hospitals and operating rooms, and they resisted making too many concessions even to basic hygiene. Many surgeons walked directly from the street to the operating room without bothering to change their clothes. Those who did shrug on a laboratory coat, however, were an even greater danger to their patients. They looped strands of silk sutures through their buttonholes for easy access during surgery, and they refused to change or even wash their coats. They believed that the thicker the layers of dried blood and pus, black and crumbling as they bent over their patients, the greater the tribute to their years of experience.

Some physicians felt that Lister's findings simply did not apply to them and their patients. Doctors who lived and worked in the country, away from the soot and grime of the industrialized cities, argued that their air was so pure they did not need antisepsis. They preferred, moreover, to rely on their own methods of treatment, which not infrequently involved applying a hot poultice of cow manure to an open wound.

Even those doctors willing to try antisepsis rarely achieved better results than they had with traditional practices. Their failure, however, was hardly a mystery. Although they dipped their instruments in carbolic acid, they used wooden handles, which could not be sterilized, and they rested them on unsterilized towels. If the surgical knife they had carefully sterilized happened to fall on the floor during an operation, they would simply pick it up and continue to use it. If a procedure required both hands, they would hold the knife in their teeth until they needed it again.

In the midst of the arrogance, distrust, and misunderstanding that characterized the American medical establishment's attitude toward Lister's theories, there was a small but growing bastion of doctors who understood the importance of practicing antisepsis, not halfheartedly but precisely. A young surgeon in New York would later write that he and his colleagues had watched with helpless horror the progress of Garfield's medical care. The president's life might have been spared, he wrote with disgust, "had the physician in charge abstained from probing Garfield's wound while he lay on a filthy mattress spread on the floor of a railroad station."

Even as far west as Kansas, Lister's followers sought to intervene on the president's behalf. In a letter to Lucretia the day after the shooting, Dr. E. L. Patee, a highly respected surgeon from Manhattan, Kansas, warned her that she must shield her husband from potentially harmful medical care. "Do not allow probing of the wound," he urged. "Probing generally does more harm than the ball." Although he lived far from what was then considered the center of medical thought in the United States, Patee had read carefully Lister's work and understood its importance. "Saturate everything with carbolic acid," he begged the first lady. "Our whole state is in . . . great grief. God help you."

Unfortunately, young, inexperienced surgeons and rural doctors had little hope of being heard. The morning after Patee wrote to Lucretia, two surgeons arrived at the White House, summoned there by Bliss. David Hayes Agnew, the chief of surgery at the University of Pennsylvania, and Frank Hamilton, a surgeon at the Bellevue Medical College in New York, were "old men," an American doctor would write, "and not likely to be pioneers in a new field of surgery." Both men had attended Lister's talk at the Centennial Exhibition, and both had made it clear that they distrusted his ideas. So vigorously had Agnew and Lister disagreed that day that a journalist covering the conference had written that "these gentlemen used no buttons to their foils. Thrusts were given in earnest." Hamilton had openly questioned the value of antisepsis, while extolling the virtues of his own practice of treating wounds with simple warm water, a common and germ-laden procedure that Lister had long warned "would in many cases sacrifice a limb or a life."

In the five years since he had heard Lister speak, Hamilton's opinions had not changed, and his arrogance, it seemed, had only grown. Soon after reaching the White House, he assured a reporter that the president's care would "bear the severest scrutiny of the experts," and that there was little danger of him dying. "The symptoms are so encouraging," Hamilton said, "that it seems to me the President now has pretty clear sailing. He is fairly in deep water, with no threatening rocks and little danger of running aground."

In his confidence, Hamilton was exceeded only by Bliss, who was impatient to present himself to the American people as the calm, competent leader of the president's medical team. Just a few days after the shooting, he settled into Joseph Stanley Brown's office with a journalist from the *New York Times.* Languidly lighting a cigar, he told the reporter, "I think that we have very little to fear." As a crowd began to gather around him, anxious for news of the president, Bliss warmed to his subject. "President Garfield has made a remarkable journey through this case, and it was a happy wound after all," he assured his audience. "I think it almost certain that we shall pull him through."

As Bliss spoke, smoke from his cigar rising in thick curls and filling the room with a heavy, pungent smell, the bright sky outside Brown's window darkened. Without warning, an afternoon thunderstorm swept through the city. Rain fell in torrents, distorting the trees and river beyond, and lightning illuminated the grounds in short, sharp flashes.

The president, Bliss said, was "the most admirable patient I have ever had. He obeys me to the letter in everything, and he never makes any complaints about my orders."

This quality above all others, Bliss believed, would serve Garfield well. As he had stressed to another reporter only a few days earlier, the president could not hope for better medical care. "If I can't save him," he said, "no one can."

As he sat in his father-in-law's house in Boston, surrounded by chattering children and a wife eager for his attention, Alexander Graham Bell's mind was still churning. Since he had learned of the assassination attempt, he had been able to think of nothing but the president. "I cannot possibly persuade him to sit, just these days," Mabel complained in a letter to her mother. "He is hard at work day and night . . . for the President's benefit."

Bell knew he could find the bullet. He just did not yet know how. His first thought was that he might be able to flood Garfield's body with light. He had read about a patient in Paris whose tumor had been revealed when his doctors inserted an electric light in his stomach, setting him aglow "like a Chinese lantern." After considering Garfield's injury, "it occurred to me," Bell wrote, "that leaden bullets were certainly more opaque than tumors." Deciding to run a few quick tests, he asked his secretary to hold a bullet and a miniature light in his mouth. As he had hoped, Bell could clearly see the bullet, a dark shadow against the young man's illuminated cheek.

In a simplistic way, the technique anticipated the medical X-ray. The problem was that, even if Bell used an intensely bright light in a darkened room, the bullet would have to be very near the surface to be discernible. If it was deep in his back, as Garfield's likely was, hidden behind dense layers of tissue and organs, it would never be seen.

As Bell worried about the flaws in his initial idea, the answer suddenly came to him. What he needed was not a light, but a metal detector. The memory of an earlier invention, he would later write, "returned vividly to my mind."

Four years earlier, while struggling to fend off interference from nearby telegraph wires, which were cluttering his telephone lines with their rapid clicking sounds, Bell had found an ingenious solution. The problem stemmed from the telegraph wires' constantly changing magnetic field, which created, or induced, corresponding currents in the telephone wires. Bell realized that if he split the telephone wire in two and placed one wire on each side of the telegraph line, the currents would cancel each other out. "The currents induced in one of the telephone conductors," he would later explain, "were exactly equal and opposite to those induced in the other." The technique, known as balancing the induction, left the line silent.

The idea had worked, and Bell had patented it in England that same year but had given it little thought since. Now, as he considered the president's wound, he recalled that his tests in 1877 had shown him that his method of balancing induction could not only achieve a quiet line, it could detect metal. "When a position of silence was established," he wrote, "a piece of metal brought within the field of induction caused the telephone to sound."

After "brooding over the problem," Bell realized that he could turn his system for reducing interference into an instrument for finding metal — the induction balance. He would loop two wires into coils, connecting one coil to a telephone receiver and the other to a battery and a circuit interrupter, thus providing the changing current necessary for induction. Then he would arrange the coils so that they overlapped each other just the right amount. He would know he had them perfectly adjusted when the buzzing sound in the receiver disappeared. If he then passed the coils over Garfield's body, the metal bullet would upset the balance, and Bell would literally be able to hear it through the receiver. In this manner, the telephone, his most famous and frustrating invention, would "announce the presence of the bullet."

Bell's instincts told him that the induction balance would work, but he could not be certain until he tested it. Feeling frustrated and helpless in Boston, without his laboratory, his equipment, or his assistant, he once again turned to Charles Williams's electrical shop, where he had met both Watson and Tainter, and where, just seven years earlier, he had built the first telephone. At "great personal inconvenience," Williams did everything he could to help Bell, giving him laboratory space, equipment, and his best men.

Bell, however, still wanted his own man. Tainter, who had continued to work in the Volta Laboratory since the shooting, "received an urgent request from A. G. Bell . . . to join him." The next day, he was on a train bound for Boston. Both men knew that, if they were to have any hope of helping the president, they had to work quickly. Although still little more than an idea in Bell's mind, their invention would be Garfield's only hope of avoiding death at his doctor's hands.

CHAPTER 15
BLOOD-GUILTY

We should do nothing for revenge. . . .
Nothing for the past.

JAMES A. GARFIELD

From his cell deep in the District Jail, Guiteau was gratified to learn that, as he had predicted, General William Tecumseh Sherman had sent out his troops. The heavily armed company of artillery that flanked the somber stone building, however, was there not to free the president's would-be assassin, but to make sure he wasn't dragged outside and lynched. So great was the fear that a mob would overwhelm the prison that its guards had at first denied that Guiteau was even there. "Information had reached them," the *New York Times* reported, "that, should the fact be made known that he was there, the building would be attacked."

After the initial shock of the president's

shooting, the prevailing feeling throughout the country was one of unfettered rage. The fact that Guiteau had been captured and was in jail, awaiting trial, did little to satisfy most Americans' desire for immediate revenge. "There were many who felt intensely dissatisfied that the indignant crowd in Washington was not permitted to wreak summary vengeance on the assassin of the President," one reporter wrote. "Many declared that the proper disposition of him would have been to have held him under the grinding wheels of the railroad train which was to have carried President Garfield away."

Although Guiteau was widely assumed to be insane, the thought that he was alive while the president lay dying was unbearable. "While it seems incredible that a sane man could have done so desperate and utterly inexcusable a deed," a newspaper reported, "the feeling is quite general that it would be best to execute him first and try the question of his sanity afterward." In Brooklyn, as a "roar of indignation went up that echoed from end to end of the town," the mayor declared that "the wretch ought to be hanged whether he was insane or not." Rumors spread that a group of six hundred black men had already formed a lynching party, determined to settle the matter themselves.

Aside from occasional interviews with reporters in the warden's office, Guiteau rarely left his cell, which was even more difficult to reach than Garfield's sickroom in the White House. On the top floor of the prison's south wing, Cell Two belonged to a grim block of seventeen cells known as Murderers' Row. Guiteau's door was sunk three feet into a brick wall and barred with an L-shaped bar, a steel catch, and a lock that held five tumblers. In fact, so famously escape-proof was Guiteau's cell that fifteen years later the renowned magician Harry Houdini would thrill onlookers by escaping from it after allowing himself to be stripped, searched, and locked in.

Although prison officials went to elaborate lengths to make sure their most famous prisoner could not escape, their efforts were unneeded. Guiteau was not going anywhere. He was perfectly content to be in the prison — safe, comfortable, and well fed — while he waited for his friends to free him. In an interview on July 4 with the district attorney and his own lawyer, Guiteau said that Chester Arthur was "a particular friend of mine." At the very least, the vice president would make certain that he would not be punished for his crime. Soon after settling into his cell, Guiteau wrote Arthur a lighthearted letter, giving some advice on the selection of his cabinet and offering a friendly reminder that, without his help, Arthur would not be about to assume the presidency.

While Guiteau planned Arthur's first term, Arthur, unaware of what had happened, was concerned about the political career of only one man — Roscoe Conkling. Since the New York legislature had refused to reinstate Conkling after his dramatic resignation from the Senate, he had embarked on a desperate campaign to regain his seat. Although Conkling was widely known to be the president's fiercest detractor, Arthur had made no effort to conceal his support. On the contrary, so intimately had he been involved in Conkling's reelection bid that he was jeered in the press for "lobbying like any political henchman." *Harper's Weekly* had run a front-page cartoon of Arthur wearing an apron while he shined Conkling's shoes.

Even in the moment when he learned that the president had been shot, Arthur was with Conkling. The two men had just stepped off an overnight steamer from Albany to Manhattan, where they had planned to take a brief break from their lobbying, when Arthur was handed a telegram. As he scanned the message, a reporter waiting anxiously on the dock for his reaction watched as his face blanched with shock.

The thought of Garfield dying terrified Arthur. The vice presidency was a prominent but undemanding job that had suited him well. Now, however, with the president near death, Arthur's position had been suddenly elevated to one of far greater importance than he, or anyone else, had ever believed possible.

Clutching the telegram in his hand, Arthur reacted instinctively, turning, as he always had, to Conkling for direction. Far from frightened by this sudden turn of events, Conkling tucked Arthur even more tightly under his wing. Flagging down a taxi, he quickly steered Arthur into the carriage and climbed in next to him. Rather than seeing the vice president to the train station so that Arthur might take the first express into Washington, or even taking him home, Conkling ordered the driver to take them directly to the Fifth Avenue Hotel, and not spare the whip.

As soon as they arrived at the hotel, however, Conkling could tell that even this bastion of Republican stalwartism had already changed. Across the street, the sidewalk was choked with people struggling to see the front windows of a telegraph office that had posted the most recent bulletins about the president's condition. As Conkling and Arthur entered the hotel and walked through its ornate, marbled lobby, they were greeted not by warm, collegial smiles but by faces fixed in fear and anger. The library, sitting rooms, and bar were overflowing with more than a hundred anxious men, all fighting for a position near a small telegraph office and a beleaguered stock indicator, both of which produced bulletins at excruciatingly long intervals.

A reporter who had spent the morning at the hotel, interviewing powerful political men and listening in on their heated conversations, noticed that the general thinking had already begun to shift. The idea had taken root that something other than insanity may have been behind the president's shooting. "More than one excited man declared his belief," the reporter wrote, "that the murder was a political one." If politics was involved, even tangentially, it followed that only one man could be to blame. "This is the result of placating bosses," a man standing in the hotel bar growled. "If Conkling had not been placated at Chicago, President Garfield would not now be lying on his deathbed."

So suffocatingly crowded was the main lobby that it took Arthur and Conkling ten minutes just to reach the reception desk. By the time Conkling had his hands on the hotel register, he and Arthur were encircled by reporters shouting questions. Quickly signing his name, Conkling, his jaw set and teeth clenched, dropped the pen and strode toward the stairs, a knot of reporters at his heels.

Conkling no doubt assumed that Arthur would be right behind him, but, for the first time since he had taken office, the vice president did not follow his mentor. Making a visible effort to calm himself, Arthur turned to the reporters gathered around him and, his voice shaking, asked what news they had of the president. After hearing the most recent bulletin, Arthur expressed his "great grief and sympathy," and then hurried up the stairs toward Conkling's suite.

As the vice president hunkered down in New York, and Garfield fought for his life in Washington, the nation began to realize that, at any moment, its fate might be suddenly thrust into the hands of Chester Arthur. Across the country, among men and women of both parties, the prospect of Arthur in the White House elicited reactions of horror. Even a prominent Republican groaned, "Chet Arthur? President of the United States? Good God!"

Arthur had never been seen as anything more than Conkling's puppet, with no mind or ambition of his own. A large man with a long, fleshy face, carefully groomed sideburns that swept to his chin, and a heavy mustache that drooped dramatically, Arthur put nearly as much thought into his appearance as did the famously preening Conkling. He had even changed his birth date, quietly moving it forward a year out of what a biographer would term "simple vanity."

Arthur was also widely known as a man of leisure, someone who liked fine clothes, old wine, and dinner parties that lasted late into the night. As collector of the New York Customs House, he had rarely arrived at work before noon. In stark contrast to Garfield, he had been a lackluster student, and even now seemed to have little interest in the life of the mind. "I do not think he knows anything," Harriet Blaine wrote disdainfully of Arthur. "He can quote a verse of poetry or a page from Dickens or Thackery, but these are only leaves springing from a root out of dry ground. His vital forces are not fed, and very soon he has given out his all."

During the campaign, there had been some discussion about the fact that, were Garfield elected, Arthur would be next in line to the presidency, but the possibility of something happening to Garfield had seemed so remote as to be hardly worth considering. He was in the prime of his life, the picture of health and strength, and would be president during a time of peace. Arthur would be constrained by the limits of his office, where he could do little harm. "There is no place in which the powers of mischief will be so small as in the Vice Presidency," E. L. Godkin, the famously acerbic editor of the *Nation,* had then written. "It is true General Garfield . . . may die during his term of office, but this is too unlikely a contingency to be worth making extraordinary provisions for."

Now the unthinkable had happened, and Arthur could become president at any moment. The very idea caused hearts to sink and shoulders to shudder. After giving his readers a cursory review of Arthur's political career, Godkin now wrote with disgust, "It is out of this mess of filth that Mr. Arthur will go to the Presidential chair in case of the President's death."

The unavoidable comparison to Garfield, moreover, did not help Arthur's case. Garfield was "a statesman and a thorough-bred gentleman . . . a man whose mind was filled with great ideas for the good of all," a man at the Fifth Avenue Hotel told a reporter. "Gen. Arthur appears as a politician of the most ordinary character, a man whose sole thought is of political patronage, and a man who has for his bosom friends and intimate companions those with whom no gentleman should associate."

It was Arthur's friends, and, in particular, his close ties to Conkling, that worried Americans even more than his own questionable character. "Republicans and Democrats alike are profoundly disturbed at the probable accession to the Presidency of Vice-President Arthur, with the consequence that Conkling shall be the President de facto," one newspaper reported. In his diary, former president Hayes, whose one term in the White House had been made miserable by Conkling, choked with rage at the thought of his nemesis in such proximity to power. "Arthur for President!" he scrawled in horror in his diary. "Conkling the power behind the throne, superior to the throne!"

Conkling's attacks on the president, which

had continued to make headlines as he fought for reelection to the Senate, now seemed not just petty and vicious, but darkly suspicious. Rumors linking the former senator and the vice president to Guiteau quickly spread. "There is a theory, which has many adherents," a reporter noted, "that the attempted assassination was not the work of a lunatic, but the result of a plot much deeper and darker than has been suspected."

Given the country's tense political situation, this theory may have sprung up without any encouragement at all, but those looking for a conspiracy had been given all the evidence they needed in the words of Guiteau himself. It was already widely known that, as he was being hurried away from the train station, the would-be assassin had shouted, "I am a Stalwart, and Arthur will be president!" Although Guiteau insisted he had acted alone, and both Conkling and Arthur quickly denied any relationship with him, in the minds of the American people the connection had been made.

The rumors and accusations, moreover, were not whispered between friends but shouted from every street corner. Newspapers openly accused Conkling and Arthur of being directly to blame for the tragedy that had befallen the nation. "This crime is as logically and legitimately the result of doctrines of Conkling and his followers as the murder of Lincoln was the result of the teachings of Secessionists," the *Cleveland Herald* charged. "It was not the hand of this miserable office-seeker that armed the deadly blow at the life of Garfield, but the embodied spirit of selfishness, of love of rule, of all that is implied by 'the machine' and the 'one man power,' in a word, of Conklingism and its teachings."

Criticized for going too far and calling Conkling a murderer, the *New York Tribune* denied that it had ever used the word. That said, it wrote, "when a child, in its mad rage, kicks over a table, upsets a lamp, sets the house on fire, and burns people to death, nobody supposes that the child intended murder. Mr. Conkling has been acting like a child in a fit of passion."

So rapidly did the rumors spread that it became dangerous simply to be known as a Stalwart, especially in Conkling's own state. "Men go around with clenched teeth and white lips," one newspaper reported. "If any Stalwart in New York should be seen rejoicing he would be immediately lynched." In a New York prison, two inmates fought so savagely over the possibility of Arthur assuming the presidency that one man killed the other, bludgeoning him to death with an ax.

It did not take Conkling long to understand that neither he nor Arthur was safe from the nation's fury. The lynching parties being formed, he realized, were not for Guiteau alone. "While there is no intimation that Conkling is blood-guilty in this calamity," a reporter in Albany, where Conkling was seeking reelection, wrote, "the country will hold him in a degree blamable."

Even the Fifth Avenue Hotel, where Conkling had for years wielded his political power with the confidence of a king in his palace, no longer promised any refuge. After he had escaped to his rooms on the day of the shooting, Conkling rarely left them. Armed police detectives suddenly appeared, pacing the corridor outside his door. It was clear to everyone present, one reporter wrote, "that the ex-Senator had asked for protection."

Downstairs in the lobby, the hotel's proprietors received an anonymous note. Scrawled on a card, the handwritten message, which had been signed "THE COMMITTEE," read, "Gens: We will hang Conkling and Co. at nine P.M. sharpe."

Born into abject poverty, James Garfield paid for his first year of college by working as the school's carpenter and janitor, but so extraordinary was his academic achievement that by his second year he was promoted to assistant professor of literature and ancient languages. Just before his wedding to Lucretia Rudolph he was made the school's president, at twenty-six years of age.

(Right) Little more than a year after he accepted a seat in the Ohio state senate, Garfield joined the Union Army to fight in the Civil War. Although his service was hailed as heroic and he was quickly promoted to brigadier general, Garfield was haunted by the memory of the young soldiers he had seen killed in battle. "Something went out of him," he told a friend, "that never came back; the sense of the sacredness of life and the impossibility of destroying it."

In 1876, Garfield attended the Centennial Exhibition in Philadelphia to see some of the world's most ambitious scientific and artistic inventions, including the towering hand and torch that were then all that had been completed of the Statue of Liberty. Also at the exhibition were twenty-nine-year-old Alexander Graham Bell and the renowned British surgeon Dr. Joseph Lister.

At the 1880 Republican Convention, Garfield (standing center stage, right side of the photograph) gave the nominating address for John Sherman, then secretary of the treasury. Speaking to a rapt audience, Garfield, who was not a candidate himself, asked a simple question: "And now, gentlemen of the Convention, what do we want?" To his dismay and the crowd's delight, one man shouted, "We want Garfield!"—starting a cascade of support that ended in his nomination.

Three days after Garfield's surprise nomination, a dangerously delusional young man named Charles Guiteau boarded the steamship *Stonington* for an overnight crossing from Connecticut to New York that ended tragically in a fiery maritime disaster. To Guiteau, his survival meant that he had been chosen by God for a task of great importance.

On November 2, 1880, Garfield was elected the twentieth president of the United States. Although he approached his presidency with a characteristic sense of purpose, he mourned the quiet, contemplative life he was about to lose. "There is a tone of sadness running through this triumph," he wrote, "which I can hardly explain."

(Left) The greatest threat to Garfield's presidency came from within his own party, in the person of Roscoe Conkling, a preening senior Republican senator from New York and arguably the most powerful man in the country. Although he expected the new president to bend to his will, Conkling found in Garfield a surprisingly unyielding opponent. "Of course I deprecate war," Garfield wrote, "but if it is brought to my door the bringer will find me at home."

(Below) Conkling's most loyal minion was Garfield's own vice president, Chester Arthur. Arthur, who had been forced upon Garfield as a running mate, did nothing to disguise his loyalties, even after the election. Others bewailed his lack of credentials, noting that Arthur "never held an office except the one he was removed from."

Never comfortable in her role as first lady, Lucretia Garfield was as quiet and reserved as her husband was warm and expansive. The early years of their marriage had been difficult, but over time Garfield had fallen deeply in love with his wife. "The tyranny of our love is sweet," he wrote to her. "We waited long for his coming, but he has come to stay."

When they moved into the White House after Garfield's inauguration, James and Lucretia brought with them their five children (from left to right: Abram, James, Mollie, Irvin, and Harry), as well as James's widowed mother, Eliza. "Slept too soundly to remember any dream," Lucretia wrote in her diary after her family's first night in the White House. "And so our first night among the shadows of the last 80 years gave no forecast of our future."

(Below) Although thousands of office seekers flooded Brown's office, one man stood out as an "illustration of unparalleled audacity." Charles Guiteau visited the White House and the State Department nearly every day, inquiring about the consulship to France he believed the president owed him. Finally, after months of polite but firm discouragement, Guiteau received what he felt was a divine inspiration: God wanted him to kill the president.

(Above) At just twenty-three years of age, Joseph Stanley Brown was the youngest man ever to hold the office of private secretary to the president. Brown's most difficult job was keeping at bay the hoards of office seekers who demanded to see the president. "These people," Garfield told his young secretary, "would take my very brains, flesh and blood if they could."

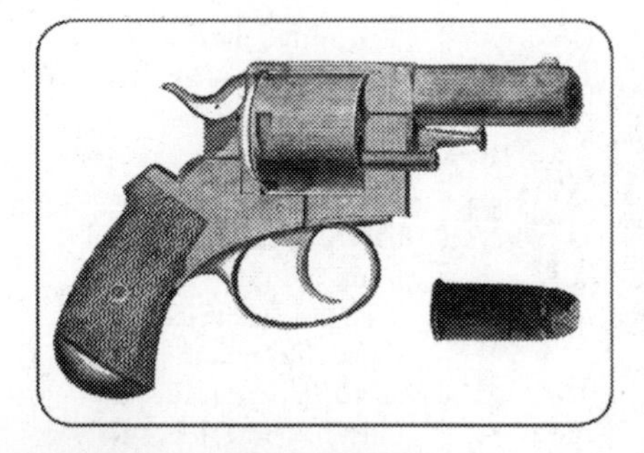

In mid-June, Guiteau, who had survived for years by slipping out just before his rent was due, borrowed fifteen dollars and bought a gun—a .44 caliber British Bulldog with an ivory handle. Having never before fired a gun, he took it to the Potomac River and practiced shooting at a sapling. "I knew nothing about it," he said, "no more than a child."

On the morning of July 2, Garfield and his secretary of state, James Blaine *(left)*, arrived at the Baltimore and Potomac train station *(below)*, where Guiteau, who had been stalking the president for more than a month, was waiting for him. The assassin's gun was loaded, his shoes were polished, and in his suit pocket was a letter to General William Tecumseh Sherman. "I have just shot the President . . . ," it read. "Please order out your troops, and take possession of the jail at once."

Just moments after Garfield and Blaine entered the waiting room, Guiteau pulled the trigger. The first shot passed through the president's right arm, but the second sent a bullet ripping through his back. Garfield's knees buckled, and he fell to the train station floor, bleeding and vomiting, as the station erupted in screams.

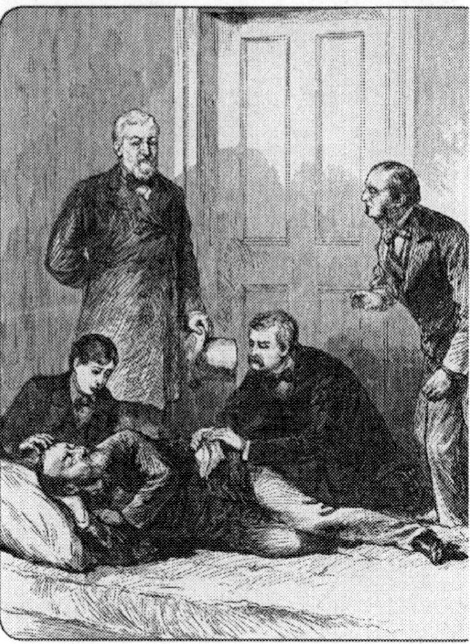

(Right) While Guiteau was quickly captured and taken into custody, Garfield was carried on a horsehair mattress to an upstairs room in the train station. Surrounded by ten different doctors, each of whom wanted to examine the president, Garfield lay, silent and unflinching, as the men repeatedly inserted unsterilized fingers and instruments into the wound, searching for the bullet.

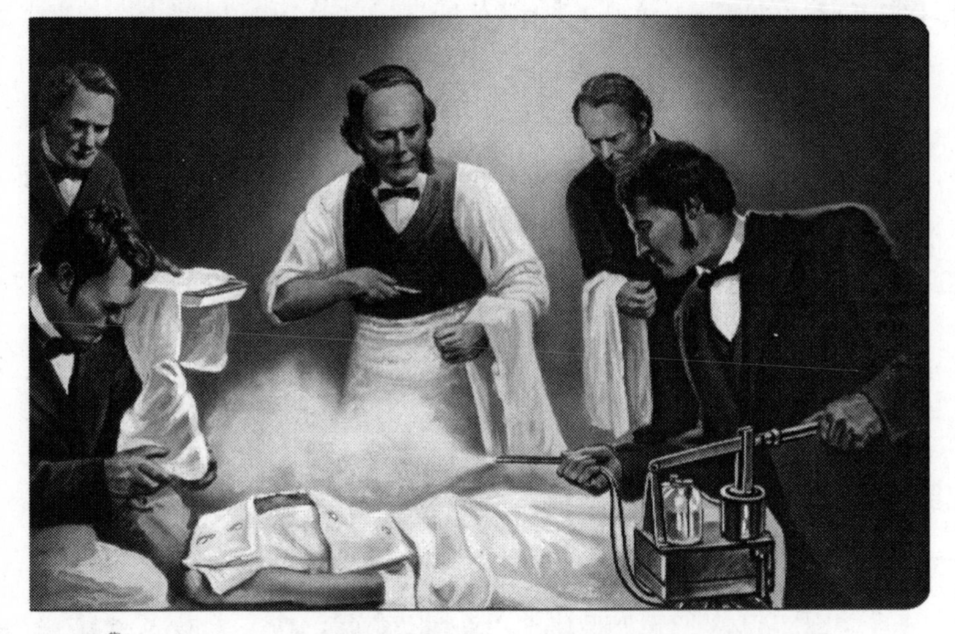

Sixteen years before Garfield's shooting, Joseph Lister had achieved dramatic results using carbolic acid to sterilize his operating room, and his method had been adopted in much of Europe. In the United States, however, the most experienced physicians still refused to use Lister's technique, complaining that it was too time-consuming, and dismissing it as unnecessary, even ridiculous.

Although a crowd of nervous doctors hovered over Garfield at the train station, Robert Todd Lincoln, Garfield's secretary of war and Abraham Lincoln's only surviving son, quickly took charge, sending his carriage for Dr. D. Willard Bliss *(left)*, one of the surgeons who had been at his father's deathbed. Bliss, a strict traditionalist, was confident that the president could not hope to find a better physician. "If I can't save him," he told a reporter, "no one can."

Soon after Garfield was brought to the White House, Bliss dismissed the other doctors, keeping only a handful of physicians and surgeons who reported directly to him. Dr. Susan Edson, one of the first female doctors in the country and Lucretia's personal physician, insisted on staying, even though Bliss refused to let her provide anything but the most basic nursing services to the president.

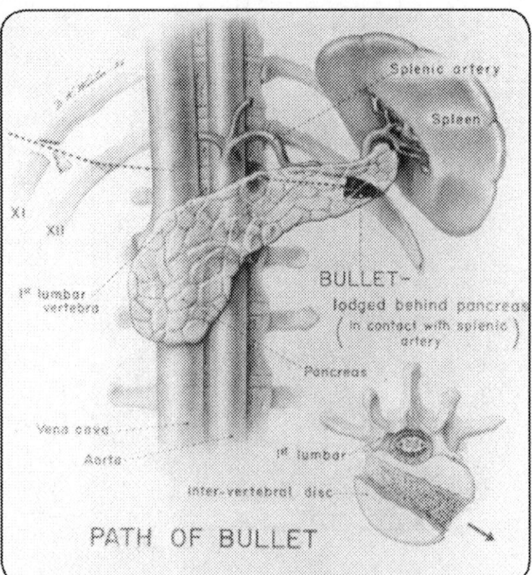

Guiteau's bullet *(above)*, which entered Garfield's back four inches to the right of his spinal column, broke two of his ribs and grazed an artery. Miraculously, it did not hit any vital organs or his spinal cord as it continued its trajectory to the left, finally coming to rest behind his pancreas. The bullet had done all the harm it was going to do, but Bliss had only begun.

After returning Garfield to the White House, which although crumbling and rat infested was preferable to the overcrowded hospitals, Bliss continued to search for the bullet. Garfield had survived the shooting, but he now faced an even more serious threat to his life: the infection that his doctors repeatedly introduced as they probed the wound in his back.

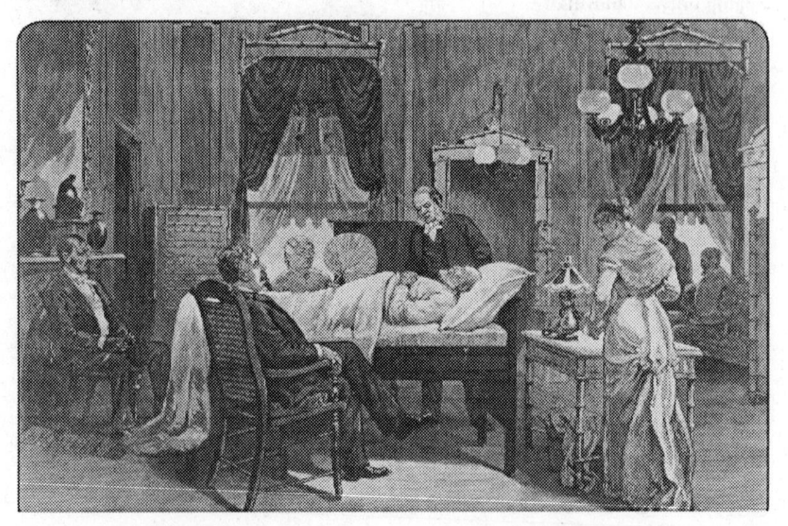

Although he allowed almost no one to visit the president, Bliss regularly issued medical bulletins, which were posted at telegraph offices and on wooden billboards outside newspaper buildings. “Everywhere people go about with lengthened faces,” one reporter wrote, “anxiously inquiring as to the latest reported condition of the president.”

As soon as he learned of the shooting, Alexander Graham Bell *(left)*, who had a laboratory in Washington, D.C., began to think of ways the bullet might be found. Sickened by the thought of Garfield's doctors blindly "search[ing] with knife and probe," he reasoned that "science should be able to discover some less barbarous method." Bell quickly decided that what he needed was a metal detector. Four years earlier, he had invented a device to get rid of the static in telephone lines, and he now recalled that, when a piece of metal came near the invention, it caused the sound to return. Bell was confident that the invention, which he called an induction balance *(right)*, could be modified to "announce the presence of the bullet."

Bell (at right, with his ear to the telephone receiver) twice attempted to find the bullet in Garfield using the induction balance. Bliss, however (leaning over Garfield with the induction balance), allowed Bell to search only the president's right side, where Bliss believed, and had publicly stated, the bullet was lodged.

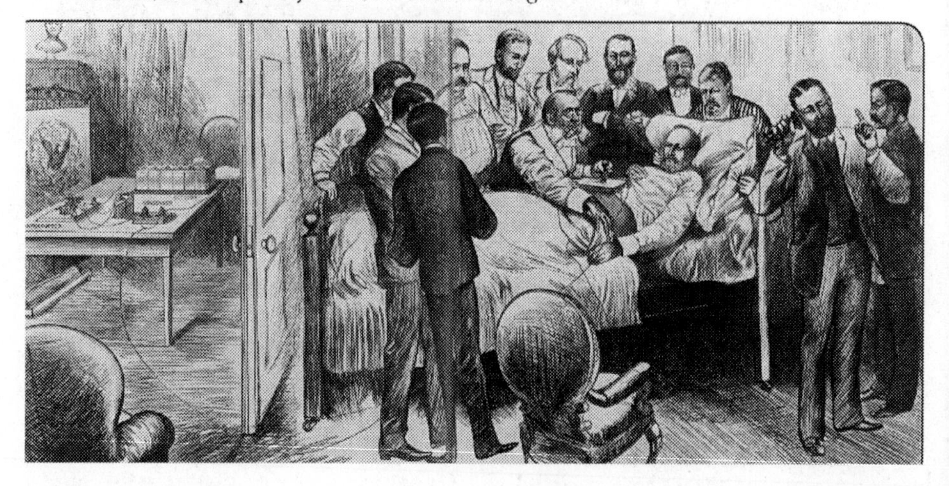

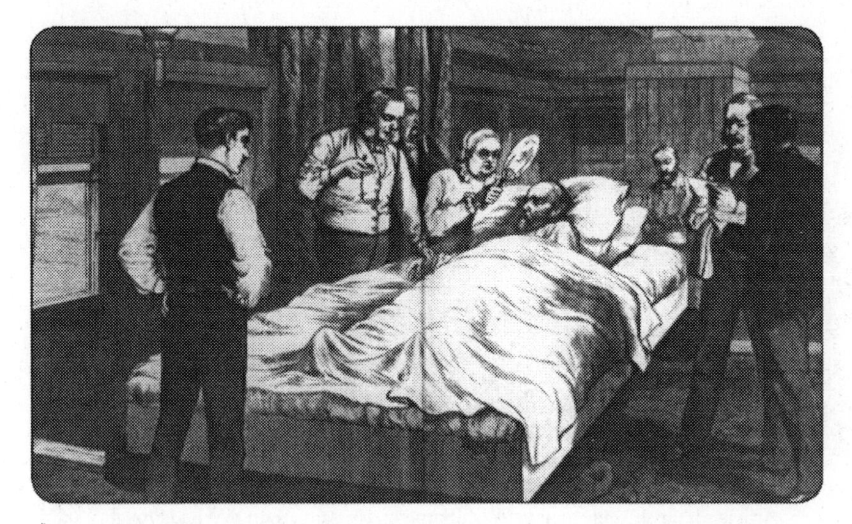

After spending two months in his sickroom in the White House, Garfield finally insisted that he be moved. A wealthy New Yorker offered his summer home in Elberon, New Jersey, and a train was carefully renovated for the wounded president. Wire gauze was wrapped around the outside to protect him from smoke, and the seats inside were removed, thick carpeting laid on the floors, and a false ceiling inserted to help cool the car.

When the train reached Elberon, it switched to a track that would take it directly to the door of Franklyn Cottage. Two thousand people had worked until dawn to lay the track, but the engine was not strong enough to breach the hill on which the house sat. "Instantly hundreds of strong arms caught the cars," Bliss wrote, "and silently . . . rolled the three heavy coaches" up the hill.

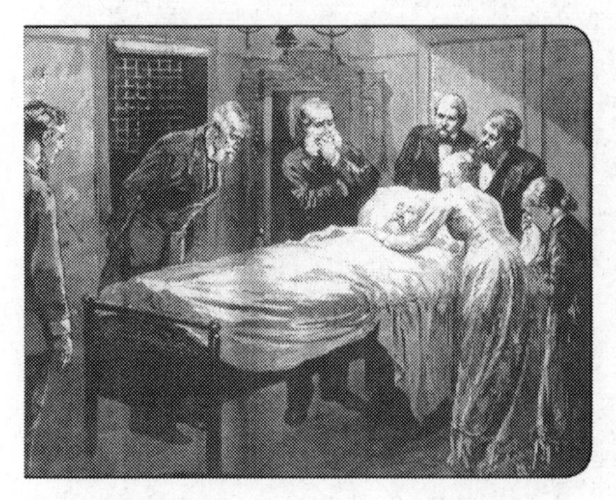

At ten o'clock on the night of September 19, Garfield suddenly cried out in pain. Bliss rushed to the room, but the president was already dying. As Garfield slipped away, "a faint, fluttering pulsation of the heart, gradually fading to indistinctness," he was surrounded by his wife and daughter, and his young secretary, Joseph Stanley Brown—"the witnesses," Bliss would later write, "of the last sad scene in this sorrowful history."

Garfield's body was returned to Washington on the same train that had brought him to Elberon just two weeks earlier. Thousands of people lined the tracks as the train, now swathed in black, passed by. The White House was also draped in mourning, as were the buildings through which a procession of some one hundred thousand mourners wound, waiting to see the president's body as it lay in state in the Capitol rotunda.

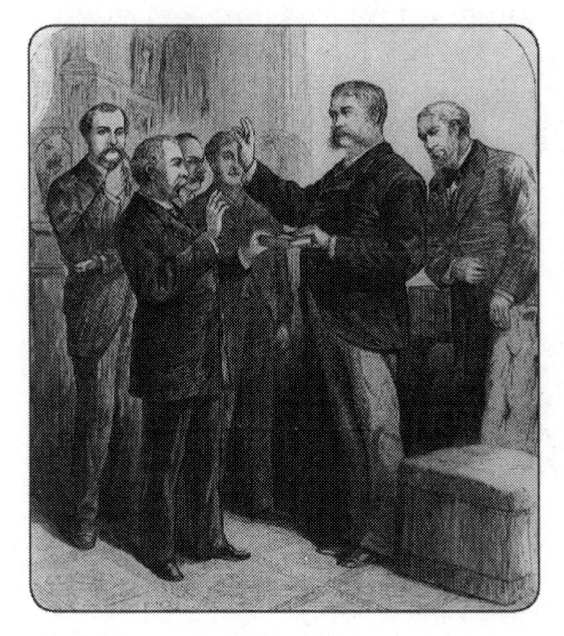

When news of Garfield's death reached New York, reporters rushed to Arthur's house, but his doorkeeper refused to disturb him. The vice president was "sitting alone in his room," he said, "sobbing like a child." A few hours later, at 2:15 a.m., Arthur was quietly sworn into office by a state judge in his own parlor.

After a trial that lasted more than two months, Guiteau was found guilty and sentenced to death. Twenty thousand people requested tickets to the execution. Two hundred and fifty invitations were issued. Guiteau was hanged on June 30, 1882, two days before the anniversary of Garfield's shooting.

Wardens' Office U. S. Jail,
Washington, D. C.

Mr. C. V. Henry.
U S Marshal + Deputies, You are respectfully invited to witness the execution of Charles J. Guiteau, at this jail Friday June 30th 1882;
between the hours of 12 M., and 2 o'clock P. M.

John S. Crocker
Warden.

Had it not been for her children, "life would have meant very little" to Lucretia after her husband's death. When this photograph was taken of the former first lady with her grandchildren in 1906, she had already been a widow for a quarter of a century. Lucretia would live another twelve years, thirty-seven years longer than James.

In the years following Garfield's death, Bell continued to invent, helped to found the National Geographic Society, established a foundation for the deaf, and did what he could for those who needed him most. In 1887, he met Helen Keller and soon after helped her find her teacher, Annie Sullivan. Keller would remember her meeting with Bell as the "door through which I should pass from darkness into light."

Part Four: Tortured for the Republic

Chapter 16
Neither Death nor Life

> I love to believe that no heroic sacrifice is ever lost, that the characters of men are moulded and inspired by what their fathers have done.
>
> JAMES A. GARFIELD

Just two weeks after the attempt on the president's life, Alexander Graham Bell was back in Washington. Although his wife, Mabel, was nearing the advanced stages of her pregnancy and he worried over her, admonishing her not to use the stairs more than necessary and to rest as often as possible, he had not hesitated to leave her. He had promised that they would spend the hottest part of the summer in Maine, but that trip, like everything else in his life, would now have to wait.

A few days earlier, he had contacted Dr. D. Willard Bliss to offer his help in locating the bullet inside the president. Although

Bliss was not in the habit of consulting with inventors, Bell had two factors in his favor — his fame and Bliss's fear. As he watched Garfield's temperature ominously rise, Bliss had quietly agreed to meet with the young scientist.

As his train pulled into the station, Bell knew that the president's private secretary, Joseph Stanley Brown, would be waiting for him. Brown quickly spotted Bell and his assistant Tainter in the rush of people pouring from the train and led them to a carriage that was waiting to take them directly to the White House. As they left the station, Bell could see that the hysteria he had witnessed on the day of the shooting had passed. Left in its wake was a palpable feeling of tension and nervousness. The usually noisy, chaotic city was somber and strangely quiet, as if every man were holding his breath. The only pockets of bustling activity were around telegraph stations and newspaper offices, where Bliss's bulletins were posted on enormous wooden billboards. "Everywhere people go about with lengthened faces, anxiously inquiring as to the latest reported condition of the president and sadly speculating at the probable outcome of this terrible affair," one newspaper reported.

The entire city was on a deathwatch, and

everything, from day-to-day activities to special events, had been postponed, or, in many cases, canceled altogether. Even the Fourth of July celebrations had been called off, for the first time in the city's history. That morning, the only outward recognition of Independence Day in the nation's capital had been the raising of the flag on the White House grounds, and even that had been nothing more than a quiet message to a terrified people that their president still lived. "Men looked eagerly to the flagpole this morning," a reporter had written that day, "fearing to see the ensign at half mast, and breathed a sigh of relief when they found it floated from the top of the pole."

When the carriage reached the White House, it became clear that the nation had changed not just suddenly, but fundamentally and irretrievably. Where once an old policeman and a young secretary had been the only barriers between a president and his people, there now stood armed sentinels, flanking the White House as if it were the palace of a king. A reporter mournfully described the sun rising on the capital and looking "down upon the Executive Mansion of a free country guarded by soldiers." As frightening and un-American as this sight seemed, it did not keep people away. On the contrary, hundreds of people were sprawled out on the lawns just outside the White House gates, many with picnic baskets and blankets, some who had clearly been sleeping there for days, anxious for news.

Bell's carriage was quickly ushered through the gates, but his meeting with Bliss was brief. The two men discussed the basic theory behind the induction balance and then made arrangements for the doctor to visit the Volta Laboratory to see the invention for himself. Before leaving, Bell turned to Brown and handed him a small gift he had carried on his lap from Boston — a basket of grapes that Mabel had sent for Lucretia. Attached was a note that read, "To Mrs. Garfield, a slight token of sympathy from Mr. & Mrs. Alexander Graham Bell." Brown assured Bell that the first lady would receive the gift. Then he handed Bell something in return, something that he had given to only a very few people — a card that gave the bearer access to the White House at any time, day or night.

As Bell climbed back into the carriage, eager to return to his laboratory and begin work, Garfield lay in his isolated room on the south side of the White House, where he had been confined to his bed for nearly two weeks, unable to walk or even sit up. Although his temperature had fallen slightly, he was still sweating profusely, his arms and legs were cold, and pus was freely flowing through the drainage tube that his surgeons had inserted that day. On Bliss's orders, he had been given rum, wine, and an injection of morphine, which he had received at least once a day, every day, since the shooting.

Although Garfield rarely mentioned it, his doctors knew that he was in excruciating pain. He suffered from what Bliss described as "severe lancinating," or stabbing, pains in his "scrotum, feet and ankles." Garfield admitted that the pain felt like "tiger's claws" on his legs, but tried to reassure those around him. "They don't usually stay long," he told his friend Rockwell after waking from a fitful sleep one night. "Don't be alarmed."

More difficult for Garfield to deny than the pain was the violent vomiting that often seized him. On the morning of the Fourth of July, as plans for celebrations were being hastily canceled, the president vomited every twenty minutes for two hours. Since then, the vomiting and nausea had slowed, but continued to come in unpredictable waves.

Garfield had for years suffered from severe stomach ailments. He had endured chronic dysentery during the Civil War and later battled dyspepsia so extreme that at one point he was confined to bed for nearly two weeks. Finally, a doctor told him that he would have to have a section of his intestines removed. Garfield had avoided such drastic measures, but he carefully controlled his diet, even carrying with him to Congress a lunch that his doctors had prescribed — a sandwich of raw beef on stale bread.

Under Bliss's care, however, the president's diet changed dramatically and, for the victim of a gunshot wound, inexplicably. He received a wide variety of rich foods, from bacon and lamb chops to steak and potatoes. Boynton, Garfield's cousin and one of the doctors whom Bliss had demoted to nursing status, openly criticized the way the president was being fed. "He was nauseated . . . with heavy food," Boynton told the *New York Herald.* "He was given a dose of brandy that capped the climax, and he threw up everything, and a severe fit of vomiting followed."

Although Garfield was dangerously ill, the idea of taking him to a hospital was never considered. Hospitals were only for people who had nowhere else to go. "No sick or injured person who could possibly be nursed at home or in a medical man's private residence," one doctor wrote, "would choose . . . to enter the squalid and crowded wards of the public institutions." They were dimly lit, poorly ventilated, and vastly overpopulated. The stench was unbearable, and ubiquitous. "Patients, no matter how critical their need," one reporter noted, "dread the very name of hospital."

Unfortunately for Garfield, the White House was not much better. The structure had been built into sloping ground, and water constantly trickled in, keeping three layers of floors, two of which were made of unmortared brick, perpetually damp. The servants' living quarters were dark, cold, and dank. The kitchen, which was underneath the central hallway, was almost beyond repair, with whitewash peeling from the ceilings and sifting down into the cooking pots.

Over the years, the moist rooms and rotting woodwork had proved irresistible to the rats that roamed the city and woods. By the time Garfield and his family had moved in, the entire house was, in the words of one reporter, "packed with vermin from cellar to garret." At night, when the office seekers had finally abandoned their hopes for the day and the staff had retired to their rooms, the family could hear rats scampering under the floorboards and rustling in the pantries.

Worse than the whitewash in the soup or even the rats in the flour bins, however, was the house's antiquated plumbing system. An inspection found that it did not even meet the most basic "sanitary requirements of a safe dwelling." Much of the plumbing, one inspector noted, was "defective — not a little of it radically so." The plumbing system had been built nearly half a century earlier and could not hope to hold up under the daily demands of waste from seven bathrooms in the primary living quarters, as well as the servants' chambers, the kitchen, and the pantries. Many of the pipes had long since disintegrated, leaving the soil under the basement saturated with "foul matters."

The decrepit condition of the White House was no secret to the outside world. One New York newspaper referred to it derisively as a "pest house" and argued that it should be torn down altogether. "The old White House is unfit for longer use as a Presidential residence," the *Washington Post* declared. "Indeed, it has not, for many years, been suitable for such occupancy."

Even if the mansion itself had been in good repair, its location was among the worst in Washington. The south lawn ended at the edge of the Potomac's infamous tidal marsh. Although no one then understood that malaria was carried by mosquitoes, they had made the link between the "bad air" for which the disease was named and the marsh. When the "notoriously unhealthy" house had been blamed for Lucretia's illness, former president Hayes had rushed to its defense, insisting that it was a perfectly safe place to live. Even Hayes, however, had moved to the Soldiers' Home in the higher, cooler northwest section of the city every summer, from early July until after the first frost in October, as had Presidents Lincoln and Buchanan before him.

There was now deep concern that the president was being "greatly influenced by the miasma generated by the marshes." Four servants in the White House had already fallen ill with malaria, and Garfield's doctors felt certain that if he were to contract the disease, he would not survive it. In a desperate effort to ward off malaria, they gave him five to ten grains of quinine every day. Unfortunately, the dangers of the drug are many. Not only can quinine be toxic if taken in large doses, but it can also bring on severe intestinal cramping, thus causing further trauma to Garfield's already ravaged digestive system.

Even away from the marsh, the city itself seemed noxious and diseased. Raw sewage floated down the Potomac, coating the thick summer air with a hazy stench, and dust and dirt settled over everything, from buildings to people. "You can't imagine anything so vile as Washington," Harriet Blaine wrote in disgust. "It seems like a weed by the wayside, covered with dust, too ugly for notice." The temperature hovered at 90 degrees. "Scarcely a breath of air was stirring," one reporter moaned, "and the air was heavy and sultry." The little breeze there was, moreover, came from the north, never reaching Garfield's room on the White House's southern side.

The oppressive heat, and the misery they knew it must be causing the president, prompted many Americans to write to the first lady, suggesting ways in which she might help her husband. "Sitting to day on my piazza, suffering from the great heat, my mind turned to Mr. Garfield," one man wrote from Georgia, "and it occurred to me that the air of his sick room might be cooled to any degree you wish by having sufficient ice in [the] room over his room, and let cold air down by pipes." Others suggested hanging sheets that had been dipped in ice water in Garfield's room, piling ice on the floor, and even placing large pieces of marble on the furniture.

Finally, a corps of engineers from the navy and a small contingent of scientists, which included Garfield's old friend, the famed explorer and geologist John Wesley Powell, stepped in and designed what would become the country's first air conditioner. To cool Garfield's room, which was twenty feet long, twenty-five feet wide, and eighteen feet high, the men determined that they would need at least three tons of ice. In the president's office, they set up an elaborate system comprised of a thirty-six-inch electric fan that forced air through cheesecloth screens that had been soaked in ice water and placed in a six-foot-long iron box. The cooled air was then conducted into the president's room through a series of tin pipes.

Although the system worked, cooling the air to a miraculous 55 degrees as it entered the pipes, the first trials brought Garfield more misery than relief. The damp cheesecloth made the air not just cool but heavily humid. Worse, although the air conditioner was in the president's office, its perpetual grinding and whirring filled his bedroom with an ear-splitting racket. So deafening was the sound that Garfield, summoning the little strength he had, finally called out for someone to turn the contraption off.

Unbowed, the engineers set to work to fix the problems. First, they placed a 134-gallon icebox between the iron box and the pipes, which, one scientist happily reported, produced air that was "cool, dry, and ample in supply." Then, realizing that the tin pipes amplified the noise, they quickly replaced them with ones made of canvas-covered wire, which absorbed the sounds, leaving Garfield, at long last, in relatively cool, quiet peace.

No one appreciated all that was being done to ease his suffering and save his life more than Garfield himself. Despite the fact that his health, his work, and quite possibly his life had been suddenly and senselessly taken from him, he remained unfailingly cheerful and kind, day after day. His doctors marveled at him, calling him a "wonderfully patient sufferer." Bliss would later recall that, throughout Garfield's illness, he "never approached him without meeting an extended hand, and an expression of thankful recognition of the efforts being made for his comfort and recovery." Each time, after the doctors had dressed his wounds, a long and painful daily process, Garfield would always say, in a hearty voice, "Thank you, gentlemen."

While Garfield's body had begun to fail him, his courtesy never did, nor his sense of humor. He had always been "witty, and quick at repartee," a former college classmate recalled, "but his jokes . . . were always harmless, and he would never willingly hurt another's feelings." Garfield now used humor to put those around him at ease. He gave his attendants affectionate nicknames, teasingly referring to one particularly fussy nurse as "the beneficent bore." "The vein of his conversation was . . . calculated to cheer up his friends and attendants," a reporter wrote, recalling how, when a messenger sent to buy a bottle of brandy returned with two, Garfield joked that he would now have to receive a "double allowance."

Garfield was painfully aware of the widespread fear and suffering on his behalf, and he wanted desperately to lighten the burden, even on those who had made themselves his enemies. Although they had done their best to destroy his presidency, Garfield made it clear that he did not for a moment believe the rumors linking Chester Arthur and Roscoe Conkling to Guiteau. Too weak to read the newspaper himself, he often listened as Lucretia read to him. One day, she stumbled upon a paragraph that directly blamed the vice president and former senator for the shooting. Hearing this, Garfield vehemently shook his head. "I do not believe that," he said.

Although Garfield rarely mentioned the man who had tried to assassinate him, he could not help but wonder why anyone would do something so strange and inexplicably cruel. Finally, turning to Blaine, he asked, "What motive do you think that man could have had?" His old friend replied quietly, "I do not know Mr. President. He says he had no motive. He must be insane."

Chapter 17
One Nation

> There is no horizontal Stratification of society in this country like the rocks in the earth, that hold one class down below forevermore, and let another come to the surface to stay there forever. Our Stratification is like the ocean, where every individual drop is free to move, and where from the sternest depths of the mighty deep any drop may come up to glitter on the highest wave that rolls.
>
> JAMES A. GARFIELD

For the first time in their memory, certainly since the earliest beginnings of the Civil War, Americans facing the shared tragedy of Garfield's ordeal felt a deep and surprising connection to one another. Divided by vast stretches of dangerous wilderness and stark differences in race, religion, and culture, there had been little beyond severely strained notions of common citizenship to unite them. The assassination of Abraham Lincoln sixteen years earlier had only deepened that divide. But the attempt on Garfield's life aroused feelings of patriotism that many Americans had long since forgotten, or never knew they had.

The waves of emotion that swept over the country, moreover, were fed not only by the fact that America's president had been attacked in the train station that morning, but that that president had been Garfield. To his countrymen, a staggeringly diverse array of people, Garfield was at the same time familiar and extraordinary, a man who represented both what they were and what they hoped to be. Although he had been elevated to the highest seat of power, he was still, and would always be, one of their own.

A nation of immigrants, the United States found in Garfield a president who knew well the brutal indignities of poverty, and the struggle to overcome them. Between 1850 and 1930, the country's foreign-born population would rise from more than two million to more than fourteen million. This flood of people, known as the "new immigrants," came from a broader range of countries and with a greater number of languages than ever before. In Garfield's humble origins, remarkable rise, and soaring erudition, they found justification for their sacrifices, and hope for their children.

In the West, those Americans who had endured the perils and hardship of the frontier to find a better life knew Garfield not only as a child of poverty but as the son of pioneers. Although it was still a long and difficult journey from any part of the West to Washington, Garfield himself was a powerful link to the world of covered wagons and dirt farms. Since he had taken office, settlers, living on land they had cleared themselves and which, every day, they fought to defend, had felt secure in one thing at least, that they would not be forgotten in their nation's capital.

For freed slaves, an impoverished and, until recently, almost entirely powerless segment of the population, Garfield represented freedom and progress, but also, and perhaps more importantly, dignity. As president, he demanded for black men nothing less than what they wanted most desperately for themselves — complete and unconditional equality, born not of regret but respect. "You were not made free merely to be allowed to vote, but in order to enjoy an equality of opportunity in the race of life," Garfield had told a delegation of 250 black men just before he was elected president. "Permit no man to praise you because you are black, nor wrong you because you are black. Let it be known that you are ready and willing to work out your own material salvation by your own energy, your own worth, your own labor."

Even in the South, where he had once been hated and feared as an abolitionist and Union general, there was a surprising pride in Garfield's presidency. Although he had made it clear from the moment he took office, even in his inaugural address, that he would not tolerate the discrimination he knew was taking place in the South, what he promised was not judgment and vengeance but help. The root of the problem, he believed, was ignorance, and it was the responsibility, indeed "the high privilege and sacred duty," of the entire nation, North and South, to educate its people.

Garfield's plan was to "give the South, as rapidly as possible, the blessings of general education and business enterprise and trust to time and these forces." The South had taken him at his word, and, for the first time in decades, had accepted the president of the North as its president as well. With Garfield in the White House, the *New York Times* wrote, Southerners "felt, as they had not felt before for years, that the Government . . . was their Government, and that the chief magistrate of the country had an equal claim upon the loyal affection of the whole people."

Although each of these disparate groups trusted Garfield, it was not until they were plunged into a common grief and fear that they began to trust one another. Suddenly, a contemporary of Garfield's wrote, the nation was "united, as if by magic." Even Jefferson Davis, the former president of the Confederacy and a man whom Garfield had voted to indict as a war criminal, admitted that the assassination attempt had made "the whole Nation kin."

Together, Americans waited for news of the president's condition, helpless to prevent what they feared most. Although Garfield had not died in the attack, neither had he yet been saved. He was in an agonizing place in between, and as he suffered, so did his countrymen. Unable to rejoice or mourn, they waited in silence, and prayed as if they were at the sickbed not of a president but a brother.

What made the suffering even harder to bear was that, despite the fury directed at men like Conkling and Arthur, it was devastatingly clear that there was nothing and no one to blame. In no man's mind save the assassin's had the shooting achieved anything. It had not been carried out in the name of personal or political freedom, national unity, or even war. It had addressed no wrong, been the consequence of no injustice.

Garfield's shooting had also revealed to the American people how vulnerable they were. In the little more than a century since its inception, the United States had become a powerful and respected country. Yet Americans suddenly realized that they still had no real control over their own fate. Not only could they not prevent a tragedy of such magnitude, they couldn't even anticipate it. The course of their lives could be changed in an instant, by a man who did not even understand what he had done.

As he waited cheerfully in Cell Two, Charles Guiteau felt no remorse for his actions, or even fear for his life. He was, in fact, happier now than he had ever been. Having long thirsted for fame and recognition, he found the intense interest in his life and the frenzy of activity that surrounded him at the District Jail not terrifying but thrilling. "I felt lighthearted and merry the moment I got into that cell," he would later say.

Although reporters visited him on Murderers' Row in a steady stream, they recoiled when they met him. Even the most seasoned journalists were sickened by the arrogance and enthusiasm with which he recounted his plans to murder the president. "His vanity is literally nauseating," one reporter, Edmund Bailey, wrote. "Guiteau has an idea that the civilized world is holding its breath waiting to hear of the minutest details of his career."

Anxious to control what he was asked and how he was perceived, Guiteau wrote up a list of subjects that he wanted to cover, and brought the list with him to interviews. He also encouraged reporters to describe him in detail, from his dress to his demeanor, and he labored to give them his best stories, told with an almost theatrical flourish. "He spoke with deliberation," Bailey recalled, "occasionally emphasizing, somewhat dramatically, with his voice or by gesture, a remark which he deemed of transcendent importance, or chuckling at the mention of some incident which he considered amusing."

As much as he was enjoying himself, Guiteau expected to be shown respect during the interviews, even deference. He saw himself not as a man reviled by an entire country but as a national hero and the object of widespread fascination. "He objected strenuously to the 'continuity of his thought' being disturbed by interruption," Bailey wrote, "and frequently stated so in a most imperious way, intimating that the interruption had placed in immediate jeopardy of destruction some thought of vital interest and importance to the community."

Guiteau's desire for control extended even to the photographer who was sent to the prison to take his picture. He had always been extremely particular about how he was photographed, giving detailed instructions about every feature and flaw. "I want you to be sure and take a good picture of me," he once told a photographer. "Be sure you get the right expression of my face and eyes, and I think you had better not take a side view." Now, with the world watching, he was almost frantic in his concern that the picture be flattering. "I don't want to appear strained and awkward," he said as he sat down before the camera in the prison's rotunda. "If my picture is taken at all it must be a good one." Before returning to his cell, he asked the photographer for a $25 royalty fee.

Having lived most of his adult life in dire poverty, surviving only by stealing, cheating, and borrowing, Guiteau spent much of his time in prison planning ways to make money. He believed that he would be released on bail by the fall, at which time he planned to go on a speaking tour that, he was confident, would earn tens of thousands of dollars. He also expected to now generate a considerable income from sales of his book, *The Truth.* Nor was he above selling personal items. In particular, he hoped to auction off the thin, ragged suit he had been wearing when he shot the president, which he hoped would bring a high price because of its historical value.

Beyond his financial needs, Guiteau did not worry about his own fate. As soon as Arthur was made president, he expected grateful Stalwarts to begin visiting him "by the hundreds." He also insisted that the American people were on his side. He was not allowed to read newspapers while in prison, the one deprivation he felt, but even if he had seen the countless editorials that demanded his hanging or the articles that described angry mobs forming across the country, Guiteau would not have believed them. He vowed that, if he were to be tried — and he did not think Arthur would let that happen — "a conviction would shock the public."

So carefree was Guiteau, he was quickly

putting on weight. While the president was unable to keep anything down, had literally begun to starve, his would-be assassin ate everything he could get his hands on. By the time the summer was out, Guiteau would gain 10 pounds, a substantial amount of weight for a man who had been only 135 pounds when he was brought through the prison gates.

Guiteau also began to make plans for his future. Although by now he was used to being alone, he felt that it was time to remarry, and that he should take advantage of his newly won fame to find a wife. Having offered his autobiography for publication to the *New York Herald,* he tacked onto the end a personal note. "I am looking for a wife and see no objection to mentioning it here. I want an elegant Christian lady of wealth, under thirty, belonging to a first-class family. Any such lady can address me in the utmost confidence."

Guiteau also used his autobiography to announce his candidacy for president, a decision he believed the American people would not only welcome but actively encourage. "For twenty years, I have had an idea that I should be President," he wrote. "My idea is that I shall be nominated and elected as Lincoln and Garfield were — that is, by the act of God. . . . My object would be to unify the entire American people, and make them happy, prosperous and God-fearing."

While Guiteau sank deeper into delusion and the country staggered under the weight of shock and grief, a thin ray of hope shone late into the night, every night, in a small laboratory on Connecticut Avenue. From the moment he had left the White House, Alexander Graham Bell had begun work in earnest, thrilled to be back in his own laboratory, where there was little danger of interruption or distraction. He had often worked under intense pressure, under the threat of humiliation, even professional and financial ruin, but he had never before felt the weight of another man's life in his hands.

Bent over a long, rectangular work bench made of unpainted wood, Bell stared at the latest incarnation of his induction balance, modified to find a bullet in a man's back. He had been wrestling with the design for weeks and had solicited advice from some of the world's most respected scientists. He was in contact with everyone from the British inventor David Hughes to the renowned mathematician and astronomer Simon Newcomb to inventors at Harvard, Johns

Hopkins, and the *Scientific American.* "Alec says he telegraphed all leading physicists here and in London and all here at least have answered with suggestions and expressions of interest and desire to help," Mabel wrote to her mother. "No one thinks they can do enough to help the President."

At this point in his experiments, Bell had made some significant changes to his original design, most of which revolved around the coils. He had tried winding the primary coil into a conical shape. He had adjusted the coils' size, making them "enormous" at one point, and as small as a bullet at another. Most important, he had decided to borrow an idea from Hughes and use four coils — two exploring and two balancing — rather than two. He was concerned that if he used his original instrument to search for a bullet, especially over a broad area such as the president's back, the movement might upset the coils' delicate balance. By using Hughes's four-coil design, he could rigidly attach the two exploring coils to each other. Any necessary adjustments could be made to the balancing coils, which would sit on a nearby table, undisturbed.

The result of Bell's experiments was the instrument that sat before him now. The exploring arm of the invention consisted of a handle, rounded at the top and narrower at its base, attached to a disk carved from walnut. On the other side of the disk were the exploring coils, which he had stacked on top of each other — the larger, primary coil against the disk and the smaller, secondary coil against the primary. Four wires from the coils had been threaded up through a hole Bell had hollowed into the handle. The wires stretched out like tentacles, connecting one coil to the telephone receiver and a balancing coil, and the other to a battery, the second balancing coil, and an automatic circuit interrupter.

Bell and Tainter had already begun testing the design. Before each test, they would fire a bullet against a board, to ensure that it was flattened like the bullet inside Garfield, and then conceal it in their subject. Bell had never hesitated to use unorthodox test subjects. Seven years earlier, while working on a phonautograph, a distant cousin of the phonograph, he had used a dead man's ear, soaking it in glycerin and water to make it pliable. Now, for Garfield, he used everything from a bag stuffed with wet bran to mimic the electrical resistance of a human body to a massive joint of meat that he had bought from a butcher in an effort to "more nearly approximate the dreadful reality."

On July 20, as promised, Bliss visited the Volta Laboratory, as had Joseph Stanley Brown the day before. Bliss, who had brought for the inventor two lead bullets exactly like the one lodged in Garfield, watched in silence as Bell repeated a number of his tests. Gripping the induction balance's handle in one hand, Bell carefully ran the instrument over his subjects. Every time, it found its mark, emitting its now-familiar buzzing through the telephone receiver.

Just days after Garfield's shooting, Bell had begun carefully detailing his work on the induction balance in a laboratory notebook. He used a modest, bound book with a pebbled cover and a white label that, in handwriting that shook and swerved with each bump in the leather, read "Volta Lab Notes." On July 9, before he had even returned to Washington, he had expressed his confidence in his invention, scrawled over half an unlined page. "Ball can certainly be located by Induction Balance," he had written. "See it clearly."

There was no question that the invention worked. The problem was that it did not yet work well enough. Not only did the induction balance have to detect metal, it had to detect lead, which, among the metals, is one of the poorest conductors of electricity. What Bell yearned for was, quite literally, a silver bullet. "If people would only make their bullets of silver or iron," he complained, "there would be no difficulty in finding them in any part of the body!"

In its earliest form, the induction balance could detect lead buried only slightly more than an inch deep. After weeks of struggle, Bell had been able to increase that range to just over two inches. His fear was that the bullet in Garfield lay deeper than that.

Convinced that he could stretch the range even farther, Bell rarely left his laboratory, and the strain was apparent. He had dragged his fingers through his black hair and beard so many times, they stood out at sharp, odd angles, like untrimmed trees. Always a serious young man, he had never managed to look youthful. Even when he had fallen in love with Mabel, her family had assumed that he was nearly ten years older than he was. Six years later, as he hunched over the induction balance, his face seemed to be set in a permanent scowl of concentration. No one would have guessed that the dour scientist had only recently celebrated his thirty-fourth birthday.

The Volta Laboratory, moreover, was far from an ideal work environment. Despite

Bell's renovations, the building seemed less like a laboratory than a horse stable, which is what it had been. Bell used the saddle posts that still hung from the walls as coat hooks, but there was little he could do about the smell. No amount of scrubbing could free the small building from the stubborn odor of manure, which seemed to cling to the walls, attracting clouds of flies that drove Bell and Tainter to distraction with their soft, buzzing hum. So unhealthy was the laboratory, in fact, that just a few weeks earlier it had been reported to the board of health.

Bell hardly noticed the clutter or even the smell, but he could not ignore the heat. For a man who suffered blinding headaches brought on by heat, spending the hottest days of summer in Washington, D.C., was excruciating. The summer before, he had complained that his "headache has taken root in my left eye and is flourishing!" Even when he could not bear the sound of a slamming door or ringing telephone, however, he had refused to stop working. "Alec says he would rather die than leave work," his exasperated wife had written to his mother.

So engrossed had Bell become in his work that he had little time to think about anything else, even his wife, who was pregnant and miserable in sweltering Boston. After not writing to her for more than a week, he apologized for his "epistolary silence," but then quickly lapsed back into it. Mabel, on the other hand, wrote frequently — both to Bell and about him. "Alec says he is well and bearing the heat well," she wrote to her mother. "Still I shall be glad to have him home again and his work accomplished. I fear he won't have the rest he so much needs after all."

Mabel understood the importance of her husband's work, but she also knew that he would literally work himself to death before he would give up. She had seen him sick with worry and determination too many times before, and it frightened her to know that this invention, and the good it could accomplish, meant as much to him as anything he had ever done. "I want to know how you are personally," she wrote to Alec a few days after he had left for Washington. "I fancy you are so eager and excited that you don't feel the heat as you otherwise would. Only for my sake do take care and don't wear yourself all out. I . . . would think the President's life a poor exchange for yours."

Chapter 18
"Keep Heart"

> If wrinkles must be written upon our brows, let them not be written upon the heart. The spirit should not grow old.
>
> JAMES A. GARFIELD

While Mabel's anxiety for her husband grew, Lucretia's fears for James slowly began to ease. As the weeks passed and the president, whom few had believed would survive the first night, lived on, clear-eyed and cheerful if too weak even to sit up, the sharp terror that had seized her began to loosen its grip. "I hope the dangers are nearly passed," she wrote to a friend on July 14. "My heart is full of gratitude . . . so full that I have no words wherewith to express it." By late July, she had settled into a nervous but steady vigilance. Although she continued to spend the greater part of her days and evenings at James's bedside, he had convinced her to sleep in a room in another corner of the house, apart from the shuffling and whispering attendants who always surrounded him, and even to venture out on occasion, taking quiet rides through the city.

When she was not with her family, Lucretia had always preferred to be alone. Since becoming first lady, she had dreaded public functions, painfully aware that she paled in comparison to her immediate predecessors, Julia Grant and Lucy Hayes, who were effortless and enthusiastic hostesses. "I hope I shall not disappoint you," Lucretia had told a group of women who had called on her after James's inauguration. She also found the rules of etiquette that accompanied her position confusing and almost impossible to follow. In her last diary entry before James was shot, she had lamented a small misstep in protocol that had been quickly reported in the newspapers. "Blundered!" she wrote. "I wonder if I shall ever learn that I have a position to guard!"

After the assassination attempt, Lucretia endured a far more intense and prolonged public scrutiny than any first lady before her. In the midst of it, she won not only the approval of the American people, but their hearts as well. Throughout the country, families who had lost fathers, sons, and brothers to the Civil War, or had watched them suffer and survive, took pride in Lucretia's courage, knowing far too well how difficult it was to sustain, day after day. "In these few weeks of trial and anxiety," the *New York Times* wrote, "Mrs. Garfield has achieved a distinction grander and more lasting than ever before fell to the lot of a President's wife." Although worry had taken its toll, and Lucretia was even thinner and paler than before, she seemed to those around her to have an almost supernatural strength. "She must be a pretty brave woman," Mabel wrote admiringly to Bell. "The whole nation leans upon her courage."

Lucretia's courage was buoyed by genuine hope. She refused to be lied to or shielded in any way, and she had never been one to pretend that things were better than they were. She now felt, however, that she had real reason for optimism. Not only had her husband survived the initial trauma of the shooting, but his natural vitality and strength had made it possible for him to fight off the early infection introduced by the bullet, and his doctors' fingers, in the train station. Since July 6, Garfield had been making slow but undeniable progress. His pulse and temperature had been steady. He had been eating and sleeping well, and the pain in his feet and legs had eased. "His gradual progress towards recovery is manifest," Bliss's morning bulletin announced on July 13, "and thus far without complications."

Hope filled the White House, and, as the nation eagerly read Bliss's bulletins, which were posted several times a day, every day, it radiated throughout the country. Every day, newspapers ran headlines proclaiming that the president was "On the Road to Recovery" and announcing that his condition was "More and More Hopeful." So confident of Garfield's survival was the governor of Ohio that he wrote to his fellow governors suggesting that all thirty-eight states designate a "day of thanksgiving for the recovery of the President."

Garfield himself made every effort to assure those around him that he was not only well but content. "You keep heart," he told Lucretia. "I have not lost mine." He endured without complaint excruciating pain and daily humiliations. "Every passage of his bowels and urine required the same attendance bestowed upon a young infant," one of his doctors would recall. He could not bend his spine, so, in an effort to avoid bed sores, his large body was rolled from one side to another as often as a hundred times a day, a ritual that required at least three people and the strongest linen sheets the White House could find. Garfield, however, "rarely spoke of his condition," an attendant wrote, "seldom expressed a want."

The president's only complaint was loneliness. Although Garfield appeared to have improved dramatically, Bliss continued to deny him any visitors. For a man who cherished his friends and delighted in long, rambling conversations, this isolation was more painful than anything else he had had to endure. His only link to the outside world was through the one window not obscured by the screens Bliss had placed around his bed. It was the same view he had had from his office — a stretch of trees on the White House grounds, the unfinished Washington Monument, and a silver thread of the Potomac. Now, however, as he lay on his back, unable to sit up, his bamboo bed frame lifting him just high enough to see out the window, the scene must have seemed lonely and remote, almost unfamiliar.

Turning to his friend Rockwell, Garfield asked for something with which to write. After handing him a clipboard and a pencil, Rockwell watched as the president wrote his name in a loose, drifting hand that was almost unrecognizable as his signature.

Then, underneath his name, he scrawled the words *"Strangulatus pro Republica"* — Tortured for the Republic. "There was never a moment that the dear General was left alone," Rockwell would later write, "and yet, when one thinks of the loneliness in which his great spirit lived, the heart is almost ready to break."

Bliss permitted no one to see the president but the handful of friends and family members who had become his nurses. His children, whom he ached to see, were allowed only rare visits. Even Blaine had not seen Garfield since the day he had knelt over him in the train station. Finally, nearly a month after the shooting, Garfield insisted that he see his secretary of state. On a Friday morning in late July, Blaine was ushered into the president's darkened sickroom. He was relieved to see that Garfield looked better than he had feared, but he had time to do little more than reassure himself that his friend was still alive. Just six minutes after Blaine had entered the room, Garfield's doctors politely showed him back out.

In part, Bliss defended his decision to keep the president isolated by insisting that it was dangerous for Garfield to talk. By talking, he said, Garfield moved his diaphragm, which in turn moved the liver, the region where Bliss believed the bullet had lodged. "But I move the diaphragm every time I breathe," Garfield had pointed out. Yes, he was told, but breathing was a gentle movement, while talking was violent.

Garfield did his best to follow his doctors' instructions, but as his old friend Swaim sat by his bed one night, trying to conjure a small breeze with a fan, he could not resist talking to him. Terrified that Garfield would somehow further injure himself, Swaim asked him several times to stay silent. Finally, when the president tried to strike up yet another conversation, Swaim snapped at him, "I won't talk to you and won't listen to you." Garfield laughed, laid his hand on his friend's arm, and said, "I will make a treaty with you. If you keep my mouth filled with ice I will keep quiet."

By late July, Garfield had seemed so strong and steady, so much like himself for so long, that it seemed impossible that he would not recover. Friends and family members in Ohio who had been packing their bags, expecting to go to Washington to be of support and help to Lucretia in her mourning, began canceling their travel plans. "Everywhere," one reporter wrote, "hope and confidence have taken the place of alarm and doubt." On July 21, Lucretia told Harriet Blaine that she considered her husband to be "out of danger."

The very next day, in a descent that seemed as sudden and mysterious as it was terrifying, Garfield began to lose all the ground he had gained. When his wound was dressed that morning, a "large quantity" of pus escaped, carrying with it fragments of cloth that the bullet had dragged into his back and a piece of bone that was about an eighth of an inch long. By evening, he was uncharacteristically restless and so tired he did not even try to speak.

Bliss was not concerned about the pus. On the contrary, he considered it to be a good sign, as did many like-minded surgeons at that time. Just two years earlier, William Savory, a well-regarded British surgeon and prominent critic of Joseph Lister, had proclaimed in a speech to the British Medical Association that he was "neither ashamed nor afraid to see well formed pus." A wound, he declared, was "satisfactory under a layer of laudable pus." Bliss could not have agreed more heartily. Garfield's wound, the medical bulletin announced that night, "was looking very well," having "discharged several ounces of healthy pus."

By the next morning, however, even Bliss's confidence had begun to fade. At 7:00 a.m., the president's temperature was 101 degrees. By 10:00 a.m., it had risen to 104. "He is feverish and quite restless," one of Bliss's attending physicians noted, "and has vomited three times this morning a fluid tinged with bile."

Quietly, Bliss sent for his surgeons, David Hayes Agnew and Frank Hamilton, who arrived in Washington by a quarter past eight that evening. As Garfield lay in his bed, "drenched with a profuse perspiration," the two surgeons examined his back and found a small pus sac about three inches below the wound. Using only a sulphuric ether, sprayed directly onto the site, to lessen the pain, Agnew made a deep incision into Garfield's back and inserted a large drainage tube.

Bliss's bulletin that day announced that "the President bore the operation well," and was "much relieved." Garfield's condition, however, continued to deteriorate. He vomited repeatedly and was constantly bathed in sweat. Two days after the first surgery, Agnew again operated on the president, enlarging the opening he had earlier made over his rib and pulling out fragments of muscle, connective tissue, and bone, one piece of which was an inch long.

Bliss, Agnew, and Hamilton would later insist that, as they examined and operated on the president, they used an adequate degree of antisepsis. Occasionally, they sprayed Garfield's back with carbolic acid or rinsed the wound with a "weak solution of car bolic [*sic*] acid (one-fourth of 1 per cent)." Like the surgeons who sterilized their knives and then held them in their teeth, however, the doctors' efforts did little more than give the appearance of antisepsis. Each time they inserted an unsterilized finger or instrument into Garfield's back, something that happened several times every day, they introduced bacteria, which not only caused infection at the site of the wound, but entered Garfield's bloodstream.

Unbeknownst to his doctors, cavities of pus had begun to ravage the president's body. One cavity in particular, which began at the site of the wound, would eventually burrow a tunnel that stretched past Garfield's right kidney, along the outer lining of his stomach, and down nearly to his groin. An enormous cavity, six inches by four inches, would form under his liver, filling with a greenish-yellow mixture of pus and bile.

Nearly a month had passed since the

shooting, but Bliss and his team of doctors were still probing Garfield's wound in the hope of answering one question: Where was the bullet? Eager to help solve the mystery, Americans flooded the White House with letters not just of concern and sympathy but medical advice. "We received every morning literally bushels of letters," one doctor in the White House would later recall. "Every crank . . . in the country seemed to think himself called upon to offer to cure the president." One man sent the doctors plans for a suction device that he assured them would suck the bullet right out of Garfield. Another suggested that they simply hang the president upside down until the bullet fell out. A man in Maryland wrote to Bliss saying that there was no reason for concern. The bullet was not in Garfield at all, but with him in Annapolis.

Although Bliss admitted that he could not be certain where the bullet lay, he had made it clear from the moment he took charge of the case that he believed it was in or near Garfield's liver. In this belief, he was joined by nearly every other doctor who had examined the president. While Garfield was still at the train station, one doctor had claimed that he could feel his liver as he probed the wound with his little finger.

Hamilton had told a reporter that he "had a suspicion, founded upon a good deal of evidence, that the ball was in the right iliac region, not far above the right groin." So convincing were the doctors that, soon after the shooting, the *New York Times* had announced that the "bullet has pierced the liver, and it is a fatal wound."

At least one doctor in Washington, however, believed strongly that the bullet wasn't anywhere near the president's liver — that it was, in fact, on the opposite side of his body. Frank Baker, a young man who had recently completed his medical degree and taken a position as an "assistant demonstrator of anatomy" at Columbian University (now George Washington University), had been carefully following Garfield's case since the day of the shooting. After considering the president's symptoms and applying some of the basic theories he had learned in medical school, he concluded that, although the bullet had entered Garfield's back on the right, it had come to rest on the left.

Baker even drew up a diagram, which traced with remarkable accuracy the course of the bullet. On July 7, just five days after the assassination attempt, he showed it to three doctors, one of whom was Smith

Townsend, who had been the first doctor to examine Garfield at the train station. Although he had little doubt that he was right, Baker never shared his theory with Bliss, or with any of the doctors caring for the president at the White House. Acutely aware of his own modest position, he worried that it would be disrespectful to question men of their stature. "I felt," he would later explain, "that it was improper to urge views which were diametrically opposed to those of gentlemen of acknowledged skill and experience."

As Baker had guessed, Bliss would not have welcomed his help. Even the physicians Bliss had personally invited to advise him on Garfield's care were strongly discouraged from disagreeing with him. Bliss's medical bulletins, which were uniformly optimistic, even when there was clear cause for concern, were a central point of contention. "These bulletins were often the subject of animated and sometimes heated discussion between Dr. Bliss and the other attending surgeons," one of the doctors would later admit. "The surgeons usually taking one side of the question and Dr. Bliss the other."

Bliss argued that he was only protecting the president, who had the newspapers read to him every morning. "If the slightest unfavorable symptom was mentioned in one of the bulletins," one of Garfield's surgeons recalled Bliss saying, "it was instantly telegraphed all over the country, and appeared in every newspaper the next morning."

Bliss expected the greatest possible discretion from everyone involved in the president's care, even Alexander Graham Bell. In Bell's case, however, he need not have worried. The inventor was well aware that his reputation too was at risk. In that respect, in fact, he had more to lose than Bliss, as he was by far the more famous man. By trying a new and largely untested invention on a dangerously wounded president, Bell was jeopardizing the respect and admiration he had so recently won. If the induction balance did not work, it would be his failure alone.

Reporters had been following Bell closely since the day he had arrived in Washington. "Your arrival and 'Professor' Tainter's was in the papers yesterday," Mabel had warned him on July 16. "Also a full account of what was said to be the instrument you would use." The day before, the *Washington Post* had printed a brief description of the induction balance and promised that "the experiment will be watched with great interest."

In an attempt to retain some privacy, Bell had avoided sending telegrams. "Ordinary telegrams I presume are private enough," he explained to Mabel in a long-awaited letter, "but in the case of my telegrams to you concerning the experiments to locate the bullet in the body of the President — I have no doubt they are all discussed by the employees of the Telegraph Company — and thus run a great chance of leaking out to the public Press."

In truth, reporters had little idea what Bell was up to, as he spent every day holed up in his laboratory, desperately trying to perfect his invention so that it would be ready when Bliss was. Since he had agreed to a brief interview with a few reporters nearly a week earlier, the only people Bell had allowed in the lab besides his assistants were fellow scientists and envoys from the White House. That would change on July 22, when he welcomed his first live test subject.

That day, a veteran of the Civil War named Lieutenant Simpson knocked on the door of the Volta Laboratory. Bliss had recommended Simpson to Bell because he had "carried a bullet in his body for many years." Bell found a "sonorous spot" on the lieutenant's back, but he worried that it was too faint to be trusted. He ran the test several times, asking Tainter, his father, and even Simpson himself to try to replicate the results. He also attempted a blindfold test, in which Tainter "closed his eyes and turned away." Tainter thought that he heard something in the same area Bell had noted, but Bell was skeptical. "I find that very feeble sounds like that heard are easily conjured up by imagination and expectancy," he wrote to Bliss the following day.

Bell needed more time, but as Garfield's condition continued to worsen, Bliss began to panic. Finally, at noon on July 26, he sat down and wrote a letter to the inventor, avoiding, as had Bell, the telegraph station. "Will you do us the favor to call at the Executive Mansion at about 5 p.m. today and work the experiment with the Induction Balance on the person of the President?" he wrote in an elegant, slanting hand on White House stationery. "We would be glad to have the experiment tried at the time of the dressing changing, about six p.m."

That morning, Bell had slept until eleven. He felt "tired, ill, dispirited and headachy," and had crawled into bed the night before "thoroughly exhausted from several days of hard labour." He was still hunched over his breakfast when Tainter arrived, carrying Bliss's letter, which had been sent to the laboratory by White House courier. As he held the letter in his hands, Bell regarded it with a mingled sense of excitement and fear. "Our last opportunity for improving the apparatus had come!" he would write Mabel later that night. Throwing on some clothes, he rushed to the laboratory with Tainter at his side and immediately set to work. He had one objective in mind: improving the induction balance's hearing range, so that it could detect an even deeper-seated bullet.

The day before, Professor Henry Rowland, who occupied the chair of physics at Johns Hopkins University in Baltimore, had visited Bell to make a suggestion. If Bell added a condenser, which can store and quickly release an electric charge, to the induction balance's primary circuit, he could increase the current's rate of change, and probably obtain a clearer sound. Bell didn't have a condenser and didn't have time to find one. That morning, however, in a moment of inspiration, he suddenly remembered that, when returning from his last trip to England, he had brought with him a large induction coil. Inside the coil was a condenser.

Breaking open the instrument, Bell removed the condenser, attached it to his invention, and was thrilled with what he found. Not only did it improve the sound, it increased the induction balance's range. Bell could now detect a bullet nearly three inches deep in the president's back. That, he hoped, would be enough.

As he left the laboratory, Bell made a rare stop at the telegraph station. Deciding to try his hand at subterfuge, he wrote to Mabel that the "trial of the apparatus on [the] President" would not take place for several days. The telegram, he later told her, was "intended not for you at all — but for the employees of the Telegraph Company."

A few hours later, Bell and Tainter arrived at the White House. Between them, they carried the newly improved induction balance, with all of its many parts and a tangle of wires. Approaching the house, they headed not for the front door, where they would risk being seen by the crowds of people still camped out in the park across the street, but to a private entrance in the back.

Bell was uncomfortably aware that the president had expressed reservations about this test. "Mr. Garfield himself is reported to have said that he was much obliged, but did not care to offer himself to be experimented on," Mabel had written to her mother a week earlier. "Of course not, but Alec isn't going to experiment upon him." The test, however, was an experiment. Bell's invention was less than a month old and had undergone significant changes only that afternoon. He had tested it, moreover, on only one other person, a man who had been perfectly well for many years.

After being quickly ushered inside, Bell and Tainter were shown up the narrow servants' staircase to the president's room. When Bell walked in the door, he was astonished by what he saw. The president lay sleeping, a peaceful expression on his face. He looked "so calm and grand," Bell later wrote Mabel, "he reminded me of a Greek hero chiselled in marble." Garfield, however, bore little resemblance to the man Bell had seen so many times before in pictures and paintings, always with the appearance of vibrant health — "the look of a man who was accustomed to work in the open air." The man before him now was an "ashen gray colour," Bell wrote, "which makes one feel for a moment that you are not looking upon a living man. It made my heart bleed to look at him and think of all he must have suffered to bring him to this."

While the president slept, Bell worked quickly in an adjoining room to set up the induction balance. Having sent Tainter to the basement with the interrupter, which was too loud to have nearby as they performed the test, he now arranged the battery, condenser, and balancing coils on a simple wooden table. After everything had been connected, Bell lifted the telephone receiver to his ear. To his horror, what he heard was not the cool silence of a balanced induction, but a strange sputtering sound he had never heard before.

Frantically, Bell tried everything he could think of to get rid of the sound. He sent Tainter back to the basement to check on the interrupter, and he carefully adjusted each of the four coils. No matter what he did, the sputtering remained. Pulling a lead bullet out of his pocket, he quickly ran a test and found, to his tremendous relief, that the invention appeared to work. The sound, however, was distracting, and Bell was concerned that the induction balance's hearing distance might be affected as well.

Before Tainter could even return from the basement, Bell turned to find Garfield's doctors standing in the door that separated the two rooms, beckoning him to come in.

Gripping the handle of the induction balance's round, wooden detector in one hand and the telephone receiver in the other, Bell stepped back into the president's room, wires snaking behind him. Bliss had ordered the screen that surrounded the president's bed to be removed. Garfield was now awake, his wound had been dressed, and he was looking directly at Bell.

Taking in the long wires that stretched out the door and down the hallway, and were about to be draped over his body, Garfield asked Bell to explain to him how the instrument worked. After listening intently, the president allowed himself to be rolled over onto his left side so that the test could begin. He rested his head on an attendant's shoulder, supporting the weight of his body by clasping his arms around the man's neck. "His head was so buried on the gentleman's shoulder," Bell would later recall, "that he could not see any person in the room."

Garfield's bed was surrounded by doctors, eager to see as much of the procedure as possible. The focus of their attention, however, was not just the president and Bell, but Bliss. After carefully pulling Garfield's dressing gown to one side so that his back was exposed down to his thighs, the doctor turned expectantly to Bell, who handed him the induction balance's exploring arm. Although it made more sense for Bell to search for the bullet himself while he listened through the telephone receiver, as he had done many times before, Bliss had made it understood that he would be the one to handle the exploring arm, and to decide which areas would be explored.

As everyone in the room looked on in silence, Bliss took the wooden disk by its handle and slowly began to run the coils along the president's spine, starting at the wound and traveling downward. Bell stood behind Garfield's bed, the telephone receiver pressed to his ear. Although he waited to hear the distinctive buzzing sound that he knew would indicate the presence of a bullet, the only sound that reached him was the same faint, maddening sputter that had earlier appeared without warning.

Turning Garfield over onto his back, they tried again, this time passing the coils over his abdomen. At one point, Bell thought he heard a "sharp and sudden reinforcement of sound," but he was unable to find it again. "That horrid unbalanced spluttering kept coming & going," Bell would later write in bitter frustration. Finally, with the President quickly tiring, he had no choice but to end the experiment.

Although Bliss asked him to try again at another date, Bell felt the sharp sting of humiliation. "I feel woefully disappointed & disheartened," he admitted to Mabel that night. The only consolation lay in knowing that he would "go right at the problem again tomorrow."

Returning to his laboratory early the next morning, Bell was sickened to find that the problem lay not in the induction balance at all, but simply in the way he had set it up. In his haste to improve the invention, Bell had added the condenser at the last minute. While setting up the induction balance at the White House, he had connected the condenser to only one side of the instrument. Had he connected it to both sides, the sputtering sound would have been banished immediately, and the instrument would have worked perfectly.

More than ever, Bell was convinced of the necessity for secrecy. He had worked as hard as he possibly could, using every conceivable resource and idea, and still he had made a devastating mistake. Although, in his letter to Mabel, Bell described as faithfully as he could all that had happened at the White House that night, even drawing a sketch of the room, he sternly reminded her that the letter was intended for no one but her. “Private and confidential,” he wrote in a postscript. “Don’t tell any one the contents.”

Chapter 19
On a Mountaintop, Alone

Light itself is a great corrective. A thousand wrongs and abuses that are grown in darkness disappear like owls and bats before the light of day.

JAMES A. GARFIELD

On July 23, three days before Bell arrived at the White House with his induction balance, Conkling had woken early in his room at the Fifth Avenue Hotel in New York, already seething with anger. While most of the hotel's occupants still slept, Conkling sat down to breakfast dressed in his customary black cutaway suit, yellow waistcoat, and brightly colored butterfly bow tie, an array of newspapers spread before him. As he did every day, his private secretary had carefully marked with blue pencil any article in which Conkling's name appeared. On that day, the papers were awash in blue.

Conkling, who had always worked in the

shadows, demanding secrecy and anonymity, had rarely approved of anything that was written about him. Now, the mere sight of his name in print could be relied on to leave him trembling with rage. Picking up the *New York Times,* he saw, printed in bold letters across the front page, the words "ROSCOE CONKLING BEATEN." It was a headline no New Yorker, least of all Conkling himself, had ever expected to see.

Since his dramatic resignation in May, Conkling had called in every favor and used every opportunity for intimidation to win back his Senate seat. For more than two months, the citizens of New York had been forced to wait for the New York legislature to hold an election while Conkling and his men, including the vice president of the United States, had made promises, threats, and even alliances with Democrats. After the president's shooting, Conkling was rarely seen in public, but had redoubled his efforts behind the scenes, forcing those Stalwarts who were still loyal to him to meet every morning at ten to "renew their pledges of firmness and adherence."

Despite the desperate efforts of what one New York newspaper mockingly referred to as "Conkling's Servile Band," an election had finally taken place on July 22. Not only had Conkling failed to regain his seat that day, but he had lost it to a rumpled, overweight, little-known congressman named Elbridge Lapham, a man to whom he scarcely would have deigned to speak in the past.

The fact that Lapham was a professed Stalwart only further enraged Conkling. Simply by accepting the seat, he railed, Lapham showed himself to be a traitor, and he "must not reap the reward of his perfidy!" The contest, however, had been decided, and Conkling was astonished to find himself powerless to change it.

Finishing his breakfast, Conkling stood up from the table and walked across the room to where his suitcase sat, already packed. Despite the early hour, a clutch of reporters waited in the hotel lobby for him, watching as he descended the stairs looking "moody and fretful." He quickly paid his bill and then turned to leave, ignoring the men hovering nervously around him. In answer to their questions, he would say only that he was going away. "No one," one reporter wrote, "dared to ask him his destination."

Conkling was going home to Utica, to the three-story gray stone mansion on the Mohawk River that he had bought with a single year's salary when he was practicing law. His wife, a quiet, practical woman who recoiled from her husband's political and social intrigues, lived there with their daughter in relative seclusion. Since taking his place in the Senate fourteen years earlier, Conkling had made only rare and brief appearances in Utica, and he did not plan to stay long now.

Although, in the wake of his humiliating defeat, he vowed that he was "done with politics now and forever," no one who knew him believed that he was about to bow out gracefully. Conkling would never again debase himself by asking for a single vote. Fortunately, votes were no longer necessary. He had, he believed, something much more valuable than a Senate seat. He had Chester Arthur.

Like Conkling, Arthur had largely disappeared from view after Garfield's shooting. It was widely assumed that he was in close and constant discussions with the man who had made him, planning for the day when he would be king, and Conkling his Cromwell. So little respect was there for the vice president, and so openly had he aligned himself with the president's fiercest enemy, that to accuse him now of conspiring with

Conkling was simply stating the obvious. "I presume that if Mr. Arthur should become President, in his ignorance and inexperience he would be compelled to rely on some one more capable than himself," the political writer George William Curtis shrugged. "Obviously that person would be Mr. Conkling."

Hatred for Conkling and Arthur grew with each setback Garfield suffered. Newspapers only fueled the fire, assuring readers that, while they prayed for their president's recovery, these two men plotted how best to take advantage of the tragedy. "Disguise it as they may seek to do," one article read, "the men who have chosen to assume an attitude of hostility to the Administration are speculating hourly upon the chances of Garfield's life or death."

Enraged by the very idea of Arthur taking over the presidency, Americans across the country readied themselves as if for battle. Some took a tactical approach, frantically trying to revive the rumor, started during the campaign, that the vice president had been born in Canada, and so was constitutionally prohibited from becoming president. Others were ready to take more drastic measures. Police departments prepared their men for riots as agitated crowds gathered in city streets. In Ohio, men angrily proclaimed that they would not hesitate to "shoulder their muskets and go to Washington to prevent the inauguration of Arthur."

As they oiled their guns, however, the object of their wrath, the once-preening politician whom they pictured waiting hungrily in the wings, sat alone in a borrowed house, terrified and distraught. To the few people who were able to see him in those first days after the shooting, Arthur seemed not just concerned or saddened, but shattered. His friends were reminded of the dazed, hollow man he had been little more than a year earlier, when he had lost his wife to pneumonia. "There is no doubt that he is suffering keenly," one man confided to a reporter. "No one can look on him for a moment without being convinced of that fact. He cannot, if he would, control the evidences of his feelings."

The day after the shooting, Arthur had arrived in Washington at 8:00 a.m. and gone directly to the White House. Although Bliss had refused to let him see the president, Arthur had stayed for nearly two hours. A senator waiting in Joseph Stanley Brown's office caught sight of him as he paced the halls and noted with astonishment that the vice president "seemed to be overcome." Before Arthur left, Lucretia agreed to see him. Eager to express his sympathy to the first lady, he found to his embarrassment that he was "unable to conceal his emotion," tears filling his eyes and his voice tightening as he tried to speak.

After leaving the White House, Arthur returned to the house on Capitol Hill where he was staying, the enormous granite home of Senator John Jones, a Stalwart Republican from Nevada. For the next few days, he did not leave, turning away a stream of visitors and causing an undercurrent of alarm that ran just below the surface of the larger national crisis. This was the man who could be called upon at any moment to lead the nation, and he had effectively disappeared.

Finally, a journalist from New York managed to gain entry into Senator Jones's home. Jones and his family, who had fled the heat and filth of the summer, intending to return a few months later, had left the house in a state of complete disarray. The little light that slanted through cracks in the shuttered windows revealed furniture shoved into corners or piled in the middle of rooms. Arthur, who was as famously fastidious in his home decor as he was his dress, had done nothing to make sense of the confusion.

Stepping into one of the home's several parlors, the reporter finally found the vice president, sitting on a sofa, "his head bowed down and looking vacantly out through a low, open window." At the sound of footsteps, Arthur looked up in surprise, and the reporter could see with startling clarity "the impression which the calamity . . . had left on his countenance." Arthur's eyes were bloodshot and rimmed with tears, and it was clear from the streaks on his face that he had been crying. "His whole manner," the reporter would later write, "rather than the words he uttered, showed a depth of feeling . . . which would astonish even many of those who think they know the man well."

Although he soon returned to New York, anxious to allay fears that he was about to seize control of the White House, Arthur had already begun a transformation so complete that few would have believed it possible. He had, whether out of fear or force of habit, continued to help Conkling try to regain his Senate seat, but as soon as the election was over, he had begun to pull away. Conkling had "received no visit from the Vice-President since the news of the election of Mr. Lapham was received in this City," the *New York Times* reported, "and this was remarked as very queer conduct for Gen. Arthur."

Not only had Arthur begun to pull away from Conkling, but he had started taking political advice from a very different and, even to him, completely unknown source. After Garfield's shooting, he had received a letter from a woman named Julia Sand. Although he had never met Sand and knew nothing about her, Arthur read the letter, and was surprised to find in it a reflection of his own tortured thoughts. "The hours of Garfield's life are numbered — before this meets your eye, you may be President," Sand had written. "The day he was shot, the thought rose in a thousand minds that *you* might be the instigator of the foul act. Is not that a humiliation which cuts deeper than any bullet can pierce?"

Sand, Arthur would later learn, was an unmarried, thirty-two-year-old invalid. For the past five years, she had felt "dead and buried," but the attempt on Garfield's life and Americans' complete lack of faith in Arthur had inspired her to attempt to inspire him. She was as brutally honest in her assessment of the situation as she was galvanizing. "Your kindest opponents say: 'Arthur will try to do right' — adding gloomily — 'He won't succeed, though —

making a man President cannot change him,' " she wrote. "But making a man President can change him! Great emergencies awaken generous traits which have lain dormant half a life. If there is a spark of true nobility in you, now is the occasion to let it shine. Faith in your better nature forces me to write to you — but not to beg you to resign. Do what is more difficult & more brave. Reform!"

Arthur not only read Sand's letters, he kept them. Over the years, he would keep twenty-three of her letters, each one urging him to be a better man than he had once believed he could be. "It is not the proof of highest goodness never to have done wrong," Sand assured him, "but it is a proof of it . . . to recognize the evil, to turn resolutely against it." Arthur had been given an extraordinary opportunity, and he had found in Sand perhaps the one person in the nation who believed him capable of change. "Once in awhile there comes a crisis which renders miracles feasible," she wrote. "The great tidal wave of sorrow which has rolled over the country, has swept you loose from your old moorings, & set you on a mountaintop, alone."

As long as Garfield's survival lay in doubt, however, Arthur felt as though he were standing not on a mountaintop, but a precipice. So intense and apparent was his distress that it led to a rumor that the president had died and, prostrate with grief, Arthur had poisoned himself. Both men still lived, but for Arthur, the only relief from the despair that had settled over him was the occasional glimmer of hope from the White House.

"As the President gets better," he told Blaine, "I get better, too."

The president, however, was not getting better — a fact that his doctor, unable to change, was desperate to disguise. For nearly a month, Bliss had rarely left Garfield's bedside, making every decision regarding his care, from what medicine he would receive, to what he could eat, to whom he could see. In a futile effort to have the decaying room "thoroughly aired and cleaned," he insisted that all the carpets and upholstered furniture be removed, and he ordered the other doctors to take off their shoes so that the sound of their footsteps would not disturb the president's rest.

As he grew increasingly nervous, Bliss no longer trusted even the doctors he had handpicked to help him. Soon after taking charge of the case, he had given Robert

Reyburn, a professor of surgery at Howard University and a close friend of his, the task of taking the president's temperature several times a day. So many times had Reyburn walked into Garfield's room holding a thermometer that the president had begun referring to him as "Old Temperature." Now, Bliss took over even that menial duty, personally taking the president's vital signs and writing the results in his daily medical bulletins. The other doctors were expected to take Bliss's word for it that the bulletins were accurate, and sign them without having examined the president themselves.

So tight was Bliss's grip on the president's case that it seemed as if he were fighting not for Garfield's survival, but his own. In a confidential note to a friend, written on White House stationery, Bliss complained that he was "devoting all my professional skills — ability — time & thoughts to this case." With little sleep and no relief from worry, his own health had begun to suffer, as had his medical practice, which he had completely neglected since the shooting. He had risked everything he had to treat the president, and, he wrote, underlining not just the sentence but each word with a heavy hand, "I can't afford to have him die."

What Bliss needed now, as he watched

Garfield's temperature rise and fall like a churning sea, was some good news. On July 30, after instructing Hamilton to insert a drainage tube "farther into the cavity of the [President's] wound," Bliss wrote once again to Bell, asking him to return to the White House for a second test of the induction balance on the president.

Bell was eager to try again, but he had not forgotten the humiliation of his first, failed test. "Courage," Mabel had urged him as soon as she heard the news. "From failure comes success," she wrote. "Be worthy of your patient."

When Bliss's letter arrived, Bell was literally knee-deep in his work. Piles of wire coils littered the laboratory, and battery cells, which consisted of electrodes resting in jars of noxious liquid, sloshed threateningly every time he bumped a table. He was running a new series of experiments, following less scientific theory than empirical method. What he had found was that, not only might it help to double his battery voltage — from four cells to eight — but, more important, he would be better off without the balancing coils. Without the extra coils, he could reduce the resistance, which significantly strengthened the current, and increased the hearing range.

The results, he wrote in his laboratory notebook, barely able to contain his excitement, were "Splendid!" In just four days, he had managed to extend the instrument's range to more than five inches. The problem was that the only way to balance the induction with just two coils was to overlap them, and they were extraordinarily sensitive to the slightest movement in relation to one another.

By this point the last thing Bell was worried about was aesthetics, but the induction balance had to be portable. Using what he would later describe as "forced exertions," he and Tainter managed to encase the coils in two rectangular wooden blocks, held together by four pins made of ebonite, a type of hard rubber. The wires now emerged from the sides of the blocks rather than through the top of the handle, but there was no time to make a new handle, so the original one, with an empty hole through the center, would have to do. "In its present form," Bell admitted to Bliss, the instrument was a "very clumsy affair."

On July 31, the day before he was scheduled to return to the White House, Bell tested his redesigned invention on a man who lived at the Soldiers' Home, a veterans' retirement compound that included the summer cottage where Lincoln had written the final draft of the Emancipation Proclamation. The test subject this time was Private John McGill, who, for nearly twenty years, had lived with a bullet from the Civil War battle of Gaines' Mill. Bell had "no difficulty," he wrote to Bliss that night, "in finding a sonorous spot in his back, where undoubtedly the bullet lies imbedded." After the test Bell found that, in this case, he could actually confirm the results simply by pressing his fingers on the "sonorous spot," and feeling the bullet beneath McGill's skin.

At about nine o'clock that night, after sending Mabel a ringingly confident telegram, declaring that there was "no need of further secrecy," Bell allowed a reporter from the *Boston Herald* to join him in his laboratory. Welcomed with a hail "Come up and see us" from Bell himself, the reporter made his way to the door of the brick building, which was nearly hidden behind overgrown trees and shrubs. After stopping for a moment to admire the light streaming from the windows, marveling that "every room was in use," he was led into the laboratory, where Bell, his father, and Tainter stood, surrounded by the detritus of their work.

Every surface, from tables to chairs to cabinets, even the floor they stood on, was covered with "coils of wire, batteries, instruments and electrical apparatus of every sort," the reporter marveled. "The light from the jets, burning brilliantly in the centre of the room, was reflected from a hundred metallic forms. It was reflected too from the smiling faces of the great electrician and his assistant, who saw success almost within their grasp."

Bliss was waiting for Bell when he and Tainter arrived at the White House the next morning, carrying between them the induction balance, awkwardly shaped and roughly hewn but working perfectly, and with nearly twice the range it had had just four days earlier. For the first time since he had begun work on this invention, Bell felt calm and confident. "My new form of Induction Balance," he had written to Bliss the day before, "gives brilliant promise of success."

Bliss, however, had a very specific definition of success. He expected Bell not only to find the bullet, but to find it where Bliss believed it to be. He would not allow the inventor and his assistant to waste his time or the president's energy on fruitless efforts. It was understood that they were to search the right side of Garfield's body, and only the right. Bliss agreed to let Bell and Tainter conduct the test themselves this time, but he would be standing next to the president's bed, closely watching the examination.

As Bell slowly ran the induction balance over what he referred to as the "suspected spot," he suddenly heard a faint pulsating sound. He tried again several times over the same area, and each time got the same result. Tainter, "the only other person present whose ear had been sufficiently trained to be reliable in such an emergency," repeated the test a number of times as well, assuring Bell that he heard the same sound. Still, Bell wanted another opinion. Finally, he asked the first lady to press her ear to the telephone receiver and tell him what she heard. Lucretia agreed that there seemed to be something there.

This spot, Bell knew, was exactly where Bliss wanted him to find the bullet. Despite that fact — or more likely because of it — he hesitated. There was, he would later write, "a general expectation that the bullet would be found in that part of the body." His fear was that that expectation might lead him to "imagine a difference that did not exist."

As far as Bliss was concerned, they had

their answer. Like the rest of the city, he had certainly seen the *Washington Post* article that morning, announcing that, "if success crowns the effort, and the ball is where it is now very strongly suspected to be, the original diagnosis of the wound will be upheld." It was no secret that that diagnosis had come from the president's chief physician.

Without wasting any time, Bliss issued a bulletin to announce the successful test of Alexander Graham Bell's invention. It was "now unanimously agreed," he wrote, "that the location of the ball has been ascertained with reasonable certainty, and that it lies, as heretofore stated, in the front wall of the abdomen, immediately over the groin, about five inches below and to the right of the navel."

As Bliss declared victory, Bell struggled with a nagging sense of unease. Whatever it was that he had heard as he tested the president, he had never heard it before. It certainly was not the faint but distinct buzzing sound that, after weeks of testing, he would have recognized immediately. Unfortunately, it had been clear to everyone in the room that Bell had heard something, and he had been unable to explain what else it could be. "In the absence of any other apparent cause for the phenomenon I was forced to agree in the conclusion that it was due to the presence of the bullet," he would later write. "I was by no means satisfied, however, with the results."

After returning to his laboratory, Bell felt none of the triumph he had felt the night before. As he turned the memory of the test over and over in his mind, trying to understand what had been different this time, he began to wonder if the problem had been some sort of outside interference. The next day, he returned to the White House and asked urgently to speak to Garfield's surgeons. Were they "perfectly sure," he asked, "that all metal had been removed from the neighborhood of the bed." "It was then recollected," Bell would later write, "that underneath the horse-hair mattress on which the President lay was another mattress composed of steel wires."

The revelation stunned Bell, who had had no way to anticipate such an unusual and potentially disastrous factor in his work. Box springs would not become common in the United States for another twenty years. As Bell knew, however, it would be difficult to find a better way to interfere with an induction balance than a mattress made of metal. Still, Bell was not convinced that it was the entire source of the problem. It seemed to him that, since Garfield had been lying on the mattress, he would have heard the pulsating sound everywhere he tested, rather than in just a small area near the wound. He asked the White House to send him an exact duplicate of the president's mattress for testing.

Acutely aware that time was running out, Bell returned to his lab and threw himself into meeting this new challenge. He had just begun, however, when he received an urgent message from Boston. Mabel, who was in the third trimester of her pregnancy, had fallen ill. She had been pleading with him to visit her and their children for more than a month. Now the situation had taken an ominous turn. Determined to find a way to keep working, Bell left Tainter with detailed instructions and then rushed aboard a train, already planning to ask Charles Williams for his old work space in the machine shop.

Waiting for Bell in Boston, however, was a tragedy that was far more personal than the one he was leaving behind, and which would leave him powerless to help Garfield, or indeed himself.

Chapter 20
Terror, Hope, and Despair

I have sometimes thought that we cannot know any man thoroughly well while he is in perfect health. As the ebb-tide discloses the real lines of the shore and the bed of the sea, so feebleness, sickness, and pain bring out the real character of a man.

JAMES A. GARFIELD

In his sickroom in the White House, Garfield was exhausted and weakened by the suffering he endured, but he was not surprised. He had been poor, and he had been a soldier, and like any man who had known want or war, he understood that the cruelest enemy was disease. "This fighting with disease," he had written to Lucretia nearly ten years earlier, after watching twenty-two of his men die from typhoid fever during the Civil War, "is infinitely more horrible than battle."

Now, his body, which had miraculously survived the initial trauma of the bullet wound, was so riddled with infection that he was literally rotting to death. Although Bliss closely tracked the spikes in the president's temperature, the chills, restlessness, vomiting, pounding heart, and profuse sweating, he either did not know, or refused to acknowledge, that they were symptoms of severe septicemia. He also insisted that he was not worried about the small, pus-filled lumps that dotted Garfield's back and arms. Known as "septic acne," they were yet another indication of blood infection. When a reporter, who had seen them mentioned in the bulletins, asked Bliss about them, the doctor dismissed them as being fairly common. "They will not be allowed to get large," he said, "but will be opened as they may form."

On August 8, a few days after Bell left for Boston, Bliss directed Agnew to again operate on the president, to "facilitate the escape of pus." When Bliss told Garfield that he would need to undergo another operation, Garfield, with "unfailing cheerfulness," replied, "Very well; whatever you say is necessary must be done." Using a long surgical knife with an ivory handle, Agnew made a deep incision down to and slightly past Garfield's twelfth rib, following what he believed to be the track of the bullet, but which was, in fact, a long, vertical cavity that had been created by the doctors' own fingers and instruments, and filled with infection. Before closing the incision, Agnew inserted two drainage tubes, which, Bliss noted with satisfaction, quickly issued "a profuse discharge of pus and bloody serum." Garfield, Bliss recalled with astonishment, endured the procedure "without an anæsthetic, and without a murmur, or a muscular contraction."

Neither the incisions the surgeons made, however, nor even the drainage tubes they inserted could keep up with the copious amounts of pus Garfield's body was producing. Just two weeks after the surgery, another abscess formed, this one on Garfield's right parotid gland, the largest salivary gland, which lies between the mouth and ear. Within days, the abscess had become so filled with pus that it caused his eye and cheek to swell and paralyzed his face. Finally, it ruptured, flooding Garfield's ear canal and mouth with so much pus, mixed with thick, ropy saliva, that it nearly drowned him.

So toxic was the infection in Garfield's body that it was a danger even to those who were treating him. One morning, while dressing the president's wound, Bliss reached for a knife that was partially hidden under some sheets. Unable to see the blade, he accidentally sliced open the middle finger of his right hand. "It is thought that some pus from the President's wound penetrated the cut," the *New York Times* reported the next day, "and produced what is known as pus fever." The resulting infection caused Bliss's hand to become so painfully swollen that he had to carry it in a sling.

Before his hand had even had a chance to fully heal, Bliss gave an interview in which he proclaimed that there was no evidence of blood infection in the president. "Not the minutest symptom of pyæmia has appeared thus far in the President's case," he told a reporter. "The wound," he said, "is healthier and healing rapidly. . . . In a word, the wound is in a state that causes us no apprehension whatever."

What did cause Bliss apprehension was the very real possibility that the president might die — not from infection, but starvation. In less than two months, Garfield had lost more than a third of his body weight, plunging from 210 pounds to 130. The barrel-chested, broad-shouldered former soldier who had taken office just five months earlier, radiating health and vitality, was now a near skeleton, so weak he could hardly hold a pen. The president, one of his doctors privately told a reporter, had reached "the limit of what a man can lose and yet live."

Not only did Garfield continue to suffer from violent bouts of vomiting, but he had long since lost any interest in eating. Edson, Lucretia's doctor who had agreed to serve as a nurse so that she could watch over the president, had told the *New York Herald* earlier in the month that, "at the best meal he has had lately, after the couple of mouthfuls he would ask to have it removed." Most days, Garfield was able to keep down a little bit of oatmeal. Unfortunately, that happened to be the one food he despised.

Although Garfield found it difficult to eat anything, for a while at least he seemed to relish drinking a glass of milk. He dutifully swallowed the koumiss, a drink made from fermented horse milk, that Bliss gave him nearly every day, but he strongly preferred cow's milk. Eager to help in any way, Americans latched onto this small piece of information. So that the president might have the freshest possible milk, a company in Baltimore sent him an Alderney cow, which could be seen tied up on the White

House lawn. The White House cook, who was the only Catholic among the staff, poured a large glass of milk for Garfield every day. Just before she carried his tray up the winding servant stairs to his sickroom, she quietly sprinkled holy water into his glass.

Realizing that he urgently needed to find a way to feed the president, Bliss came up with an alternative to food: "enemata," or rectal feeding. He mixed together beef bouillon — predigested with hydrochloric acid — warmed milk, egg yolk, and a little bit of opium, to help with retention. The solution, which, if absorbed, would provide protein, fatty acids, and saline, was injected into the president rectally every four hours, night and day. For a stretch of eight days, Garfield had nothing but enemata.

Then Bliss began altering the mixture. On one day he added 5 drams, or roughly 1.25 tablespoons, of whiskey. On another, he removed the egg yolk, which had been causing the president gastric pain, and replaced it with a small amount of charcoal. The danger was that, if the solution was too thick, this type of feeding could actually contribute to malnutrition rather than combat it. At first, Garfield seemed to rally, but as the days passed, he continued to lose weight at an alarming rate.

As well as being malnourished, Garfield was almost certainly suffering from profound dehydration. He had lost a dangerous amount of fluid through profuse bleeding on the day he was shot, and had continued to lose water every day, through vomiting, fever, drenching sweats, frequent enemas, and nearly constant drainage of his wound. Bliss had also been giving him almost daily doses of alcohol, from brandy to claret to whiskey, all of which are dehydrating. Not only was Garfield losing large quantities of fluid, he was not ingesting nearly enough. In a modern hospital, a sweating, feverish patient would be given at least two quarts of intravenous fluid every day. Garfield's daily fluids never amounted to more than a single quart.

While newspapers continued to print Bliss's assurances that the only danger to the president now was exhaustion, it was painfully apparent to anyone who saw Garfield that he could not live long. "This dreadful sickness will soon be over," Harriet Blaine wrote to her son in late August. "Every night when I go to bed I try to brace for that telephone which I am sure before morning will send its shrill summons through our room. The morning is a little reassuring, for light itself gives courage."

Each time she stepped into the White House, however, Harriet felt even that small source of strength slip away. It seemed that everyone she encountered, from the cook to cabinet members, had already succumbed to despair. Dr. Edson, who had spent many long nights by Garfield's side, admitted to Harriet in a private conversation that she no longer held out hope. Robert Todd Lincoln's "darkness," she told her family, "is unillumined by one ray of courage." Even Almon Rockwell, who, since the day of the shooting, had reacted with anger and indignation at the slightest suggestion that Garfield might not survive, looked as though he had already lost his old friend. His "feathers," Harriet wrote sadly, "I imagined drooped."

So desperate had the situation become that her husband felt that, as secretary of state, he was obliged to ask Chester Arthur to take over the president's responsibilities, at least temporarily. "Your father [is] much exercised on the question of disability," Harriet wrote to her daughter. "Should Arthur be brought to the front, and how?"

The Constitution was of no help. Nothing in it offered any guidance on how to determine when a president was no longer able to perform his duties. Nor was there any precedent. Only three other presidents had died while in office. Lincoln had lived only a few hours after he was shot; Zachary Taylor had succumbed to cholera in just a few days; and William Henry Harrison had survived only one month after contracting pneumonia while giving the longest inaugural address in history on a cold, rainy day. Garfield — much younger, stronger, and with a family to care for — had already lived twice as long as Harrison.

Finally, Blaine sent a cabinet member to New York to discuss the transition with the vice president. Arthur, however, made it clear that he would not even consider taking over the presidency while Garfield still lived. He refused even to return to Washington, concerned that it would appear as if he were preparing for his own inauguration. "Disappoint our fears," his young invalid friend, Julia Sand, had urged him. "Force the nation to have faith in you. Show from the first that you have none but the purest of aims."

In the White House, Blaine found it impossibly painful to talk to the president about any of this. Garfield, however, had no illusions about his chances of survival. When asked if he knew that he might not live, he had replied simply, "Oh, yes, I have always been conscious of that." What worried him now was not his own death, but the suffering it would bring to those he loved most. The last letter he would write was to his mother, in the hope that he could bolster her spirits, if only for a short time. Taking a pen, he began writing in a thin, shaky script that slipped down the page.

> Dear Mother,
>
> Don't be disturbed by conflicting reports about my condition. It is true I am still weak, but I am gaining every day, and need only time and patience to bring me through.
>
> Give my love to all the relatives & friends, & especially to sisters Hetty and Mary.
>
> Your loving son,
> James A Garfield

Only to his wife did Garfield admit his weariness. "I wonder," he told her one night, "if all this fight against death is worth the little pinch of life I will get anyway." Lucretia knew that what her husband wanted more than anything now was to escape, not just from this dreary, lonely room, but from

Washington altogether. He dreamed of returning to his farm in Ohio, seeing his old friends, sitting in the shade of his neighbor's maple trees, maybe even having a slice of his aunt's homemade bread.

If he could not go home, he hoped to go to the sea. He had never lost his childhood love of the ocean, which had seemed almost mythical to a boy from Ohio, and he wanted to see it one last time. "I have always felt that the ocean was my friend," he had written in his diary just a few weeks before the assassination attempt. "The sight of it brings rest and peace."

Bliss, however, terrified that Garfield would not survive the trip, refused. "It would not now be prudent," he told the president. He could leave Washington as soon as his stomach was stronger.

"It's all right now," Garfield replied. "I want to get away."

Although Harriet seemed to speak for everyone in the White House when she admitted to her daughter that she had lost "heart and spirit," there remained two people who refused to surrender. Lucretia had been so sick with worry for so long that her hair had begun to fall out, forcing her finally to cover her head with a scarf. Still, a reporter from the *Evening Star* marveled, she seemed to have "banished despair, and hopes even when to everyone else there was no hope."

The only person in the White House whose determination equaled Lucretia's was Garfield's young secretary, Joseph Stanley Brown. Although he would describe this time in his life as "one prolonged, hideous nightmare," Brown would allow no one, not even the members of Garfield's cabinet, to express anything but optimism in his presence. At a meeting of the cabinet members in late August, "despair," a reporter noted, "was in their countenance, and in their speech. They said, 'He must die.' " Brown, who had not yet turned twenty-four, stood and addressed the men, each one old enough to be his father. "Let nothing but words of cheer ever reach the President," he reprimanded them. "He will not die."

Brown rarely left the White House, sleeping, when he slept at all, on the small sofa in his office. Garfield wanted Brown near him, so the young man divided his days and nights between the sadness of the sickroom and the madness of his own office, where he replied to thousands of letters and telegrams, fielded journalists' questions, and greeted dignitaries. "During all this terror, hope, despair, and rush at the White House," a reporter for the *Evening Critic* wrote, Brown has been "the ruling spirit of the Mansion, and his young hand, guided by his wise head and kind heart, has been upon all."

One night, as Brown was working, a member of the White House staff brought him a message that the first lady wished to see him. When he appeared before her, Lucretia did not at first speak, waiting "until control of her voice was assured." Finally, she asked, "Will you tell me just what *you* think the chances are for the General's recovery?"

Brown took one look in Lucretia's "anguished face," he would later say, and "threw truthfulness to the winds, and lied and lied as convincingly and consolingly as I could." Then, as quickly as possible — "as soon as decency permitted" — he excused himself and left the room. "Once beyond the door," he admitted, "all restraint gave way." He could not bear to tell Lucretia the truth, but he could no longer hide it from himself. He was, he would acknowledge years later, "utterly shattered and broken."

CHAPTER 21
AFTER ALL

Despite the prayers and tears, and
earnest pleading,
And piteous protest o'er a hero's fall,
Despite the hopeful signs, our hearts
misleading,
Death cometh after all

Over the brightest scenes are clouds
descending;
The flame soars highest ere its deepest
fall;
The glorious day has all too swift an
ending;
Night cometh after all

O'er bloom or beauty now in our
possession
Is seen the shadow of the funeral
pall;
Though Love and Life make tearful
intercession,

Death cometh after all

ANONYMOUS POEM, UPON THE DEATH OF PRESIDENT GARFIELD, SEPTEMBER 1881

While Lucretia was forced to watch the slow, cruel approach of death, for Bell it came suddenly, blindsiding him while he was caught up in another man's tragedy. Although he had returned to Boston to be with Mabel, he continued to work feverishly on the induction balance at his old work space in Charles Williams's machine shop.

Just a week after Bell returned from Washington, Mabel suddenly went into labor. That day she gave birth to a little boy, whom they named Edward. He was, Mabel would later write wistfully, a "strong and healthy little fellow." As the baby struggled to breathe, however, it was immediately apparent that he had been born too soon. After Bell had seen his son for the first time, he sent his parents in Washington a telegram with the wrenching news.

LITTLE BOY BORN PREMATURELY THIS AFTERNOON DIED IN THREE HOURS. MABEL DOING AS WELL AS CAN BE EXPECTED. NO NEED TO COME ON.

A GRAHAM BELL

Years later, Alec would admit to Mabel

that he had yet to recover from the death of their son, and did not think he ever would. He was haunted by the belief that his selfishness had brought about their tragedy. "Nothing will ever comfort me for the loss," he wrote, "for I feel at heart that *I was the cause.*"

Engulfed in his own grief and mourning, Bell responded by plunging even more deeply into his quest for an answer to the president's suffering. After his son's funeral, he returned immediately to his work. He devised an attachment to the induction balance, and he wanted Tainter to re-create it in their laboratory in Washington so that he could take it to the White House.

Just three days after Edward's death, Tainter successfully tested the induction balance's new attachment for one of Garfield's surgeons, Frank Hamilton, in the Volta Laboratory in Washington. But with Garfield's condition deteriorating gravely, and Bell stranded in Boston with his devastated family, unable to force the issue in person, his desperate, single-minded race to save the president came to an end. Bliss refused to let Tainter try the invention on Garfield. The president was too weak, he said. He would not risk the exhaustion that another test might cause.

Unwilling to accept defeat, Bell redoubled his efforts from Boston, still believing that the president's life could be saved or, failing that, that his invention would prove to have lasting value for others. Perfecting the induction balance was a personal and scientific obligation, and he was not about to abandon it now, whatever the cost. "Heartless science," he would write years later, "seeks truth, and truth alone, quite apart from any consequences that may arise."

As a practical matter, however, Bell knew that whatever benefits the induction balance might have, they would come too late for President Garfield. The clock had run out, and there was simply nothing more that Bell could do.

At the White House, the siegelike atmosphere surrounding the stricken president's sickbed only seemed to worsen with each passing day. Strenuously resisting anything that might further weaken Garfield, Bliss was outraged when, upon entering the sickroom one day, he found a barber cutting the president's hair. Bliss "stopped the proceedings immediately," a reporter wrote, "much to the barber's disgust." Try as he might, however, Bliss could do nothing to banish the unbearable heat, which was sapping what little strength his patient had left. In the city, it was 90 degrees in the shade. Inside the president's room, even with the help of the air conditioner the navy had built for him, the temperature was never below 80.

Finally, Garfield had had enough. When Bliss walked into his room on the morning of September 5, the president made it clear that he would be going to the sea, with or without Bliss. "Well," he said, "is this the last day in the White House?" Bliss tried to calm him, promising that he "might soon be so far recovered as to make the journey." Garfield, however, was not going to be put off any longer. He was still the president, and he demanded to have some control over whatever was left of his own life. "No, no," he said. "I don't want any more delay."

At two o'clock the next morning, a specially equipped train pulled into the Baltimore and Ohio depot. It had been prepared weeks earlier so that it would be ready to take the president wherever he wished to go, whenever he was ready. Finally, the time had come. That day, Garfield was to be taken to Elberon, New Jersey, "in the hope," a member of the White House staff wrote, "that the air and the sight of the sea might do for him what the doctors could not."

The train, which pulled four cars — three passenger and one baggage — had been thoroughly renovated for the sick president. One of the principal concerns was dust, both from the tracks and from the train itself. To protect Garfield, the train had been outfitted with an engine that used only clean-burning anthracite coal. Wire gauze had been wrapped around the outside of his car, and heavy curtains had been hung inside.

The president's car, number 33, bore almost no resemblance to a normal train car. The seats had been removed, and thick Brussels carpet laid on the floors. Taking up most of the space was a new bed with strong springs to try to soften the tracks' jolts and bumps. In an attempt to keep Garfield cool, ice had been placed in the car, and a false ceiling had been installed a few inches from the actual ceiling to encourage air circulation.

Before he would allow the president to be moved, Bliss insisted that everything be tested. The train was driven nearly twenty miles in a trial trip, to "determine," Bliss explained, "the amount and nature of the motion of the bed." The attendants who had been chosen to carry Garfield — among them, Swaim and Rockwell, his closest friends — were drilled over and over again, so "as to make a mistake almost impossible." Bliss even considered having tracks laid from the White House door. He finally decided, however, that the "perfectly even surface of Pennsylvania Avenue really rendered such an expenditure needless."

Finally, at 6:00 a.m., Bliss walked into Garfield's room and said, "Mr. President, we are ready to go." Garfield replied, "I am ready." Edson, who had spent that night watching over the president, vividly recalled the scene in his room that morning. It was, she would later write, "the saddest I have ever witnessed. The patient, while he spoke cheerfully, had a sad expression of countenance which was so unusual for him, but which I do not think indicated that he had given up hope, but rather that he had realized the danger of the situation."

Garfield was carried, Bliss wrote, "by no strange hands." Standing on either side of his bed, Rockwell and Swaim grasped the sheet on which he lay, lifted it, and gently placed him on a stretcher, which they then carried down the stairs and out the door. Members of the White House staff filled the windows with tear-streaked faces, watching the solemn procession to the express wagon that waited on the gravel drive. As they looked down, Garfield looked up, caught sight of them, and lifted his hand in a feeble but warm wave. "A last token of amity," one of the staff wrote, "from a man who loved the world and the people in it."

The train ride to Elberon had been planned as carefully as Garfield's transfer from the White House to the station. Every conductor and engineer in the region stood ready, waiting for word that the president's train had left the Baltimore and Ohio. As soon as they heard that Garfield was on his way, they switched off their engines and waited for him to pass so that their trains would not disturb him in any way. "No sound of bell or whistle was heard," Bliss wrote. The doctor had also arranged to have private homes available for his patient all along the route, so that, if Garfield needed to stop, he would have a safe, clean place to stay. "I must now say," Bliss would later write, "that this whole journey was a marvel even to myself."

The American people were acutely aware that their president was being moved from the White House. "At every station crowds of men and women appeared," Bliss would later recall, "the former uncovered, with bowed heads, the latter often weeping."

Thousands of people stood in silence along the train tracks. "It was indeed a strange and affecting journey," a doctor traveling with Garfield would write, "as we silently sped along."

When the train finally reached Elberon, it switched to a line of railroad track that had been laid just the night before. Two thousand people had worked until dawn to lay 3,200 feet of track so that the president's train could take him to the door of Franklyn Cottage, the twenty-two-room summer home a wealthy New Yorker had offered for as long as it was needed. While determining where the track would have to go, a surveyor had realized that he would need to cut through a neighboring garden, and he apologized to the owner. "I am willing that you should ruin my house," she replied, "all I have — if it would help to save him."

Before the train could reach its final destination, however, it stopped short. The cottage sat at the top of a hill, and the engine was not strong enough to breach it. No sooner had the problem become apparent than, out of the crowd of people who had waited all day in the tremendous heat for Garfield's arrival, two hundred men ran forward to help. "Instantly hundreds of strong arms caught the cars," Bliss wrote, "and silently . . . rolled the three heavy coaches" up the hill.

When he was carried into his room, the first thing Garfield noticed was that the bed was turned away from the window. He asked to have it moved, so that he could look out at the sea. A few days later, when he was lifted into a chair so that he could better see the wide expanse of ocean just beyond the cottage walls, he was thrilled. "This is delightful," he said. "It is such a change."

Despite the relentless suffering Garfield had endured for more than two months, he had maintained not only the strength of his mind, but the essence of his personality. "Throughout his long illness," Rockwell would later recall, "I was most forcibly impressed with the manner in which those traits of his character which were most winning in health became intensified." Even as he lay dying, Garfield was kind, patient, cheerful, and deeply grateful.

When Bliss told him that a fund was being raised for Lucretia, Garfield was overcome with gratitude. "What?" he said in surprise. Then, turning his face to his pillow to hide his emotion, he continued, "How kind and thoughtful! What a generous people!" Garfield was then "silent and absorbed for a long time," Bliss remembered, "as if overwhelmed with the thought."

Garfield was also deeply grateful to the people who had cared for him for so long, and with such devotion. One day, he placed his hand on the head of one of his attendants and said, "You have been always faithful and forebearing." For Bliss, who was visibly weakened by exhaustion and worry, he tried to provide a measure of comfort. "Doctor, you plainly show the effect of all this care and unrest," he said. "Your anxious watching will soon be over."

Bliss still refused to admit that he could not save the president's life. A few days after they arrived in Elberon, he issued a bulletin announcing that the last of the attending physicians had been dismissed, leaving him with only occasional assistance from the surgeons Agnew and Hamilton. Garfield was doing so well, Bliss explained in his bulletin, that he wished to relieve the doctors "from a labor and responsibility which in his improved condition he could no longer impose upon them." To a reporter from the *Washington Post,* Bliss said that Garfield had a "clearer road to recovery now than he ever has had." There was "no abscess, no pus cavity, no pyemia," he insisted. "The trouble has now passed its crisis, and is going away."

Bliss's assurances, however, no longer went unquestioned. "Despite the announcements that the condition of the President is hopeful and that he is making slight gains daily," a reporter for the *Medical Record* wrote, "it is quite evident that his chances for ultimate recovery are very poor indeed." Even Agnew admitted to a friend that he thought the president had very few days left to live. He "may live the day out," he said, "and possibly tomorrow, but he cannot live a week."

Garfield was "perfectly calm, sentient," Bliss wrote, content to live out his last days in this borrowed cottage, gazing at the sea. The president could not help but wonder, however, if, after such a brief presidency, he would leave behind any lasting legacy. "Do you think my name will have a place in human history?" he asked Rockwell one night. "Yes," his friend replied, "a grand one, but a grander place in human hearts."

Rockwell was again with Garfield on the evening of September 19. The president had been suffering from chills, fever, and a persistent cough, but still he longed for companionship. Looking over at his old friend, with whom he had passed many happy evenings, he lifted his hands slightly above the bedcovers and wistfully pantomimed dealing a deck of cards. Soon after, Swaim arrived to relieve Rockwell for the night, and Garfield fell asleep.

At 10:00 p.m., as Swaim sat in silence in the president's room, he suddenly heard Garfield make a gasping sound, as if he were struggling to speak. Rushing to his bedside, he saw, by the light of a single candle, Garfield open his eyes and look at him for a moment. "Well, Swaim," he said, and then, suddenly pressing his hand to his heart, he cried out, "Oh my! Swaim, what a pain I have right here."

Bliss was in his room, reading through the day's multitude of letters offering sympathy and medical advice — "wonderful productions of the human imagination" — when one of Garfield's attendants appeared at the door. "General Swaim wants you quick!" he said. As soon as he reached the room, Bliss knew that there was nothing he could do. Garfield was unconscious, his breathing shallow and fast. "My God, Swaim!" Bliss cried.

Moments later, Lucretia, who had been woken by the attendant, was standing next to Bliss, looking at her husband in terror. "Oh!" she said, "What is the matter?" For once, Bliss had no words of encouragement to offer the first lady. "Mrs. Garfield," he replied quietly, "the President is dying."

As Lucretia bent over James, kissing his brow, the attendant sent word throughout the house and to nearby cottages. One of the first to come was Joseph Stanley Brown. For the rest of his life, Brown would write, he could "hear the long, solemn roll of the sea on the shore as I did on that night of inky darkness, when I walked from my cottage to his bedside." Before many minutes had passed, the room was filled with everyone who had come with them to Elberon — Garfield's surgeons, his friends, and his fourteen-year-old daughter, Mollie. They were, Bliss would later write, "the witnesses of the last sad scene in this sorrowful history."

As Bliss tried in vain to stop what was happening, he could feel Garfield slipping away. "A faint, fluttering pulsation of the heart," he would remember, "gradually fading to indistinctness." For several minutes, the only sound in the room was the president's ragged, irregular breathing. Finally, at 10:35 p.m., Bliss raised his head from Garfield's chest. "It is over," he said.

There was not a movement or a sound, even of crying. "All hearts," Bliss would write, “were stilled.” After a moment, the room slowly began to empty, until Lucretia was left alone with James. She sat by his bed for more than an hour, staring at his frail and lifeless body. Finally, Rockwell returned and, gently touching her arm, “begged her to retire.” Without a word, she stood, and allowed him to lead her away.

Chapter 22
All the Angels of the Universe

If a man murders you without provocation, your soul bears no burden of the wrong; but all the angels of the universe will weep for the misguided man who committed the murder.

JAMES A. GARFIELD

Just after midnight, as he worked late at his house in Washington, Alexander Graham Bell's concentration was suddenly interrupted by a newsboy's shout ringing through the streets. "Extra Republican!" the boy cried. "Death of General Garfield!"

Unable to bear his isolation in Boston any longer, Bell had finally made his way back to the city the day before. Although he was still mourning the death of his son, his thoughts about the induction balance continued to churn urgently even as he had rattled into Washington on the Baltimore and Potomac. "Please hunt in the study and see if you can find [a] bundle of letters and papers in [a] large envelope concerning [the] Induction Balance," he had written quickly to Mabel as the capital came into view. "If so please send me the names and addresses of the poor people who want to have bullets located. . . . One especially is from the father of a little boy who was shot last year."

Now, as he listened to the newsboy's cries, an exhausted Bell could only reflect on the injustice of the ordeal he had witnessed from such a personal vantage point. "How terrible it all is," he wrote to Mabel, who was still at home in Boston. "After seventy-nine days of suffering to be obliged to give up at last. I hope indeed that there may be an immortality for that brave spirit. It is too horrible to think of annihilation and dust."

Science had not been able to prevent the president's death, Bell conceded, but neither had religion. "If prayers could avail to save the sick," he reasoned sadly, "surely the earnest heartfelt cry of a whole nation to God would have availed in this case."

At four o'clock that afternoon, Garfield's doctors assembled in the Franklyn Cottage for what Brown would refer to as "the final agony." The president's autopsy was performed by Dr. D. S. Lamb of the Army Medical Museum, with the assistance of a local doctor and six of Garfield's original physicians, including Bliss, Hamilton, and Agnew. Brown was also there, having agreed to represent "the official household," but was so grief-stricken and horrified by the "ghoulish business" that he found it almost impossible to bear.

In the end, the autopsy would take four excruciating hours to complete. As afternoon turned to evening, Lamb, working slowly and painstakingly, finally had to ask for more lamps to be brought into the room. Across the street, on the porch of the Elberon Hotel, a growing crowd stood peering at the cottage in the fading light, anxious to know why they had lost their president after months of hope and prayers.

The results of the autopsy would surprise no one more than Garfield's own doctors. Soon after they had opened his abdomen, with a long, vertical incision and then another, transverse cut, they found the track of the bullet. "The missile," they realized with sickening astonishment, "had gone to the left." Following its destructive path — as it shattered the right eleventh and twelfth ribs, moved forward, down, and to the left, through the first lumbar vertebra, and into connective tissue — they finally found Guiteau's lead bullet. It lay behind Garfield's pancreas, safely encysted, on the opposite side of the body from where they had been searching.

Running down the right side of Garfield's body was a long channel, which Bliss and eleven other doctors had probed countless times, convinced that, at the end of it, lay the bullet. The autopsy report stated that, while "this long descending channel was supposed during life to have been the track of the bullet," it was "now clearly seen to have been caused by the burrowing of pus from the wound." Pus, however, does not burrow. It simply follows an open path, which, in this case, was made by the doctors' own fingers and instruments. Alongside the channel lay Garfield's liver, slightly enlarged but untouched. There was, the report noted, "no evidence that it had been penetrated by the bullet."

What was perhaps as stunning to the doctors as the location of the bullet was the infection that had ravaged Garfield's body. Evidence of the proximate cause of his death, profound septic poisoning, was nearly everywhere they looked. There were collections of abscesses below his right ear, in the middle of his back, across his shoulders, and near his left kidney. He had infection-induced pneumonia in both of his lungs, and there was an enormous abscess, measuring half a foot in diameter, near his liver. "The initial point of this septic condition probably dates as far back as the period of the first chill," one of Garfield's doctors would later admit. "The course of this . . . infection was practically continuous, and could only result in inevitable death."

The immediate cause of Garfield's death was more difficult to determine. After removing most of his organs, they finally found it — a rent, nearly four-tenths of an inch long, in the splenic artery. The hemorrhage had flooded Garfield's abdominal cavity with a pint of blood, which by now had coagulated into an "irregular form . . . nearly as large as a man's fist." This, they realized, had been the cause of the terrible pain that had forced him to cry out to Swaim just before his death.

After the examination was finally complete, Agnew silently approached the president's body. As everyone in the room watched, he reached out with one hand and ran his little finger down Garfield's spinal column. The finger "slipped entirely through the one vertebra pierced by the bullet," Brown would later recall. Dropping his hand, Agnew turned to the men standing around him and said, "Gentlemen, this was the fatal wound. We made a mistake." Without another word, he left the room.

In New York, as soon as the press learned of the president's death, reporters rushed to Chester Arthur's house on Lexington Avenue, eager for his reaction. His doorkeeper, however, not only refused to let them in but would not even bring them a statement from the vice president. "I daren't ask him," he said. "He is sitting alone in his room sobbing like a child with his head on his desk and his face buried in his hands."

That morning, Arthur had received a telegram from Washington warning him that Garfield's condition was perilous. Still, he had not been prepared when a messenger had knocked on his door late that night. Just a few hours later, he found himself standing in his parlor, its green blinds closed to the newsmen gathered outside, with a New York state judge standing before him, swearing him into office. By 2:15 a.m. on September 20, Arthur had become the twenty-first president of the United States.

Two days later, in the presence of two former presidents, seven senators, six representatives, and several members of Garfield's cabinet, Arthur delivered his inaugural address at the Capitol. To the surprise of everyone present, the new president made it clear that he had no wish to strike a different path from his predecessor. On the contrary, he seemed to hope for nothing more than to be the president that Garfield would have been, had he lived. "All the noble aspirations of my lamented predecessor which found expression in his life," Arthur said, "will be garnered in the hearts of the people, and it will be my earnest endeavor to profit, and to see that the nation shall profit, by his example."

Although Arthur was well aware that, had they been given the opportunity, his countrymen never would have elected him, he was grateful that they now seemed willing to accept him, perhaps even trust him. Even the governor of Ohio, Garfield's proud and devastated state, predicted that "the people and the politicians will find that Vice-President Arthur and President Arthur are different men."

After his inaugural address, Arthur received another letter from his mysterious young adviser, Julia Sand. "And so Garfield is really dead, & you are President," she began. Her advice now was not action, but compassion. The American people were exhausted and grief-stricken, and Arthur must let them mourn. "What the nation needs most at present, is rest," Sand wrote. "If a doctor could lay his finger on the public pulse, his prescription would be, perfect quiet."

Garfield's body, which was returned to Washington by the same train, now swathed in black, that had carried him to Elberon, lay in state in the Capitol rotunda for two days and nights. The line to see the president stretched for more than a quarter mile, snaking through the hushed streets of Washington, under flags bordered in black and flying at half-mast, and in the shadow of buildings wrapped in so much dark fabric they were nearly hidden from view. "The whole city was draped in mourning," Garfield's daughter Mollie would write in her diary. "Even the shanties where the people were so poor that they had to tear up the[ir] clothes in order to show people the deep sympathy and respect they had for Papa. . . . All persons are friends in this deep and great sorrow."

The scene near the Capitol, a reporter wrote, was "in many respects the most remarkable that has ever been witnessed in the United States." More extraordinary even than the size of the crowd, said to include some one hundred thousand mourners, was its unprecedented diversity. "The ragged and toil-stained farm hands from Virginia and Maryland and the colored laborers of Washington," the reporter marveled, "stood side by side with the representatives of wealth and fashion, patiently waiting for hours beneath the sultry September sun for the privilege of gazing for a minute on the face of the dead President."

Only one man had no place in this national mourning. In fact, he was told nothing of the president's death. For Charles Guiteau there was no official notification, nor even a word spoken in passing. He overheard the news from a guard who happened to be standing near his cell at the District Jail. As soon as he realized what had happened, he fell to his knees, desperately mumbling a prayer.

Even before the president's death, Guiteau's fantasy that he had the support and sympathy of the American people had begun to crack. More than a week earlier, as he had been standing at his cell window, watching three wagonloads of fresh troops pull up to the prison to stand guard through the night, he suddenly saw a flash and heard the distinct ripping sound of a bullet as it shot past him. Missing his head by just an inch, the bullet sliced through a coat hanging from a nail and slammed into the whitewashed wall.

The bullet, "a great big musket-bullet," Guiteau would later complain, had come from the gun of one of his own guards, Sergeant William Mason. Although he would later be sentenced to eight years in prison, Mason never expressed regret for his actions. He was tired, he said, of coming to work every day, only to protect a dog like Guiteau.

Throughout the country, there was little condemnation for Mason's act, and widespread sympathy for his feelings of frustration. Newspapers were filled with letters suggesting creative ways to make Guiteau not only pay for his crime, but suffer in the process. One man proposed that he be thrown to a pack of dogs. Another wanted him to be forced to consume himself, by being fed two ounces of his own flesh every day. Others simply wanted to see him dead, as quickly and with as little fanfare as possible. "There is an American judge whose decisions are almost always just, and whose work is always well done," one editorial read. "His name is Judge Lynch; and if he ever had a job that he ought to give his whole attention to, he has it waiting for him in Washington."

Lucretia tried to feel some Christian sympathy for Guiteau, and she urged her children to do the same. Her daughter, however, found it almost impossible. "Mama says he ought to be pitied — Pitied!" Mollie wrote. "I suppose Mama darling is right. But I can not feel that way." Mollie, who had watched her father die a long and agonizing death, wished for nothing more than a tortured end for his assassin. "I suppose I am wicked but these are my feelings," she confessed in her diary. "Guiteau ought to be made to suffer as much and a thousand times more than Papa did. . . . Nothing is to[o] horrible for him, & I hope that everything that can be done to injure him, will be done."

One of the few voices of calm and reason was that of General William Tecumseh Sherman, who had organized the troops now protecting Guiteau. His request for restraint, however, was couched in terms that made it clear that he fully understood how difficult it was to wait for justice. "For this man Guiteau I ask no soldier, no citizen, to feel one particle of sympathy," he wrote in an open letter that was printed in papers across the country. "On the contrary, could I make my will the law, shooting or hanging would be too good for him. But I do ask every soldier and citizen to remember that we profess to be the most loyal Nation on earth to the sacred promises of the law. There is no merit in obeying an agreeable law, but there are glory and heroism in submitting gracefully to an oppressive one."

Now that Garfield was dead, Americans' greatest fear was that Guiteau would get away with murder — not because he was innocent, but because he was insane. The insanity defense was already widely known and almost uniformly despised. Even Garfield, ten years before his own murder, had expressed deep skepticism about the plea. "All a man would need to secure immunity from murder would be to tear his hair and rave a little," he had written, "and then kill his man."

The legal standard for determining insanity — known as the M'Naghten Rule — had been established nearly forty years earlier, across the sea. The rule was named for Daniel M'Naghten, a Scottish woodworker who, believing that he was the target of a conspiracy between the pope and the British prime minister Robert Peel, had attempted to assassinate Peel. Instead, he had shot and mortally wounded Peel's private secretary,

Edward Drummond. M'Naghten's lawyers had successfully argued that he was insane, and so not responsible for his actions. M'Naghten would live another twenty-two years, finally dying in an insane asylum in 1865, from "gradual failure of heart's action."

The verdict had sparked immediate outrage in England, and awakened bitter memories of the trial of Edward Oxford just three years earlier. Oxford, who had attempted to shoot Queen Victoria while she was riding in a carriage, pregnant with her first child, had also been found not guilty by reason of insanity. "We have seen the trials of Oxford and MacNaughtan [spelling variation] conducted by the ablest lawyers of the day," Queen Victoria had written in disgust to Peel after the M'Naghten ruling, "and they allow and advise the Jury to pronounce the verdict of Not Guilty on account of Insanity, — whilst everybody is morally convinced that both malefactors were perfectly conscious and aware of what they did!" Before her eventual death in 1901, at the age of eighty-one, Queen Victoria would survive several more assassination attempts. Her husband, who had lived to witness four of them, was convinced that the would-be assassins had been encouraged by Oxford's acquittal.

The House of Lords, in agreement with the queen, decided that the country needed a clear, strict definition of criminal insanity. Less than four months after M'Naghten's trial, the judges of the British Supreme Court ruled that, in essence, the difference between a sane man and one who was insane lay in the ability to distinguish between right and wrong. A defendant, they declared, could use the insanity defense only if, "at the time of the committing of the act, the party accused was labouring under such a defect of reason, from a disease of the mind, as not to know the nature and quality of the act he was doing; or, if he did know it, that he did not know he was doing what was wrong."

The M'Naghten Rule, while quickly adopted in the United States as well as in England, did little to improve the reputation of the insanity defense. In America, it became known as the "insanity dodge," the refuge not of the mad but of the guilty. Celebrity cases only made matters worse. In 1859, Congressman Daniel Edgar Sickles was found not guilty by reason of temporary insanity after shooting to death Philip Barton Key, the son of Francis Scott Key, author of "The Star-Spangled Banner."

Thirteen years later, Edward Stokes, the man who murdered James Fisk, Jay Gould's partner, used the same defense and spent only four years in prison.

It came as no surprise, therefore, when, on October 14, Garfield's assassin submitted his plea to Judge Walter Cox. "I plead not guilty to the indictment," Guiteau stated, in a plea that he had drafted himself. His first and primary defense was "Insanity, in that it was God's act and not mine. The Divine pressure on me to remove the president was so enormous that it destroyed my free agency, and therefore I am not legally responsible for my act." Although Guiteau laid blame for the shooting squarely on God's shoulders, he made it clear that his faith in divine intervention — at least when his own life was at stake — remained unshaken. "I have entire confidence in His disposition to protect me," he wrote in the plea, "and to send me forth to the world a free and innocent man."

Guiteau would follow the lead of M'Naghten, Oxford, Sickles, and Stokes, and attempt to use his insanity to save his life. Legally, he was allowed this argument, and there was nothing anyone could do to prevent it. It was clear to all involved in the case, however, that the American people would accept no verdict but guilty, no sentence but death. "Guiteau should have a fair trial. Everything that can be urged in his behalf should be patiently heard. It is the right of the meanest thing that bears a human form," one editorial argued. "But such a trial, such a hearing, in a community of intelligent beings can have but one result."

The case of the *United States v. Charles J. Guiteau* began on the morning of November 14, less than two months after Garfield's death. Guiteau's attorney was his brother-in-law, George Scoville, who had come to his rescue countless times in the past with a place to live and loans to keep him alive and out of prison. Scoville was a patent lawyer, and knew almost nothing about the criminal justice system, but he was one of the few lawyers in the country willing to represent the president's assassin. Even Scoville admitted, "If I didn't think the unfortunate man was insane, I would not defend him at all."

As difficult as it was to find a competent defense attorney, it had been nearly impossible to assemble a dispassionate jury. When asked if he would be able to render an impartial verdict in the trial of Guiteau, one prospective juror had replied, "I think he ought to be hung or burnt or something else. . . . I don't think there is any evidence in the United States to convince me any other way." It took three days of jury selection and 175 men to find 12 jurors. In the end, however, Guiteau faced a jury that was, if not unbiased, at least diverse. Deciding his fate were a machinist, two grocers, three merchants, an iron worker, a retired businessman, a restaurant manager, a cigar dealer, and two plasterers. Eleven of the men were white, and one was black.

Before the trial began at 10:00 a.m., a crush of people gathered outside the courtroom, clutching tickets and staring at the closed doors. Deputy marshals wearing bright red badges surrounded the throng, checking the authenticity of their tickets and examining media passes, which, "for the first time in anyone's memory," journalists were required to carry.

The courtroom itself had been renovated just for the trial. A temporary floor had been installed, and more seating added. Half the seats were reserved for lawyers, distinguished guests — a group that included even Frederick Douglass — and journalists. The rest were first come, first served. Those fortunate enough to find seats were so worried that they would lose them during the noon recess that they carried picnic baskets when they arrived in the morning, and had their lunch on their laps.

Guiteau had planned to make an opening statement that day, but the judge refused to allow it. Frustrated, he turned to the long row of reporters seated behind him and handed them his statement. It was not a defense of his actions, or even an argument for insanity, but an indictment of the men who were, he argued, the president's true murderers — his doctors.

The situation, Guiteau insisted, was perfectly clear. "General Garfield died from malpractice," he wrote. "According to his own physicians, he was not fatally shot. The doctors who mistreated him ought to bear the odium of his death, and not his assailant. They ought to be indicted for murdering James A. Garfield, and not me." A few days later, Guiteau would himself announce his argument to the courtroom, interrupting a witness who was describing the scene at the train station when Garfield was shot. "I deny the killing, if your honor please," he said. "We admit the shooting."

Day after day, as the trial slowly advanced, Guiteau repeatedly tried to insert himself into the proceedings. Often, his outbursts were harsh, humiliating critiques of his brother-in-law's legal skill. "Now, don't spoil the matter on cross-examination," he shouted at Scoville at one point. "That is the way you generally do. You spoil everything by cross-examination. . . . You are a jackass on the question of cross-examination. I must tell you that right in public, to your face."

When he wasn't attacking his own attorney, Guiteau attempted to question witnesses, refute testimony, address the judge directly, and even make public appeals for legal and financial assistance. After learning that a fund had been established for Lucretia and her children, he made an announcement to the courtroom. "The rich men of New York gave Mrs. Garfield $200,000 or $300,000," he said. "It was a splendid thing — a noble thing. Now, I want them to give me some money."

Finally, Scoville himself asked the court to force his client to keep quiet. Judge Cox, determined that there not be any possible grounds for appeal, was reluctant to remove Guiteau from the courtroom. There was little he could do, therefore, beyond issuing repeated warnings and moving the defendant farther from the witness stand. Guiteau's "declarations," the judge would later complain, "could not have been prevented except by resorting to the process of gagging him."

The more Guiteau spoke, the more apparent his insanity became. He was highly intelligent and surprisingly articulate, but his mind did not work like that of a sane man. "All the links in the chain are there," George Beard, a psychiatrist who would interview Guiteau on four separate occasions, explained, "but they are not joined, but rather tossed about hither and thither, singly, like quoits, each one good and strong of itself, but without relation to any other." When Guiteau speaks, Beard said, "his insanity forces itself constantly to the front, breaking in upon his eloquence."

Guiteau spent nearly a week on the stand, talking about his childhood, his years at the commune, his life as a traveling evangelist, and his motivations for shooting the president. The prosecution did everything in its power to prove that he was not insane, but simply immoral. Scoville countered by tracing the history of insanity in Guiteau's family — from an uncle who had died in an asylum to several aunts, cousins, and even Guiteau's own mother.

Before the trial had ended, thirty-six experts would testify on the subject of

Guiteau's sanity. Scoville placed most of his hope in a controversial but widely admired young neurologist named Edward Spitzka, who had studied in Vienna and Leipzig and was well known for openly questioning, even attacking, the most powerful psychiatrists in the nation. Even before meeting Guiteau, Spitzka had written in a medical journal that, if the defendant, "with his hereditary history, his insane manner, his insane documents and his insane actions were to be committed to any asylum in the land, he would be unhesitatingly admitted as a proper subject for sequestration." In the courtroom, after Spitzka testified that he had examined Guiteau and found him to be insane, Scoville asked, "Did you have any question on that subject?" Without hesitating, Spitzka replied, "Not the slightest."

Determined to drown out men like Spitzka, the prosecution brought to the stand nearly twice as many experts as the defense. The star witness for the prosecution was Dr. John Purdue Gray, the superintendent of the New York State Lunatic Asylum. Gray had spent two days interviewing Guiteau, and was convinced that his only ailment was moral depravity. "A man may become profoundly depraved and degraded by mental habits and yet not be insane," he insisted. "It is only depravity."

Guiteau listened to these testimonies with avid interest. Although he had pleaded insanity, he was anxious to make clear that he had been insane only at the time of the shooting — not before, and certainly not after. Now, he argued, he was as sane as any man in the courtroom. As Gray attempted to define insanity for the jury, explaining that it was a "disease of the brain, in which there is a . . . change in the individual, a departure from himself," Guiteau abruptly broke in. "That is my case," he said. "I shot the President on the second of July. I would not do it again for a million dollars, with the mind I have got now."

The central question of the trial — whether or not Guiteau was insane — seemed to most Americans a waste of time. Insane or not, they wanted to see him hanged, at the very least. "Hanging is too good for you, you stinking cuss," a Union veteran had written to him. "You ought to be burned alive and let rot. You savage cannibal dog." A farmer from Maryland tried to accomplish what William Mason had failed to do. As the prison coach carried Guiteau from the courtroom back to the District Jail one day, he rode up on his horse, drew his pistol, and fired at the prisoner. Once again, the shot missed Guiteau, but left him terrified, with a singed hole in his coat.

The trial, punctuated by Guiteau's constant outbursts and heightened by testimony from members of the Senate, the secretary of state, and, by letter, even President Arthur, finally ended on January 26, 1882. At 4:35 that afternoon, after more than two months of testimony, the prosecution rested. Less than an hour later, the jury returned with a verdict.

"Gentlemen of the jury," the clerk called out, his voice harsh against the perfect silence of the courtroom, "have you agreed upon a verdict?" The foreman, a man named John Hamlin, replied that they had. "What say you," asked the clerk. "Is the defendant guilty or not guilty?" "Guilty as indicted, sir," Hamlin said.

Before Hamlin had even finished speaking, the courtroom erupted in thunderous applause. So deafening were the cheers that the bailiff's shout for order could hardly be heard. When the crowd, under threat of expulsion from the courtroom, finally quieted, one voice alone rang out. "My blood be on the head of the jury, don't you forget it," Guiteau cried. "That is my answer. . . .

God will avenge this outrage."

Even after he had been found guilty and sentenced to death, Guiteau believed that he would be set free. It was only a matter of time — and presidential influence. He had already written to Arthur several times, demanding a full pardon, but after the U.S. Supreme Court denied his appeal, he wrote again. The letter was a window into Guiteau's strained mind. "I am willing to DIE for my inspiration," he wrote, "but it will make a terrible reckoning for you and this nation. I made you . . . and the least you can do is to let me go." Then, suddenly switching tracks from dire threat to friendly advice, he offered what seemed to him a reasonable compromise. "But I appreciate your delicate position," he wrote, "and I am willing to stay here until January, if necessary."

Besides Guiteau himself, the only people who believed that his life might yet be spared were his brother and sister. John Guiteau, although he had long been deeply ashamed of his younger brother, and had often been bitterly angry with him, could not bear to see him die. "Whatever your impressions may be," he had written to Charles after the trial ended, "I want you to know that I feel towards you as a brother and a friend, and shall, in the short time remaining, do all I can to save your life." He was convinced that Charles was insane, and that if the American people could only be made to understand that fact, they would want to see him locked away in an asylum, not hanged. "The public have never had the facts, nor the Court," he wrote to Charles. "And they know not what they are about to do."

Finally, John also wrote to the president, seeking not a pardon, but simply a stay of execution. In his letter to Arthur, he asked only for enough time to present further evidence of his brother's insanity. He hoped that the president would give him "an audience before a decision is reached, that I may make a brief statement of my brother's unfortunate life, which will explain much of what now appears to his disadvantage."

Arthur refused to see John, knowing that, if he gave Guiteau's brother even a few moments of his time, there would be a public outcry. He did, however, agree to meet with the psychiatrist George Beard, and with Miss A. A. Chevaillier, an advocate for the insane. After listening to them for twenty minutes, Arthur forwarded their appeal to his attorney general, Benjamin Harris Brewster. Brewster replied almost immediately, advising Arthur to reject the appeal. Two days later, the newspapers reported that, after careful consideration, the president and his cabinet had come to the conclusion that there were "no grounds to justify Executive interference with the verdict of the jury and the action of the courts."

Frances Scoville, who had for most of her life been more of a mother to Charles than a sister, also tried desperately to stay the hand of the court. She directed her appeal, however, not to Garfield's successor, but to his widow. In a letter to Lucretia just two weeks after the verdict was read, she openly begged for her brother's life.

> Dear Madam:
>
> Humbly I address you, trusting you will not turn a deaf ear even upon despised Guiteau's sister.
>
> All these weary months I have patiently waited until the time should come for me to speak: when, after the verdict, which I believed would be "Not guilty by reason of insanity," I could say without shamefacedness, "My heart bleeds for you and the sainted dead." . . .
>
> I have counted the hours for the time when I could boldly say to you, as I have

> said from the moment when the terrible news was brought me on that dark day in July: "He was brain sick, deluded, crazy; forgive him, even as Christ shall forgive us all. . . ."
>
> In Heaven we know, as we are known. The sainted Garfield knows now that he "had to do it," and I feel sure if he could speak he would say, "Forgive that deluded man, even as I forgive him; safely keep him from doing any more harm, but forgive."

Lucretia never replied. When she could wait no longer, Frances packed a bag, took a train from Chicago to Cleveland, Ohio, walked up to the home where Garfield's widow was living, and knocked on the door. Lucretia and Mollie were down the street, and so Frances, who had traveled under the name of Mrs. Smith, was asked to wait in the library. When Lucretia returned home to find that Charles Guiteau's sister was waiting for her, she went up to her room and sent down word that she would not see her.

Mollie was sitting on the front steps when Frances left. When she later learned who the strange visitor had been, she felt nothing but fury and outrage that she had "dared to come." For her father's assassin, Mollie would write bitterly in her diary, "nothing could be too awful . . . & my heart is like *stone* toward him."

By the day of his execution, even Guiteau had accepted that there would be no stay, no pardon, no fearsome act of God to save his life. When John Crocker, the warden of the District Jail, appeared at his cell door just after twelve noon on June 30, 1882, Guiteau was sitting on his cot, wearing a black suit that he had paid a prison worker to wash and press the day before, and shoes that he had sent to be polished that morning. Beside him was Reverend Hicks, a Washington minister who had visited him every day for nearly a month, and with whom Guiteau had become so close he had made him the executor of his will. "I'm fully resigned," Guiteau had told Hicks the night before, when he had woken just before midnight and asked to see the minister. "God has smoothed over the road to glory which I will travel tomorrow."

Now, as he looked up and saw Crocker standing before him, Guiteau's face whitened, but he quickly stood and, holding Hicks's hand, listened quietly as the warden began to speak. "With the events of the past year crowding around you now, as the hours of life enfold around you," Crocker said, "I find myself called upon to perform a last solemn duty in connection with the death of our President." Then, his voice trembling slightly, he read aloud the warrant for Guiteau's death.

After Crocker had finished, Guiteau asked of him a final favor. He wanted to give the executioner's signal, to choose for himself the moment of his death. He had written a prayer that morning, he said, and planned to read it on the scaffold. When he was ready, he would drop the prayer. Crocker agreed.

A few minutes later, Hicks, Crocker, and a small contingent, which included several guards as well as the executioner, followed Guiteau as he was led from his cell to the prison's northeast corridor, where a scaffold had been erected. As they passed a window, Guiteau stopped to look out on a bright summer day, green hills swelling under a blue sky. He paused at the window for just a moment, and then, without being asked, turned away and walked on.

Finally, the procession came to a set of stairs that led down to a narrow courtyard, at the far end of which sat the scaffold. The courtyard was flanked on the east by the jail's outer wall, and on the west by tiers of cells rising sixty feet to the ceiling. The cells had been emptied, and the tall windows on the eastern wall had been covered by heavy curtains.

Twenty thousand people had requested tickets to the execution. Two hundred and fifty had been issued. More than a thousand people stood outside, waiting for the announcement of Guiteau's death, while those who had seats inside watched in silence as he made his way toward the scaffold, his footsteps echoing on the brick floor. As he ascended the steps of the scaffold, struggling a little because his arms were tied tightly behind his back, Guiteau tripped on the first step. Smiling, he turned to Hicks and said, "I stubbed my toe going to the gallows."

When they had all assembled on the scaffold, Hicks, who was visibly shaken, spoke first, giving a brief supplication. Then he held a Bible before Guiteau, who proceeded to read fourteen verses from Matthew 10, beginning with the words "And fear not them which kill the body, but are not able to kill the soul." After he had finished, Guiteau looked out at the silent, stone-faced crowd and announced that he would now read a prayer of his own composition.

He began by paraphrasing Matthew 18:3. "Except ye become as a little child," he said, "ye cannot enter into the kingdom of heaven." Then, in a falsetto meant to evoke the pleadings of a child, he began to read "Simplicity."

> I am going to the Lordy, I am so glad.
> I am going to the Lordy, I am so glad.
> I am going to the Lordy,
> Glory hallelujah! Glory hallelujah!
> I am going to the Lordy!

The poem continued for four more stanzas. Guiteau's voice, although high, remained strong until the final line. "Glory hallelujah! Glory hallelujah!" he said, his voice finally breaking. "I am with the Lord."

When Guiteau had finished, Hicks stepped forward once again to give the benediction. "God the Father be with thee," he said, "and give thee peace evermore." Nothing more was said as Guiteau's legs were bound together, a noose looped around his neck and carefully adjusted, and a heavy black hood placed over his head. He stood with his shoulders pulled back, his head held high.

"Glory, glory, glory," he called out, and

then, opening his hand, he let the prayer fall.

Epilogue: Forever and Forever More

There is nothing in all the earth that you and I can do for the Dead. They are past our help and past our praise. We can add to them no glory, we can give to them no immortality. They do not need us, but forever and forever more we need them.

JAMES A. GARFIELD, AUGUST 1880

The death of Charles Guiteau, which was greeted by a triumphant shout that echoed through the courtyard and was picked up and carried by the crowd pressed against the prison walls, accomplished nothing. It did not prevent future assassinations, brought no solace to a heartbroken nation, no comfort to Lucretia or her children, nor even lasting satisfaction to those who had screamed for vengeance.

After the doors were opened and the throng was allowed to parade past Guiteau's body, while his brother silently fanned flies from his face, he was buried in the prison courtyard. As the casket was being covered with dirt, John Guiteau did not say a word or shed a tear. Before he left, however, he bent over the grave and placed a small clutch of white flowers at its head.

A few days later, Guiteau's body was quietly exhumed and taken to the Army Medical Museum, where Dr. Lamb, the same man who had performed Garfield's autopsy, studied it for signs of insanity. Guiteau's brain was removed, divided into small sections, and sent to psychiatrists across the country. Besides a malaria-infected spleen that was twice the normal size, however, the scientists found nothing notable in the remains of Charles Guiteau.

Today, two sections of Guiteau's spleen, parts of his skeleton — including his ribs, left hand, and left foot — and a glass jar containing the pieces of his brain, which were eventually returned to Washington, remain in the Army Medical Museum, now known as the National Museum of Health and Medicine. These specimens are kept in a large metal cabinet with long, deep drawers. The drawer just below Guiteau's holds the vertebrae of another presidential assassin — John Wilkes Booth — as well as a six-inch section of Garfield's spine, which had served as an exhibit at Guiteau's trial. A red, plastic rod rests in a hole in the knobby, yellowed bone, indicating the path of the bullet.

Even as they mourned the death of their president, Americans understood that, as time passed, Garfield would begin to fade from memory. "His ultimate place in history will be far less exalted than that which he now holds in popular estimation," the *New York Times* warned its readers. More painful even than the realization that his brief presidency would be forgotten was the thought that future generations would never know the man he had been. A few years after Garfield's death, a reporter, gazing at a formal portrait of him that hung in the White House, wrote, "I fear coming generations of visitors who pass through this grand corridor will see nothing in the stern, sad face of Garfield to remind them that here was a man who loved to play croquet and romp with his boys upon his lawn at Mentor, who read Tennyson and Longfellow at fifty with as much enthusiastic pleasure as at twenty, who walked at evening with his arm around the neck of a friend in affectionate conversation, and whose sweet, sunny, loving nature not even twenty years of political strife could warp."

What has survived of Garfield, however, is far more powerful than a portrait, a statue, or even the fragment of his spine that tells the tragic story of his assassination. The horror and senselessness of his death, and the wasted promise of his life, brought tremendous change to the country he loved — change that, had it come earlier, almost certainly would have spared his life.

Garfield's long illness and painful death brought the country together in a way that, even the day before the assassination attempt, had seemed to most Americans impossible. "Garfield does not belong to the North alone," read a letter that was written by a southerner to Lucretia soon after the shooting, and printed in papers across the country. "From this common vigil and prayer and sympathy in the travail of this hour there shall be a new birth of the Nation." That prediction was realized the day Garfield's death was announced, when his countrymen mourned not as northerners or southerners, but as Americans. "This morning from the depth of their grief-stricken hearts all Americans can and will thank God that there is no North, no South, no East, no West," a minister said from his pulpit. "Bound together in one common sorrow, binding in its vastness, we are one and indissoluble."

Out of this common sorrow grew a fierce resolve to prevent such a tragedy from ever happening again. Americans did not believe, however, that Garfield had been assassinated because he had walked into the train station, just as he had traveled everywhere since the day of his election, wholly unprotected. Even after losing two presidents to assassins, the idea of surrounding them with guards, and so distancing them from the people they served, still seemed too imperial, too un-American. In fact, Secret Service agents would not be officially assigned to protect the president until after William McKinley was shot in Buffalo, New York, on September 6, 1901. The day McKinley was shot — he would die from his wounds eight days later — Robert Todd Lincoln was once again standing with the president, thus earning the dubious distinction of being the only man to be present at three of our nation's four presidential assassinations.

To Americans in 1881, the principal danger their presidents faced was not physical attack but political corruption. With a determination that shocked even the most senior politicians, they turned their wrath on the spoils system, the political practice that had made Garfield the target of the delusional ambitions of a man like Guiteau. "We do not think we have taken up a newspaper during the last ten days which has not in some manner made the crime the product of 'the spoils system,' " an article in the *Nation* had read soon after the shooting. "There has hardly been an allusion to it in the pulpit which has not pointed to the spoils system as the *fons et origo mali.* In fact, the crime seems to have acted on public opinion very like a spark on a powder-magazine. It has fallen on a mass of popular indignation all ready to explode." With Garfield's death, the cries of indignation reached such a fevered pitch that they could no longer be ignored.

Finally, civil service reform would find its most powerful advocate in the most unlikely of men — Chester Arthur. No man in the country owed more to the spoils system — or to its most powerful advocate, Roscoe Conkling — than Arthur. Since Garfield's death, however, it had become strikingly apparent that Arthur was no longer the man Conkling had made. "He isn't 'Chet Arthur' any more," one of Conkling's men mournfully said after he had taken office. "He's the President."

In his first official address as president,

Arthur called for civil service reform. Just one year later, he signed the Pendleton Civil Service Act. This act, named for the Ohio Senator who sponsored it, transformed government appointments from what men like Conkling and Guiteau believed them to be — gifts given at the pleasure of powerful officials to those who had been most useful to them — into positions won on the basis of merit. Pendleton had introduced the bill two years earlier, but Congress had ignored it. It took Garfield's assassination, the resounding defeat in 1882 of several congressmen who had publicly opposed reform, and President Arthur's support to finally make it law.

Conkling learned this too, when he visited Arthur in the White House soon after his inauguration. Now that Arthur was president, Conkling expected his protégé to redeem his reputation, and avenge his humiliating defeat at Garfield's hands. He demanded that Arthur strip William Robertson of the collectorship of the New York Customs House, the appointment that had led to his disastrous decision to resign his Senate seat, and he expected to be made secretary of state. Blaine had resigned in December, writing to a friend that Garfield's death was still a "fresh grief to me," and

Conkling relished the idea of taking up the powerful position from which his old enemy had limped away.

Arthur, however, to Conkling's amazement, not only refused to do his bidding, but was offended by the assumption that he would. Conkling's demands, he said angrily, were "outrageous." Conkling, realizing that he was suddenly powerless to control a man who had for years been his most loyal minion, stormed out of the room, sick with rage and "swearing that all of his friends have turned traitor." Even more than the loss of his Senate seat, this betrayal was, for Conkling, a staggering blow. "When I saw him *afterwards,*" his mistress, Kate Sprague, would later write to Arthur, "& saw *how he was suffering,* I urged his quitting Washington without delay. Friends who have seen him within a day or two, report him as very ill."

Arthur had, in part, found the strength to free himself from Conkling's grasp in the bold letters of his mysterious friend, Julia Sand. So much did he admire her strong, intelligent advice that he finally decided that he must meet her. After dinner on August 20, 1882, a highly polished carriage pulled up to the front door of number 46 East Seventy-Fourth Street, the house where

Sand lived with her brother. Sand was inside, stretched out on the sofa, having "disdained roast beef and scorned peach-pie," when she suddenly heard a man talking to her brother in the front parlor. She was just "wondering who that gentle-voiced Episcopal minister . . . might be" when President Arthur walked into the room. Arthur would stay for nearly an hour, pleased to finally have a face-to-face discussion with one of his most trusted advisers.

Although Arthur would go on to become a respected leader, his presidency marked by earnest effort and honest, if modest, achievement, his political career would end with his first term. In 1884, the Republican Party chose for its presidential candidate not the man who had inherited the White House, but the one who had fought longest and hardest to occupy it — James G. Blaine. Blaine, although he had promised Garfield he would never again seek the presidency, could not resist a final chance to hold the office he had hungered for most of his life. So desperately did he want to be president that, after he won the nomination, he even had his men approach Conkling, in the hope that the former senator might set aside his hatred for him to help secure the election for his party. "Gentlemen, you have been misinformed," Conkling coolly replied. "I have given up criminal law." Soon after, Blaine lost the election to Grover Cleveland, who became the first Democratic president to be elected since the Civil War.

When Arthur left the White House, after having meticulously and beautifully renovated it, he was almost unrecognizable as the man who had been Garfield's running mate and vice president. "No man ever entered the Presidency so profoundly and widely distrusted," the well-known journalist Alexander McClure wrote, "and no one ever retired . . . more generally respected." It was not until after Arthur had moved back to New York City that it became widely known that he was suffering from Bright's disease, an excruciatingly painful and, at that time, fatal kidney disease. He died two years later, at the age of fifty-six.

Although he attended Arthur's funeral, Conkling never forgave him. For years after their falling-out, he nursed a bitter grudge, jeeringly referring to Arthur as "His Accidency" and taking pleasure in refusing an appointment to the U.S. Supreme Court after Arthur had risked his reputation nominating him. After Garfield's death and Arthur's betrayal, Conkling bitterly turned his back on public life. "How can I speak into a grave?" he railed. "How can I do battle with a shroud? Silence is a duty and a doom!"

Like his life, Conkling's death, which came just two years after Arthur's, was a pitched battle for control. Early in the spring of 1888, over a period of little more than two days, New York City was buried under twenty-two inches of snow, more than twice as much snow as it had seen all winter. The wind howled at forty-five miles per hour, with gusts nearly twice as fast, and the city was littered with towering snow drifts, some as high as fifty feet. Before it was over, four hundred people along the northeastern coast would die — two hundred in New York City alone.

On March 11, while most New Yorkers stayed home, or huddled in bars or train stations — three hundred people slept in Grand Central Terminal — Conkling insisted on going to work. Then, as the storm steadily worsened, he refused a hack driver's offer to drive him for fifty dollars, and insisted on walking home. It took even Conkling, who was a famously vigorous walker, three hours to walk the three miles from his office to the New York Club at Broadway and Twenty-first Street. Moments after he walked in the door, he fell facedown onto the entryway floor. "He didn't crumble, he didn't collapse," his biographer would write. "He fell full length. For he was that kind of man."

Conkling survived that night, even returned to work, but on April 4 he fell ill again. For nearly two weeks, he fought to gain the upper hand, falling in and out of a feverish delirium. Twelve years earlier, while suffering from a severe case of malaria, Conkling had told a friend through clenched teeth, "I am *not* going to die." Now, he paced the floor of his room, fighting off those who tried to help him as his temperature soared. The battle lasted until two o'clock on the morning of April 17, when, more than a month after he had walked through one of the deadliest snowstorms in New York history, Conkling died from pulmonary edema.

Although there were many deaths in the late nineteenth century that even the most skilled physicians had no ability to prevent, Garfield's was not one of them. In fact, following his autopsy, it became immediately and painfully apparent that, far from preventing or even delaying the president's death, his doctors very likely caused it.

Bliss had a few loyal defenders, but as a

whole, the international medical community forcefully condemned the decisions he had made and the actions he had taken, particularly the repeated, unsterilized probing of the president's wound. Just six months after Garfield's death, *The Boston Medical and Surgical Journal* printed a lecture by the renowned German surgeon Friedrich Esmarch. "It seems that the attending physicians were under the pressure of the public opinion that they were doing far too little," Esmarch had said. "But according to my opinion they have not done too little but too much."

American physicians were less gentle in their assessment. Bliss had done "more to cast distrust upon American surgery than any time heretofore known to our medical history," one doctor wrote. Young surgeons, especially, were scornfully critical of Bliss's care. "None of the injuries inflicted by the assassin's bullet were necessarily fatal," wrote Arpad Gerster, a thirty-three-year-old New York surgeon who had recently been in Europe, studying the "Listerian method of wound treatment," and would write the first American surgical textbook based on that method. To the physicians of his generation, Gerster continued, Garfield's death proved with certainty that, as the poet Thomas

Gray had written more than a century earlier, "ignorance is Bliss."

Bliss, however, refused to be cowed. Garfield, he said, had died not from a massive blood infection, but as the result of a broken backbone. He insisted, moreover, that the care he had given the president had been not only adequate, but exemplary. In a document titled "Statement of the Services Rendered," Bliss and the few surgeons he had allowed to work with him argued that "he should receive, as he merits, the sympathy and goodwill (as well as the lasting confidence) of every patriotic citizen for the great skill, unequalled devotion and labor performed in this notable case, which . . . secured to the distinguished patient the perfection of surgical management."

To the astonishment of the members of Congress, Bliss confidently presented them with a bill for $25,000 — more than half a million dollars in today's currency. While caring for the president, Bliss said, he had lost twenty-three pounds, and his health was "so greatly impaired as to render him entirely unable to recover or attend to his professional duties." Congress agreed to pay Bliss $6,500, and not a penny more. Bliss, outraged, refused to accept it, bitterly complaining that it was "notoriously inadequate as a just compensation." Seven years later, Bliss would die quietly at his home following a stroke, having never recovered his health, his practice, or his reputation.

The day after her husband's funeral, Lucretia Garfield returned home to Mentor. At first, even surrounded by family and friends — her children, her mother-in-law, Rockwell and his family, and Swaim and his wife had all gone with her — the house felt achingly empty. "Now that Papa has gone," James, her second son, wrote that night, "our home will be desolate." For Lucretia, the farmhouse had always been filled with her husband's great, booming laughter, or with the happy anticipation of his return. "Had it not been that her children needed her more than at any time in their lives," Mollie would write of her mother years later, "life would have meant very little to her."

Lucretia, however, would not surrender to grief. One of the few outward concessions she would make to a life of mourning was her stationery, which, from the day of James's death until her own, would be trimmed in black. The letters she wrote, however, were strong and fearless — most often in the protection either of her children's future, or her husband's memory. She had become, in the words of Garfield's mother, James's "armed defender."

Although it was a role that Lucretia did not enjoy, she was determined to do it well. She spent countless hours correcting articles about James, keeping private letters out of books and newspapers, and trying to discourage eager but talentless portraitists. She informed one painter that his portrait of Garfield was "not very good" and that she hoped he would not let anyone else see "such an imperfect representation."

Lucretia's first concern, however, was for her husband's papers. She asked Joseph Stanley Brown for his help in organizing them, and she used some of the money from the fund that had been established for her to build an addition to the farmhouse. The second floor of this wing was made into a library, which would become the nation's first presidential library.

Within the library, Lucretia installed a fireproof vault. Today, that vault still holds the wreath that Queen Victoria sent upon Garfield's death. Among the first items Lucretia placed in it, however, were the letters that she and James had written to each other over twenty-two years of marriage. She included all that she had, even the most painful. To one small bundle of letters, she attached a note. "These are the last letters and telegrams received from My Darling," she wrote, "during the five days I remained at Elberon previous to the fearful tragedy of July 2nd, 1881."

The most precious product of her marriage to James, their children, would, under her firm guidance, grow up to live full and useful lives, lives that would have made their father exceedingly proud. Their oldest son, Harry, would become a lawyer, a professor of government at Princeton, and, like his father, a university president — of Williams College, Garfield's alma mater. James, also a lawyer, would become Theodore Roosevelt's secretary of the interior in 1907. Of James, Roosevelt would write, "He has such poise and sanity — he is so fearless, and yet possesses such common sense, that he is a real support to me." Irvin would become a lawyer as well, and Abe, the youngest, an architect. All of Garfield's sons, no matter where they settled, remained close to their mother, often visiting her and the family farm that had shaped their boyhoods.

Perhaps more than her brothers, Mollie would struggle to accept the loss of their father. "Sometimes I feel that God couldn't have known how we all loved & needed him, here with us," she wrote in her diary two months after his death. "I don't believe I shall ever learn to say 'Thy will be done' about that." The holidays were particularly painful, when she kept expecting to hear the little song, "Ring out wild bells," that her father used to sing, "to a tune he made himself." "Oh! me!" she wrote, "How I miss my darling father."

In the end, Mollie would find comfort and strength in an emotion even more powerful than grief — love. Little more than a year after her father's death, Mollie, now sixteen, wrote in her diary not a lament, but a confession. She had fallen in love with the young man who had been like a son to her father — Joseph Stanley Brown. "I believe I am in love," she wrote. "I don't believe I will ever in my life love any man as I do Mr. Brown — and it can't be merely like. For I *like* Bentley, Don, and Gaillard Hunt. And it isn't infatuation, for when I first knew Mr. Brown I didn't like him at all. No, I'm sure it is nothing but honest & true love."

Brown had turned down Arthur's request to stay on in the White House as the president's private secretary. He wished, he said, to complete the work he had begun. When he had finished that work — organizing

Garfield's papers and preparing them for binding — he left Mentor for New Haven, Connecticut, where he attended Yale's Sheffield Scientific School.

Little more than two years later, Brown returned to Ohio, a college-educated man. When Mollie arrived home after a trip to England with her mother, he was waiting for her at the dock, with a ring in his pocket. The diamond was, Mollie would later tell her daughter, "a small stone, but a *very* good one." Three months later, Mollie and Joseph were married, in a double wedding with Harry Garfield and his fiancée, Belle Hartford Mason. The wedding took place before the large bay window of the library that Lucretia had built for James.

After Garfield's death, Alexander Graham Bell stayed on in Washington, still convinced that his induction balance would save lives. The reason for its failure remained a frustrating and demoralizing mystery to Bell until the day Garfield's autopsy results were announced. "It is now rendered quite certain why it was that the result of the experiment with the Induction Balance was 'not satisfactory,' as I stated in my report," he wrote soon after to Mabel, in a letter filled with as much anger as sorrow. "For the bullet was not in any part of the area explored."

The realization that, while he had carefully searched Garfield's right side for the bullet, it had been lying on the left, was sickening to Bell. "This is most mortifying to me and I can hardly bear to think of it," he confessed to Mabel. "I feel that now the finger of scorn will be pointed at the Induction Balance and at me — and all the hard work I have gone through — seems thrown away." More painful to him than the damage to his reputation was the thought that his invention would be dismissed as useless, or even dangerous. "I feel that I have really accomplished a great work — and have devised an apparatus that will be of inestimable use in surgery," he wrote, "but this mistake will re-act against its introduction. The patients I am anxious to benefit would hardly be willing to risk an operation . . . after what has occurred."

As dejected as Bell was, however, he could not give up on his invention. On October 7, less than a month after Garfield's death, he again tested the induction balance, this time on several patients of Dr. Hamilton, who had been one of Garfield's surgeons. The tests were an unqualified success — the first time the invention had found a bullet "the position of which was previously unknown"

— and they left Bell even more convinced that, had he been permitted to search both sides of Garfield's body, he would have found Guiteau's bullet.

Bell made no further entries in his laboratory notebook about the induction balance until October 25. On that day, however, his notes covered four pages. "An old idea not previously noted came back to me with considerable significance," he wrote from a hotel room in Paris. A few days later, he returned once again to the invention, with the same determination and enthusiasm he had had from the moment of its inception.

Bell knew that the induction balance was important. His mistake was in believing that, because it had not worked on the president, no one would be willing to use it. In the years to come, the induction balance would lessen the suffering and save the lives not just of Americans but of soldiers in the Sino-Japanese War and the Boer War. Even during World War I, doctors would often turn to the induction balance when they could not find an X-ray machine, or did not trust its accuracy.

The induction balance, however, was not the only medical invention that would come out of this difficult time in Bell's life. The death of his son also inspired him to build a machine that would essentially breathe for those who, like Edward, could not breathe for themselves. The invention, which he called a vacuum jacket, consisted primarily of an airtight iron cylinder that encircled the patient's torso, and a suction pump that forced air into his lungs. The vacuum jacket was a precursor to the iron lung, which would help thousands of people breathe during the polio epidemic of the 1940s and early 1950s.

Bell, still a young man, had an astonishingly busy and productive life yet ahead of him. Soon after Garfield's death, he would become a United States citizen. In 1888, he and a small group of like-minded men would found the National Geographic Society, whose ambition it was to create "a society for the increase and diffusion of geographic knowledge." About the same time, Bell also founded the Volta Bureau, "for the increase and diffusion of knowledge relating to the Deaf." In 1893, he moved the bureau into a yellow-brick and sandstone building, now a National Historic Landmark, on Thirty-fifth Street in Washington, D.C., directly across the street from where he had earlier moved his Volta Laboratory.

Although he would continue to work on a

wide range of inventions, most strikingly with various forms of flight, for Bell, the desire to help and teach the deaf would be the overarching passion of his life. In 1886, Captain Arthur Keller traveled to Washington from Alabama to see Bell. He brought with him his six-year-old daughter, Helen, who had been left blind, deaf, and mute after contracting what may have been scarlet fever when she was nineteen months old. Years later, Helen Keller would remember that meeting with Bell as the "door through which I should pass from darkness into light." So grateful was she to Bell that sixteen years later, she would dedicate her autobiography to him.

Keller wrote her memoirs when she was just twenty-two years old, but Bell, even near the end of his life, refused to write his own. When repeatedly asked to put down on paper the extraordinary events of his life, his reply was always the same: He was "still more interested in the future than in the past."

Bell would live to be seventy-five years old, dying at his home in Nova Scotia on August 2, 1922. Alone with him in his room was his wife, Mabel. She had been by his side when he was an unknown, penniless teacher, and she was with him now, forty-five years later, as he left the world one of its most famous men. Moments before his death, Mabel, who would survive her husband by only six months, whispered to Alec, "Don't leave me." Unable to speak, he answered her by pressing her fingers with two of his own — sign language, their language, for "no."

Like Bell, Joseph Lister would live a long life, long enough to see his ideas not only vindicated, but venerated. Over the years, he would be given his country's most distinguished honors — from being knighted by Queen Victoria in 1882, to being made a baron by William Gladstone a year later, to being named one of the twelve original members of the Order of Merit, established in 1902 by Edward VII, Victoria's son, to recognize extraordinary achievement. What Lister valued above all else, however, was the knowledge that doctors around the world now practiced antiseptic surgery, and that their patients had a far greater hope of keeping their limbs, and their lives. "I must confess that, highly, and very highly, as I esteem the honors that have been conferred upon me," he would say later in life, "I regard all worldly distinctions as nothing in comparison with the hope that I may have been the means of reducing in some degree the sum of human misery."

Long before his death at the age of eighty-four, Lister would be recognized as "the greatest conqueror of disease the world has ever seen." Nowhere, however, was his contribution to science, and to the welfare of all humankind, appreciated more than in the United States, a country that had once dismissed his theory at tremendous cost. In 1902, more than twenty years after Garfield's death, the American ambassador to England would give a speech at the Royal Society in honor of the fiftieth anniversary of Lister's doctorate.

"My lord," the ambassador said, addressing Lister as he sat in an opulent hall, surrounded by powerful men and celebrated scientists, "it is not a profession, it is not a nation, it is humanity itself which, with uncovered head, salutes you."

ACKNOWLEDGMENTS

It does not take much exposure to the vast and rich collection of Garfield's papers and artifacts to understand that our twentieth president was not just a tragic figure, but an extraordinary man. The story of his remarkable life and brutal murder is told in heartbreaking detail in hundreds of diary entries, letters, and personal artifacts — a historical treasure trove that would have been lost long ago were it not for the exceptional skill and devotion of the men and women who are the keepers of our nation's great archives.

While researching this book, every time I visited one of these archives I found largely forgotten items that, more than a century after Garfield's death, brought him suddenly and vividly to life. At the Historical Society of Washington, D.C., I was shown the lead bullet, smooth and flattened by the impact with Garfield's body, that Guiteau shot from his .44 caliber gun on the morning of July 2, 1881. At the National Museum of Health and Medicine, I held in my gloved hands the section of Garfield's spine which that bullet had pierced. At the National Museum of American History, I had the great honor of being able to closely examine the many versions of Alexander Graham Bell's induction balance — in various shapes and sizes, with hanging wires and unfinished edges — that Bell had designed and built in the Volta Laboratory in a desperate attempt to save the president's life.

In the Library of Congress's Manuscript Division, I would like to thank Lia Apodaca, Fred Augustyn, Jennifer Brathodue, Patrick Kerwin, Bruce Kirby, and Joseph Jackson, with special thanks to Jeff Flannery, who patiently and kindly answered my many questions. At the National Museum of Health and Medicine, I am grateful to Kathleen Stocker, assistant archivist; Brian Spatola, anatomical collections; and, especially, the museum's chief archivist, Michael Rhode. Michael made all my research there possible, helped me find items I never would have found without his guidance, and introduced me to one of my most valued scientific advisers.

I was very fortunate to spend much of my research time at the National Museum of American History. David Haberstitch, the incredibly knowledgeable curator of photographs in the Archives Center, helped me track down the unpublished memoirs of Charles Sumner Tainter, Bell's assistant, who played a critical role in helping to build the induction balance. Judy Chelnick, associate curator in the museum's Division of Medicine and Science, first told me about the various versions of the induction balance, which Bell donated to the museum in 1898, and then made arrangements for me to see them for myself. Judy also introduced me to Roger Sherman, also an associate curator in the Division of Medicine and Science, who patiently explained to me how the induction balance, in all its many manifestations, worked. Roger has a genius not only for understanding even the most complicated and arcane historical scientific instruments, but for explaining them in a way that others too might understand. I will be forever grateful for his help.

I also had the pleasure of doing a great deal of research in Ohio, my home state, and was extremely impressed with the libraries and archives I visited there. At Hiram College — known as the Western

Reserve Eclectic Institute when Garfield was one of its students and teachers, and, later, its president — Jennifer Morrow, the college archivist, was unfailingly helpful, both while I was in the library, doing general research, and later, when I asked for her help in finding specific items long-distance. She always worked with astonishing speed, and found exactly what I was looking for. The Western Reserve Historical Society also has a large collection of Garfield papers, and I would like to thank reference supervisor Ann Sindelar for her generous help. Many thanks also go to the very knowledgeable guides at Lawnfield, Garfield's beloved farmhouse, which is now a National Historic Site. I would strongly encourage anyone visiting the area to stop and see it. It is fascinating and beautifully preserved.

Thanks also go to Richard Tuske, director of the library for the New York City Bar; Anne Thacher, library director of the Stonington Historical Society; Dale Sauter, manuscript curator of the special collections department at East Carolina University; William Bushong at the White House Historical Association; Kathie Pohl, director of marketing and community relations for the City of Mentor; Mary Kramer at Lakeview

Cemetery; Kathryn Murphy at the Alexander Graham Bell Association for the Deaf; and the staff of the Chicago Historical Society.

For help in understanding Garfield's physical condition after the shooting and his autopsy report, I am very grateful to Dr. Paul Uhlig, who generously shared his time and exceptional knowledge. For advice on the science behind the induction balance, I would like to thank David Deatherage, an electrical engineer at Pearson Kent McKinley Raaf Engineers. For sending me a copy of his fine article about the medical aspects related to Garfield's shooting, thanks go to Dr. Ibrahim Eltorai. I am also, and especially, deeply grateful to Dr. Dave Edmond Lounsbury, a brilliant internist who spent months answering my countless questions and pointing out details relating to Garfield's condition and care that I had overlooked. Dave also read and reviewed every chapter in this book.

I would also like to thank those scholars who devoted many years of their lives to studying and writing about Garfield. I am grateful to Kenneth Ackerman for his compelling book *Dark Horse,* to Ira Rutkow for *James A. Garfield* in the American Presidents Series, and to John Shaw, both for his insightful biography of Lucretia Garfield and for his careful reading and editing of James and Lucretia's letters to each other, which he compiled into a moving and illuminating book. I am indebted to Harry Garfield's daughter, Lucretia Garfield Comer, who wrote *Harry Garfield's First Forty Years,* and to Ruth Feis, Mollie Garfield's daughter, author of *Mollie Garfield in the White House,* for their beautifully written books, which give the kind of insight into Garfield's life that could come only from the members of his family. Finally, I am especially grateful to Allan Peskin, who, with his book *Garfield,* wrote what is, in my opinion, the definitive Garfield biography. I had the great pleasure to meet Allan in Cleveland, and he generously shared with me his own impressions of Garfield, after having spent a quarter of a century studying him.

Among the most enjoyable experiences I had while researching this book was the time I spent with several of Garfield's descendants. There is no doubt in my mind that James Garfield would have been exceptionally proud of the fine family that grew out of his marriage to Lucretia. The president's descendants — from great-grandchildren to great-great-great-grandchildren — were every bit as warm and kind as their famous forefather is remembered to have been. I would especially like to thank James A. Garfield III, known as Jay, who, along with his mother, Sally, and brother, Tom, generously invited me to a delicious, fascinating, and very fun family dinner. I will never forget their kindness and hospitality, or the wonderful stories they told. I am also very grateful to Rudolph Garfield, known as Bob, who shared with me details of his family's history as well as memories of his grandfather James, who had been in the train station with his father, President Garfield, on that fateful day. I would also like to thank Wyatt Garfield, whom I interviewed over the phone, and Jill Driscoll, Mollie Garfield's great-great-granddaughter, who kindly sent me a copy of the treatise that her father, a physician, wrote about the medical care Garfield received after the shooting.

For help with tracking down elusive newspaper articles, many thanks go to my very smart, resourceful friend Stacy Benson. I am grateful to Lora Uhlig for spending several painful weekends copying the nearly three thousand pages of the trial record of *United States v. Guiteau.* Thanks too to David Uhlig and Clif Wiens for helping me to understand and navigate the world of social media. I am grateful to Michelle Harris for applying her impressive and abundant research skills toward fact-checking this book. For stirring in me an early interest in history and the world outside our hometown, I would like to thank my lifelong friend Jodi Lewis. For her great warmth and kindness to my family, I will always be grateful to Betty Jacobs.

As a writer, I am extremely fortunate to have a brilliant editor in Bill Thomas, an extraordinary agent in Suzanne Gluck, and an incredibly talented publicist in Todd Doughty. I would like to thank them not only for the time and talent they have devoted to this book, but for their kindness and encouragement.

Many thanks and much love to my parents, Lawrence and Constance Millard, to whom this book is dedicated; my sisters, Kelly Sandvig, Anna Shaffer, and Nichole Millard; my mother-in-law, Doris Uhlig; and my bright, sweet, funny, precious-beyond-words children, Emery Millard Uhlig, Petra Tihen Uhlig, and Conrad Adams Uhlig.

My husband, Mark Uhlig, has been a constant source of encouragement, inspiration, and pure happiness for the past nearly twenty years of my life. He deserves more thanks than I could possibly fit into a thousand books, much less one, so I carry them all in my heart. *A tu lado.*

Finally, over the years I spent writing this book, my family and I have learned firsthand how fortunate we are to live in a time when medical science has advanced in the treatment not just of bullet wounds and infections, but of diseases as mysterious and insidious as cancer. I would like to take this opportunity to express my deepest gratitude to Dr. Gerald Woods, Cathy Burks, Dr. Brian Kushner, Dr. Margaret Smith, Lynn Hathaway, and Dr. Edward Belzer, as well as the many exceptional men and women at Children's Mercy Hospital in Kansas City and Memorial Sloan-Kettering Cancer Center in New York. From the bottom of this mother's heart, and on behalf of every member of my family, thank you, thank you, thank you.

NOTES

Prologue: Chosen

Crossing the Long Island Sound: *New York Times,* June 13, 1880.

Although most of the passengers: *Report of the Proceedings in the Case of the United States v. Charles J. Guiteau, Tried in the Supreme Court of the District of Columbia, Holding a Criminal Term, and Beginning November 14, 1881* (1882), 583–84. (Hereafter *United States v. Guiteau.*)

Absorbed in his own thoughts: Ibid.

As the *Stonington* recoiled: *Harper's Weekly,* July 3, 1880.

On board the *Narragansett: New York Times,* June 13, 1880; *Harper's Weekly,* July 3, 1880; *Manitoba Daily Free Press,* June 26, 1880.

As the passengers of the *Stonington* watched in horror: *Daily Evening Bulletin,* June 12, 1880.

In just minutes, the fire grew in intensity:

Indiana Statesman, June 17, 1880.
As the tragedy unfolded before him: *United States v. Guiteau*, 583–84.
The frightened and ill-prepared crew: *Indiana Statesman*, June 17, 1880.
When the *Stonington* finally staggered: *New York Times*, June 13, 1880.
The ship's bow had been smashed in: Notes from the Stonington Historical Society.
Guiteau, however, believed that luck: *United States v. Guiteau*, 598.

Chapter 1: The Scientific Spirit

Even severed as it was: Gross and Snyder, *Philadelphia's 1876 Centennial Exhibition*, 125; Hilton, *The Way It Was*, 190–91.
Across the lake from the statue: Garfield, *Diary*, May 10, 1876, 3:290.
Although he was a congressman: Ibid.
With fourteen acres of exhibits: Gross and Snyder, *Philadelphia's 1876 Centennial Exhibition*, 67–82.
In fact, so detailed was his interest in mathematics: Dunham, *The Mathematical Universe*, 95–101.
"The scientific spirit has cast out the Demons": Garfield, Speech to the U.S. House of Representatives, December 16, 1867.
After his first day at the exposition: Shaw,

Lucretia, 68.

With characteristic seriousness of purpose: Garfield, *Diary,* May 11, 1876, 3:291.

As fairgoers stared in amazement: Gross and Snyder, *Philadelphia's 1876 Centennial Exhibition,* 73. Edison would invent the electric light just three years later.

So incomplete and uncertain: Hilton, *The Way It Was,* 86.

Is freedom "the bare privilege of not being chained?": Quoted in Peskin, *Garfield,* 253.

"instruments for the curing": "Scenes in the Grand Hall," *New York Times,* May 14, 1876.

His first child: Garfield, *Diary,* 1:xxxvii.

With his quick, crisp stride: Gross and Snyder, *Philadelphia's 1876 Centennial Exhibition,* 22.

In many ways, Garfield had less in common: Hilton, *The Way It Was,* 189.

Next door to Machinery Hall: Gross, *Philadelphia's 1876 Centennial Exhibition,* 26–29.

Inside, at the far east end of the building: Bruce, *Alexander Graham Bell and the Conquest of Solitude,* 193–95; Mackenzie, *Alexander Graham Bell,* 119; Post, *1876,* 63; Gross, *Philadelphia's 1876 Centennial Exhibition,* 30.

Bell's school would administer: Bruce, *Alexander Graham Bell and the Conquest of Solitude,* 119.

From the moment Bell had stepped: Mackenzie, *Alexander Graham Bell,* 120.

To his horror, when he examined: Grosvenor and Wesson, *Alexander Graham Bell,* 71.

When Bell had finally reached: Mackenzie, *Alexander Graham Bell,* 119; Post, *1876,* 63.

Fearing that he would be forgotten: Mackenzie, *Alexander Graham Bell,* 121.

"How do you do, Mr. Bell?": Ibid., 122; Grosvenor and Wesson, *Alexander Graham Bell,* 72.

With the judges waiting anxiously nearby: Bell to his parents, June 27, 1876; Mackenzie, *Alexander Graham Bell,* 122.

After the group had crossed the vast hall: Bruce, *Alexander Graham Bell and the Conquest of Solitude,* 195.

As the judges gathered around him: Ibid., 196.

Leaning into a transmitter: Mackenzie, *Alexander Graham Bell,* 123.

Sitting at the table, with the iron box receiver: Bruce, *Alexander Graham Bell and the Conquest of Solitude,* 197.

Although the results were dramatic: Noble, *The Courage of Dr. Lister,* 134.

Even Dr. Samuel Gross: Gross had personally invited Lister to Philadelphia to talk about antisepsis, but apparently only as an opportunity to discredit it.

"Little, if any faith": Clarke et al., *A Century of American Medicine, 1776–1876,* 213.

There was a much-admired exhibit: Post, *1876,* 153.

"American surgeons are renowned": Ashhurst, *Transactions of the International Medical Congress of Philadelphia, 1876,* 517.

For three hours, Lister did all he could: Ibid., 535.

"It is worth some trouble": "Exsection" is a nineteenth-century term for excision.

"glad to have you convince us": Ashhurst, *Transactions of the International Medical Congress of Philadelphia, 1876,* 532.

A few weeks after Lister tried in vain: Garfield, *Diary,* September 3, 1876, 3:344.

At his home in Washington, he watched helplessly: Ibid., October 25, 1876, 3:370.

"I am trying to see through it": Ibid., October 27, 1876, 3:371.

"The children were not pleased": Ibid., November 21, 1875, 3:186.

Chapter 2: Providence

James Garfield's father, Abram: Theodore Clarke Smith, *The Life and Letters of James Abram Garfield,* 9.

It consisted of one room: Alger, *From Canal Boy to President,* 3.

Like his ancestors, who had sailed: Theodore Clarke Smith, *The Life and Letters of James Abram Garfield,* 2.

In 1819, he and his half brother: Ibid., 3; Conwell, *The Life, Speeches, and Public Services of James A. Garfield,* 34.

Although land was available: Conwell, *The Life, Speeches, and Public Services of James A. Garfield,* 37.

Soon after their arrival, they met: Ibid., 34.

In 1829 the two couples: Ibid., 37.

When Abram had seen the wildfire: Ridpath, *The Life and Work of James A. Garfield,* 21–22.

"Let us never praise poverty": Garfield to J. H. Rhodes, November 19, 1862, in Theodore Clarke Smith, *The Life and Letters of James Abram Garfield,* 36.

Between them, working as hard as they could: Ridpath, *The Life and Work of James A. Garfield,* 23.

So little did they have to spare: Alger, *From Canal Boy to President,* 5.

"received no aid, worked and won": Theodore Clarke Smith, *The Life and Letters of James Abram Garfield,* 11.

"If I ever get through a course of study": Ibid., 53.

She came from a long line: Conwell, *The Life, Speeches, and Public Services of James A. Garfield,* 35.

She donated some of her land: Alger, *From Canal Boy to President,* 6.

"Whatever else happens": Theodore Clarke Smith, *The Life and Letters of James Abram Garfield,* 15.

Although he could not swim: Ibid., 22.

Garfield's first job on the canal: Ibid., 23.

Now it was midnight: Ibid., 24.

"Carefully examining it": Ibid., 24–25.

"Providence only could have saved": *New York Times,* September 20, 1881.

"As I approached the door": Theodore Clarke Smith, *The Life and Letters of James Abram Garfield,* 25.

"I took the money": Ibid., 26.

By the fall of 1851, Garfield had transformed: The Western Reserve Eclectic Institute would become Hiram College in 1867.

"It was without a dollar of endowment": Theodore Clarke Smith, *The Life and Let-*

ters of James Abram Garfield, 44.

Unable to afford tuition: Dean, "Reminiscences of Garfield: Garfield the Student, the Eclectic Institute," Hiram College Archives.

"tread was firm and free": Theodore Clarke Smith, *The Life and Letters of James Abram Garfield,* 46.

"The ice is broken": "Rough Sketch of an Introduction to a Life of General Garfield," typescript, Hiram College Archives.

His day began at 5:00 a.m.: Theodore Clarke Smith, *The Life and Letters of James Abram Garfield,* 58.

"If at any time I began to flag": Ibid., 45.

So vigorously did Garfield: Shaw, *Lucretia,* 9.

"There is a high standard": Theodore Clarke Smith, *The Life and Letters of James Abram Garfield,* 74.

"I am aware that I launch out": Garfield, *Diary,* August 23, 1859, 1:340–41.

"no heart to think of anything": Theodore Clarke Smith, *The Life and Letters of James Abram Garfield,* 160.

Four months after Confederate: Ridpath, *The Life and Work of James A. Garfield,* 92.

"pride and grief commingled": Garfield to Lucretia Garfield, September 23, 1863, in

Shaw, *Crete and James,* 189.

"I hope to have God on my side": Perry, *Touched with Fire,* 60.

Garfield's regiment did not have: Ibid., 59–63.

After he received his orders: Conwell, *The Life, Speeches, and Public Services of James A. Garfield,* 139.

In the end, the struggle: Perry, *Touched with Fire,* 76–87.

"The [Confederate] regiment and battery": Ibid.

"resting there after the fatigue": Peskin, *Garfield,* 118–19.

"something went out of him": Ibid., 19. Although Garfield had no sympathy for the Confederates, he could not help but admire the passion with which they fought for their beliefs, no matter how misguided. "Let us at least learn from our enemies," he wrote. "I have seen their gallantry in battle, their hoping against hope amid increasing disaster, and traitors though they are, I am proud of their splendid courage when I remember that they are Americans."

"By thundering volley": Ibid., 233.

"like throwing the whole current": Garfield, *Diary,* November 2, 1855, 1:273. Although Garfield was a fierce and effective advocate for rights for freed slaves, his vocabulary at times reflected the racial prejudice of the time. While at the same time praising black men's courage and defending their right to fight for "what was always their own," he could casually refer to a neighborhood as "infested with negroes."

"trust to God and his muscle": Ibid., October 6, 1857.

"For what else are we so fearfully": Peskin, *Garfield,* 234.

"A dark day for our country": Garfield, *Diary,* December 2, 1859.

In the fall of 1862: Garfield defeated D. B. Woods 13,288 votes to 6,763.

"I have resigned my place in the army": Theodore Clarke Smith, *The Life and Letters of James Abram Garfield,* 355–56. Garfield did not hold Lincoln in high esteem. He thought the president was not strong enough, and he feared that Lincoln would lose his bid for reelection because of his "painful lack of bold and vigorous administration." Quoted in Peskin, *Garfield,* 239.

"What legislation is necessary": Peskin, *Garfield,* 234.

"who have been so reluctantly compelled": Ibid., 253.

As head of the Appropriations Committee: Theodore Clarke Smith, *The Life and Letters of James Abram Garfield,* 796.

Garfield even defended: Ibid., 826–27.

"law of life": Garfield, *Diary,* December 31, 1880, 4:499–500.

"I suppose I am morbidly sensitive": Peskin, *Garfield,* 301.

"first, I should make no pledge": Theodore Clarke Smith, *The Life and Letters of James Abram Garfield,* 140–41.

"if the Senatorship is thus": Peskin, *Garfield,* 340.

After a landslide victory: Ibid., 447.

"I have so long and so often": Garfield, *Diary,* February 5, 1879.

"wait for the future": Rockwell, "From Mentor to Elberon."

Chapter 3: "A Beam in Darkness"

"Don't fail to write me": Garfield to Lucretia Garfield, May 29, 1880, in Shaw, *Crete and James,* 369.

"The first half of my term": Hoogenboom, *Rutherford B. Hayes,* 402–3.

Hayes's abdication: Clancy, *The Presidential Election of 1880,* 82.

The Half-Breeds had two top candidates: Presidential nominees would be chosen at their party's national conventions until the mid-twentieth century.

Although the Republican Party: Andrew Johnson was a Democrat and a southerner, but to prove that they embraced all men loyal to the Union, and to ensure Abraham Lincoln's election, the Republicans had made him one of their own by choosing him to be Lincoln's vice president. He became president after Lincoln was assassinated.

The street he was walking on: Author interview with Chicago History Museum; Encyclopedia of Chicago, "Chicago's Lakefront Landfill," http://www.encyclopedia.chicagohistory.org/pages/3713.html.

At the time of the fire: PBS American Experience, "People & Events: The Great Fire of 1871," www.pbs.org/wgbh/amex/chicago/peopleevents/e_fire.html; *Encyclopædia Britannica,* online, "Chicago Fire of 1871."

Within a year of the fire: Rayfield, "Tragedy in the Chicago Fire and Triumph in the Architectural Response," http://www.lib.niu.edu/1997/iht419734.html.

"Fresh crowds arriving": Garfield, *Diary,* May 31, 1880, 4:424.

The Interstate Industrial Exposition Building: Encyclopedia of Chicago, "Places of Assembly," www.encyclopedia.chicago

history.org/pages/333.html. The Interstate Industrial Exposition Building was razed twelve years later to make room for Chicago's Art Institute.

"the cool air of the lake": "The President-Makers," *New York Times,* June 5, 1880.

Although the hall could accommodate: "The Convention and Its Work," *New York Times,* June 3, 1880; "The Story of the Ballots," *New York Times,* June 8, 1880; photograph of convention floor, published in several sources.

"Blaine! Blaine!": Quoted in Peskin, *Garfield,* 465.

"asked me to allow his brother": Garfield to Lucretia Garfield, June 2, 1880, in Shaw, *Crete and James,* 373.

"It is evident": Hoogenboom, *Rutherford B. Hayes,* 403.

"It is impossible": Theodore Clarke Smith, *The Life and Letters of James Abram Garfield,* 50–51.

"too fond of talking": Peskin, *Garfield,* 293.

"We have but faith": "Garfield's Eulogy of Lincoln," *New York Times,* July 13, 1881.

"I have arisen at 7 this morning": Garfield to Lucretia Garfield, June 2, 1880, in Shaw, *Crete and James,* 373.

Ten years earlier: Hoogenboom, *Rutherford*

B. Hayes, 324.

Since then, Conkling had personally made: Doenecke, *The Presidencies of James A. Garfield & Chester A. Arthur,* 12.

He had helped to draft: Five years earlier, when Blanche Kelso Bruce, a former slave, was sworn in to the Senate after having been elected in Mississippi, Conkling escorted him up the Senate's aisle when the senior senator from Bruce's state refused to perform that traditional duty.

"thoroughly rotten man": Quoted in Hoogenboom, *Rutherford B. Hayes,* 412.

He offended fellow senators: Ackerman, *Dark Horse,* 317n.

"some ill-bred neighbor": Conkling, *The Life and Letters of Roscoe Conkling,* 44.

"his haughty disdain": Chidsey, *The Gentleman from New York,* 91.

Even Garfield, who admired Blaine: After watching Blaine unashamedly try to prevent the publication of an article on black suffrage that Garfield had written because it would outshine Blaine's own work, Garfield noted with astonishment, "It is apparent to me that Blaine cares more about the glory . . . than having the cause of negro enfranchisement defended." Peskin, *Garfield,* 435.

"cool, calm, and after his usual fashion":

"The Struggle at Chicago," *New York Times,* June 4, 1880.

"serene as the June sun": "The Convention and Its Work," *New York Times,* June 3, 1880.

"I shall never cease to regret": "The Evening Session," *New York Times,* June 6, 1880; Peskin, *Garfield,* 467.

"folded his arms across": "The Evening Session," *New York Times,* June 6, 1880; Peskin, *Garfield,* 467.

"New York is for Ulysses S. Grant": "The Evening Session," *New York Times,* June 6, 1880.

"New York requests that Ohio's real candidate": Ackerman, *Dark Horse,* 84.

"Conkling's speech": Garfield to Lucretia Garfield, June 6, 1880, in Shaw, *Crete and James,* 376.

"I have witnessed the extraordinary": "Nomination of John Sherman," James A. Garfield Papers, Library of Congress; Hoar, *Autobiography of Seventy Years,* 393–95.

"And now, gentlemen of the Convention": "Nomination of John Sherman," James A. Garfield Papers, Library of Congress.

"I presume I feel very much as you feel": Conkling, *The Life and Letters of Roscoe Conkling,* 604.

The convention chairman: Hoar, *Autobiography of Seventy Years,* 395.

"The chair," wrote one reporter: "The Evening Session," *New York Times,* June 6, 1880.

"Never": "Two Remarks of Garfield's," *New York Times,* July 10, 1881.

"General," he said, "they are talking": Peskin, *Garfield,* 472.

The balloting began at ten: "The Story of the Balloting," *New York Times,* June 9, 1880.

Grant, as had been expected: "The Twenty-Eight Ballots," *New York Times,* June 8, 1880.

"By high noon": "The Excitement in this City," *New York Times,* June 8, 1880.

"elbow [his] way through": "Fight it Out!" *Boston Globe,* June 8, 1880.

On the thirty-fourth ballot: "The Story of the Balloting," *New York Times,* June 9, 1880.

"Mr. President": Hoar, *Autobiography of Seventy Years,* 397.

"No, no, gentlemen": "Gen. Garfield's Nomination," *New York Times,* June 15, 1880.

"No candidate has a majority": "The Story of the Balloting," *New York Times,* June 9, 1880.

"If this convention nominates me": Peskin, *Garfield,* 476.

"And then," a reporter wrote with awe, "then the stampede came": "The Story of the Balloting," *New York Times,* June 9, 1880.

"Whenever the vote of Ohio": Sherman, *Recollections of Forty Years in the House, Senate and Cabinet,* 775.

"Cast my vote for Sherman!": Peskin, *Garfield,* 476.

"Shall the nomination": "Roscoe Conkling, Political Boss," *New York Times,* April 14, 1935.

"The delegates and others on the floor": "The Story of the Balloting," *New York Times,* June 9, 1880.

"Only once," a reporter recalled, "did he express": "The Story of the Balloting," *New York Times,* June 9, 1880; "U.S.G.'s Waterloo," *Boston Globe,* June 9, 1880.

"As Garfield entered the carriage": "Gen. Garfield's Nomination," *New York Times,* June 15, 1880.

"grave and thoughtful expression": Ibid.

When the carriage pulled: "The Story of the Balloting," *New York Times,* June 8, 1880.

"pale as death": "Gen. Garfield's Wife Notified," *New York Times,* June 13, 1880.

Chapter 4: God's Minute Man

From an early age: *United States v. Guiteau,* 348, 354, 419.

"My mother was dead": Ibid., p. 547

Charles's own fanaticism grew: Carden, *Oneida,* xiii.

Like most of Noyes's followers: Ibid., 43.

"unhealthy and pernicious": Ibid., 49–54.

"up to the very moment": Ibid., 49–50.

"You prayed God": Guiteau to J. H. Noyes, no date, Library of the New York City Bar.

"I ask no one to respect me": Guiteau to "Mr. Burt," no date, Library of the New York City Bar.

"God's minute man": Guiteau to George Campbell, June 21, 1865, Library of the New York City Bar.

"in the employ of Jesus Christ": Guiteau to "The Community," no date, Library of the New York City Bar.

"Chas. J. Guiteau of England": Clark, *The Murder of James A. Garfield,* 4–5.

"the Community women": Noyes, *"Guiteau v. Oneida Community,"* 3.

In fact, so thorough: Rosenberg, *The Trial of the Assassin Guiteau,* 19.

"practically a Shaker": *United States v. Guiteau,* 549.

"egotism and conceit": Ibid., 297; Rosen-

berg, *The Trial of the Assassin Guiteau,* 19–20.
"destined to accomplish": *Guiteau v. Oneida Community,* 3.
"God and my own conscience": Guiteau to "The Community," no date.
"warm friend of the Bible": Guiteau to "The Community," April 10, 1865.
"labored there for weeks and months": *United States v. Guiteau,* 297.
"lost [his] eternal salvation": Ibid., 556.
"asked him three questions": Ibid., 299.
"The style and plea of his conduct": Beard, "The Case of Guiteau — A Psychological Study," 32.
"talked about theology": *United States v. Guiteau,* 392.
Much more than the work itself: Clark, *The Murder of James A. Garfield,* 12–13.
"I asked Mr. John H. Adams": *United States v. Guiteau,* 560.
"have been in the habit": Ibid., 566.
"failure all the way through": Ibid., 567.
After arriving in a town: Ibid., 573.
On most nights: Rosenberg, *The Trial of the Assassin Guiteau,* 33.
"You may say that this is dead beating": *United States v. Guiteau,* 570.
"I had no trouble": Ibid., 569.

"you can arrest a man for a board-bill": Ibid., 568.

"I was never so much tortured": Ibid., 558–59.

"If Mr. Scoville would let me": Guiteau to Frances Scoville, December 11, 1864.

Much larger sums of money: *United States v. Guiteau,* 562; Rosenberg, *The Trial of the Assassin Guiteau,* 30.

Searching for another target: "Scoville, Guiteau and Oneida Community," 4, Library of the New York City Bar; Rosenberg, *The Trial of the Assassin Guiteau,* 24.

"moody [and] self-conceited": *United States v. Guiteau,* 1048–49.

"If you intend to pay": Guiteau to John Humphrey Noyes, February 19, 1868.

"I infer from your silence": Guiteau to John Humphrey Noyes, March 2, 1868. Hostility against the Oneida Community grew until Noyes and his followers stopped their practice of complex marriage in 1879. A few years later, Noyes and a small group moved to Canada, where Noyes died in 1886.

"I have no ill will toward him": Rosenberg, *The Trial of the Assassin Guiteau,* 26, 30, 31.

"cut up a little wood for us": *United States*

v. Guiteau, 469.
"explosions of emotional feeling": Ibid., 352.
"I had no doubt then": Ibid., 476–77.
For the next five years: Ibid., 583.
Believing, as did most of the country: Ibid., 584.
"I remember distinctly": Hayes and Hayes, *A Complete History of the Life and Trial of Charles Julius Guiteau, Assassin of President Garfield* (hereafter, *A Complete History*), 452.

Chapter 5: Bleak Mountain

The house, which the reporters: Garfield, *Diary,* August 22, 1880, 4:445.
"regular town": Balch, *Life of President Garfield,* 314–15.
For the past three years: Garfield, *Diary,* 4:85, 88, 410.
To the house itself: National Park Service, "James A. Garfield National Historic Site," www.nps.gov/jaga/index.htm.
"You can go nowhere": Leech and Brown, *The Garfield Orbit,* 183.
"I long for time": Garfield, *Diary,* September 24, 1879, 4:298–99.
"take the stump": Peskin, *Garfield,* 482.
Happily left to his own devices: Theodore Clarke Smith, *The Life and Letters of*

James A. Garfield, 921.

"Result 475 bushels": Garfield, *Diary,* July 31, 1880, 4:432.

While Garfield worried: Three independent parties had presidential candidates that year: the Greenback-Labor Party, which, as well as supporting the continuation of paper money, argued fiercely for workers' rights; the Prohibitionists, who wanted a president who would follow in the footsteps of Hayes and ban alcohol in the White House, if not throughout the nation; and the Anti-Masons, which, as their name implied, opposed Freemasons, who they feared were trying to take over the country. Clancy, *The Presidential Election of 1880,* 157–66.

"Hancock the Superb": "The Democratic Trojan Horse," *New York Times,* July 31, 1880.

"rebel party": Peskin, *Garfield,* 277.

In fact, Garfield had turned down the stock: *The Transactions of the Credit Mobilier Company, and an Examination of that Portion of the Testimony Taken by the Committee of Investigation and Reported to the House of Representatives at the Last Session of the Forty-Second Congress which Relates to Mr. Garfield.* Washington, 1873.

"There is nothing in my relation": Theodore Clarke Smith, *The Life and Letters of James A. Garfield,* 530.

In the end, the effort to renew: Leech and Brown, *The Garfield Orbit,* 218.

"Individuals or companys": Theodore Clarke Smith, *The Life and Letters of James A. Garfield,* 1039–41.

In New York, Garfield campaign clubs: *New York Times,* October 2, 1880; September 25, 1880; October 18, 1880.

"support Gen. Garfield for President": *New York Times,* September 27, 1880.

In Washington, D.C., a former slave: *New York Times,* July 4, 1880.

"Now we'll use a Freemen's right": *Book of Election Songs,* Song 21, microfilm at the Library of Congress, Garfield Papers.

"It could not have been larger": *New York Times,* October 26, 1880.

"James A. Garfield must be our President": Ibid.

"front porch talks": Leech and Brown, *The Garfield Orbit,* 212.

"As the singers poured out": Stanley-Brown, "My Friend Garfield."

A few weeks later: Garfield, *Diary,* November 2, 1880, 4:480.

"coolest man in the room": "At General Garfield's Home," *New York Times,* November 3, 1880.

"the news of 3 a.m.": Garfield, *Diary,* November 3, 1880, 4:481.

"There is a tone of sadness": Garfield, November 8, 1880, quoted in Theodore Clarke Smith, *The Life and Letters of James A. Garfield,* 1048.

Chapter 6: Hand and Soul

As Garfield tried to accept: Grosvenor and Wesson, *Alexander Graham Bell,* 111.

"I did not realize": "Bell's 'Electric Toy,' " *New York Times,* January 2, 1905.

By the summer of 1877: Grosvenor and Wesson, *Alexander Graham Bell,* 88.

That same year, President Hayes: Gray, *Reluctant Genius,* 180–81.

"A Professor Bell explained": Mackenzie, *Alexander Graham Bell,* 193.

"the voice already carries": Quoted in Grosvenor and Wesson, *Alexander Graham Bell,* 86.

"Ladies and gentlemen, it gives me": Quoted in Mackenzie, *Alexander Graham Bell,* 160.

After Morse developed: Casson, *The History of the Telephone;* Lubrano, *The Telegraph,* 140–41.

"It can speak, but it won't!": Quoted in

MacKenzie, *Alexander Graham Bell,* 215–16.

Although Bell deeply resented: Grosvenor and Wesson, *Alexander Graham Bell,* 75.

To add insult to injury: Ibid.; Bruce, *Alexander Graham Bell and the Conquest of Solitude,* 173.

In a court of law: Gray, *Reluctant Genius,* 197. Bruce, *Alexander Graham Bell and the Conquest of Solitude,* 270.

With Western Union's defeat: Mackenzie, *Alexander Graham Bell: The Man Who Contracted Space,* p. 212.

The fighting, however, continued: MacKenzie, *Alexander Graham Bell,* 214.

"Of all the men who didn't": Quoted in ibid., 218. Although the legitimacy of Bell's telephone patent has been scrutinized in hundreds of lawsuits, and over more than a century, the question of whether or not he invented the telephone continues to be raised. Perhaps the most persistent accusation against Bell is that he took the idea of a liquid transmitter from Elisha Gray. (For the most recent of these arguments, see A. Edward Evenson's *The Telephone Patent Controversy of 1876,* and Seth Shulman's *The Telephone Gambit.*) It should be noted, however, that Bell had been using liquid transmitters in experiments for several years before he filed his patent for the telephone. Moreover, Bell did not use a liquid transmitter either in the model he presented at the Centennial Exhibition in 1876, or in the telephone his company sold commercially.

"I am sick of the Telephone": Bell to Mabel Bell, September 9, 1878, Bell Family Papers.

"hateful to me at all times": Quoted in Grosvenor and Wesson, *Alexander Graham Bell,* 88.

"first incentive to invention": Bruce, *Alexander Graham Bell and the Conquest of Solitude,* 26.

"Our earthly hopes": Alexander Melville Bell to Alexander Graham Bell, May 28, 1870, Bell Family Papers.

His mother, who had homeschooled: Bruce, *Alexander Graham Bell and the Conquest of Solitude,* 20.

"I should probably have sought": Quoted in Gray, *Reluctant Genius,* 104.

"As far as telegraphy is concerned": Quoted in ibid., 136.

"I wish very much": Eliza Bell to Alexander Graham Bell, March 7, 1880, Bell Family Papers.

"I have my periods": Bell to Mabel Bell, March 1879, Bell Family Papers.

When struggling with an invention: Gray, *Reluctant Genius,* 3.

"wee bit fiddler": *New York Times,* January 2, 1905.

"musical fever": Bruce, *Alexander Graham Bell and the Conquest of Solitude,* 22.

Even to Bell's father: Ibid., 19.

"I have serious fears": Alexander Melville Bell to Alexander Graham Bell, May 19, 1873, Bell Family Papers.

"sort of telephonic undercurrent": Gray, *Reluctant Genius,* 145.

"My mind concentrates itself": Bell to Mabel Bell, December 12(?), 1885, Bell Family Papers.

By 1880, so frustrated: Bruce, *Alexander Graham Bell and the Conquest of Solitude,* 283.

"I have been almost": Gardiner Greene Hubbard to Alexander Graham Bell, July 1880, Bell Family Papers.

"However hard and faithfully": Bruce, *Alexander Graham Bell and the Conquest of Solitude,* 284.

In February of 1881: Bell to William Forbes, February 2, 1881, Bell Family Papers.

Along with the prize: Mackenzie, *Alexander Graham Bell,* 222.

Watson had left: Bruce, *Alexander Graham*

Bell and the Conquest of Solitude, 282.

"These are germs": Bell to Alexander Melville Bell and Eliza Bell, January 18, 1881, Bell Family Papers.

"functional derangement of the heart": Bruce, *Alexander Graham Bell and the Conquest of Solitude,* 341.

"Edison was completely absorbed": Tainter, "The Talking Machine and Some Little Known Facts in Connection with Its Early Development," 12-A.

"I trust you will": Bell to Mabel Bell, September 9, 1878, Bell Family Papers.

Chapter 7: Real Brutuses and Bolingbrokes

At 2:30 in the morning: Garfield, *Diary,* March 3, 1881, 4:552.

"no less than a half-dozen": Almon F. Rockwell, "From Mentor to Elberon," *Century Magazine* 23(1882), 431.

"the staggerings of my mind": Ibid., March 1, 1881, 4:551.

With very few exceptions: During Washington's first inauguration, which was held in New York City on April 30, 1789, he established the traditions of kissing the Bible after being sworn in to office and using the phrase "So help me God." For his second inauguration, he delivered the shortest inaugural address in history, at just 135 words.

As transportation improved dramatically: The inauguration did not move to January 20 until 1933, when Congress ratified the Twentieth Amendment to the Constitution. Although the Twentieth Amendment was ratified on January 23, Franklin D. Roosevelt was still inaugurated on March 4 of that year. It wasn't until his second inauguration, in 1937, that the January 20 date was established.

By the time a crowd: *New York Times,* February 1, 1881.

Just beyond the Mall: Another three years would pass before the Washington Monument was finally finished, and by then the Army Corps of Engineers would have to use a type of marble different from that in the original construction, leaving the top two-thirds of the monument slightly darker than the bottom third.

"free from snow": "A New Chief Magistrate," *New York Times,* March 5, 1881.

"The momentous question": *New York Times,* November 18, 1880.

"the very picture": *New York Times,* March 5, 1881.

"in a deafening chorus": Ibid.

"Low bridge!": *New York Times,* December

22, 1907.

"James A. Garfield sprung from the people": *New York Times,* March 5, 1881.

"smile[d] quietly at the hard task": "How the Address Was Received," *New York Times,* March 5, 1881.

"The elevation of the negro race": James A. Garfield, *Inaugural Address,* March 4, 1881.

"black men who had been slaves": "How the Address Was Received," *New York Times,* March 5, 1881.

"The emancipated race": James A. Garfield, *Inaugural Address,* March 4, 1881.

"There was the utmost silence": "How the Address Was Received," *New York Times,* March 5, 1881.

"Mr. Garfield will doubtless leave": *New York Times,* August 6, 1881, quoted in Theodore Clarke Smith, *The Life and Letters of James Abram Garfield,* 435.

"No trades, no shackles": Garfield, *Diary,* August 9, 1880, 4:439.

"I need hardly add": Peskin, *Garfield,* 528.

On March 1, Levi Morton: Chidsey, *The Gentleman from New York,* 326; Connery, "Secret History of the Garfield-Conkling Tragedy," 152.

"Allison broke down": Garfield, *Diary,*

March 4, 1881, 4:552.

"The Senate": Henry Adams, *The Education of Henry Adams,* 309.

"The nomination of Garfield": John Sherman to Governor Foster, June 30, 1880; Sherman, *Recollections of Forty Years in the House, Senate and Cabinet,* 777–78.

"using his influence and power": "The Republican Campaign," *New York Times,* June 19, 1880.

"a little reckless": Garfield, *Diary,* March 28, 1875, 4:48.

"I ask this": Quoted in Peskin, *Garfield,* 519.

"His appointment would act": Ibid., 517, 526.

The only public position Arthur had held: Reeves, *Gentleman Boss,* 63.

"The nomination of Arthur": Ackerman, *Dark Horse,* 132.

"The Ohio men have offered": Quoted in Hudson, *Random Reflections of an Old Political Reporter,* 96–99.

"For his enemies": Rockwell, "From Mentor to Elberon," *Century Magazine,* 437.

"a stranger entering the House": Ridpath, *The Life and Work of James A. Garfield, Twentieth President of the United States,* 272–73.

"You old rascal": Peskin, *Garfield,* 322.

"determined not to be classified": Garfield,

Diary, March 23, 1881, 4:562.

"Of course I deprecate war": Quoted in Ackerman, *Dark Horse,* 324.

Chapter 8: Brains, Flesh, and Blood

From an open window: The Oval Office would not be used as the president's office until 1909, when William Howard Taft was president. Taft also renovated the room to change its shape from a rectangle to an oval.

"The eyes of Washington": "Letter from Washington," unnamed newspaper, June 3, 1881, Library of Congress.

"sat down to a good rattling talk": Lucretia Garfield, *Diary,* April 15, 1881, in Garfield, *Diary,* 4:640.

With their help, she convinced: Seale, *The President's House,* 516. Hayes's wife, Lucille, was widely known as Lemonade Lucy because she refused to serve alcohol in the White House.

"abreast of current literature": Theodore Clarke Smith, *The Life and Letters of James Abram Garfield,* 752.

"Every day I miss Spofford": Ibid., 753.

While home in Mentor: Garfield, *Diary.*

"It is a pity": Quoted in Theodore Clarke Smith, *The Life and Letters of James Abram Garfield,* 923.

For Garfield, being able to work: Feis, *Mollie Garfield in the White House,* 60.

While nine-year-old Abe: Whitcomb and Whitcomb, *Real Life at the White House,* 174. The East Room is the largest room in the White House, and as such has often been used as a playroom by presidents' children. Tad Lincoln tied a goat to a chair so that it could pull him through the room. Theodore Roosevelt's children roller-skated through it, as did Jimmy Carter's daughter, Amy.

"Whatever fate may await me": Rockwell, "From Mentor to Elberon," *Century Magazine,* 434. (*Hoc opus, hic labor est.* "That is the work, that is the task." From *The Aeneid,* Book VI.)

"I am the first mother": *New York Times,* March 23, 1881.

"cozy and home like": *New York Times,* July 8, 1881.

"Slept too soundly": Lucretia Garfield, *Diary,* March 5, 1881, in Garfield, *Diary,* 4:628.

"This is the way in which": "Patronage in Our Politics," *New York Times,* March 27, 1881.

"Almost everyone who comes to me": Quoted in Peskin, *Garfield,* 515.

"Let us go into the Executive mansion": Quoted in Mr. Lincoln's White House, http://mrlincolnswhitehouse.org.

"My day is frittered away": Garfield, *Diary,* June 13, 1880, 4:610.

"My God!": Peskin, Garfield, 551.

"beasts at feeding time": Peskin, *Garfield,* 551.

"These people would take": Stanley-Brown, "Memorandum Concerning Joseph Stanley-Brown's Relations with General Garfield," 9.

"Secretary Blaine is especially sought after": "A Crowd of Office Seekers," *Washington Post,* March 9, 1881.

"When Dr. Johnson defined patriotism": Quoted in Peskin, *Garfield,* 452–53.

The Secret Service had been established: Melanson, *The Secret Service,* 22.

"strong dispatch of sympathy": Garfield, *Diary,* March 19, 1881, 4:561.

"allusion to our own loss": Garfield, *Diary,* March 19, 1881, 4:561.

"We cannot protect our Presidents": "A Lesson," *New York Times,* July 4, 1881.

"Assassination can no more": Sherman, *Recollections of Forty Years in the House, Senate and Cabinet,* 789.

Brown had met Garfield: Stanley-Brown, "Memorandum Concerning Joseph

Stanley-Brown's Relations with General Garfield."

"Good morning, what can I do for you?": Ibid., 2.

"Aspirations for the reflected glory": Stanley-Brown, *Stanley-Brown Family History,* 1.

Brown's grandfather Nathaniel Stanley: "Scope and Content Note," Joseph Stanley-Brown Papers, 1. When Joseph, an avid genealogist, learned that his grandfather had changed his name from Stanley to Brown, he added Stanley to the end of his own name. Years later, Lucretia Garfield suggested that he hyphenate the two names, and he was thereafter known as Joseph Stanley-Brown. Feis, *Mollie Garfield in the White House,* 114–15; "Scope and Content Note," Joseph Stanley-Brown Papers, Library of Congress.

In America, Nathaniel's son: Unnamed newspaper, Hiram College archives.

When he was twelve: Stanley-Brown, "Memorandum Concerning Joseph Stanley-Brown's Relations with General Garfield," 1.

"The gracious, affectionate home life": Ibid., 4.

"Where have you been": Ibid.; Stanley-

Brown, "My Friend Garfield," 50.

"He is very bright and able": Garfield, *Diary,* January 9, 1881, 4:522.

"Well, my boy": Stanley-Brown, "Memorandum Concerning Joseph Stanley-Brown's Relations with General Garfield," 7–8.

Immediately following Garfield's nomination: "Gen. Garfield's Letters," *New York Times,* June 29, 1880.

"There was no organized staff": Stanley-Brown, "My Friend Garfield," 50.

"How the President and his Private Secretary": "An Hour Spent in the President's Private Office," unnamed newspaper, June 3, 1881.

The day after Garfield's inauguration: *United States v. Guiteau,* 630–31.

"We have cleaned them out": Ibid., 115–16.

"I have practiced law": Ibid., 210.

"Being about to marry": Beard, "The Case of Guiteau — A Psychological Study," 30–31.

While still in New York, Guiteau: *United States v. Guiteau,* 585.

"All those leading politicians": Ibid., 584.

"I have seen him at least ten times": Ibid., 896.

"on free-and-easy terms": Ibid., 896, 584–85.

Within days of his arrival in Washington:

Ibid., 208.

"No day in 12 years": Garfield, *Diary,* March 8, 1881, 4:555.

"I think I prefer Paris": *United States v. Guiteau,* 209.

"The inclosed [*sic*] speech": Ibid., 209.

"so that the President would remember": Hayes and Hayes, *A Complete History,* 424.

"Of course, [Garfield] recognized me": *United States v. Guiteau,* 586–87.

"His visits were repeated": Ibid., 208.

"very large attendance": Garfield, *Diary,* March 12, 1881, 4:557.

"the great roaring world": Lucretia Garfield, *Diary,* March 12, 1881, in Garfield, *Diary,* 4:628.

Suddenly, Lucretia heard someone say: Ackerman, *Dark Horse,* 280; Rosenberg, *The Trial of the Assassin Guiteau,* p. 29.

Guiteau had a strikingly quiet walk: Rosenberg, *The Trial of the Assassin Guiteau,* 38; "Guiteau in Jail," *New York Times,* July 3, 1881.

"one of the men that made": Ackerman, *Dark Horse,* 280.

"aching in every joint": Lucretia Garfield, *Diary,* March 12, 1881, in Garfield, *Diary,* 4:628.

"chatty and companionable": Whitcomb and Whitcomb, *Real Life at the White*

House, 175.

Chapter 9: *Casus Belli*

"She is not well": Garfield, *Diary,* May 3, 1881, 4:586.

"Crete": Ibid., May 4, 1881, 4:587.

"My anxiety for her": Ibid., May 8, 1881, 4:588.

Lucretia was the center: Shaw, *Lucretia,* 1–8.

"big, shy lad with a shock of unruly hair": Typed paragraph, apparently written by Mary "Mollie" Garfield Brown, from the Western Reserve Historical Society archives.

"over and over upon the ground": Peskin, *Garfield,* 349.

"never elated": Quoted in Shaw, *Lucretia,* 2.

"generous and gushing affection": Quoted in ibid., 31.

"The world": Shaw, *Crete and James,* xii.

"Please pardon the liberty": Ibid., 2.

"It is my desire": Ibid., xii.

"I do not think I was born": Quoted in Shaw, *Lucretia,* 2.

"For the past year": Garfield, *Diary,* September 10, 1855, 4:271–72.

"Never before did I see": Ibid., September 11, 1855, 4:272.

"I am not certain I feel": Ibid., June 24, 1854, 4:251.

"There are hours when my heart": Shaw, *Crete and James,* xii.
If their courtship was difficult: Ibid., ix, xiv.
"Before when you were away": Ibid., 165–66.
"It seemed a little hard": Ibid., 104.
"I believe after all": Ibid., 210.
"gushing affection": Ibid., 240.
"I here record": Ibid., 242–43.
"You can never know": Ibid., 374.
"Dear wife": Quoted in Shaw, *Lucretia,* 84.
"It is almost painful": Shaw, *Crete and James,* 233.
"life of my life": Garfield, *Diary,* May 13, 1881, 4:590.
"the continent, the solid land": Quoted in Peskin, *Garfield,* 347.
"to get her further from the river air": Garfield, *Diary,* May 10, 1881, 4:589.
"I am sorry to say": Harriet S. Blaine and Beale, *Letters of Mrs. James G. Blaine,* 202.
"I refused to see people": Garfield, *Diary,* May 11, 1881, 4:590.
"I try to be cheerful": Peskin, *Garfield,* 230.
Every day, Garfield consulted: Garfield, *Diary,* May 9, 1881, 4:589.
"fever powders": Ibid., May 11, 1881, 4:589–90.
"If I thought her return": Shaw, *Lucretia,* 101.

"In the majority of cases": Crook, *Through Five Administrations,* 269.
"The President says it will be impossible": *United States v. Guiteau,* 589.
"I will tell you how I do it": Ibid., 633.
The technique had worked: Ibid., 221.
"Mr. Guiteau came into my office": Ibid., 220.
"I lived": Hayes and Hayes, *A Complete History,* 459.
Despite the constant humiliations: Ibid., 513–14.
"possessed of an evil spirit": Ibid., 504.
"very proud and nice": Ibid., 499.
After years of living as a traveling evangelist: "A Great Nation in Grief," *New York Times,* July 3, 1881.
While everyone else was wearing: *United States v. Guiteau,* 446.
"somewhat haggard and weak": Ibid., 222.
When Guiteau did have an opportunity: Hayes and Hayes, *A Complete History,* 38.
"Do you know who I am?": Crook, *Through Five Administrations,* 267.
"elected the President": *United States v. Guiteau,* 445–46.
"He did not strike me": Ibid., 446.
"The first time that I see": Ibid., 446–47.
"to have a consulship": Ibid., 128–29.

"We have not got to that yet": Ibid., 647.
So frequent were Guiteau's visits: Ibid., 202.
"he had, in my opinion": Ibid., 647, 117.
Before Lucretia had fallen ill: Hinsdale, *Garfield-Hinsdale Letters,* 489.
"perfidy without peril": Shaw, *Lucretia,* 95.
Not only had Garfield not consulted: Peskin, *Garfield,* 470.
"treacherously betray[ed] a secret trust": Connery, "Secret History of the Garfield-Conkling Tragedy," 149.
"casus belli": Garfield, *Diary,* March 27, 1881, 4:565.
"I owe something": Hinsdale, *Garfield-Hinsdale Letters,* 490.
Of more than one hundred newspapers: Peskin, *Garfield,* 569.
"has recognized Republicans": "What the Newspapers Say," *New York Times,* May 6, 1881.
Just two years earlier: "Marriage Starts Bride Down Aisle to Misery," *Washington Times,* July 13, 2002. Kate Sprague's husband would eventually divorce her, leaving her not only publicly humiliated and a social pariah, but penniless. By the end of her life, she would be reduced to selling eggs door to door, and, in 1899, would die from disease and malnutrition at the age of fifty-eight.

It was not until early May: Connery, "Secret History of the Garfield-Conkling Tragedy," 146.

"Garfield has not been square": Ibid.

After Robertson's appointment: Doenecke, *The Presidencies of James A. Garfield and Chester A. Arthur,* 42.

"smiled and looked at me": Connery, "Secret History of the Garfield-Conkling Tragedy," 147.

"God will be merciful": Garfield, *Diary,* May 15, 1881, 4:592.

"rebuke the President": Peskin, *Garfield,* 571–72.

"Sir, Will you please": "A Sensation in Politics," *New York Times,* May 17, 1881.

"seemed to stupefy": Ibid.

"a great big baby": Peskin, *Garfield,* 572.

"a very weak attempt": Garfield, *Diary,* May 16, 1881, 4:593.

A few days later, he announced: Ibid., March 21, 1881, 4:561.

"Having done all I fairly could": Ibid., May 16, 1881, 4:593.

"with emphasis, it is ended": Ibid., May 31, 1881, 4:602.

"Stung with mortification": "Conkling's Few Friends," *New York Times,* June 2, 1881.

"A deep strong current": Garfield, *Diary,*

May 31, 1881, 4:602.

Chapter 10: The Dark Dreams of Presidents

"like a flash": *United States v. Guiteau,* 593.

"If the President was out of the way": Hayes and Hayes, *A Complete History,* 428.

Guiteau was certain: *United States v. Guiteau,* 597.

"with renewed force": Ibid., 593.

"no ill-will to the President": Ibid., 215.

In fact, he believed that he had given: Hayes and Hayes, *A Complete History,* 428.

"It seems to me that the only way": *United States v. Guiteau,* 210.

"Until Saturday I supposed": Ibid., 211.

"immediate resignation": Ibid., 117.

"he should be quietly kept away": Crook, *Through Five Administrations,* 266–67.

"That is the way I test the Diety": *United States v. Guiteau,* 593.

"I kept reading the papers": Hayes and Hayes, *A Complete History,* 428.

"the divinity of the inspiration": *United States v. Guiteau,* 593.

"I thought just what": Hayes and Hayes, *A Complete History,* 430.

"Two points will be accomplished": *United States v. Guiteau,* 219.

"in proper shape": Hayes and Hayes, *A*

Complete History, 429.

"a new line of thought": Guiteau, *The Truth,* preface.

"better than the Bible": *United States v. Guiteau,* 677.

Even *The Truth*'s publication: Ibid., 581; Clark, *The Murder of James A. Garfield,* 22.

The next stage of Guiteau's plan: "Eyewitness," *American Heritage,* February/March 1980.

"did not call it by name": *United States v. Guiteau,* 224.

Two days later, George Maynard: Ibid., 223, 224.

"He had a peculiar manner": Ibid., 222.

Guiteau explained that he had received: Ibid., 220–22.

That same day, Guiteau returned: Ibid., 636.

"One of the strongest pistols made": Ibid., 224–25.

After striking a deal with O'Meara: Ibid., 224.

"I knew nothing about it": Ibid., 637.

"The Lord inspired me": Ibid., 593.

"I wanted to see what kind": Ibid., 701.

"I thought it was a very excellent jail": Ibid., 701.

"It would not do to go": Hayes and Hayes, *A Complete History,* 430.

"there could not possibly be": Ibid.

A member of the Disciples of Christ: Two other presidents have also been members of the Disciples of Christ: Lyndon B. Johnson and Ronald Reagan.

He had been an active and involved parishioner: Foster, *The Encyclopedia of the Stone-Campbell Movement,* 349.

"a wise and holy purpose": "A Pastor's Tribute," *New York Times,* August 19, 1881.

Guiteau knew exactly where Garfield's church: *United States v. Guiteau,* 695.

"That," he judged, "would be good chance": Hayes and Hayes, *A Complete History,* 430.

"a very stupid sermon": Garfield, *Diary,* June 12, 1881, 4:609.

"Next Sunday": Hayes and Hayes, *A Complete History,* 430.

Before the next Sunday sermon: Ibid.

"we have concluded to take her": Garfield, *Diary,* June 16, 1881, 4:610.

"I was all ready": Hayes and Hayes, *A Complete History,* 431.

"intended to remove the President": *United States v. Guiteau,* 216.

Garfield arrived back in Washington: Garfield, *Diary,* June 27, 1881, 4:617.

"sea air is too strong for her": Ibid., June

28, 1881, 4:617.

On June 30: Taylor, *Garfield of Ohio,* 261–62; "A Great Nation in Grief," *New York Times,* July 3, 1881.

"death-like stillness about me": "Lincoln's Faith in Dreams," *New York Times,* April 7, 1898.

"an ugly dream": Shenk, *Lincoln's Melancholy,* 209.

"reveal God's meaning in dreams": "The Burden of the Presidency," *New York Times,* September 25, 1881.

"I started to plunge": Garfield, *Diary,* January 21, 1881, 4:531.

"as foolish as it does to you": "The Burden of the Presidency," *New York Times,* September 25, 1881.

The night after his cabinet meeting: Garfield, *Diary,* 4:614, n. 191.

"had never heard him speak": "The Night Before the Shooting," *New York Times,* July 20, 1881.

After Henry left: Garfield, *Diary,* 4:618–19, n. 206.

"let the matter drop": *United States v. Guiteau,* 692.

When Garfield reached Blaine's house: Hamilton, *Biography of James G. Blaine,* 516.

As he waited for Blaine: Harriet S. Blaine and Beale, *Letters of Mrs. James G. Blaine,* 215.

"Mr. Garfield had sold himself": *United States v. Guiteau,* 694.

"engaged in the most earnest conversation": Ibid., 694; Hayes and Hayes, *A Complete History,* 434.

"My mind": Hayes and Hayes, *A Complete History,* 436.

Chapter 11: "A Desperate Deed"

"as if we were in fact two babies": Comer, *Harry Garfield's First Forty Years,* 55.

"You are President": Hamilton, *Biography of James G. Blaine,* 516.

To his sons' astonishment: Comer, *Harry Garfield's First Forty Years,* 55.

"There are a few additional lines": Quoted in Feis, *Mollie Garfield in the White House,* 67.

"The work of the campaign": Stanley-Brown, "Memorandum Concerning Joseph Stanley-Brown's Relations with General Garfield," 11.

"the tact and ability": "Mr. Rogers' Successor," *Washington Post,* March 17, 1881.

"perfectly master of the situation": "Some Stylish Turn-Outs," *Washington Post,* May 1, 1881.

“with an almost pathetic longing”: Stanley-Brown, “My Friend Garfield,” 100.

“Goodbye, my boy”: Ibid.; Stanley-Brown, “Memorandum Concerning Joseph Stanley-Brown’s Relations with General Garfield,” 12.

The small caravan: Peskin, *Garfield,* 595.

“in conscious enjoyment”: Hamilton, *Biography of James G. Blaine,* 516.

When he opened his eyes at 5:00 a.m.: *United States v. Guiteau,* 631.

After reading about the president’s trip: “Riggs House Is Demolished,” *Bryan Times,* July 18, 1911.

“I can’t do anything for you to-day”: *The Attempted Assassination of President Garfield,* 34–35.

It was too early for breakfast: *United States v. Guiteau,* 705.

“I ate well”: Hayes and Hayes, *A Complete History,* 437.

“To General Sherman”: Guiteau to William Tecumseh Sherman, Library of Congress; *United States v. Guiteau,* 217.

“You can print this entire book”: *United States v. Guiteau,* 217.

“The President’s tragic death”: Ibid., 215–16.

“nice, clean shirt”: Ibid., 142, 705.

Before stepping out the door: Hayes and Hayes, *A Complete History,* 438; Clark, *The Murder of James A. Garfield,* 54.

Although he had taken his time: The station was razed in 1908, under the orders of President Theodore Roosevelt, and is now the site of the National Gallery of Art. B Street is now Constitution Avenue.

"Well, I will take you out there": Hayes and Hayes, *A Complete History,* 438.

Approaching a newsstand, he asked: *United States v. Guiteau,* 186.

"Certainly": Hayes and Hayes, *A Complete History,* 438; "Guiteau's Murderous Plans," *New York Times,* July 15, 1881.

"will wonder": Belanger, "The Railroad in the Park," 5–19.

"nuisance which ought long since": Garfield, *Diary,* October 25, 1876, 3:370.

"I did not know, since that great sorrow": Ibid., October 27, 1876, 3:371.

As the carriage carrying Garfield: *United States v. Guiteau,* 186.

"I did not think it was proper": Ibid., 121.

As the two men ascended the steps: Ibid., 120, 186.

"absolutely free": Theodore Clarke Smith, *The Life and Letters of James A. Garfield,* 46.

"He would look in one door": *United States v. Guiteau,* 141.

"His teeth were clenched": "The First Shot Struck the President," *New York Times,* July 17, 1881.

Garfield had walked only a few steps: Clark, *The Murder of James A. Garfield,* 58.

"My God! What is this?": *United States v. Guiteau,* 121.

"The expression on [his] face": "The First Shot Struck the President," *New York Times,* July 17, 1881.

Despite the wave of fear: The order in which Garfield was shot — first in his arm, then in his back — is described by Mollie Garfield in her diary, July 2, 1881, Library of Congress; also quoted in Feis, *Mollie Garfield in the White House,* 82.

The force thrust Garfield forward: *United States v. Guiteau,* 121; "A Great Nation in Grief," *New York Times,* July 3, 1881; Ridpath, *The Life and Work of James A. Garfield,* 594; *United States v. Guiteau,* 151, 156.

Chapter 12: "Thank God It Is All Over"

"Catch him!": "The First Shot Struck the President," *New York Times,* July 17, 1881.

"blanched like that of a corpse": *United*

States v. Guiteau, 121; *The Attempted Assassination of President Garfield,* 43.

The first man to catch Guiteau: Melanson, *The Secret Service,* 24. A Secret Service agent happened to be standing nearby, but did nothing to help. Later that day, he would mention in his daily report that he had noticed a strange commotion at the station that morning.

Officer Kearney, who had exchanged: *United States v. Guiteau,* 186.

"I truly believe": *The Attempted Assassination of President Garfield,* 46.

"in his eyes": *United States v. Guiteau,* 149, 187.

"I have a letter": Ibid., 180–81.

The men who had arrested Guiteau: Ibid., 171, 188; "A Great Nation in Grief," *New York Times,* July 3, 1881.

"I did not expect to go through": *United States v. Guiteau,* 702.

"You stick to me": "A Great Nation in Grief," *New York Times,* July 3, 1881.

"haunted and haunted": *United States v. Guiteau,* 601.

"Keep back!": Rockwell, "Garfield's Assassination."

"was very pale": *United States v. Guiteau,* 159.

"very hard": Ibid.

Watching Smith struggle: Ibid., 141.

As tears streamed down White's face: Ibid., 145.

Although it seemed to everyone: "The Assassination of President Garfield," National Museum of Health and Medicine, 1; Reyburn, *Clinical History of the Case of President James Abram Garfield,* 7.

Just five minutes after the shooting: Reyburn, *Clinical History of the Case of President James Abram Garfield,* 11.

Townsend's first concern: Bliss et al., "Record of the Post-mortem Examination of the Body of President J. A. Garfield," 2.

When Garfield was alert enough: "A Great Nation in Grief," *New York Times,* July 3, 1881.

After he made his initial examination: Ibid.

A group of men who worked: Rutkow, *James A. Garfield,* 84.

As they lifted the president: *The Attempted Assassination of President Garfield,* 44; Rockwell, "Garfield's Assassination."

"I think you had better telegraph to Crete": Rockwell, "Garfield's Assassination."

"I recognized the man": *United States v. Guiteau,* 122.

Although he was only thirty-nine: Medicine

.howard.edu; encyclopedia.jrank.org.

Now, as he leaned over Garfield: Bliss's notes, p. 3, archives of the National Museum of Health and Medicine

"the calmest man in the room": Robert Todd Lincoln to a friend, July 28, 1881, Library of Congress.

"One chance in a hundred": "Some Hope at Midnight," *New York Times,* July 3, 1881.

"My God," he murmured: "A Great Nation in Grief," *New York Times,* July 3, 1881.

Suddenly, Lincoln decided: "Dr. Bliss's Authority," *National Republic,* July 4, 1882.

"an earnest, industrious boy": Paulson, "Death of a President and His Assassin," *Journal of the History of the Neurosciences* (2006): 80.

Years later, when he was a congressman: Kaufman, *Homeopathy in America,* 88–90; "Who the Doctors Are," *Washington Post,* July 5, 1881.

In the end, Bliss could not hold up: Soper, "Dr. Willard Bliss."

Although it seemed that his occupation: "How Dr. Bliss Got His Name," *New York Times,* July 9, 1881. After Bliss was born, the nurses attending his mother suggested that she name her son after the man who had delivered him — Dr. Willard. Bliss's mother, taking the suggestion perhaps a little too literally, named her child Doctor Willard Bliss.

While at the Armory Square Hospital: Soper, "Dr. Willard Bliss."

"Cundurango!": Ibid.

As soon as Bliss arrived: Bliss et al., "Record of the Post-mortem Examination of the Body of President J. A. Garfield," 1–2.

"In attempting to withdraw the probe": Ibid., 2.

"what appeared to be lacerated tissue": Ibid.

"downward and forward": Ibid.; Ackerman, *Dark Horse.*

Chapter 13: "It's True"

Lucretia was packing her bags: Peskin, *Garfield,* 146.

"The President wishes me to say": *Harper's Weekly* 25 (1881); "A Great Nation in Grief," *New York Times,* July 3, 1881; Rockwell, "Garfield's Assassination."

"Tell me the truth": Shaw, *Lucretia,* 103.

still nursing a grudge: A few days later, Grant made a late and extremely brief appearance at a reception that was held for Garfield. He kept his wife waiting in their carriage while he stepped into the hall, shook Garfield's hand, and quickly made his exit.

"I do not think he can afford": Garfield, *Diary,* June 24, 1881, 4:615.

"so overcome with emotion": "Sending for Mrs. Garfield," *New York Times,* July 3, 1881.

Finally, he was able to tell Lucretia: Ackerman, *Dark Horse,* 387.

Hurriedly finishing her packing: "Mrs. Garfield's Narrow Escape," *New York Times,* July 5, 1881.

By the time they reached the station: "Sending for Mrs. Garfield," *New York Times,* July 3, 1881.

"All along the route": *The Attempted Assassination of President Garfield,* 45.

"Conductors passed quietly": Comer, *Harry Garfield's First Forty Years,* 57.

"We have not said a word": "At the President's House," *New York Times,* July 3, 1881.

In the second-story room: Reyburn, *Clinical History of the Case of President James Abram Garfield,* 12.

"The crowd about the depot": *The Attempted Assassination of President Garfield,* 43.

Within ten minutes of the shooting: *Chicago Tribune,* July 3, 1881.

As soon as Garfield appeared: "Removal of

Mr. Garfield," *Washington Post,* July 3, 1881.

"I think I can see now": Reyburn, *Clinical History of the Case of President James Abram Garfield,* 11.

Hoping to spare the president: Seale, *The President's House,* 521.

"sufferings must have been intense": *Chicago Tribune,* July 3, 1881.

"haltingly and timidly": Stanley-Brown, "My Friend Garfield."

"Oh, Mr. Secretary": Ibid.

"Even in moments of greatest misery": Ibid.

"temporary but adequate": Stanley-Brown, "Memorandum Concerning Joseph Stanley-Brown's Relations with General Garfield," 12.

"full and accurate information": Stanley-Brown, "My Friend Garfield."

"miniature hospital": Ibid.

"abounding in health": Stanley-Brown, "Memorandum Concerning Joseph Stanley-Brown's Relations with General Garfield," 13.

A dozen men lifted above their heads the mattress: Seale, *The President's House,* 522.

"The upper story is alright": "A Great Nation in Grief," *New York Times,* July 3, 1881.

"the Pullman car": "Mrs. Garfield's Narrow Escape," *New York Times,* July 5, 1881.

"That's my wife!": Brown, *The Life and Public Services of James A. Garfield,* 220.

"Mrs. Garfield came, frail, fatigued": Blaine, *Letters of Mrs. James G. Blaine,* 211.

"evidently . . . making a strong effort": "A Great Nation in Grief," *New York Times,* July 3, 1881.

"will not probably live": "A Great Nation in Grief," *New York Times,* July 3, 1881.

"I am here to nurse you": Seale, *The President's House,* 522.

Chapter 14: All Evil Consequences

While most of the country heard: Tainter, "The Talking Machine and Some Little Known Facts in Connection with Its Early Development," 17. (Hereafter "The Talking Machine.")

"President Garfield," the caller said: Ibid.

"belonged to us": Eliza Bell to Alexander Graham Bell, July 8, 1881, Bell Family Papers.

"Everybody ran hither and thither": McCabe, *Our Martyred President,* 535.

Determined to find out for himself: Tainter, "The Talking Machine," 17.

"no one could venture to predict": Bell, *Upon the Electrical Experiments,* 1.

"Nature did all she could": Girdner, "The Death of President Garfield," *Munsey's Magazine,* 548.

"none the worse for it": "What Surgeon J. F. May Says," *New York Times,* July 8, 1881.

"had been a 'tough' ": Girdner, "The Death of President Garfield," 547.

"the crowds were rapidly increasing": "A Great Nation in Grief," *New York Times,* July 3, 1881.

Inside the White House: Seale, *The President's House,* 522.

"President Garfield was shot and killed": Clark, *The Murder of James A. Garfield,* 64.

At the top of his list of potential competitors: "The President's Physicians," *New York Times,* July 13, 1881.

When Baxter arrived at the White House: Bliss, *Statement of the Services Rendered by the Surgeons in the Case of the Late President Garfield,* 19.

"Why, doctor": Ibid., 19.

"He is my patient": Bliss's wife to her brother, August 28, 1881.

"I know your game": "The President's Physicians," *New York Times,* July 13, 1881.

"Dear Doctor": D. W. Bliss to doctors, July 3, 1881.

"He just took charge of it": "President Garfield's Case," *American Observer,* 494.

"select such counsel": Reyburn, *Clinical History of the Case of President James Abram Garfield,* 15.

To his mortification, however: Clark, *The Murder of James A. Garfield,* 99.

Lucretia, in fact, had taken matters: Dr. Edson was a homeopathic physician. Like other homeopaths, her philosophy was in direct opposition to that of allopathy, the type of medicine that Bliss, Baxter, and the vast majority of American doctors then practiced. In medical school, she had been taught that "like cures like." When treating a patient, she tried to prescribe medicines that produced the same symptoms in her patients as the diseases from which they were suffering. More important, she believed in the "law of infinitesimals" — the smaller the dose, the more effective the treatment. Although homeopathic medicine did little good, neither did it cause much harm, certainly in comparison to allopathy. In the late nineteenth century, American allopathic doctors still relied heavily on "heroic measures" — not as a last resort, but as a first step. They vigorously argued the benefits of bleeding, blistering, and scarification. Purging was also considered highly therapeutic, brought on by doses so toxic that they caused violent vomiting and, occasionally, death.

The stout, bespectacled doctor: Feis, *Mollie Garfield in the White House,* p. 70.

"Mrs. Dr. Edson": Balston, *Life of President Garfield,* Supplementary Chapter by Edson, 612.

Dr. Silas Boynton: Garfield had an especially high regard for Boynton because the doctor had "burst the narrow barriers of homeopathy."

"Please to have you come": Deppisch, "Homeopathic Medicine and Presidential Health," 6.

"I had a taste of what has been": Pasteur and Lister, *Germ Theory and Its Applications to Medicine,* 144.

"all evil consequences": Bankston, 35.

"In order to successfully practice": Clark, *The Murder of James A. Garfield,* 72.

"Judging the future by the past": Ibid.

"good old surgical stink": Ibid., 70; Guthrie, *From Witchcraft to Antisepsis,* 32.

Some physicians felt that Lister's: Rutkow, *James A. Garfield,* 110.

They preferred, moreover: Haller, *American Medicine in Transition, 1840–1910,* ix.

Even those doctors willing to try: Rothstein, *American Physicians in the Nineteenth Century,* 256; Clark, *The Murder of James A. Garfield,* 73.

"had the physician in charge abstained": Gerster, *Recollections of a New York Surgeon,* 206.

"Do not allow probing": Dr. E. L. Patee to Lucretia Garfield, July 3, 1881, James A. Garfield Papers, Library of Congress. Patee understood gunshot wounds as well as any of the doctors circling the White House, and better than most. Just a few years after graduating from Ohio's Western Reserve Eclectic Institute, which he had attended at the same time as Garfield, and the Starling Medical College in Columbus, Patee had moved to western Kansas. A devoted abolitionist, he had been among the first to enlist in the Union Army at the start of the Civil War. During the war, he had established a hospital on the front lines and, afterward, had devoted much of his time to treating the freed slaves who flooded into Kansas.

"old men": Girdner, "The Death of President Garfield," *Munsey Magazine,* 547.

Both men had attended Lister's talk: Paulson, "Death of a President and His Assassin," 81.

"these gentlemen used no buttons": Godlee, *Lord Lister,* 391.

"would in many cases sacrifice": Pasteur and Lister, *Germ Theory and Its Applications to Medicine,* 136.

"bear the severest scrutiny": "Dr. Hamilton Much Pleased," *New York Times,* July 6, 1881.

"I think that we have": "A Medical View of the Case," *New York Times,* July 8, 1881.

As Bliss spoke, smoke from his cigar: "Still Brighter Prospects," *New York Times,* July 8, 1881.

"the most admirable patient": "A Medical View of the Case," *New York Times,* July 8, 1881.

"If I can't save him": Quoted in Ackerman, *Dark Horse,* 403.

"I cannot possibly persuade him to sit": Mabel Bell to her mother, July 8, 1881, Bell Family Papers.

"like a Chinese lantern": Bell, *Upon the Electrical Experiments,* 47.

Deciding to run a few quick tests: Bruce, *Alexander Graham Bell and the Conquest of Solitude,* 344; Tainter, "The Talking Machine," 18.

In a simplistic way, the technique anticipated: In November 1895, Wilhelm Conrad Röntgen took an X-ray of his wife's hand, which showed her bones and wedding ring.

The problem was that: Bell, *Upon the Electrical Experiments,* 47–48.

"returned vividly to my mind": Ibid., 4.

"The currents induced": Ibid., 2–3.

"When a position of silence": Ibid., 3.

"brooding over the problem": Ibid., 4.

"great personal convenience": Ibid.

"received an urgent request": Tainter, "The Talking Machine," 18.

Chapter 15: Blood-Guilty

"Information had reached them": "Guiteau in Jail," *New York Times,* July 3, 1881.

"There were many who felt": "A Cloud upon the Holiday," *New York Times,* July 3, 1881.

"While it seems incredible": Ibid.

"roar of indignation": "Brooklyn Much Disturbed," *New York Times,* July 3, 1881.

Rumors spread that a group: "Bulletins Still Eagerly Watched," *New York Tribune,* July 6, 1881, cited in Menke, "Media in America," 652.

On the top floor: Kalush, *The Secret Life of Houdini,* 177.

"a particular friend": "A Talk with the Assassin," *New York Times,* July 5, 1881.

Soon after settling into his cell: "A Great

Nation in Grief," *New York Times,* July 3, 1881.

"lobbying like any henchman": Ackerman, *Dark Horse,* 363.

As he scanned the message: "Garfield Shot," *Milwaukee Daily Sentinel,* July 2, 1881.

Across the street, the sidewalk: "Seeking for the Latest News," *New York Times,* July 4, 1881.

As Conkling and Arthur entered the hotel: "At the Fifth Avenue Hotel," *New York Times,* July 3, 1881.

"More than one excited man": Ibid.

So suffocatingly crowded: Ibid.

By the time Conkling had his hands: *Chicago Tribune,* July 3, 1881.

"great grief and sympathy": Ackerman, *Dark Horse,* 384–85.

"Chet Arthur?": Whitcomb and Whitcomb, *Real Life at the White House,* 181.

"simple vanity": Reeves, *Gentleman Boss,* 5.

Arthur was also widely known: Karabell, *Chester Alan Arthur,* 30.

"I do not think he knows anything": Harriet S. Blaine and Beale, *Letters of Mrs. James G. Blaine,* 309.

"There is no place in which the powers of mischief": Quoted in Reeves, *Gentleman Boss,* 241.

"a statesman and a thorough-bred gentleman": "Seeking for the Latest News," *New York Times,* July 4, 1881.

"Republicans and Democrats alike": "A Cloud Upon the Holiday," *New York Times,* July 3, 1881.

"Arthur for President!": Williams, *Diary and Letters of Rutherford B. Hayes,* 23.

"There is a theory": "Guiteau in Jail," *New York Times,* July 3, 1881.

"I am a Stalwart": "A Great Nation in Grief," *New York Times,* July 3, 1881.

"This crime is as logically and legitimately": *Cleveland Herald,* July 3, 1881.

"when a child": Quoted in Chidsey, *The Gentleman from New York,* 354.

"Men go around with clenched teeth": Quoted in Ackerman, *Dark Horse,* 385.

In a New York prison, two inmates: *New York Times,* September 16, 1881.

"While there is no intimation": "Thunderbolt at Albany," *New York Times,* July 3, 1881.

"that the ex-Senator had asked": "The Scenes Up Town," *New York Times,* July 5, 1881.

"Gens: We will hang": Platt, *The Autobiography of Thomas Collier Platt,* 163.

Chapter 16: Neither Death nor Life

As his train pulled into the station: Bell to Mabel Bell, July 17, 1881, Bell Family Papers.

"Everywhere people go about": "A Cloud Upon the Holiday," *New York Times,* July 3, 1881.

Even the Fourth of July celebrations: Celebrations had also been canceled in nearly every other city in the nation.

"Men looked eagerly to the flag-pole": "The Events of Yesterday," *New York Times,* July 5, 1881.

"down upon the Executive Mansion": Ibid.

"To Mrs. Garfield, a slight token": Bell to Mabel Bell, July 17, 1881, Bell Family Papers.

Although his temperature had fallen slightly: Doctors' notes, July 14, 1881, National Museum of Health and Medicine.

"severe lancinating": Ibid., July 3, 1881.

"tiger's claws": "At the Patient's Bedside," *New York Times,* July 5, 1881.

More difficult for Garfield to deny: Doctors' notes, July 4, 1881, National Museum of Health and Medicine.

Garfield had for years suffered: Garfield, *Diary,* June 15–July 19, 1875, 3:85.

Finally, a doctor told him: Ibid., May 24, 1875, 3:85.

Garfield had avoided such drastic: Peskin, *Garfield,* 433.

He received a wide variety of rich foods: Bliss's notes, 11, National Museum of Health and Medicine.

"He was nauseated": Quoted in Clark, *The Murder of James A. Garfield,* 89.

"No sick or injured person": Gaw, *A Time to Heal,* 8.

"Patients, no matter how critical": Ibid.

The structure had been built into sloping ground: Seale, *The President's House,* 536.

"packed with vermin": Clark, *The Murder of James A. Garfield,* 80.

"sanitary requirements of a safe dwelling": "Condition of the White House," *New York Times,* September 7, 1881.

The plumbing system had been built: Seale, *The President's House,* 536.

"pest house": Feis, *Mollie Garfield in the White House,* 74.

"The old White House is unfit": Quoted in Clark, *The Murder of James A. Garfield,* 80.

"notoriously unhealthy": Hoogenboom, *Rutherford B. Hayes,* 469.

"greatly influenced by the miasma": Reyburn, *Clinical History of the Case of President James Abram Garfield,* 578.

Four servants in the White House: Mackenzie, *Alexander Graham Bell,* 236.

In a desperate effort to ward off malaria: Paulson, "Death of a President and His Assassin," 83; Deppisch, "Homeopathic Medicine and Presidential Health," 3.

"You can't imagine anything so vile": Harriet S. Blaine and Beale, *Letters of Mrs. James G. Blaine,* 229.

"Scarcely a breath of air": "Another Weary Night Watch," *New York Times,* July 6, 1881.

"Sitting to day on my piazza": Stephen Upson to Lucretia Garfield, July 3, 1881.

Others suggested hanging sheets: Letters to Lucretia Garfield, Library of Congress, Garfield papers.

Finally, a corps of engineers: *Reports of Officers of the Navy: Ventilating and Cooling of Executive Mansion,* 4. Nine years later, Willis Haviland Carrier designed the first system for controlling not only temperature, but also humidity.

In the president's office: Telegram from Joseph Stanley Brown to R. J. Jennings, the owner of a company in Baltimore that had a cooling device, quoted in Clark, *The Murder of James A. Garfield,* 83.

Although the system worked: Seale, *The President's House,* 523–24. "They found some kind of compressed air machine," Garfield's fourteen-year-old daughter, Mollie, complained in her diary, "& it made a horrible noise when it became full of air." James A. Garfield Papers, Library of Congress.

"cool, dry, and ample": Seale, *The President's House,* 524.

"wonderfully patient sufferer": Paulson, "Death of a President and His Assassin," 79.

"never approached him": Bliss, "The Story of President Garfield's Illness," 301.

"Thank you, gentlemen": Rockwell, "From Mentor to Elberon," *Century Magazine,* 437.

"witty, and quick at repartee": Ibid.

"The vein of his conversation": "A Great Nation in Grief," *New York Times,* July 3, 1881.

"I do not believe that": "At the Patient's Bedside," *New York Times,* July 5, 1881.

Although Garfield rarely mentioned: Rockwell, "From Mentor to Elberon," *Century Magazine.*

"What motive do you think": "A Great Nation in Grief," *New York Times,* July 3, 1881.

Chapter 17: One Nation

"You were not made free merely": "Colored Men Visit Garfield," *New York Times,* October 21, 1880.

"the high privilege and sacred duty": Garfield, *Inaugural Address,* March 4, 1881.

"give the South, as rapidly as possible": De Santis, "President Garfield and the 'Solid South,' " 449.

"felt, as they had not felt before": "Southern Sympathy," *New York Times,* July 20, 1881.

"united, as if by magic": Bundy, *The Nation's Hero, in Memoriam,* 242–43.

"the whole Nation kin": "Jefferson Davis on Guiteau's Crime," *New York Times,* July 16, 1881.

"I felt lighthearted and merry": *United States v. Guiteau,* 601.

"His vanity is literally nauseating": Hayes and Hayes, *A Complete History,* 405–6.

"He spoke with deliberation": Ibid.

"He objected strenuously": Ibid., 406.

"I want you to be sure": Ibid., 499.

"I don't want to appear strained": Quoted in Ackerman, *Dark Horse,* 406.

Before returning to his cell: Clark, *The Murder of James A. Garfield,* 65.

He believed that he would be released: Rosenberg, *The Trial of the Assassin Gui-*

teau, p. 46.

"by the hundreds": Clark, *The Murder of James A. Garfield,* 91.

"a conviction would shock the public": *United States v. Guiteau,* 2246.

So carefree was Guiteau: Rosenberg, *The Trial of the Assassin Guiteau,* 45.

"I am looking for a wife": Hayes and Hayes, *A Complete History,* 451.

"For twenty years, I have had an idea": Hayes and Hayes, *A Complete History,* 452.

He was in contact with everyone: Mackenzie, *Alexander Graham Bell,* 235.

"Alec says he telegraphed": Mabel Bell to her mother, July 20, 1881, Bell Family Papers.

At this point in his experiments: Bell, *Upon the Electrical Experiments,* 15.

He had adjusted the coils' size: Ibid., 8–11.

Most important, he had decided to borrow: Ibid., 5.

Bell and Tainter had already begun testing: Mackenzie, *Alexander Graham Bell,* 236.

Seven years earlier, while working: Bruce, *Alexander Graham Bell and the Conquest of Solitude,* 121.

"more nearly approximate": Bell to Mabel Bell, July 17, 1881, Bell Family Papers; Mackenzie, *Alexander Graham Bell,* 236.

On July 20, as promised: Bell, "Volta Lab

Notes," July 19, 1881.

Bliss, who had brought for the inventor: Clark, *The Murder of James A. Garfield,* 86. The bullets are in the collection of the National Museum of American History.

"Ball can certainly be located": Bell, "Volta Lab Notes," July 9, 1881.

"If people would only make their bullets": Bell, *Upon the Electrical Experiments,* 46.

In its earliest form, the induction balance: Ibid., 7, 11.

Always a serious young man: Grosvenor and Wesson, *Alexander Graham Bell,* 62.

The Volta Laboratory, moreover, was far: Gray, *Reluctant Genius,* 217.

So unhealthy was the laboratory: Mabel Bell to Eliza Bell, June 23, 1881, Bell Family Papers.

"headache has taken root": Bruce, *Alexander Graham Bell and the Conquest of Solitude,* 201.

"Alec says he would rather die": Mabel Bell to Eliza Bell, June 23, 1881, Bell Family Papers.

"epistolary silence": Bell to Mabel Bell, July 26, 1881, Bell Family Papers.

"Alec says he is well and bearing": Mabel Bell to her mother, July 20, 1881, Bell Family Papers.

"I want to know how you are personally":

Mabel Bell to Alexander Graham Bell, July 16, 1881, Bell Family Papers.

Chapter 18: "Keep Heart"

"I hope the dangers are nearly passed": Lucretia Garfield to Mrs. Logan, July 14, 1881.

Although she continued to spend: Feis, *Mollie Garfield in the White House,* 88.

"I hope I shall not disappoint you": Shaw, *Lucretia,* 91.

"Blundered!": Lucretia, *Diary,* April 20, 1881, in Garfield, *Diary,* 641, 4:641.

"In these few weeks of trial and anxiety": "The President's Wife," *New York Times,* Aug. 28, 1881.

"She must be a pretty brave woman": Mabel Bell to Alexander Graham Bell, July 25, 1881, Bell Family Papers.

"His gradual progress": Reyburn, *Clinical History of the Case of President James Abram Garfield,* 31.

"day of thanksgiving for the recovery": "Thanksgiving for the President," *New York Times,* July 13, 1881.

"You keep heart": "A Typical American Family," *New York Times,* July 25, 1881.

"Every passage of his bowels": Reyburn, *Clinical History of the Case of President James Abram Garfield,* 18.

"rarely spoke of his condition": Ibid., 14.

His only link to the outside world: "Still Brighter Prospects," *New York Times,* July 8, 1881.

"Strangulatus pro Republica": Theodore Clarke Smith, *The Life and Letters of James Abram Garfield,* 2:1193.

"There was never a moment": Rockwell, "From Mentor to Elberon."

Finally, nearly a month after the shooting: Harriet S. Blaine and Beale, *Letters of Mrs. James G. Blaine,* p. 220.

"But I move the diaphragm": "Still Brighter Prospects," *New York Times,* July 8, 1881.

"I won't talk to you": "At the Patient's Bedside," *New York Times,* July 5, 1881.

Friends and family members in Ohio: "The Feeling in Cleveland," *New York Times,* July 4, 1881.

"Everywhere," one reporter wrote, "hope and confidence": "The President's Fight for Life," *New York Times,* July 7, 1881.

"out of danger": Harriet S. Blaine and Beale, *Letters of Mrs. James G. Blaine,* 221.

"large quantity": Reyburn, *Clinical History of the Case of President James Abram Garfield,* 38–39.

"neither ashamed nor afraid": Fisher, *Joseph Lister,* 130.

"was looking very well": Reyburn, *Clinical History of the Case of President James Abram Garfield,* 39.

"he is feverish": Ibid., 40.

"drenched with a profuse perspiration": Ibid., 41.

"the President bore": "Complete Medical Record of President Garfield's Case Containing All of the Official Bulletins," 25–26.

He vomited repeatedly: Reyburn, *Clinical History of the Case of President James Abram Garfield,* 43.

"weak solution of car bolic [*sic*] acid": Ibid., 42.

Unbeknownst to his doctors: Autopsy of James A. Garfield, 4.

An enormous cavity: Ibid., 3.

"We received every morning": Reyburn, *Clinical History of the Case of President James Abram Garfield,* 23.

One man sent the doctors plans: Ibid.

A man in Maryland wrote to Bliss: Prichard and Herring, "The Problem of the President's Bullet," *Surgery, Gynecology, and Obstetrics,* 2 (May 1951), 625–33.

Although Bliss admitted: Ibid., 626.

"had a suspicion": Ibid., 627.

"bullet has pierced the liver": "A Great Nation in Grief," *New York Times,* July 3, 1881.

At least one doctor in Washington: Baker, *President Garfield's Case,* 1–8.

Baker even drew up a diagram: Ibid.

"I felt," he would later explain, "that it was improper": Quoted in Rutkow, *James A. Garfield,* 117.

"These bulletins were often the subject": Reyburn, *Clinical History of the Case of President James Abram Garfield,* 19.

"If the slightest unfavorable symptom": Reyburn, *Clinical History of the Case of President James Abram Garfield,* 19.

"Your arrival and 'Professor' Tainter's": Mabel Bell to Alexander Graham Bell, July 16, 1881, Bell Family Papers.

"the experiment will be watched": "Search for the Pistol Ball," *Washington Post,* July 15, 1881.

"Ordinary telegrams I presume": Bell to Mabel Bell, July 26, 1881, Bell Family Papers.

Since he had agreed to a brief interview: Bell, "Volta Lab Notes," July 18, 1881.

"carried a bullet in his body": Bell, *Upon the Electrical Experiments,* 18.

"sonorous spot": Bell to D. W. Bliss, July 23, 1881, quoted in Bell, *Upon the Electri-*

cal Experiments, 54.

"Will you do us the favor": D. W. Bliss to Alexander Graham Bell, July 26, 1881, Bell Family Papers.

"tired, ill, dispirited": Bell to Mabel Bell, July 26, 1881, Bell Family Papers.

If Bell added a condenser: What was then known as a condenser is today called a capacitor.

Breaking open the instrument: Bell to Mabel Bell, July 26, 1881, Bell Family Papers.

Not only did it improve the sound: Bell, *Upon the Electrical Experiments,* 20.

Bell could now detect a bullet: Bell, *Upon the Electrical Experiments,* 16–20; Bruce, *Alexander Graham Bell and the Conquest of Solitude,* 345.

"trial of the apparatus": Bell to Mabel Bell, July 26, 1881, Bell Family Papers.

"Mr. Garfield himself is reported": Mabel Bell to her mother, July 17, 1881, Bell Family Papers.

"so calm and grand": Bell to Mabel Bell, July 26, 1881, Bell Family Papers.

"the look of a man": Ibid.

Frantically, Bell tried everything: Bell, *Upon the Electrical Experiments,* 55.

The sound, however, was distracting: Bell

to Mabel Bell, July 26, 1881, Bell Family Papers.

Taking in the long wires: Mackenzie, *Alexander Graham Bell,* 237.

"His head was so buried": Bell to Mabel Bell, July 26, 1881, Bell Family Papers.

After carefully pulling: Ibid.

As everyone in the room: Ibid.

"sharp and sudden reinforcement": Bruce, *Alexander Graham Bell and the Conquest of Solitude,* 346.

Finally, with the president quickly tiring: Bell, *Upon the Electrical Experiments,* 55.

"I feel woefully disappointed": Bruce, *Alexander Graham Bell and the Conquest of Solitude,* 346.

Returning to his laboratory: Bell, *Upon the Electrical Experiments,* 55.

"Private and confidential": Bell to Mabel Bell, July 26, 1881, Bell Family Papers.

Chapter 19: On a Mountaintop, Alone

On July 23: "Conkling and His Friends," *New York Times,* July 24, 1881.

Conkling, who had always worked: Chidsey, *The Gentleman from New York,* 3.

"renew their pledges": "Roscoe Conkling Beaten," *New York Times,* July 23, 1881.

"must not reap the reward": Chidsey, *The Gentleman from New York,* 355.

"moody and fretful": "Conkling and His Friends," *New York Times,* July 24, 1881.

"done with politics": Conkling, *The Life and Letters of Roscoe Conkling,* 306; Chidsey, *The Gentleman from New York,* 115.

"I presume that if Mr. Arthur": Chidsey, *The Gentleman from New York,* 354.

"Disguise it as they may seek to do": "The Senatorial Contest," *New York Times,* July 6, 1881.

Some took a tactical approach: "Arguing About Possibilities," *New York Times,* July 6, 1881. Arthur had been born in Vermont.

"shoulder their muskets": *Chicago Tribune,* July 3, 1881, quoted in Ackerman, *Dark Horse,* 394.

"There is no doubt that he is suffering keenly": "Vice President Arthur," *New York Times,* July 5, 1881.

"seemed to be overcome": Reeves, *Gentleman Boss,* 242.

"unable to conceal his emotion": "Gen. Arthur in Washington," *New York Times,* July 4, 1881.

Finally, a journalist from New York: *New York Times,* July 5, 1881.

"his head bowed down": Ibid.

"received no visit": "Conkling and His

Friends," *New York Times,* July 24, 1881.

"The hours of Garfield's life are numbered": Julia Sand to Chester Arthur, August 27, 1881, Chester Arthur Papers.

"dead and buried": Reeves, *Gentleman Boss,* 296.

"Your kindest opponents say": Julia Sand to Chester Arthur, August 27, 1881, Chester Arthur Papers.

Over the years, he would keep: Reeves, *Gentleman Boss,* 478.

"It is not the proof of highest goodness": Julia Sand to Chester Arthur, August 27, 1881, Chester Arthur Papers.

"As the President gets better": Reeves, *Gentleman Boss,* 242.

"thoroughly aired and cleaned": Clark, *The Murder of James A. Garfield,* 9; Reyburn, *Clinical History of the Case of President James Abram Garfield,* 44.

Soon after taking charge of the case: Rockwell, "From Mentor to Elberon."

Now, Bliss took over: "President Garfield's Case," *American Observer,* 494.

"devoting all my professional skills": D. W. Bliss, on White House stationery, August 13, 1881.

"farther into the cavity": Reyburn, *Clinical History of the Case of President James Abram Garfield,* 46.

"Courage": Mabel Bell to Alexander Graham Bell, July 29, 1881, Bell Family Papers.

When Bliss's letter arrived: *Boston Herald,* quoted in Bruce, *Alexander Graham Bell and the Conquest of Solitude,* 347; author interview with Roger Sherman, National Museum of American History.

"Splendid!": Bell, "Volta Lab Notes," July 30, 1881.

In just four days, he had managed: Bell, *Upon the Electrical Experiments,* 24, 29.

"forced exertions": Ibid., 26–27.

"In its present form": Bell to D. W. Bliss, July 31, 1881, in Bell, *Upon the Electrical Experiments,* 56.

On July 31: Bell, "Volta Lab Notes," July 31, 1881.

"no difficulty": Bell to D. W. Bliss, July 30, 1881, in Bell, *Upon the Electrical Experiments,* 57. Just the day before, Bell had tested McGill with no success, writing dejectedly in his laboratory notebook that he had been able to "get no indication" of the bullet in McGill.

"no need of further secrecy": Bell to Mabel Bell, July 31, 1881, Bell Family Papers.

"Come up and see us": *Boston Herald,* quoted in Bruce, *Alexander Graham Bell and the Conquest of Solitude,* 346–47.

"My new form of Induction Balance": Bell to D. W. Bliss, July 31, 1881, in Bell, *Upon the Electrical Experiments,* 56.

"suspected spot": Bell, *Upon the Electrical Experiments,* 32; "The President's Case," *Washington Post,* August 1, 1881.

"the only other person present": Bell, *Upon the Electrical Experiments,* 32.

Finally, he asked the first lady: *Harper's Weekly,* August 13, 1881.

"a general expectation": Bell, *Upon the Electrical Experiments,* 32–33.

"if success crowns the effort": Ibid., 32–33.

"now unanimously agreed": Prichard and Herring, "The Problem of the President's Bullet," 627.

"In the absence": Bell, *Upon the Electrical Experiments,* 33.

"perfectly sure": Ibid.

Still, Bell was not convinced: Ibid.

He had just begun: Ibid., 34.

Determined to find a way to keep working: Tainter, "The Talking Machine," 37.

Chapter 20: Terror, Hope, and Despair

"This fighting with disease": Garfield to Lucretia Garfield, February 23, 1862, quoted in Shaw, *Crete and James,* 126.

"They will not be allowed to get large":

"The Doctors' Reasons for Hope," *New York Times,* Aug. 30, 1881.

"facilitate the escape of pus": Bliss, "The Story of President Garfield's Illness," 301.

Using a long surgical knife with an ivory handle: Garfield exhibit at National Museum of Health and Medicine.

"a profuse discharge": Reyburn, *Clinical History of the Case of President James Abram Garfield,* 53.

"without an anæsthetic": Bliss, "The Story of President Garfield's Illness," 301.

Neither the incisions: Reyburn, *Clinical History of the Case of President James Abram Garfield,* 67–71; Rutkow, *James A. Garfield,* 119–20.

"It is thought that some pus": "Steps Toward Recovery," *New York Times,* August 13, 1881; D. W. Bliss to [??], August 13, 1881.

"Not the minutest symptom": "The Surgeons' Confidence," *New York Times,* August 20, 1881.

What did cause Bliss apprehension: The infection contributed to Garfield's starvation by itself consuming calories.

In less than two months: Herr, "Ignorance Is Bliss," 459.

The barrel-chested: Ibid.; *The Death of*

President James A. Garfield, National Museum of Health and Medicine.

"the limit of what a man can lose": "The Doctors' Reasons for Hope," *New York Times,* August 30, 1881.

"at the best meal": *New York Herald,* August 16, 1881, quoted in Clark, *The Murder of James A. Garfield,* 100.

Most days, Garfield was able: Clark, *The Murder of James A. Garfield,* 89.

Although Garfield found it difficult: Ibid.; Comer, *Harry Garfield's First Forty Years,* 60.

The White House cook: Seale, *The President's House,* 525.

Realizing that he urgently needed: "Dr. Bliss Reassured," *New York Times,* August 17, 1881.

For a stretch of eight days: Prichard and Herring, "The Problem of the President's Bullet," 628.

Then Bliss began altering the mixture: Ibid.; Clark, *The Murder of James A. Garfield,* 101.

The danger was that: Author interview with David Lounsbury, MD; Eltorai, "Fatal Spinal Cord Injury of the 20th President of the United States," 336.

At first, Garfield seemed: Clark, *The Murder*

of James A. Garfield, 101.

As well as being malnourished: Author interview with David Lounsbury, MD; Reyburn, *Clinical History of the Case of President James Abram Garfield.*

While newspapers continued: "The Fight for Life," *Evening Star,* August 23, 1881.

"This dreadful sickness": Harriet S. Blaine and Beale, *Letters of Mrs. James G. Blaine,* 233–34.

It seemed that everyone: Clark, *The Murder of James A. Garfield,* 93.

"darkness," she told her family: Harriet S. Blaine and Beale, *Letters of Mrs. James G. Blaine,* 225.

"Your father [is] much exercised": Ibid., 236–37.

The Constitution was of no help: The government did not tackle the issue of presidential disability until 1967, when it finally ratified the Twenty-Fifth Amendment to the Constitution. The amendment had been spurred by the assassination of President John F. Kennedy four years earlier.

Finally, Blaine sent a cabinet member: Ackerman, *Dark Horse,* 421.

"Disappoint our fears": Julia Sand to Chester Arthur, August 27, 1881, Chester Arthur Papers.

"Dear Mother": Garfield to his mother, August 11, 1881.

"I wonder": Theodore Clarke Smith, *The Life and Letters of James A. Garfield,* 2:1193.

He dreamed of returning: "Longing to Be at Lawnfield," *New York Times,* August 21, 1881.

"I have always felt": Garfield, *Diary,* June 19, 1881, 4:613.

"It would not now be prudent": Medical Bulletin, August 25, 1881.

"It's all right now": Reyburn, *Clinical History of the Case of President James Abram Garfield,* 68.

Lucretia had been so sick: Seale, *The President's House,* p. 526.

"banished despair": *Evening Star,* August 1881.

"one prolonged, hideous nightmare": Stanley-Brown, "My Friend Garfield," 101.

"despair," a reporter noted: *Evening Star,* August 1881.

Brown rarely left the White House: *Sunday Herald,* July 5, 1881; *Evening Critic,* July 19, 1881.

"During all this terror, hope, despair": *Evening Critic,* July 15, 1881.

"until control of her voice": Stanley-Brown, "My Friend Garfield," 101.
"anguished face": Ibid.

Chapter 21: After All

Although he had returned: Bruce, *Alexander Graham Bell and the Conquest of Solitude,* 347.
"strong and healthy little fellow": Gray, *Reluctant Genius,* p. 222.
"Little boy born prematurely": Bell to his father, August 15, 1881, Bell Family Papers.
"Nothing will ever comfort me": Bell to Mabel Bell, December 12, 1885, Bell Family Papers.
After his son's funeral: Tainter, "Home Notes," 37.
Just three days after Edward's death: Tainter, "Home Notes," 37. Bell's attachment for the induction balance was, in Tainter's words, "an electrical attachment to be made to the ordinary exploring needle so that when the point of the needle touched the bullet it would be indicated upon a telephone placed in the circuit."
Bliss refused to let Tainter: Bruce, *Alexander Graham Bell and the Conquest of Solitude,* 347.

"Heartless science": Bell, "Science and Immortality," *The Christian Register Symposium,* 96.

"stopped the proceedings immediately": McCabe, *Our Martyred President,* 592.

In the city, it was 90 degrees: Reyburn, *Clinical History of the Case of President James Abram Garfield,* 57.

"Well," he said, "is this the last day": Bliss, "The Story of President Garfield's Illness," 302.

"No, no," he said: Reyburn, *Clinical History of the Case of President James Abram Garfield,* 80.

At two o'clock the next morning: Ibid.

"in the hope": Crook, *Through Five Administrations,* 274.

The train, which pulled four cars: Reyburn, *Clinical History of the Case of President James Abram Garfield,* 80.

The president's car, number 33: Ibid.; Clark, *The Murder of James A. Garfield,* 105.

"determine," Bliss explained: Bliss, "The Story of President Garfield's Illness," 302.

It was, she would later write, "the saddest": Edson, "The Sickness and Nursing of President Garfield," 620.

"by no strange hands": Bliss, "The Story of

President Garfield's Illness," 302.

"A last token of amity": Crook, *Through Five Administrations,* 274.

The train ride to Elberon: Reyburn, *Clinical History of the Case of President James Abram Garfield,* 81.

"No sound of bell or whistle": Bliss, "The Story of President Garfield's Illness," 303.

"At every station": Ibid.

"It was indeed": Reyburn, *Clinical History of the Case of President James Abram Garfield,* 82.

When the train finally reached Elberon: *United States v. Guiteau,* 124.

"I am willing that you should ruin": Brown, *The Life and Public Services of James A. Garfield,* 241.

Before the train could reach: Ackerman, *Dark Horse,* 425.

"Instantly hundreds of strong arms": Bliss, "The Story of President Garfield's Illness," 303.

When he was carried into his room: Reyburn, *Clinical History of the Case of President James Abram Garfield,* 84.

"This is delightful": Ibid., 89.

"Throughout his long illness": Rockwell, "From Mentor to Elberon."

When Bliss told him that a fund: The fund

had been started by Cyrus W. Field, an American financier who helped found the Atlantic Telegraph Company, the first company to attempt to lay a telegraph cable across the Atlantic. The fund for Lucretia eventually reached $350,000. She used it not only to live on and to send her children to college, but to help establish Garfield's library, the first presidential library, in their home in Mentor.

"What?": Bliss, "The Story of President Garfield's Illness," 301.

"Doctor, you plainly show": Ibid., 303.

"from a labor and responsibility": Medical Bulletin, September 8, 1881, 6:00 p.m.

"clearer road to recovery": Quoted in Clark, *The Murder of James A. Garfield,* 107.

"Despite the announcements": Quoted in ibid., 98.

"may live the day out": Peskin, *Garfield,* 606.

"Do you think my name": Ibid., 607.

Rockwell was again with Garfield: Ibid.

"Well, Swaim"; Reyburn, *Clinical History of the Case of President James Abram Garfield,* 95.

"wonderful productions": Bliss, "The Story of President Garfield's Illness," 304.

Moments later, Lucretia: Ibid.

"hear the long, solemn roll": Stanley-Brown, "My Friend Garfield," 101.

"the witnesses of the last sad scene": Bliss, "The Story of President Garfield's Illness," 304.
"A faint, fluttering pulsation": Ibid.
"All hearts," Bliss would write, "were stilled": Ibid.
"begged her to retire": Ibid., 305.

Chapter 22: All the Angels of the Universe

"Extra Republican!": Bell to Mabel Bell, September 19, 1881, Bell Family Papers. Bell began this letter to Mabel earlier in the evening of the 19th. As he was writing, it turned midnight, and soon after he heard the newsboy's cry, announcing Garfield's death.
"Please hunt in the study": Ibid.
"How terrible it all is": Ibid.
"the final agony": Stanley-Brown, "My Friend Garfield," 101.
In the end, the autopsy: "The Result of the Autopsy," *New York Times,* September 21, 1881.
"The missile": Bliss et al., "Record of the Post-mortem Examination of the Body of President J. A. Garfield," 4.
"this long descending channel": Ibid.
"no evidence that it had been penetrated": Ibid., 3.
Evidence of the proximate cause: Ibid.;

Author interview with Dr. David Lounsbury, June 29, 2010.

"The initial point of this septic condition": Reyburn, *Clinical History of the Case of President James Abram Garfield,* 97.

"irregular form": Bliss et al., "Record of the Post-mortem Examination of the Body of President J. A. Garfield," 5.

This, they realized: "Official Bulletin of the Autopsy," 1.

"slipped entirely through": Stanley-Brown, "My Friend Garfield," 101.

"I daren't ask him": Reeves, *Gentleman Boss,* 247.

"All the noble aspirations": Ibid., 244.

"the people and the politicians": Ibid., 245.

"And so Garfield is really dead": Julia Sand to Chester Arthur, September 28, 1881, Chester Arthur Papers.

Garfield's body, which was returned: Ridpath, *The Life and Work of James A. Garfield,* 657.

"The whole city was draped in mourning": Mollie Garfield diary, September 29, 1881, quoted in Feis, *Molly Garfield in the White House,* 101.

"in many respects": "Looking Upon the Dead," *New York Times,* September 23, 1881.

Only one man had no place: Rosenberg, *The Trial of the Assassin Guiteau,* 48.

More than a week earlier: *United States v. Guiteau,* 599.

"a great big musket-bullet": After hitting the wall, the bullet was said to have been flattened into a nearly perfect likeness of Guiteau's profile. An enterprising man, R. A. Whitehand, made molds from the bullet and sold facsimiles, whose authenticity was certified by John Crocker, the warden of the District Jail, and by Guiteau himself.

Although he would later: There was an outcry against Mason's sentence, and a fund was established for his defense.

He was tired, he said: Clark, *The Murder of James A. Garfield,* 107.

"There is an American judge": Rosenberg, *The Trial of the Assassin Guiteau,* 50–52.

"Mama says he ought": Quoted in Feis, *Molly Garfield in the White House,* 95.

"For this man Guiteau": "Gen. Sherman's Timely Counsel," *New York Times,* September 19, 1881.

"All a man would need": Rosenberg, *The Trial of the Assassin Guiteau,* 98.

The legal standard for determining insanity: There is considerable disagreement about the spelling of M'Naghten's name. Richard Moran, who wrote what is likely the definitive book on the case — *Knowing Right from Wrong* — devotes several pages to a discussion of this controversy. His conclusion is that the correct spelling is "McNaughtan," and he makes a very compelling argument. However, the most common spelling is M'Naghten.

"gradual failure of heart's action": Moran, *Knowing Right from Wrong,* 186.

"We have seen the trials": Quoted in ibid., 21.

"at the time of the committing": Ibid., 22–24.

In America, it became known: Clark, *The Murder of James A. Garfield,* 118.

In 1859, Congressman Daniel Edgar Sickles: Mitchell, "The Man Who Murdered Garfield," 470.

"I plead not guilty to the indictment": Clark, *The Murder of James A. Garfield,* 116.

"Guiteau should have a fair trial": "Guiteau's Trial," *New York Times,* November 14, 1881.

"If I didn't think the unfortunate man was insane": Clark, *The Murder of James A. Garfield,* 117.

"I think he ought to be hung": Rosenberg,

The Trial of the Assassin Guiteau, 114.
It took three days: Ibid., 116.
"for the first time in anyone's memory": Taylor, "Assassin on Trial," 3.
The courtroom itself had been renovated: Ibid.
The rest were first come, first served: Clark, *The Murder of James A. Garfield,* 121–22.
Guiteau had planned to make: Ibid., 122.
"General Garfield died from malpractice": Quoted in ibid., 122–23.
"I deny the killing": *United States v. Guiteau,* 226.
"Now, don't spoil the matter": Ibid., 1730.
"The rich men of New York": Ibid., 1110.
Finally, Scoville himself asked the court: Ibid., 163.
"could not have been prevented": Ibid., 2330–31.
"All the links in the chain are there": Beard, "The Case of Guiteau," 22.
Before the trial had ended: Rosenberg, *The Trial of the Assassin Guiteau,* 71–72.
"with his hereditary history": Taylor, "Assassin on Trial," 5. The psychiatrist George Beard, who was convinced that Guiteau was not only insane now, but had been since he was eighteen years old, would go even further. Those who knew Guiteau best, he said, and had failed to have him

admitted to an asylum, were to blame for his actions. "On his friends rests the real responsibility for the assassination," Beard charged. "Mr. Scoville is the real murderer of President Garfield."

"Did you have any question": *United States v. Guiteau,* 965.

"A man may become profoundly depraved": Taylor, "Assassin on Trial," 6.

"disease of the brain": *United States v. Guiteau,* 1591.

"Hanging is too good for you": Rosenberg, *The Trial of the Assassin Guiteau,* 50.

A farmer from Maryland tried: "A Shot at the Assassin," *New York Times,* November 21, 1881. Additional men had been assigned to guard Guiteau, and he was moved to a different cell, but he grew increasingly nervous. He attempted to hide a knife, asked to be vaccinated as protection against infection that might reach him through the mail, and insisted on making another announcement in court. "I understand that there are one or two disreputable characters hanging around this court, intending to do me harm," he said, interrupting testimony about the gun he had used to shoot the president. "I want to notify all disreputable persons that if they attempt to injure me they will probably be shot dead by my body-guard. . . . There has been considerable loose talk on this subject this week, and I wish the public to understand it."

"My blood be on the head": Rosenberg, *The Trial of the Assassin Guiteau,* 223.

"I am willing to DIE": Quoted in ibid., 233–34.

"Whatever your impressions may be": John Guiteau to Charles Guiteau, June 20, 1882.

"The public have never had the facts": John Guiteau to Charles Guiteau, May 31, 1882.

"an audience before a decision": John Guiteau to Chester Arthur, June 23, 1882.

Arthur refused to see John: Clark, *The Murder of James A. Garfield,* 141.

"no grounds to justify": "The President's Decision in Guiteau's Case," *New York Herald,* June 25, 1882.

"Dear Madam: Humbly I address you": Frances Guiteau to Lucretia Garfield, February 12, 1882, quoted in unnamed newspaper found in the Hiram College Archives.

When she could wait no longer: Mollie Garfield diary, June 29, 1882, quoted in Feis, *Mollie Garfield in the White House,* 107.

"dared to come": Ibid., 106.

By the day of his execution: Rosenberg, *The Trial of the Assassin Guiteau,* 234n.

"I'm fully resigned": "A Great Tragedy Ended," *New York Times,* July 1, 1882.

"With the events of the past year": "The Drop Falls," unnamed newspaper, "Special Dispatch to the Inquirer," June 30, 1882.

After Crocker had finished: "Final Moments of Life," *Washington Post,* July 1, 1882; Fox, *The Crime Avenged,* 62.

A few minutes later, Hicks: "The Drop Falls," unnamed newspaper, "Special Dispatch to the Inquirer," June 30, 1882, Hiram College Archives.

Twenty thousand people: "The Gallows Prepared," *New York Times,* June 30, 1882.

"I stubbed my toe": "The Drop Falls," unnamed newspaper, "Special Dispatch to the Inquirer," June 30, 1882, Hiram College Archives; *Alienist and Neurologist* 4 (October 1882): 554.

"Except ye become": "Final Moments of Life," *Washington Post,* July 1, 1882.

Epilogue: Forever and Forever More

After the doors were opened: "Guiteau's Grave," *Washington Post,* July 2, 1882.

"His ultimate place in history": "Garfield

and Arthur," *New York Times,* Sept. 25, 1881.

"I fear coming generations": *Century Magazine* (April 1884): 807.

"Garfield does not belong": Quoted in Comer, *Harry Garfield's First Forty Years,* 62–63.

"This morning from the depth": Quoted in Comer, *Harry Garfield's First Forty Years,* 62–63.

In fact, Secret Service agents: Congress had allowed Secret Service agents to guard Grover Cleveland during his second term, in the mid-1890s, but it had not been an official assignment. Melanson, *The Secret Service,* 138.

The day McKinley was shot: Although Robert Todd Lincoln was not at Ford's Theatre when his father was shot, he was by his side when President Lincoln died.

"We do not think": Quoted in Hoogenboom, *Outlawing the Spoils,* 209.

"fresh grief to me": Ackerman, *Dark Horse,* 448.

"outrageous": Hudson, *Random Recollections of an Old Political Reporter,* 125–27.

"When I saw him *afterwards*": Reeves, *Gentleman Boss,* 256–57.

"disdained roast beef": Ibid., 296.

"Gentlemen, you have been misinformed":

Chidsey, *The Gentleman from New York,* p. 374.

"His Accidency": Chidsey, *The Gentleman from New York,* 357.

"He didn't crumble": Ibid., 384.

"I am *not* going to die": Conkling, *The Life and Letters of Roscoe Conkling,* 512.

Now, he paced the floor: Chidsey, *The Gentleman from New York,* 380–86.

"It seems that the attending physicians": Quoted in Clark, *The Murder of James A. Garfield,* 112–13.

"more to cast distrust": Quoted in Rutkow, *James A. Garfield,* 131.

"None of the injuries inflicted": Gerster, *Recollections of a New York Surgeon,* 206.

"ignorance is Bliss": Quoted in Herr, "Ignorance Is Bliss," 460.

Bliss, however, refused: Rutkow, *James A. Garfield,* 128.

"Statement of the Services Rendered": Bliss, *Statement of the Services Rendered by the Surgeons in the Case of the Late President Garfield,* 10–11.

"so greatly impaired": Ibid., 7.

Seven years later: "At the Point of Death," *Washington Post,* February 21, 1889.

"Now that Papa has gone": Comer, *Harry Garfield's First Forty Years,* 63.

"Had it not been that her children": Quoted in Shaw, *Lucretia,* 107.
"armed defender": Ibid., 109.
"not very good": Ibid., 111.
She asked Joseph Stanley Brown: Ibid., 110.
The second floor of this wing: Presidential libraries would officially begin fifty-eight years later, in 1939, with Franklin Delano Roosevelt's library.
"These are the last letters": Shaw, *Crete and James,* 390.
"He has such poise and sanity": Shaw, *Lucretia,* 116.
"Sometimes I feel that God": Quoted in Feis, *Mollie Garfield in the White House,* 108.
"I believe I am in love": Ibid., 110.
"a small stone": Ibid., 113.
Three months later, Mollie and Joseph: Ibid., 116.
"It is now rendered quite certain": Bell to Mabel Bell, 1881, Bell Family Papers.
"This is most mortifying to me": Ibid.
"An old idea": Bell, "Volta Lab Notes," October 25, 1881.
In the years to come: Bruce, *Alexander Graham Bell and the Conquest of Solitude,* 348.
In 1886, Captain Arthur Keller: Ibid., 400.
"door through which I should pass": Mackenzie, *Alexander Graham Bell,* viii.

Bell would live to be seventy-five years old: Bruce, *Alexander Graham Bell and the Conquest of Solitude,* 491.

"I must confess that": "Lister Was the Father of Antiseptic Surgery," *New York Times,* September 4, 1927.

"the greatest conqueror of disease": "Lister and Surgery," *New York Times,* October 5, 1913.

"My lord": Keen, "Before and After Lister," *Science,* June 18, 1915, 885. Keen attributes the quote to Thomas Bayard, as do several other sources, but Joseph Hodges Choate was the American ambassador to Great Britain in 1902. Bayard had died four years earlier.

BIBLIOGRAPHY

Manuscript Sources

The Alexander Graham Bell Family Papers, Library of Congress, Manuscript Division

Charles Sumner Tainter Papers, National Museum of American History

Chester Arthur Papers, Library of Congress, Manuscript Division

Chicago Historical Society

East Carolina University, Special Collections Department

Hiram College Archives

Historical Society of Washington, D.C.

James A. Garfield Papers, Library of Congress, Manuscript Division

Joseph Stanley-Brown Papers, Library of Congress

Library of the New York City Bar

Library of the Stonington Historical Society

Lucretia Garfield Papers, Library of Congress, Manuscript Division

National Museum of American History

National Museum of Health and Medicine
Western Reserve Historical Society
White House Historical Association

Select Bibliography

Ackerman, Kenneth D. *Dark Horse: The Surprise Election and Political Murder of President James A. Garfield.* New York: Carroll & Graf, 2003.

Adams, Henry. *The Education of Henry Adams.* 1907; reprint, Boston: Massachusetts Historical Society, 2007.

Adams, J. Howe. *History of the Life of D. Hayes Agnew.* Philadelphia: The F. A. Davis Company, 1892.

Agnew, D. Hayes. *The Principles and Practice of Surgery, Being a Treatise on Surgical Diseases and Injuries.* Philadelphia: J. B. Lippincott & Co., 1883.

Alger, Horatio. *From Canal Boy to President.* New York: Dodo Press, 1881.

Angelo, Bonnie. *First Families: The Impact of the White House on their Lives.* New York: Harper, 2007.

Ashhurst, John, ed. *Transactions of the International Medical Congress of Philadelphia, 1876.* Philadelphia: Printed for the Congress, 1877.

The Attempted Assassination of President

Garfield. Philadelphia: Barclay & Co., 1881.

Autopsy of James A. Garfield, National Museum of American History.

Baker, Frank. *President Garfield's Case: A Diagnosis Made Two Days after the Injury.* Washington, DC: Judd & Detweiller, 1882.

Balch, William Ralston, ed. *Garfield's Words: Suggestive Passages from the Public and Private Writings of James Abram Garfield.* Boston: Houghton, Mifflin, 1881.

———. *Life of President Garfield.* Philadelphia: Hubbard Bros., 1881.

Baskett, Thomas F. "Alexander Graham Bell and the Vacuum Jacket for Assisted Respiration." *Resuscitation* (November 2004), 115–17.

Beard, George M. "The Case of Guiteau — A Psychological Study." *Journal of Nervous and Mental Disease* 9 (January 1882).

Belanger, Dian Olson. "The Railroad in the Park: Washington's Baltimore & Potomac Station, 1872–1907," *Washington History* 15 (Spring 1990).

Bell, Alexander Graham. "Science and Immortality," The Christian Register Symposium. Boston: Geo. H. Ellis, 1887.

———. *Upon the Electrical Experiments to*

Determine the Location of the Bullet in the Body of the Late President Garfield; and upon a Successful Form of Induction Balance for the Painless Detection of Metallic Masses in the Human Body. Washington: Gibson Brothers, 1882.

———. "Volta Lab Notes," June 25, 1881–July 29, 1881. The Alexander Graham Bell Family Papers.

Bennett, Tracey Gold. *Washington, D.C., 1861–1962,* Black America Series. Charleston, SC: Arcadia, 2006.

Blackmon, Douglas A. *Slavery by Another Name: The Re-Enslavement of Black Americans from the Civil War to World War II.* New York: Anchor Books, 2008.

Blaine, Harriet S., and Harriet S. Blaine Beale, ed. *Letters of Mrs. James G. Blaine,* vol. 1. New York: Duffield and Company, 1908.

Blaine, James G. *Arrangements for the Memorial Address on the Life and Character of James Abram Garfield,* February 27, 1882.

Bliss, D. W. *Statement of the Services Rendered by the Surgeons in the Case of the Late President Garfield and a Brief Review of the Official Action of the "Board of Audit."* Washington: Gibson Bros., 1888.

———. "The Story of President Garfield's

Illness," *Century Magazine* 25 (1881): 299–305.

———, J. K. Barnes, J. J. Woodward, Robert Reyburn, and D. S. Lamb. "Record of the Post-mortem Examination of the Body of President J. A. Garfield, made September 20, 1881, commencing at 4:30 P.M., eighteen hours after death, at Franklyn Cottage, Elberon, New Jersey." *The Medical Record,* October 8, 1881.

Boettinger, H. M. *The Telephone Book: Bell, Watson, Vail and American Life, 1876–1976.* Croton-on-Hudson, NY: Riverwood, 1977.

Boller, Paul F. *Presidential Anecdotes.* New York: Oxford University Press, 1996.

Brandt, Nat. "The Great Blizzard of '88," *American Heritage* 28 (February 1977).

Brooks, Stewart M. *Our Murdered Presidents: The Medical Story.* New York: Frederick Fell, 1966.

Brown, E. E. *The Life and Public Services of James A. Garfield, Twentieth President of the United States.* Boston: D. Lothrop and Company, 1881.

Bruce, Robert V. *Alexander Graham Bell and the Conquest of Solitude.* Ithaca, NY: Cornell University Press, 1973.

Bundy, J. M. *The Nation's Hero, in Memo-*

riam. New York: A. S. Barnes & Co., 1881.
Carden, Maren Lockwood. *Oneida: Utopian Community to Modern Corporation.* New York: Harper Torchbooks, 1971.
Casson, Herbert N. *The History of the Telephone.* Chicago: McClurg, 1910.
Chaitkin, Anton. *Treason in America: From Aaron Burr to Averell Harriman.* Washington: Executive Intelligence Review, 1998.
Chidsey, Donald Barr. *The Gentleman from New York: A Life of Roscoe Conkling.* New Haven, CT: Yale University Press, 1935.
Clancy, Herbert J. *The Presidential Election of 1880.* Chicago: Loyola University Press, 1958.
Clark, James C. *The Murder of James A. Garfield: The President's Last Days and the Trial and Execution of His Assassin.* Jefferson, NC: McFarland & Company, 1993.
Clarke, Edward H., Henry J. Bigelow, Samuel D. Gross, T. Gaillard Thomas, and J. S. Billings. *A Century of American Medicine, 1776–1876.* New York: Burt Franklin, 1876.
Clemmer, Mary. *Ten Years in Washington: Life and Scenes in the National Capital, as a Woman Sees Them.* Hartford, CT: The Hartford Publishing Company, 1882.
Collier, Leslie. *The Lister Institute of Preven-*

tive Medicine: A Concise History. Hertfordshire, UK: The Lister Institute of Preventive Medicine, 2000.

Comer, Lucretia Garfield. *Harry Garfield's First Forty Years: A Man of Action in a Troubled World.* New York: Vantage Press, 1965.

Conkling, Alfred R. *The Life and Letters of Roscoe Conkling: Orator, Statesman and Advocate.* New York: Charles L. Webster & Company, 1889.

Connery, T. B. "Secret History of the Garfield-Conkling Tragedy." *Cosmopolitan Magazine* 23 (June 1897): 145–62.

Conwell, Russell H. *The Life, Speeches, and Public Services of James A. Garfield, Twentieth President of the United States.* Portland, ME: George Stinson & Company, 1881.

Cox, Jacob Dolson. *Military Reminiscences of the Civil War,* 2 vols. Kessinger Publishing.

Crapol, Edward P. *James G. Blaine: Architect of Empire.* Wilmington, DE: Scholarly Resources, 2000.

Crook, William H. *Through Five Administrations: Reminiscences of Colonel William H. Crook.* Edited by Margarita Spalding Gerry. New York: Harper & Brothers, 1907.

"Crude and Curious Inventions at the Centennial Exhibition," *Atlantic Monthly* 39 (June 1877): 517.

Davis, Harold E. *Garfield of Hiram: A Memorial to the Life and Services of James Abram Garfield.* Hiram, OH: Hiram Historical Society Publication, 1931.

Day, Richard H. "Review of the Surgical Treatment of President Garfield." *New Orleans Medical and Surgical Journal* 10 (August 1882): 81–95.

Dean, "Reminiscences of Garfield: Garfield the Student, the Eclectic Institute," Hiram College Archives.

The Death of President James A. Garfield: An Exhibition to Commemorate the 125th Anniversary of His Assassination. National Museum of Health and Medicine Online Exhibition, 2006.

Denton, Hal P. "When the Nation's Eyes Were Fixed on Mentor," typescript, October 7, 1928, Hiram College.

Deppisch, Ludwig M. "Homeopathic Medicine and Presidential Health: Homeopathic Influences upon Two Ohio Presidents." *Pharos of Alpha Omega Alpha* (Fall 1997): 5–10.

De Santis, Vincent P. "President Garfield and the Solid South." *North Carolina Historical Review* 36 (October 1959).

Doctors' notes on shooting and subsequent care, National Museum of Health and Medicine.

Doenecke, Justus D. *The Presidencies of James A. Garfield & Chester A. Arthur.* Lawrence: University Press of Kansas, 1981.

"Dr. Bliss's Authority." *National Republican,* July 4, 1882.

Dunham, William. *The Mathematical Universe.* New York: John Wiley & Sons, 1994.

Edson, C. A. [Susan Ann]. "The Sickness and Nursing of President Garfield with Many Interesting Incidents Never Before Given to the Public." In William Ralston Balch, *Life of President Garfield,* Philadelphia: Hubbard Bros., 1881, 612–620.

Eltorai, Ibrahim M. "Fatal Spinal Cord Injury of the 20th President of the United States: Day-by-Day Review of his Clinical Course, with Comments." *Journal of Spinal Cord Medicine* 27 (2004): 330–41.

Farmer, Laurence. *Master Surgeon: A Biography of Joseph Lister.* New York: Harper & Row, 1962.

Feis, Ruth S. B. *Mollie Garfield in the White House.* Chicago: Rand McNally & Company, 1963.

Fisher, Richard B. *Joseph Lister: 1827–1912.*

New York: Stein and Day, 1977.

Flint, Austin. "The First Century of the Republic: Medical and Sanitary Progress." *Harper's New Monthly Magazine* (June 1876).

Foster, Douglas A., Paul M. Blowers, Anthony L. Dunnavant, D. Newel Williams, eds. *The Encyclopedia of the Stone Campbell Movement.* Cambridge: Wm. B. Eerdmans Publishing, 2004.

Fox, Richard K. *The Crime Avenged: Full History of the Jail Life, Trial and Execution of Charles J. Guiteau.* New York: Police Gazette, 1882.

Garfield, James A. *The Diary of James A. Garfield,* 4 vols. Edited by Harry James Brown and Frederick D. Williams. East Lansing: Michigan State University Press, 1967.

———. "Pons Asinorum." *New-England Journal of Education* (April 1, 1876).

Gariepy, Thomas P. "The Introduction and Acceptance of Listerian Antisepsis in the United States." *Journal of the History of Medicine and Allied Sciences* 49 (1994): 167–206.

Gaw, Jerry L. *A Time to Heal: The Diffusion of Listerism in Victorian Britain.* Philadelphia: American Philosophical Society, 1999.

Gerster, Arpad Geyza. *Recollections of a New York Surgeon.* New York: Paul. B. Hoeber, 1917.

Giberti, Bruno. *Designing the Centennial: A History of the 1876 International Exhibition in Philadelphia.* Lexington: University Press of Kentucky, 2002.

Girdner, John H. "The Death of President Garfield," *Munsey's Magazine* 26 (October 1901–March 1902): 546–49.

Godlee, Rickman John. *Lord Lister.* London: St. Martin's Street, 1918.

Goff, John S. *Robert Todd Lincoln: A Man in His Own Right.* Norman: University of Oklahoma Press, 1969.

Gray, Charlotte. *Reluctant Genius: Alexander Graham Bell and the Passion for Invention.* New York: Arcade Publishing, 2006.

Gross, Linda P., and Theresa R. Snyder. *Philadelphia's 1876 Centennial Exhibition.* Charleston, SC: Arcadia Publishing, 2005.

Grosvenor, Edwin S., and Morgan Wesson. *Alexander Graham Bell: The Life and Times of the Man Who Invented the Telephone.* New York: Harry N. Abrams, 1997.

Guiteau, Charles J. *The Truth: A Companion to the Bible.* Boston: D. Lothrop and Company, 1879. [Although this book bears the imprint of D. Lothrop and

Company, Guiteau simply had the book printed, and used the publisher's name without its consent or knowledge.]

Guiteau, John. "Letters and Facts, not Heretofore Published, Touching the Mental Condition of Charles J. Guiteau Since 1865," unpublished ms., submitted to the President of the United States, 1882.

Guthrie, Douglas. *From Witchcraft to Antisepsis: A Study in Antithesis.* Lawrence: University of Kansas Press, 1955.

———. *A History of Medicine.* London: Thomas Nelson and Sons, 1945.

Haller, John S. *American Medicine in Transition, 1840–1910.* Urbana: University of Illinois Press, 1981.

Hamilton, Gail. *Biography of James G. Blaine.* Norwich: Henry Bill Publishing Company, 1895.

Hammond, William A. "Reasoning Mania: Its Medical and Medico-Legal Relations; with Special Reference to the Case of Charles J. Guiteau." *Journal of Nervous and Mental Disease* 9 (January 1882).

Hayes, H. G., and C. J. Hayes. *A Complete History of the Trial of Guiteau, Assassin of President Garfield.* Philadelphia: Hubbard Bros., 1882.

Hazard, Sharon. *Long Branch,* Postcard History Series. Charleston, SC: Arcadia Publishing, 2007.

Henry, Laurin L. "The Awkward Interval," *American Heritage* 19 (October 1968).

Herr, Harry W. "Ignorance Is Bliss: The Listerian Revolution and Education of American Surgeons," *Journal of Urology* 177 (February 2007): 457–60.

Hilton, Suzanne. *The Way It Was: 1876.* Philadelphia: Westminster Press, 1975.

Hinsdale, B. A. "The Life and Character of James A. Garfield." Unpublished manuscript, Hiram College Archives.

Hinsdale, Mary L., ed. *Garfield-Hinsdale Letters: Correspondence Between James Abram Garfield and Burke Aaron Hinsdale.* Ann Arbor: University of Michigan Press, 1949.

Hoar, George F. *Autobiography of Seventy Years,* 2 vols. New York: Charles Scribner's Sons, 1903.

Hoogenboom, Ari. *Outlawing the Spoils: A History of the Civil Service Reform Movement, 1865–1883.* Urbana: University of Illinois Press, 1961.

———. *Rutherford B. Hayes: Warrior and President.* Lawrence: University of Kansas, 1995.

Hoyt, Edwin P. *James A. Garfield.* Chicago:

Reilly & Lee Co., 1964.
Hudson, William C. *Random Recollections of an Old Political Reporter.* New York: Cupples & Leon Company, 1911.
Hughes, C. H. "The Simulation of Insanity by the Insane." *American Journal of Insanity* (April 1860): 1110–26.
In Memoriam: Gems of Poetry and Song on James A. Garfield. Columbus: J. C. McClenahan & Company, 1881.
Kalush, William and Larry Sloman. *The Secret Life of Houdini: The Making of America's First Superhero.* New York: Atria Books, 2006.
Karabell, Zachary. *Chester Alan Arthur.* New York: Henry Holt and Company, 2004.
Kaufman, Martin. *Homeopathy in America: The Rise and Fall of a Medical Heresy.* Baltimore: Johns Hopkins Press, 1971.
Keen, W.W. "Before and After Lister," *Science* (June 18, 1915): 881–91.
Kessin, Richard H. "How Antiseptic Surgery Arrived in America." *Physicians and Surgeons* 28 (Winter 2008).
Kingsbury, Robert. *The Assassination of James A. Garfield.* New York: Rosen Publishing Group, 2002.
Kozoi, Robert A. "Frank Hastings Hamilton: Medical Educator and Surgeon to

President Garfield." *American Journal of Surgery* (June 1986): 759–60.

Kuhfeld, Albert W. "For Whom the Bell Toils: Medical Imaging by Telephone." *IEEE Engineering in Medicine and Biology* 10 (March 1991): 88–89.

Lachman, Charles. *The Last Lincolns: The Rise and Fall of a Great American Family.* New York: Union Square Press, 2008.

Leech, Margaret, and Harry J. Brown. *The Garfield Orbit: The Life of James A. Garfield.* New York: Harper & Row, 1978.

Lister, Joseph. "Antiseptic Surgery: Report of Remarks Made Before the Surgical Section, During the Adjourned Discussions on Dr. Hodgen's Paper." *Transactions of the International Medical Congress.* Philadelphia: Printed for the Congress, 1877.

———. *The Autobiography of Joseph Lister, of Bradford in Yorkshire.* Edited by Thomas Wright. London: John Russell Smith, 1842.

———. *The Collected Papers of Joseph, Baron Lister,* 2 vols. Oxford: Clarendon Press, 1909.

Lodge, E. A. "President Garfield's Case: Dr. Boynton's Statement." *American Observer* (November 1881): 492–502.

Lubrano, Annteresa. *The Telegraph: How*

Technology Innovation Caused Social Change, Garland Studies on Industrial Productivity. London: Routledge, 1997.

Mackenzie, Catherine. *Alexander Graham Bell: The Man Who Contracted Space.* Boston: Houghton Mifflin, 1928.

McCabe, James D. *Our Martyred President: The Life and Public Services of Gen. James A. Garfield . . . Together with the History of His Assassination.* Philadelphia: National Publishing Company, 1881.

McCulloch, Earnest C. *Disinfection and Sterilization.* Philadelphia: Lea & Febiger, 1936.

Melanson, Philip H. *The Secret Service: The Hidden History of an Enigmatic Agency.* New York: Carroll & Graf, 2002.

Menke, Richard. "Media in America, 1881: Garfield, Guiteau, Bell, Whitman." *Critical Inquiry* 31 (Spring 2005).

Mentor: The First 200 Years. Mentor, OH: Mentor Bicentennial Committee, 1997.

Miller, Jason T., Scott Y. Rahimi, and Mark Lee. "History of Infection Control and Its Contributions to the Development and Success of Brain Tumor Operations." *Neurosurgical Focus* 18 (April 2005): 1–5.

Mitchell, Stewart. "The Man Who Murdered Garfield," *Proceedings of the Mas-*

sachusetts Historical Society. Boston: Massachusetts Historical Society, 1945.

Moldow, Gloria. *Women Doctors in Gilded Age Washington: Race, Gender, and Professionalization.* Urbana: University of Illinois Press, 1987.

Monroe, William Henry Harrison. "Reminiscences of James A. Garfield." Unpublished manuscript, Hiram College Archives.

Moran, Richard. *Knowing Right from Wrong: The Insanity Defense of Daniel McNaughtan.* New York: Free Press, 1981.

Murphy, Jay W. *What Ails the White House: An Introduction to the Medical History of the American Presidency.* Overland Park, KS: Leathers Publishing, 2006.

Noble, Iris. *The Courage of Dr. Lister.* New York: Julian Messner, 1960.

Noyes, "Guiteau vs. Oneida Community."

Nuland, Sherwin B. *Doctors: The Biography of Medicine.* New York: Vintage, 1988.

Parker, Owen W. "The Assassination and Gunshot Wound of President James A. Garfield." Washington, DC: National Museum of Health and Medicine, March 1951.

Pasteur, Louis, and Joseph Lister. *Germ Theory and Its Applications to Medicine &*

on the Antiseptic Principle of the Practice of Surgery. 1878; reprint, New York: Prometheus Books, 1996.

Paulson, George. "Death of a President and His Assassin: Errors in Their Diagnosis and Autopsies." *Journal of the History of the Neurosciences* 15 (2006): 77–91.

Perley Poore, Benjamin. *Perley's Reminiscences of Sixty Years in the National Metropolis.* Philadelphia: Hubbard Brothers, 1886.

Perry, James M. *Touched with Fire: Five Presidents and the Civil War Battles That Made Them.* New York: Public Affairs, 2003.

Peskin, Allan. "The First Media Circus." *Ohio Magazine* 12 (July 1989): 45–49.

———. *Garfield.* Kent, OH: Kent State University Press, 1978.

———. "James A. Garfield, Historian." *Historian* 43 (1981): 483–92.

———. "Who Were the Stalwarts?" *Political Science Quarterly* 99 (Winter 1984–85): 703–16.

Platt, Thomas C. *The Autobiography of Thomas Collier Platt.* New York: B. W. Dodge & Company, 1910.

Porter, Roy. *The Cambridge History of Medicine.* Cambridge: Cambridge University

Press, 2006.
Post, Robert C. *1876: A Centennial Exhibition.* Washington, DC: National Museum of History and Technology, Smithsonian Institution, 1976.
Prichard, Robert W., and A. L. Herring. "The Problem of the President's Bullet." *Surgery, Gynecology and Obstetrics* 92 (May 1951): 625–33.
Ray, Isaac. "The Responsibility of the Insane for their Criminal Acts." *Transactions of the International Medical Congress of Philadelphia, 1876.* Philadelphia: Printed for the Congress, 1877.
Rayfield, Jo Ann. "Tragedy in the Chicago Fire and Triumph in the Architectural Response." Illinois Periodicals Online, www.lib.niu.edu/1997.
Reeves, Thomas C. *Gentleman Boss: The Life and Times of Chester Alan Arthur.* Newton, CT: American Political Biography Press, 1975.
Remini, Robert V. *The House: The History of the House of Representatives.* New York: HarperCollins, 2006.
Reports of Officers of the Navy on Ventilating and Cooling the Executive Mansion During the Illness of President Garfield. Washington, DC: U.S. Government Printing Of-

fice, 1882.

Report of the Proceedings in the Case of the United States vs. Charles J. Guiteau, Tried in the Supreme Court of the District of Columbia, Holding a Criminal Term, and Beginning November 14, 1881. Washington, DC: U.S. Government Printing Office, 1882.

Review of the Transactions of the Credit Mobilier Company, and an Examination of that Portion of the Testimony Taken by the Committee of Investigation and Reported to the House of Representatives at the Last Session of the Forty-Second Congress which Relates to Mr. Garfield. Washington, DC: U.S. Government Printing Office, 1873.

Reyburn, Robert. *Clinical History of the Case of President James Abram Garfield.* Washington, DC: Otis Historical Archives, 1893.

Ridpath, John Clark. *The Life and Work of James A. Garfield, Twentieth President of the United States.* Cincinnati: Forshee & McMakin, 1881.

Ringenberg, William C. "The Religious Thought and Practice of James A. Garfield." In *The Stone-Campbell Movement, an International Religious Tradition,* edited by Michael W. Casey and Douglas A. Foster. Knoxville: The University of Ten-

nessee Press, 2002.
Robertson, Constance Noyes. *Oneida Community: The Breakup, 1876–1881.* Syracuse: Syracuse University Press.
Robinson, Victor. *The Story of Medicine.* New York: New Home Library, 1943.
Rockwell, Almon. "From Mentor to Elberon," *Century Magazine* 23 (1882): 431–38.
Roll of Delegates and Alternates to the Republican National Convention, Chicago, June 2, 1880.
Rosenberg, Charles E. *The Trial of the Assassin Guiteau: Psychiatry and the Law in the Gilded Age.* Chicago: University of Chicago Press, 1968.
Rothstein, William G. *American Physicians in the Nineteenth Century: From Sects to Science.* Baltimore: The Johns Hopkins University Press, 1972.
"Rough Sketch of an Introduction to a Life of General Garfield," typescript, Hiram College Archives.
Rushford, Jerry. "James A. Garfield: The Early Years." *Restoration Quarterly* (1977[?]). In Hiram College Archives.
Rutkow, Ira. *Bleeding Blue and Gray: Civil War Surgery and the Evolution of American Medicine.* New York: Random House, 2005.

———. *James A. Garfield.* New York: Henry Holt, 2006.

Schlereth, Thomas J. *Victorian America: Transformations in Everyday Life.* New York: HarperPerennial, 1991.

Seale, William. *The President's House: A History,* 2 vols. Washington, DC: White House Historical Association, 1986.

Shaw, John, ed. *Crete and James: Personal Letters of Lucretia and James Garfield.* East Lansing: Michigan State University Press, 1994.

———. *Lucretia.* New York: Nova History Publications, 2004.

———. "Lucretia and Her Letters: The Garfield Correspondence." *Hiram Broadcaster Magazine* (Spring 1986): 8–12.

Shenk, Joshua Wolf. *Lincoln's Melancholy: How Depression Challenged a President and Fueled His Greatness.* Boston: Houghton Mifflin, 2005.

Sherman, John. *Recollections of Forty Years in the House, Senate and Cabinet,* 2 vols. Chicago: Werner, 1895.

Shrady, George F. "Is Guiteau Insane?" *Medical Record* 20 (October 22, 1881): 500–1.

———. "The Late President Garfield's Case." *Medical Record* 20 (October 8,

1881): 410–11.
———. “The Lesson of the Bullet.” *Medical Record* 20 (October 15, 1881): 436–37.
———. “Surgical and Pathological Reflections on President Garfield’s Wound.” *Medical Record* 20 (October 1881): 404–6.
Smalley, E. V. “The White House.” *Century Magazine* 27 (April 1884): 803–15.
Smith, Stephen. “Telephonic Bullet-Probe.” *Dublin Journal of Medical Science* 96 (July–December 1893): 106.
Smith, Theodore Clarke. *The Life and Letters of James Abram Garfield.* 2 vols. New Haven, CT: Yale University Press, 1925.
Soper, Steve. “Dr. Willard Bliss.” Men of the 3rd Michigan Infantry (blog), http://thirdmichigan.blogspot.com/2007/10/d-willard-bliss.html.
Stanley-Brown, Joseph. “Memorandum Concerning Joseph Stanley-Brown’s Relations with General Garfield.” New York: Library of Congress, June 24, 1924.
———. “My Friend Garfield.” *American Heritage* 22 (August 1971).
———. *Stanley-Brown Family History.* Washington, DC: Library of Congress.
Sutherland, Daniel E. *The Expansion of Everyday Life, 1860–1876.* New York: Harper & Row, 1989.

Tainter, Charles Sumner. "Home Notes," n.d. Charles Sumner Tainter Papers, National Museum of American History.

———. "The Talking Machine and Some Little Known Facts in Connection with Its Early Development," n.d. Unpublished memoir, Charles Sumner Tainter Papers, National Museum of American History.

Taylor, John M. "Assassin on Trial." *American Heritage* 32 (June/July 1981).

———. *Garfield of Ohio: The Available Man.* New York: W. W. Norton, 1970.

Thayer, William M. *From Log-Cabin to the White House.* Boston: James H. Earle, 1881.

Tousey, Sinclair. *Medical Electricity Röntgen Rays and Radium, with a Practical Chapter on Phototherapy.* Philadelphia: W. B. Saunders, 1921.

"The Treatment of the Late President's Wound." *Medical Gazette* (June 31, 1882).

Truax, Rhoda. *Joseph Lister: Father of Modern Surgery.* Indianapolis: Bobbs Merrill, 1944.

Trunkey, Donald. "Medical and Surgical Care of Our Four Assassinated Presidents." *Journal of the American College of Surgeons* 201 (December 2005): 976–89.

Watkins, T. H. "Eyewitness." *American Heri-*

tage 31 (February/March 1980).

Weiner, Bradley K. "The Case of James A. Garfield: A Historical Perspective." *Spine: An International Journal for the Study of the Spine* 28 (May 15, 2003): E183-E186.

Weisse, Faneuil D. "Surgico-Anatomical Study of the Gunshot Wound of President Garfield." *Medical Record* 20 (October 1881).

West, Donald J., and Alexander Walk, eds. *Daniel McNaughton: His Trial and the Aftermath.* London: Royal College of Psychiatrists, 1977.

Whitcomb, John, and Claire Whitcomb. *Real Life at the White House: 200 Years of Daily Life at America's Most Famous Residence.* New York: Routledge, 2000.

Williams, Charles Richard, ed. *Diary and Letters of Rutherford B. Hayes, Nineteenth President of the United States,* vol. 1: *1834–1860.* Columbus: The Ohio State Archaeological and Historical Society, 1922.

Young, Donald. *American Roulette: The History and Dilemma of the Vice Presidency.* New York: Holt, Rinehart and Winston, 1965.

PHOTO INSERT ILLUSTRATION CREDITS

Page 1, top: The Western Reserve Historical Society
Page 1, center: The New York Public Library
Page 1, bottom: Print and Picture Collection, Free Library of Philadelphia
Page 2, top: Library of Congress
Page 2, bottom: Stonington Historical Society, Stonington, Connecticut
Page 3: The New York Public Library
Page 4, top: Library of Congress
Page 4, center: U.S. Historical Archive
Page 4, bottom: U.S. Historical Archive
Page 5, top: Library of Congress
Page 5, center: *Mollie Garfield in the White House,* Ruth S. B. Feis
Page 5, bottom: Library of Congress
Page 6, top: Corbis
Page 6, center: Library of Congress
Page 6, bottom: Library of Congress
Page 7, top: Library of Congress
Page 7, bottom: Corbis

Page 8: Corbis
Page 9, top: National Museum of Health and Medicine (NCP 1858)
Page 9, bottom: Library of Congress
Page 10, top: The Historical Society of Washington, D.C.
Page 10, center: National Museum of Health and Medicine (NCP 1860)
Page 10, bottom: Library of Congress
Page 11: Special Collections, University of Virginia Library
Page 12, top, left: Library of Congress
Page 12, top right: Division of Political History, National Museum of American History, Smithsonian Institution
Page 12, bottom: Library of Congress
Page 13, top: Library of Congress
Page 13, bottom: Hiram College Archives
Page 14, top: National Museum of Health and Medicine (NCP 1861)
Page 14, center: Hiram College Archives
Page 14, bottom: The White House Historical Association
Page 15, top: Library of Congress
Page 15, bottom: Hiram College Archives
Page 16, top: Library of Congress
Page 16, bottom: Library of Congress

ABOUT THE AUTHOR

Candice Millard is the bestselling author of *The River of Doubt,* which was named a Best Book of the Year by the *New York Times Book Review, The Washington Post Book World,* and *San Franciso Chronicle, The Christian Science Monitor, USA Today,* and *The Kansas City Star.* A former editor and writer at *National Geographic* magazine, she lives in Kansas City with her husband and three children.